GAME DEVELOPMENT ESSENTIALS

AN INTRODUCTION

THIRD EDITION

Jeannie Novak

DELMAR
CENGAGE Learning

Australia • Brazil • Japan • Korea • Mexico • Singapore • Spain • United Kingdom • United States

DELMAR
CENGAGE Learning

Game Development Essentials:
An Introduction, Third Edition
Jeannie Novak

Vice President, Editorial: Dave Garza

Director of Learning Solutions:
Sandy Clark

Senior Acquisitions Editor: Jim Gish

Managing Editor: Larry Main

Associate Product Manager: Meaghan Tomaso

Editorial Assistant: Sarah Timm

Vice President, Marketing:
Jennifer Baker

Marketing Director: Deborah Yarnell

Marketing Manager: Erin Brennan

Marketing Coordinator:
Erin DeAngelo

Senior Production Director:
Wendy Troeger

Senior Content Project Manager: Glenn Castle

Senior Art Director: Joy Kocsis

Technology Project Manager:
Christopher Catalina

Cover Image **Uncharted 2: Among Thieves**,
courtesy of Naughty Dog, Inc.

For product information and technology assistance, contact us at
Cengage Learning Customer & Sales Support, 1-800-354-9706

For permission to use material from this text or product,
submit all requests online at **www.cengage.com/permissions.**

Further permissions questions can be e-mailed to
permissionrequest@cengage.com

Library of Congress Control Number: 2010941933

ISBN-13: 978-1-1113-0765-3

ISBN-10: 1-1113-0765-2

Delmar
5 Maxwell Drive
Clifton Park, NY 12065-2919
USA

Cengage Learning is a leading provider of customized learning solutions with office locations around the globe, including Singapore, the United Kingdom, Australia, Mexico, Brazil, and Japan. Locate your local office at:
international.cengage.com/region

Cengage Learning products are represented in Canada by Nelson Education, Ltd.

To learn more about Delmar, visit **www.cengage.com/delmar**

Purchase any of our products at your local college store or at our preferred online store **www.cengagebrain.com**

Printed in Canada
1 2 3 4 5 6 7 14 13 12 11

CONTENTS

Chapter 3   Goals & Genres:
what are the possibilities? 57

Chapter 4   Player Elements:
who plays and why? 87

Part II: Scenarios
creating compelling content . . . 121

Chapter 5 Story & Character Development:
creating the narrative 123

Chapter 7 Levels: creating the world 213

Chapter 8 Interface: creating the connection 235

Chapter 9 Audio: creating the atmosphere 277

Part III: Strategy team, process, and community 309

Chapter 10 Roles & Responsibilities: developing the team 311

Chapter 11 Production & Management: developing the process ... 351

Introduction

Game Development:
a new era in entertainment—
and in education

When asked if he could change one aspect of the game industry, Richard "Lord British" Garriott responded, "Education—I really wish schools would catch up and support our industry, by teaching more aspects of interactive game design."

This book was written to help fulfill a wish—one that many game industry professionals and educators have had: to help students become better prepared for careers in the game industry by providing them with a thorough background in all aspects of the game industry and the game development and interactive design process.

Game industry revenues, which some have estimated exceed $30 billion per year worldwide, have surpassed film box office and music concert revenues in the United States alone—making games the fastest-growing segment of the entertainment market, and an excellent field for career advancement. According to an industry impact study conducted by the International Game Developers Association (IGDA), in several countries, exports from game sales represent one of the highest exports—and well over 100,000 people are employed worldwide in the game industry.

In response to this rapid growth, hundreds of colleges and universities in the United States have launched accredited game development programs in the last few years— and textbooks providing support to these programs are in great demand. I wrote this book to satisfy the need for a comprehensive introductory text on game development for the educational and trade markets. The first edition of *Game Development Essentials* also launched the series of the same name (now boasting over 15 titles)—which is intended to help provide educators with a logical sequence of topics that might be taught in a game development curriculum. This third edition contains expanded sections on the newest trends in game development—such as social and serious games, new consoles and mobile platforms, and emerging technologies (including 3D, motion control, augmented reality, game engines, and development tools). This edition also contains updated screenshots, photos, illustrations, and diagrams—and new profiles, case studies, and tips from educators and industry professionals.

As more schools continue to create game programs, this book—and the companion books in this series—will become even more *essential* to game education and careers. Not limited to the education market, this series is also appropriate for the trade market, and for those who have a general interest in the game industry.

Jeannie Novak
Santa Monica, CA

About the *Game Development Essentials* Series

The *Game Development Essentials* series was created to fulfill a need: to provide students and creative professionals alike with a complete education in all aspects of the game industry. As more creative professionals migrate to the game industry, and as more game degree and certificate programs are launched, the books in this series will become even more essential to game education and career development.

Not limited to the education market, this series is also appropriate for the trade market and for those who have a general interest in the game industry. Books in the series contain several unique features. All are in full-color and contain hundreds of images—including original illustrations, diagrams, game screenshots, and photos of industry professionals. They also contain a great deal of profiles, tips and case studies from professionals in the industry who are actively developing games. Starting with an overview of all aspects of the industry—*Game Development Essentials: An Introduction*—this series focuses on topics as varied as story & character development, interface design, artificial intelligence, gameplay mechanics, level design, online game development, simulation development, and audio.

Jeannie Novak
Lead Author & Series Editor

About *Game Development Essentials: An Introduction*

This introductory book provides an overview of the game development process—complete with a historical framework, content creation strategies, production techniques, and future predictions.

This book contains the following unique features:

- Key chapter questions that are clearly stated at the beginning of each chapter
- Coverage that surveys the topics of planning, production, prototyping, playtesting, marketing, and management of player communities
- Thought-provoking review and study questions appearing at the end of each chapter that are suitable for students and professionals alike to help promote critical thinking and problem-solving skills
- A wealth of case studies, quotations from leading professionals, and profiles of game developers that feature concise tips and problem-solving exercises to help readers focus in on issues specific to game development
- Discussions that go beyond general game development topics into emerging areas such as serious, online, mobile, and social game development

- An abundance of full-color images throughout that help illustrate the concepts and techniques discussed in the book
- Detailed review exercises that appear at the end of each chapter (with annotated responses included in the Instructor Resources)

There are several general themes associated with this book that are emphasized throughout, including:

- Differences between games and other entertainment media (such as film)
- Usability and player control as primary aspects of game development
- Gameplay as a new form of storytelling
- Widening game market demographics and content features
- Disappearance of the "games as violent entertainment" stigma
- Uniqueness of game development team roles

Who Should Read This Book?

This book is not limited to the education market. If you found this book on a shelf at the bookstore and picked it up out of curiosity, this book is for you, too! The audience for this book includes students, industry professionals, and the general interest consumer market. The style is informal and accessible, with a concentration on theory and practice—geared toward both students and professionals.

Students that might benefit from this book include:

- College students in game development, interactive design, entertainment studies, communication, and emerging technologies programs
- Art, design and programming students who are taking introductory game development courses
- Professional students in college-level programs who are taking game development overview courses
- First-year game development students at universities

The audience of industry professionals for this book include:

- Graphic designers, animators, and Web developers who are interested in becoming game artists
- Programmers and Web developers who are interested in becoming game programmers
- Music composers, sound designers, and voice actors who are interested in becoming involved in this industry
- Professionals in other arts and entertainment media—including film, television, and music—who are interested in transferring their skills to the game development industry. These professionals might include writers, producers, artists, and designers.

How Is This Book Organized?

This book consists of three parts—focusing on industry background, content creation, and production/business cycles.

Part I   Setup: Building the Foundation—Focuses on providing a historical and structural context to game development. Chapters in this section include:

- **Chapter 1   Historical Elements: How Did We Get Here?**—provides a historical overview of electronic game development, from the arcade era to the online multiplayer games of today

- **Chapter 2   Platforms & Player Modes: What Is the Framework?**—evaluates platforms, time intervals, and player modes

- **Chapter 3   Goals & Genres: What Are the Possibilities?**—breaks down a wide variety of game goals and genres

- **Chapter 4   Player Elements: Who Plays and Why?**—explores player motivation, geographics, demographics, and psychographics

Part II   Scenarios: Creating Compelling Content—Focuses on how game developers create compelling content. Chapters in this section include:

- **Chapter 5   Story & Character Development: Creating the Narrative**— explores story structure, non-linear and collaborative storytelling, visual and verbal character development, and character archetypes

- **Chapter 6   Gameplay: Creating the Experience**—explains game theory, challenges, strategies, interactivity modes, balance, and economies

- **Chapter 7   Levels: Creating the World**—analyzes structure, environmental design, perspective, style, temporal and spatial features

- **Chapter 8   Interface: Creating the Connection**—discusses player control, manual and visual interface design, and usability

- **Chapter 9   Audio: Creating the Atmosphere**—breaks down music, sound design, and dialogue production

Part III   Strategy: Team, Process & Community—Focuses on team development, production cycles, and community management. Chapters in this section include:

- ■ **Chapter 10   Roles & Responsibilities: Developing the Team**—highlights the roles and responsibilities of companies and development team members, along with associated tools

- ■ **Chapter 11   Production & Management: Developing the Process**—outlines phases in the game development cycle (including planning, production, prototyping, and playtesting), along with project management and game documentation

- ■ **Chapter 12   Marketing & Maintenance: Developing the Community**—focuses on marketing, advertising, public relations, sales, and promotion—along with the role of player communities (including fan-produced content, modding, and fan sites)

The book concludes with **The Future: Where Are We Going?**—which presents diverse views and predictions of the future of the game industry from experts profiled in the book—followed by a **Resources** section, which includes a list of game development news sources, guides, directories, conferences, articles, and books related to topics discussed in this text.

How to Use This Text

The sections that follow describe text elements found throughout the book and how they are intended to be used.

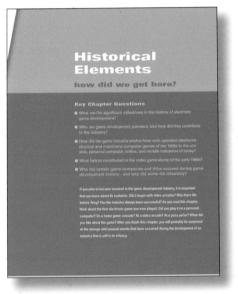

key chapter questions

Key chapter questions are learning objectives in the form of overview questions that start off each chapter. Readers should be able to answer the questions upon understanding the chapter material.

sidebars

Sidebars offer in-depth information from the authors on specific topics—accompanied by associated images.

tips

Tips provide advice and inspiration from industry professionals and educators, as well as practical techniques and tips of the trade.

quotes

Quotes contain short, insightful thoughts from players, students, and industry observers.

18

chapter 1   Historical Elements: how did we get here?

The Video Game Slump & a New Golden Age

Several theories have been attributed to the video game industry slump of the early 1980s. Perhaps the industry just experienced a temporary decline, and the platforms and titles introduced were just not revolutionary enough to reverse it. Oversupply might have also contributed to the slump; over 50 software companies produced cartridges, saturating the market with titles. There was also a lack of innovation—and low-quality and derivative games flooded the marketplace. Market conditions forced the price of games to be lowered to $5 to stay competitive. Many video game developers were also concerned that home computers would take over the home gaming market altogether. Because this industry had never experienced a decline, the general public started questioning its legitimacy—wondering whether home gaming was simply a fad, like the short-lived "hula hoop" craze!

Nintendo

Nintendo's entry into the console business in 1985 breathed new life into the home gaming industry—but it also helped push the arcade business into extinction. The system was far superior to consoles of the previous era, and the titles were graphically advanced—with compelling storylines and characters. Titles such as the *Super Mario Bros.* arcade conversion, *The Legend of Zelda*, and *Punch-Out!* (where players had the thrill of bashing boxing legend Mike Tyson) were engrossing—with seemingly limitless environments. Over 50 million NES systems were sold. The release of the improved Super NES (SNES) in 1991 solidified Nintendo's presence in the marketplace. A year later, Nintendo released *Super Mario Bros. 3*, the most successful non-bundled game cartridge of all time.

The NES became so successful in the marketplace that the former industry leader Atari established Tengen, a subsidiary that exclusively focused on developing games for the NES. Soon afterward, Tengen discovered a way to bypass Nintendo's "lockout chip" and produce NES-compatible games without Nintendo's approval. Tengen then acquired the rights to sell the extremely popular puzzle game, *Tetris*. After it was discovered that Tengen bought the rights from Mirrorsoft (which did not actually own the rights), the game was removed from the marketplace—and Nintendo, which had acquired the legitimate rights to the game, released it under its own label.

The Nintendo Entertainment System (NES) revolutionized the console industry.

> The first real video game I ever played was the *Super Mario Bros.* that came with the original NES system. I played it night and day, and I even taped my final victory against King Kazapa. It was quite an achievement for me back then.
>
> —Robert Ferguson (game art and design student)

Role-Playing Games

Role-playing games (RPGs) originate from the tradition of the *Dungeons & Dragons* paper-and-pencil fantasy role-playing games that originated in the 1970s. In these games, players take on roles such as fighters, wizards, priests, elves, or thieves. Players also explore dungeons, kill monsters (such as dragons and ogres), and gather treasure. One player, the Dungeon Master (later known as a Game Master), sets up the game world and takes on the roles of the other (non-player) characters in the game.

The Game Master

The term *Game Master* (GM), which originated from paper-and-pencil role-playing games, is currently used in online multiplayer games to refer to those who play an important role in supporting players online.

Like adventure games, RPGs are characterized by containing strong storylines—but RPGs also contain player-characters that improve throughout the course of the game. Due to the strong emotional character development—and because winning is tied in with this character advancement—RPG players usually experience close emotional involvement with their characters. The genre's presentation is diverse, ranging from simpler arcade-style games such as *Dungeon Siege* to the graphically rich environments in *Final Fantasy*. Themes in RPGs are usually variations on "save the world"—such as finding the person responsible for a murder, rescuing someone who's been kidnapped, destroying a dangerous object, or killing monsters.

The characters in RPGs are often termed heroes because they engage in heroic quests—usually in a team, known as a guild in online multiplayer versions of this genre. Combat is one way in which the heroes advance—gaining strength, experience, and money to buy new equipment. Chapter 5 goes into more depth on character development in all genres.

Dragon Age 2 is a huge role-playing game with a rich environment and in-depth characters.

Is an RPG Always Fantasy?

Why do most RPGs take place in fantasy worlds—and involve killing monsters, embarking on quests, and saving someone or something (usually the world)? Many RPGs such as *Star Wars Galaxies* allow for other goals (fame, wealth, and power) and roles (musician, smuggler, doctor, bounty hunter, storm trooper). What about creating a modern-day RPG? If you were to create an RPG, where would it take place—and what roles would exist?

75

Goals & Genres: what are the possibilities   chapter 3

---

notes

Notes contain thought-provoking ideas provided by the authors that are intended to help the readers think critically about the book's topics.

---

case studies

Case studies contain anecdotes from industry professionals (accompanied by game screenshots) on their experiences developing specific game titles.

Massively Multiplayer Online Games

In Chapter 2, you learned about technology issues related to massively multiplayer online games (MMOs). Now let's look at the content and genre characteristics of these games. Under the MMO umbrella, there are several variations on some genres we've already discussed—known as massively multiplayer online role-playing games (MMORPGs), massively multiplayer first-person shooters (MMOFPSs), and massively multiplayer real-time strategy games (MMORTSs).

One of the biggest issues in MMO development is balancing social interaction with immersion. This poses a problem for MMORPGs in particular. Traditional RPG players want to escape into a fantasy world and become involved in rich storylines and character development. If MMORPG players discuss real-world topics during the game or don't stay in character, other more traditional players might not enjoy the experience of playing. Does a developer try to enforce role-play, or do the players have to accept that the game cannot be fully immersive? Issues related to story and immersion are discussed further in Chapter 5.

With millions of subscribers, World of Warcraft is the most popular MMO on the market.

Yohoho! Puzzle Pirates: The First MMORPG?

> I created *Puzzle Pirates* because of my love of pirates—both as a concept and pretending to be a pirate—combined with the realization that puzzle games made the ideal gameplay backbone to an MMOG. My girlfriend at the time becoming pathologically addicted to *Bejeweled* was a tip-off. [Author's Note: Although *Puzzle Pirates* contains elements associated with MMORPGs, its incorporation of puzzles into the game could make it the first of its kind—an MMOPG (puzzle game)!
>
> —Daniel James (Chief Executive Officer, Three Rings Design)

81

Goals & Genres: what are the possibilities   chapter 3

profiles

Profiles provide bios, photos and in-depth commentary from industry professionals and educators.

chapter review

A *chapter review* section at the end of each chapter contains a combination of questions and exercises, which allow readers to apply what they've learned. Annotations and answers are included in the instructor's guide, available separately (see next page).

About the Companion DVD

The companion DVD contains the following media (or links to the most current versions of these media):

- Game engines: Torque 3D (GarageGames), Game Maker 7 (Mark Overmars/ YoYo Games Limited), GameSalad Creator (GameSalad Inc.), Unity 3 (Unity Technologies), and 3DVIA Studio (Dassault Systemes)
- Modeling and animation software: 3ds Max 2012 and Maya 2012 (Autodesk)
- Game design documentation: GDD template (Chris Taylor/Gas Powered Games), *Sub Hunter* (Michael Black/Torn Space), *City of Heroes/City of Villains* (NCsoft), *Dungeon Runners* (NCsoft), *Guild Wars* (NCsoft), *Tabula Rasa* (NCsoft), *EVE Online* (CCP Games, Inc.), and *Furcadia* (Dragon's Eye Productions)
- Game design articles: Harvey Smith/Witchboy's Cauldron and Barrie Ellis/One Switch Games

- Game demos: *America's Army* (U.S. Army), *Myst Online: Uru Live* (Cyan Worlds, Inc.), *EVE Online* (CCP Games, Inc.), *Magic: The Gathering Online* (Wizards of the Coast), *Multiwinia* (Introversion Software), *New Star Soccer 4* (New Star Games Ltd.), *Mount & Blade: Warband* (TaleWorlds Entertainment), *World of Goo* (2D Boy), *Zombie Shooter* (Sigma Team), *The Spirit Engine 2* (Mark Pay), *Solipskier* (Mikengreg Games Co.), *Fortix 2* (Nemesys Games), *Toys* (Christoffer Hedborg), *e7* (Jonas Richner/JGames), *A House in California* Jake Elliott/Cardboard Computer), *Hazard: The Journey of Life* (Alexander Bruce), *The Dream Machine* (Cockroach Inc.), *Loop Raccord* (Nicolai Troshinsky), *Fract* (Richard E Flanagan/ Phosfiend Systems), *Super Crate Box* (Vlambeer), *Octodad* (Kevin Zuhn), *Desktop Dungeons* (QCF Design), *Vanessa Saint-Pierre Delacroix & Her Nightmare* (Bad Pilcrow), *Gate* (One Girl, One Laptop), and *Melonauts* (The Voxel Agents)
- Mobile apps and videos: *PewPew* (Jean-Francois Geyelin), *Trucks & Skulls* (Appy Entertainment), *FaceFighter* (Appy Entertainment), *TuneRunner* (Appy Entertainment), *Zombie Pizza* (Appy Entertainment), *Zen Bound 2* (Secret Exit Ltd.), *Train Conductor* (The Voxel Agents), *Train Conductor 2: USA* (The Voxel Agents), *Time Travel Treasure Hunt* (The Voxel Agents), *Pocket Legends* (Spacetime Studios), *180* (Headcase Games), *Ghost Ninja: Zombie Beatdown* (Gabagool Games), *Agiliste* (Bushi-Go, Inc.), *Parkade* (One Girl, One Laptop), *Speedx 3D* (HyperBees Ltd.), *Aces Cribbage* (Concrete Software, Inc.), *Aces Jewel Hunt* (Concrete Software, Inc.), and *Ash Lite* (SRRN Games)
- Accessibility videos and games: *Alice Amazed* (michi.nu), *Aurikon* (Aggressive Game Designs), *Mini Golf: One Button Style* (Apocalyptic Coders), *Orbit Racers* (Pug Fugly Games), *Strange Attractors 2* (Ominous Development), *Dork* (Moo Job Inc.), *Terraformers* (Pin Interactive), *Driver* (AudioGames.net), *Win Pong* (AudioGames.net), and *Access Invaders* (Human-Computer Interaction Laboratory [HCI Lab] / Foundation for Research & Technology - Hellas [FORTH])

About the Instructor Resources

The instructor resources (available separately on DVD) was developed to assist instructors in planning and implementing their instructional programs. It includes sample syllabi, test questions, assignments, projects, PowerPoint files, and other valuable instructional resources.

Order Number: 1-1113-0765-2

About the Author

Photo credit: Mark Bennington

Jeannie Novak is the Lead Author & Series Editor of the widely acclaimed *Game Development Essentials* series (with over 15 published titles), co-author of *Play the Game: The Parent's Guide to Video Games*, and co-author of three pioneering books on the interactive entertainment industry—including *Creating Internet Entertainment*. She is also Co-Founder of Novy Unlimited and CEO of Kaleidospace, LLC (d/b/a Indiespace, founded in 1994)—where she provides services for corporations, educators, and creative professionals in games, music, film, education, and technology. Jeannie oversees one of the first web sites to promote and distribute interactive entertainment and a game education consulting division that focuses on curriculum development, instructional design, and professional development for higher education and secondary school.

As Online Program Director for the Game Art & Design and Media Arts & Animation programs at the Art Institute Online, Jeannie produced and designed an educational business simulation game that was built within the *Second Life* environment—leading a virtual team of more than 50 educators, students, and industry professionals. She was a game instructor and curriculum development expert at UCLA Extension, Art Center College of Design, Academy of Entertainment & Technology at Santa Monica College, DeVry University, Westwood College, and ITT Technical Institute—and she has consulted for several educational institutions and developers such as UC Berkeley Center for New Media, Alelo Tactical Language & Culture, and GameSalad. Jeannie has also worked on projects funded by the National Science Foundation and Google for Lehigh Carbon Community College and the University of Southern California (USC) Information Sciences Institute.

An active member of the game industry, Jeannie has served as Vice Chair of the International Game Developers Association-Los Angeles chapter (IGDA-LA), executive team member at Women in Games International (WIGI), Game Conference Chair for ANIMIAMI, advisory board member at the Game Education Summit (GES), and session chair at SIGGRAPH. She has participated on the Online Gameplay selection committee for the Academy of Interactive Arts & Sciences' DICE awards since 2003 and has developed game workshops, panels, and breakout sessions in association with events and organizations such as the Penny Arcade Expo (PAX), Game Education Summit (GES), International Game Developers Association (IGDA), GDC Online (formerly GDC Austin), Macworld Expo, Digital Hollywood, USC's Teaching Learning & Technology Conference, and the Los Angeles Games Conference. Jeannie was chosen as one of the 100 most influential people in technology by MicroTimes magazine—and she has been profiled by CNN, *Billboard Magazine*, *Sundance Channel*, *Daily Variety*, and *The Los Angeles Times*.

Jeannie received an M.A. in Communication Management from USC's Annenberg School (where her thesis focused on using massively multiplayer online games as online distance learning applications) and a B.A. in Mass Communication/Business Administration from UCLA (where she graduated summa cum laude/Phi Beta Kappa and completed an honors thesis focusing on gender role relationships in toy commercials). A native of Southern California, Jeannie grew up in San Diego and currently resides in Santa Monica with her husband, Luis Levy. She is also an accomplished composer, recording artist, performer, and music instructor (piano/voice).

Acknowledgements

I would like to thank the following people for their hard work and dedication to this project:

Jim Gish (Senior Acquisitions Editor, Delmar/Cengage Learning), for making this series happen.

Meaghan Tomaso (Senior Product Manager, Delmar/Cengage Learning), for her management help during all phases of this project.

Glenn Castle (Senior Content Project Manager, Delmar/Cengage Learning), for his assistance during the production phase.

Chris Catalina (Technology Product Manager, Delmar/Cengage Learning), for his reliability and professionalism during the DVD QA phase.

Joy Kocsis (Senior Art Director, Cengage/Learning), for her help with the cover and DVD label creation and approval process.

Sarah Timm (Editorial Assistant, Delmar/Cengage Learning), for her ongoing assistance throughout the series.

Ann Fisher, for managing the survey review process in preparation for this edition.

David Ladyman (Media Research & Permissions Specialist), for his superhuman efforts in clearing the media for this book.

IMGS, Inc., for all the diligent work and prompt response during the layout and compositing phase.

Jason Bramble, for his help with DVD design, authoring, and implementation.

Per Olin, for his organized and aesthetically pleasing diagrams.

Ben Bourbon, for his clever and inspired illustrations.

David Koontz (Publisher, Chilton), for starting it all by introducing Jeannie Novak to Jim Gish.

A big thanks also goes out to all the many people who contributed their thoughts and ideas to this book:

Aaron Marks (On Your Mark Music)

Aaron Nash

Alex Brandon (Funky Rustic)

Allen Varney

Allison P. Thresher (Harmonix)

Andy Nealen (Rutgers University)

Anne Toole (The Write Toole)

Anthony Borquez (Grab Games; University of Southern California)

Arash John Sammander

Arturo Sanchez-Ruiz (University of North Florida)

Aujang Abadi (SRRN Games)

Barrie Ellis (One-Switch)

Belinda Van Sickle (GameDocs; Women in Games International)

Bill Amend

Bill Brown

Bill Buckley (Neversoft Entertainment)

Bill Louden (Austin Community College)

Bill Shribman (WGBH Educational Foundation)

Billy Joe Cain (Sneaky Games)

Bjorn Billhardt (Enspire Learning)

Bob Bergen

Brandii Grace (Engaging Designs)

Brenda Laurel (California College of the Arts)

Brian Reynolds (Zynga)

Carissa Gerardo

Carly Staehlin (Burrow Owl Trading)

Chad Mossholder (Sony Online Entertainment)

Chance Thomas (HUGEsound)

Chang Liu (Ohio University)

Chris Avellone (Obsidian Entertainment)

Chris Klug (Carnegie Mellon University)

Chris Lenhart

Chris Swain (University of Southern California)

Christian Allen (WB Games)

Chris Taylor (Gas Powered Games)

Chris Ulm (Appy Entertainment)

Christopher Bretz

Craig Ferguson

Daniel James (Three Rings Design)

David Brin (Epocene)

David Javelosa (Santa Monica College)

David Perry (Gaikai, Inc.)

David Sushil (Bad Pilcrow)

Deborah Baxtrom (Art Institute of Pittsburgh Online)

Denis Papp (TimeGate Studios)

Don Daglow

Drew Davidson (Carnegie Mellon University)

Ed Del Castillo (Liquid Entertainment)

Ed Magnin

Edward Castronova (Indiana University)

Elizabeth Butler

Emmy Jonassen (3DVIA/Dassault Systemes)

Frank T. Gilson (Kabam)

George "The Fat Man" Sanger

Gordon Walton (Playdom)

Graeme Bayless (Big Ego Games)

Grant Collier

Greg Costikyan

Greg O'Connor-Read (Top Dollar PR)

Harvey Smith (Arkane Studios)

Henning Nugel

Hope Levy

Hugh Hancock (Strange Company)

Ivo Gerscovich (Paramount Pictures Interactive & Mobile Entertainment)

Jack Snowden (Art Institute of Seattle)

Jacques A. Montemoino (Gideon Games)

Jake Elliott (Cardboard Computer)

James Owen Lowe (ZeniMax Online Studios)

James Paul Gee (Arizona State University)

James Portnow (Rainmaker Games; DigiPen Institute of Technology)

James Stevenson (Insomniac Games)

Jamie Lendino (Sound For Games Interactive)

Jan McWilliams (Art Institute of California–Los Angeles)

Jason Bramble (Deadman Games, Inc.)

Jason Kay (Monkey Gods LLC)

Jay Gawronek (Bluepoint Games)

Jennifer Penton

Jennifer Wadsworth (Art Institute of
California-Los Angeles)

Jesse Schell (Schell Games; Carnegie
Mellon University)

Jessica Mulligan (Frogster America)

John Ahlquist (Ahlquist Software)

John Comes (Uber Entertainment)

John Davies (Codemasters)

John Hight (Sony Computer
Entertainment America)

John Murphy

Jose P. Zagal (DePaul University)

Justin Mette (21-6 Productions)

Karl Kapp (Bloomsburg University)

Kevin Perry (Alelo)

Kevin D. Saunders (Alelo)

Kevin Zuhn

Kimberly Unger (Bushi-Go)

KyungMin Bang (Electronic Arts - Seoul)

Lars Doucet

Lennart E. Nacke (University of Ontario
Institute of Technology)

Lennie Moore

Lisa Hathaway

Louis Castle (Zynga)

Luis Levy (Novy Unlimited)

Marc Taro Holmes

Marianne Krawczyk (Monkeyshines
Entertainment)

Mark C. Barlet (AbleGamers Foundation)

Mark Chuberka (GameSalad)

Mark Overmars (YoYo Games)

Mark Precious

Mark Soderwall

Mark Terrano (Hidden Path
Entertainment)

Mary-Margaret Walker

Matt MacLean (Obsidian Entertainment)

Michael Black (Torn Space)

Michael Blackledge (Electronic Arts)

Mike Pondsmith (R. Talsorian Games;
DigiPen Institute of Technology)

Nathan Madsen

Patricia A.Pizer (ZeeGee Games)

Pete Markiewicz (Art Institute of
California-Los Angeles)

Quinn Dunki (One Girl, One Laptop)

Rade Stojsavljevic (Jet Set Games, Inc.)

Rebecca Voss

Rich Ragsdale

Richard "Lord British" Garriott
(Portalarium)

Richard Bartle (University of Essex)

Richard E. Flanagan (Phosfiend Systems)

Richard Jacques

Richard Wainess (UCLA/CRESST)

Rob Cairns (Associated Production Music)

Robert Ferguson

Robert Florio

Rocksan Lessard (Secrets of Gaia)

Ron Alpert (Headcase Games)

Ron Jones

Russell Burt (Art Institute of California-
Los Angeles)

Sara Borthwick (CBS Interactive)

Scott Snyder (Edge of Reality)

Shahnaz Kamberi (DeVry University)

Sheri Graner Ray (Schell Games)

Simon Joslin (The Voxel Agents)

Starr Long (The Walt Disney Company)

Stephanie Spong (Moksa Ventures)

Stephen Jacobs (Rochester Institute of
Technology)

Sue Bohle (The Bohle Company)

Titus Levi (United International College)

Tommy Tallarico (Tommy Tallarico
Studios; Game Audio Network Guild)

Tom Salta (Persist Music)

Tom Sloper (Sloperama Productions;
University of Southern California)

Tracy Fullerton (University of Southern
California)

Travis Castillo

Troy Dunniway (Globex Studios)

Virginia R. Hetrick

Warren Spector (Junction Point - Disney
Interactive Studios)

Watson Wu

Thanks to the following people for their tremendous help with referrals and in securing permissions, images, and demos:

Book Content:

Michelle Amores (Fragapalooza)

Ken Fontana (Skate Estate)

Marissa Hill (Electronic Arts)

Carrie Hollenberg (Strategic Business Insights)

Kevin Jones & Jeremiah Heneghan (VirtualHeroes)

Valerie Massey (CCP Games)

Jodie McIntyre (MPOGD.com)

Arne Meyer (Naughty Dog)

Martin Mir (Introversion Software)

Nintendo

PARS International Corp.

Christine Seddon (ESRB)

Vikki Vega (Sony Computer Entertainment America)

Genevieve Waldman (Microsoft Corporation)

Nicole Wasowski (Lewis PR for Emotiv)

Chase Webb (Runic Games Fansite)

DVD Content:

Aujang Abadi (SRRN Games)

Ron Alpert (Headcase Games)

Michael Black (Torn Space)

Fernando Blanco (Spacetime Studios)

Alexander Bruce (Demruth)

Mark Chuberka (GameSalad Inc.)

Danny Day (QCF Design)

Dr. Cat & Emerald Flame (Dragon's Eye Productions)

Sandy Duncan (YoYo Games Limited) & Mark Overmars

Quinn Dunki (One Girl, One Laptop)

Jake Elliott (Cardboard Computer)

Barrie Ellis (One-Switch)

Richard E Flanagan (Phosfiend Systems)

Erick Fritz (GarageGames)

Jean-François Geyelin

Kyle Gabler (2D Boy)

Anders Gustafsson (Cockroach)

Tom Higgins (Unity Technologies ApS)

Rami Ismail (Vlambeer)

Emmy Jonassen (Dassault Systèmes)

Simon Joslin (Voxel Agents)

Szabolcs Jozsa (Nemesys Games)

Jani Kahrama (Secret Exit)

Valerie Massey (CCP Games)

Michael Murashov (Sigma Team)

John Murphy & Kevin Zuhn (The DePaul Game Experience)

NCsoft

Mark Pay

Simon Read (New Star Games Ltd.)

Sebastian Santacroce (Gabagool Games)

Steven Sargent (Appy Entertainment, Inc.)

Harvey Smith (Witchboy's Cauldron)

David Sushil (Bad Pilcrow)

Chris Taylor (Gas Powered Games)

Nicolai Troshinsky

Kimberly Unger (Bushi-Go)

Armagan Yavuz (TaleWorlds Entertainment)

Delmar Cengage Learning and I would also like to thank the following reviewers for their valuable suggestions and technical expertise:

Tom Bledsaw
National Chair School of Design
ITT Educational Services
Fishers, IN

John Bowditch
Director – The Game Research and Immersive Design Lab and Game Design and Development
Professor in the School of Media Arts and Studies
Ohio University
Athens, OH

Kim Callery
Faculty
International Academy of Design & Technology
Troy, MI

Edward Castronova
Professor
Indiana University
Bloomington, IN

Ola Gardner
Professor of Game Art and Design
The Art Institute of Atlanta
Atlanta, GA

Markus Harmon
Assistant Dean, Game Programs
Westwood College Online
Westminster, CO

Celeste Masinter
Instructor, Game Art and Design
Art Institute of Tampa
Tampa, FL

Mary Rasley
Professor of Computer Information Systems
Lehigh Carbon Community College
Schnecksville, PA

Arturo Sanchez
Associate Professor
University of North Florida
Jacksonville, FL

Lee Sheldon
Associate Professor, Co-Director
Games & Simulations Program
Indiana University
Bloomington, IN

Lee Wood
Course Director – Game Planning and Architecture
Full Sail University
Winter Park, FL

Questions and Feedback

We welcome your questions and feedback. If you have suggestions that you think others would benefit from, please let us know and we will try to include them in the next edition.

To send us your questions and/or feedback, you can contact the publisher at:

Delmar Cengage Learning
Executive Woods
5 Maxwell Drive
Clifton Park, NY 12065
Attn: Graphic Arts Team
(800) 998-7498

Or the author at:

Jeannie Novak
Founder & CEO
INDIESPACE
P.O. Box 5458
Santa Monica, CA 90409
jeannie@indiespace.com

DEDICATION

This book is dedicated to my family and friends for their support and understanding, to my students and colleagues for their enthusiasm and creativity—and to Luis for always challenging and inspiring me to explore and innovate.

—*Jeannie Novak*

Part I:
Setup

building the foundation

CHAPTER

1

Historical Elements

how did we get here?

Key Chapter Questions

- What are the significant *milestones* in the history of electronic game development?

- Who are game development *pioneers*, and how did they contribute to the industry?

- How did the game industry evolve from coin-operated electromechanical and mainframe computer games of the 1960s to the console, personal computer, online, and mobile industries of today?

- What factors contributed to the *video game slump* of the early 1980s?

- Why did certain game companies and titles succeed during game development history—and why did some fail miserably?

If you plan to become involved in the game development industry, it is important that you learn about its evolution. Did it begin with video arcades? Was there life before *Pong*? Has the industry always been successful? As you read this chapter, think about the first electronic game you ever played. Did you play it on a personal computer? On a home game console? At a video arcade? At a pizza parlor? What did you like about the game? After you finish this chapter, you will probably be surprised at the strange and unusual events that have occurred during the development of an industry that is still in its infancy.

Before the Arcades

The first electronic games were not played at home or even at video arcades. Instead, research departments at universities, labs, military installations, and defense contractors provided the backdrop for this industry. At military bases, electromechanical games were provided for the recruits to escape from the rigors of basic training. Meanwhile, a few bleary-eyed, overworked students, programmers, faculty, and researchers in academic and government institutions turned their mainframe computers into game machines—providing them relief from traditional duties such as performing complex mathematical calculations for research. Late at night, these pioneers spawned what would become one of the most compelling forms of entertainment in history.

BigStock   BigStock

The first electronic games were played at military bases such as the Marine Corp Air Station Kaneohe (left) and at academic institutions such as the Massachusetts Institute of Technology (right).

Two distinct segments of the electronic game industry developed in parallel, starting in the 1950s. One of these segments began in 1951 when Marty Bromley, who managed game rooms at military bases in Hawaii, bought electromechanical machines and launched SEGA (an abbreviation for SErvice GAmes). This segment of the industry grew into the coin-op video arcade industry, which experienced a boom in the 1970s. Electronic versions of arcade favorites marked the beginning of what was to become the console game industry of today.

The other segment of the electronic game industry started with mainframe computer games developed by faculty and students at universities who wanted to either hone their programming skills or entertain each other during breaks from the long hours spent working on their dissertations. Although an adaptation of one of the early mainframe games (*Spacewar!*) became the first coin-op video arcade game in the United States, it was not until the personal computer revolution that mainframe games were adapted for personal computers. It was then that the computer game industry was born.

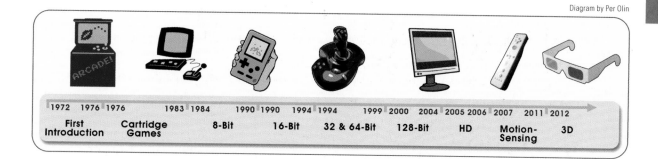

Diagram by Per Olin

1972 1976 1976	1983 1984	1990 1990	1994 1994	1999 2000	2004 2005 2006	2007	2011 2012
First Introduction	Cartridge Games	8-Bit	16-Bit	32 & 64-Bit	128-Bit	HD	Motion-Sensing	3D

Many companies and developers made significant contributions in the creation of game systems and content. You might recognize many companies that were formed in that era, and you might even have played some games that were developed during that time. What companies made a difference in the evolution of this industry? Who were the pioneering designers, artists, programmers, and producers responsible for developing compelling games that continue to inspire developers today?

A few companies were ready to plunge in just as the electronic game industry began. Some of them maintain a significant presence in the industry. You might be surprised at how they began—and how they continued to develop. Some of them initially had nothing to do with games, or even entertainment. Others tried, and failed, to dominate every segment of the game industry. Many came and went, and a few are still going strong. Some stepped out of the picture for a while, only to return with a vengeance during the second "golden age" of the industry. As we look at the arcade phenomenon, we'll focus on some of these companies and the popular games they developed.

:::::: They're *All* Video Games Now!

The term "video game" came out of the arcade business and gravitated toward the home console game business. There was a demarcation between games played on personal computers (*computer games*) and those played on home consoles (*video games*)—with electronic being used to refer to both. Although sometimes you'll still see a distinction made between "computer" and "video" games, today's electronic games are often referred to as "video games" across the board.

BigStock iStock Photo   iStock Photo

The Arcade Phenomenon

The public was first introduced to electronic games not through home game consoles or personal computers, but through public arcades. Before video games were introduced, the most popular arcade games were electromechanical pinball machines. Arcades were often located in small amusement parks, attracting children and teenagers—who challenged each other to pinball matches as part of a regular weekend social event. As video games became more popular, arcades became more accessible. Conveniently located near schools and residential areas, arcades became flooded with teens after school. At the height of the craze, kids spent hours at the arcades—sometimes into the night, forgetting to eat, or to do their homework!

:::::: Sega: Setting the 25-Cent Standard

Sega

In 1956, just a few years after Marty Bromley started SEGA, Rosen Enterprises' David Rosen began importing coin-operated electromechanical games to Japan—launching the country's coin-op business and becoming Japan's largest amusement company. In 1964, Rosen Enterprises merged with SEGA to form Sega Enterprises. Acting as a bridge between the United States and Japan, Sega Enterprises released the first Japanese export, *Periscope*, in the United States. It is interesting that the high shipping costs of this export were what made U.S. arcade owners charge 25 cents to play the game—setting a standard for future arcade games. Sega was purchased by Gulf & Western in 1969—but David Rosen and partner Isao Okawa bought it back in 1984. The price tag: $38 million.

Several games are considered milestones of this era. Although limited by the technology of the time, these games were innovative—inspiring new trends in content, genres, gameplay, and development techniques that had never been considered. Some of these games were extremely popular—successfully capturing a broad market that went far beyond the stereotypical "male teen" demographic. They provided hope for the future of electronic games as a mass entertainment medium. Many of these games are considered so nostalgic by gamers from this era that they have been re-released in console, computer, or handheld format so that they can be experienced again. You might recognize a few of them!

Computer Space

In 1961, MIT student Steve Russell developed *Spacewar!*—the first interactive computer game—on the university's mainframe computer. Nolan Bushnell, who later founded Atari, saw the game and decided to bring it to a larger market by adapting it into a stand-alone arcade coin-op game. Calling his version *Computer Space*, Bushnell sold the idea to Nutting Associates in 1971. The game, which consisted simply of trying to shoot a flying saucer, might not have been as compelling as a pinball game—and its low sales reflected this. However, Bushnell started the coin-op video arcade industry by bringing an elitist form of entertainment that had remained enclosed within the ivory tower of the university system out to the masses. In 1978, after video game arcade technology became more sophisticated, Cinematronics released *Space Wars*—another arcade adaptation of Russell's mainframe game.

JN

:::::Atari's Wild Ride

After *Computer Space*, Bushnell left Nutting Associates to start Atari with partner Ted Dabney. (The word "Atari" is from the board game *Go* and means roughly, "Look out! The move I'm about to make will be dangerous to you"—similar to "check" in chess.) After surviving a legal dispute with Magnavox over the rights to the first successful video game (*Pong*), Atari became the most prolific presence in the arcade business—churning out games such as *Asteroids*, which became the first blockbuster video game and forever associated the name "Atari" with the

Atari Interactive, Inc.

video arcade. After Bushnell left the company to start several ventures, Atari was purchased by Warner Communications in 1976, and began spending more energy on business affairs and marketing than design and development. Concerned about the growth of the console and personal computer industries, Atari also began shifting its focus away from its arcade business and toward console systems (such as the VCS/2600) and personal computers. In 1984, Atari was sold to Commodore founder Jack Tramiel—who in turn sold it to disk drive manufacturer JTS, who then filed for bankruptcy in 1999 and sold it to Hasbro Interactive. The Atari name was revived when Infogrames took over Hasbro in 2000 and completed its acquisition of Atari in 2008. Nolan Bushnell came full circle in April 2010 after replacing former Atari CEO, David Gardner, as a member of the board of directors.

Pong

The beginnings of the first memorable—and controversial—electronic game appeared in 1958 when Willy Higinbotham of Brookhaven National Laboratories in New York showcased his table tennis–style game (*Tennis for Two*) on an analog computer. Almost

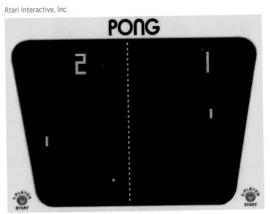

Atari Interactive, Inc.

a decade later, Ralph Baer of Sanders Associates began researching ideas for an interactive "table tennis" television system. He patented his idea in 1968, and Magnavox licensed it from him in 1970. The Magnavox Odyssey interactive game console—featuring Baer's "table tennis" game—was demonstrated in 1972. The first Atari game, *Pong* (designed by Atari engineer Al Alcorn) was released that same year. The controller was a two-direction rotary dial, and the rules of the game were simply "use your paddle to avoid missing ball for high score." *Pong* soon became the first successful coin-op arcade game. Magnavox sued Atari that same year, claiming that Bushnell had stolen the idea. The case was settled out of court.

Pong—the first successful arcade game.

:::::Ralph Baer & *Simon*

Hasbro, Inc.

Ralph Baer, who invented the Magnavox Odyssey (the first home console system), was inspired by the Steven Spielberg film *Close Encounters of the Third Kind* when he created the successful musical memory game, Simon—released by Milton-Bradley during the holiday season in 1977. Baer also invented the first light-gun game.

As a young child in the late 1970s, I encountered my first video game, *Pong*, prominently displayed in the children's clothing section of Macy's Department Store in San Leandro, California. I was entranced, excited to play, and mesmerized as I watched my hand control a rectangle that bounced a square to my opponent. Both of us gleefully volleyed the square back and forth, feverishly trying to get the other to miss a shot—as *Pong's* simple "beeps" and "blips" added to our delight.

—*Jennifer Penton (Creative Director, i2i Communications)*

Asteroids

Although *Space Invaders* (1978) was the first arcade game that recorded high scores, *Asteroids* (1979), was the first to allow players to enter their initials into a high score table. *Asteroids* (designed by Ed Logg) utilized monochrome vector graphics, which allowed the game to display fast-moving objects made up of very sharp lines instead of the crude pixel graphics common in video games of that time. (Vector graphics would later come back as polygons—and 3D games!)

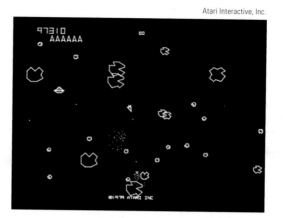
Atari Interactive, Inc.

> **M**y first experience with an electronic game was the original *Asteroids*. It was on the second floor of my mom's racquetball club in Cincinnati. The most memorable thing about the game was that for years I only got the chance to dream about destroying the "real detailed" silvery-looking asteroids because I was never allowed to insert 25 cents. My mom thought video games were a waste of money.
>
> —*Rebecca Voss (Harris Corporation - Defense Communications Systems)*

Pizza & Mechanical Animals: The Family Arcade Experience

In an attempt to remove the stigma associated with the public's idea of arcades, Atari founder Nolan Bushnell opened up a string of pizza parlors initially known as Pizza Time Theater. Eventually becoming Chuck E. Cheese, these family restaurants offered game tokens with every meal, a video arcade for kids who would play while waiting for the pizza, and a "live" floor show featuring Chuck E. Cheese himself (along with other mechanical robot animals) for the whole family to enjoy while eating.

Galaxian

Bally/Midway imported some of the most popular "slide and shoot" games to video arcades. *Space Invaders* was the first blockbuster video game, and *Galaxian* was the first video game with a full-color monitor. *Galaxian* was followed by several sequels—including *Galaga*, *Galplus*, *Galaga '88*, and *Galaxian 3*.

Namco Bandai Games America Inc

In 1976, the first public controversy over video game violence occurred in response to the Exidy Games release of *Death Race*, in which players drove over "stick figures" representing pedestrians. (Compare this to the *Grand Theft Auto* series!) The game was inspired by the 1975 cult film, *Death Race 2000* (starring David Carradine and Sylvester Stallone in one of his first roles)—in which pedestrians are run down for points in a cross-country car race of the future. Protests were so widespread that even *60 Minutes* did a story on *Death Race*—bringing video games into public awareness. The publicity didn't help the game, though—since nervous arcade owners eventually refused to carry it.

:::::"A" for "Activision"

Activision

It is not uncommon for employees in the game industry to leave one company and start a new one so they can retain creative leadership. Activision, one such company, was the first third-party game publisher, and was established in 1980 by former Atari programmers. The name was specifically chosen because it came before "Atari" alphabetically.

Pac-Man

In 1980, Namco released *Pac-Man*—which appealed to a much wider market, in part because it did away with the "shooting" theme that pervaded most other games. The game's controller consisted only of a multi-directional joystick. Instead of shooting spaceships, *Pac-Man* ate power pills—which allowed him to munch on his ghostly enemies for a short while. *Pac-Man* was developed primarily by Namco employee Toru Iwatani over a period of 18 months. Over 300,000 units were sold worldwide—making *Pac-Man* the most popular arcade game of all time. As players successfully completed one maze, they moved up a level—which contained the same maze, but play was more difficult. *Pac-Man* spawned an even more popular and inclusive sequel: *Ms. Pac-Man*, the first game to star a female character. Instead of the increasingly difficult maze used in

Namco Bandai Games America Inc

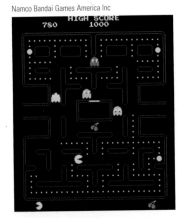

Pac-Man is one of the most popular arcade games of all time.

levels of play in the original game, there were four different mazes used in *Ms. Pac-Man*. The game even incorporated a rough three-act plot structure that featured animated sequences (a primitive form of the cinematics used in today's games) as dividers. In Act I, Pac-Man and Ms. Pac-Man meet; in Act II, Pac-Man woos Ms. Pac-Man by chasing her around the screen; and in Act III, Pac-Man, Jr. is born. The game had great crossover appeal, helping to further widen the market to include girls and families. Boys played it, too—finding the game even more challenging and addictive than its predecessor.

Arcade Graphics Evolution

Arcade games evolved from the static screen and horizontal movement of *Space Invaders*, to the limited vertical movement of *Centipede* and, finally, to the scrolling screen of *Xevious*.

Taito Corporation   Atari Interactive, Inc.   Atari Interactive, Inc.

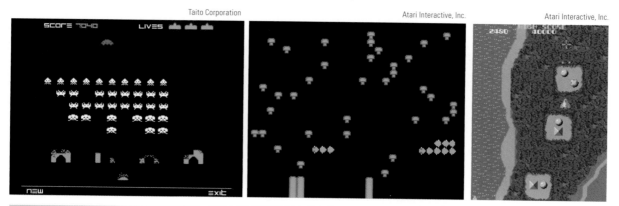

Women Enter the Arcade World

Released by Atari in 1981, *Centipede* was the first arcade game co-designed by a woman. Dona Bailey and Ed Logg teamed up to create a game with the goal of shooting quick-moving centipedes as they appeared at the top of the screen and tried to snake their way down. Each time a segment of the centipede was hit, it turned into a mushroom. The game was designed in a unique pastel color scheme.

> **M**y friends and I would go to the local arcade and play games till we ran out of money or our hands developed blisters and went numb. I would get so excited when I played that I would get drenched in my own sweat and have to walk around trying to dry off so that my mom wouldn't find out that I had been at the arcade.
>
> —*Arash John Sammander (game design and production graduate student, Aalto University of Art & Design [TAIK] - Finland)*

Donkey Kong

In 1977, Shigeru Miyamoto was hired as Nintendo's first staff artist. The company initially assigned him to *Radarscope*—a submarine game that consisted of repetitive button-pushing without any real story or characters. Although this was the typical game style of the time, Miyamoto wanted to create something unique. The result was, a game that represented a cross between *King Kong* and *Beauty and the Beast*. In, an ape steals his keeper's girlfriend and runs away. The player takes on the role of the keeper (Mario)—who becomes the hero of the story as he attempts to rescue his girlfriend (Pauline) from the clutches of the beast.

Nintendo

Donkey Kong kicked off a successful franchise still wildly popular.

Nintendo

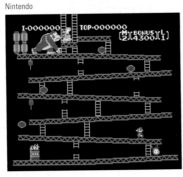

Nintendo made its phenomenal entry into the U.S. market with *Donkey Kong*. Like *Pac-Man*, the popularity of this game resulted in a series of successful, although confusing, sequels. Mario (originally called Jumpman) first appeared as the heroic carpenter whose goal was to rescue his girlfriend. The game's sequel, *Donkey Kong Junior*, switched the roles of Mario and the ape so that Mario was the enemy—an evil carpenter who had caged the now apparently innocent ape from the original game. The player took on the role of the baby ape who attempts to rescue his father (the ape from *Donkey Kong*) from Mario's evil clutches. In the third game, *Mario Bros.* (released in 1983), more confusion arose. Instead of being a carpenter, Mario was a plumber. He and his brother, Luigi, were known as the "Mario Bros." (Was Mario's full name "Mario Mario"?) The action takes place in a sewer, where two players take on the roles of Mario and Luigi to battle each other and an infinite supply of creatures (e.g., turtles and crabs) that emerge from the surrounding sewer pipes.

After *Donkey Kong*, Shigeru Miyamoto went on to develop a series of Mario titles. In fact, each time a new game system is introduced by Nintendo (starting with the original NES—discussed later in this chapter), Miyamoto designs a Mario game as its flagship title. Miyamoto's credits also include *Zelda*, *Star Fox*, *Pikmin*, and *Metroid Prime*.

Why *"Donkey Kong"*?

You might wonder why a game involving a gorilla and a carpenter would be called *Donkey Kong*. Since the gorilla in the original game was "stubborn," Shigeru Miyamoto—creator of *Donkey Kong*—wanted to call the game *Stubborn Gorilla*. In search of a more snappy English translation, Miyamoto found that "donkey" could represent "stubbornness" and "kong" could represent a gorilla (as in the film, *King Kong*)!

The U.S. arcade business reached its peak in 1981, as revenues reached $5 billion and Americans spent more than 75,000 hours playing video games. But the following year, the business experienced a decline from which it never fully recovered.

:::::: Nintendo: Ancient History

Nintendo, which became one of the "big three" in today's console wars—and a major contender in the handheld market—

Nintendo

was established in 1889 by Fusajiro Yamaguchi to manufacture and distribute Japanese playing cards known as *Hanafuda*. It wasn't until 1980 that Minoru Arakawa opened Nintendo of America. Nintendo jumpstarted the second "golden age" of the video game industry by releasing the Nintendo Entertainment System (NES) home console.

leighjevans (Photobucket)

Tron

Released in 1982 by Bally Midway, *Tron* was the first video arcade game to be licensed from a film studio. The film itself was about characters going inside games and competing with each other, so the tie-in with an arcade game was fitting!

:::::: Collecting Quarters for *Pole Position*

In 1982, Namco released *Pole Position*—which pioneered the "chase-cam" and became the first wildly successful driving game. One of these arcade games was in the breakroom at a now-defunct but then-successful recording studio in Los Angeles. During breaks from recording, famous bands and artists played the game incessantly—always putting a quarter in the slot per play. Little did they know that this wasn't necessary because the owner had deactivated the coin box control. (The staff knew about it, and they just played for free!) Every few months, the staff used the quarters to pay for a big company dinner—thanks to its clients' video game addiction!

Namco Bandai Games America Inc

The Birth of Console Games

Although the Magnavox Odyssey—the first home game console—was released in 1972, it wasn't until the late 1970s that the home console industry began to take shape. Pre-dating the video arcade industry boom, the Odyssey was ahead of its time. The video arcade industry was business-to-business—with machines sold to arcade operators rather than to consumers. The high price tag on standalone arcade machines made it prohibitive for all but the wealthiest consumers to own them. However, it became clear that selling directly to consumers (business-to-consumer) could expand the industry tremendously—so video arcades began moving into the home in the form of affordable game consoles. These systems used the television as a monitor and competed for market share much like Sony (PlayStation), Microsoft (Xbox), and Nintendo (GameCube).

Atari VCS/2600

Although the first programmable home game to use cartridges (Channel F) was released in 1976 by Fairchild Camera & Instrument, the inexpensive Atari VCS (Video Computer System)/2600 took off one year later—successfully launching the home game console industry. Atari kept the price of the hardware low and made most of its money from the game titles it developed for the console. Popular titles included *Adventure* (where a block-shaped knight searched for keys and a magic chalice, always on the lookout for angry dragons) and *Yar's Revenge* (where a race of mutated houseflies that had relocated to space sought revenge on an army setting up camp on the right side of the screen). When Atari adapted the blockbuster arcade game *Space Invaders* for the VCS format in 1980, the practice of selling home versions of arcade games began. Atari followed up with its less-successful 5200 in 1982, and the 7800 in 1984.

Atari Interactive, Inc.

The Atari VCS/2600 successfully launched the home game console industry.

::::::The Hidden "Easter Egg"

The first video game "in joke" (known as an "Easter egg") was programmed by Warren Robinett in the VCS game *Adventure*. The hidden information was Robinett's credit; it symbolized the need for game developers to get the credit they deserved for their work. It turned out that Robinett made one pixel on a wall in a room active—linking to a hidden room containing his credit. When the Easter egg was discovered by a teenager—who wrote Atari an excited letter about it—other developers were inspired to hide their names and other messages in games. The tradition continues (whether or not the game companies know about i

FoxTrot by Bill Amend
Courtesy of Universal Press Syndicate

It was love at first sight when I laid eyes on *Vanguard* for the Atari 2600 (cue Jekyll-Hyde transformation). I never thought blasting those 16-color panels in *River Raid* could be so fulfilling. It was like "bending space and time." I started playing at about 8 a.m.—and suddenly it was 3 p.m. My friend's mom was shooing us out for being inside all day. (I believe it's some sort of singularity like a black hole; neither light nor time can escape!)

—*Aaron Nash (game art and design student)*

Mattel Intellivision

Atari had some competition two years after the release of the VCS when Mattel released an arguably superior (and more expensive) console system known as Intellivision. Instead of a joystick (like the VCS), the Intellivision was equipped with an "intelligent" controller consisting of a keypad and a movement disc resembling the "track pad" on some of today's laptops. Game-specific plastic overlays were available to slide over the controllers, and the system even had rudimentary voice synthesis (with the purchase of an attachable component—the Intellivoice). In 1984, Mattel Electronics was shut down after heavy losses and sold to a Mattel vice president, Terry Valeski, who renamed it Intellivision Inc.

Mattel, Inc.

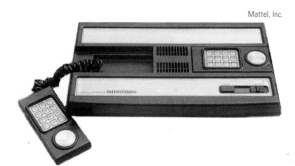

Mattel's Intellivision game console used a keypad and movement disc instead of a joystick.

:::::: Mattel's Handhelds: One Sport at a Time

In 1977, the same year that Atari released the VCS/2600, Mattel launched the handheld game industry by releasing a series of LED- (light emitting diode) based portable games. Unlike cartridge-based handhelds, these systems could contain only one game! If you wanted to play another game, you had to buy another portable. Fortunately, the games were inexpensive! Some popular titles were *Auto Race*, *Basketball*, *Bowling*, *Football*, and *Sub Chase*.

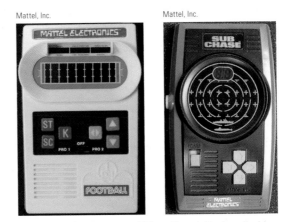

Mattel, Inc.   Mattel, Inc.

Football and *Sub Chase*—two of Mattel's popular handheld games.

Around 1984 (I was six years old), I took a handheld football game away from my male cousin. I remember feeling a sense of excitement being a girl playing a boy's game, especially when I beat all the neighborhood boys' scores.

—*Carissa Gerardo (Operations Supervisor, Integrated Marketing Services)*

ColecoVision

Coleco's entry into the console market was ColecoVision—containing mushroom-like joystick controllers and superb graphics. Blending the best of the VCS/2600 and Intellivision, ColecoVision soon became the standard for reproducing the arcade experience at home. Nintendo's wildly popular arcade game, *Donkey Kong*, was included with every ColecoVision. Most of the early titles were adaptations of other memorable arcade titles such as *Venture*, *Mr. Dot*, *Lady Bug*, and *Space Fury*.

:::::: Cobbler to Cabbage Patch: Coleco's Diverse History

The Connecticut Leather Company (later shortened to Coleco) was established in 1932 by Russian immigrant Maurice Greenberg to distribute leather products to shoemakers. The company

River West Brands

soon began making leather craft kits for kids based on popular icons Howdy Doody and Davy Crockett. After competing in the first console wars of the home gaming industry with a superior system (ColecoVision) and releasing the successful Cabbage Patch Kids toys, Coleco filed for bankruptcy in 1988.

In the 1970s and 1980s, Coleco released some of the most memorable handheld games, including mini tabletop arcade games of popular titles such as *Zaxxon*, *Frogger*, and *Galaxian*. These mini arcade games were cleverly designed to emulate the look and feel of real stand-up arcade games, down to the joystick controller and cabinet art.

> The first electronic game I remember playing was *Smurfs* on ColecoVision. I think I was about six years old. I thought I was so cool—as I jumped over the fences and ducked under the bats that swooped down on me!
>
> —*Elizabeth Butler (game art and design student)*

Sega

Mattel, Inc.

Coleco's ColecoVision blended the best of the VCS/2600 and Intellivision console systems.

Sega's *Zaxxon* was just one of the arcade games transformed into a mini tabletop game by Coleco.

Just when it seemed like the video game industry was unstoppable, it halted. The entire industry—including arcades and the home console segment—experienced a "slump" during the early 1980s. The arcades never recovered from it, although the home console segment experienced an amazing recovery in the mid-1980s. What happened, and why?

The Video Game Slump & a New Golden Age

Several theories have been attributed to the video game industry slump of the early 1980s. Perhaps the industry just experienced a temporary decline, and the platforms and titles introduced were just not revolutionary enough to reverse it. Oversupply might have also contributed to the slump; over 50 software companies produced cartridges, saturating the market with titles. There was also a lack of innovation—and low-quality and derivative games flooded the marketplace. Market conditions forced the price of games to be lowered to $5 to stay competitive. Many video game developers were also concerned that home computers would take over the home gaming market altogether. Because this industry had never experienced a decline, the general public started questioning its legitimacy—wondering whether home gaming was simply a fad, like the short-lived "hula hoop" craze!

Nintendo

Nintendo's entry into the console business in 1985 breathed new life into the home gaming industry—but it also helped push the arcade business into extinction. The system was far superior to consoles of the previous era, and the titles were graphically advanced—with compelling storylines and characters. Titles such as the *Super Mario Bros.* arcade conversion, *The Legend of Zelda*, and *Punch-Out!!* (where players had the thrill of bashing boxing legend Mike Tyson) were engrossing—with seemingly limitless environments. Over 50 million NES systems were sold. The release of the improved Super NES (SNES) in 1991 solidified Nintendo's presence in the marketplace. A year later, Nintendo released *Super Mario Bros. 3*, the most successful non-bundled game cartridge of all time.

Nintendo

The Nintendo Entertainment System (NES) revolutionized the console industry.

> The first real video game I ever played was the *Super Mario Bros.* that came with the original NES system. I played it night and day, and I even taped my final victory against King Koopa. It was quite an achievement for me back then.
>
> —*Robert Ferguson (game art and design student)*

The NES became so successful in the marketplace that the former industry leader Atari established Tengen, a subsidiary that exclusively focused on developing games for the NES. Soon afterward, Tengen discovered a way to bypass Nintendo's "lockout chip" and produce NES-compatible games without Nintendo's approval. Tengen then acquired the rights to sell the extremely popular puzzle game, *Tetris*. After it was discovered that Tengen bought the rights from Mirrorsoft (which did not actually own the rights), the game was removed from the marketplace—and Nintendo, which had acquired the legitimate rights to the game, released it under its own label.

:::::: Alexey Pajitnov & *Tetris*

Tetris originated in Russia around 1985 and was never patented. At the time, intellectual property rights were not established in the former Soviet Union for private individuals. The original author of *Tetris* was Alexey Pajitnov, assisted by Dmitry Pavlovsky and Vadim Gerasimov. *Tetris* has been embroiled in a strangely large number of legal battles since its inception. The IBM PC version eventually made its way to Budapest, Hungary, where it was ported to various platforms and was "discovered" by a British software house named Andromeda. They attempted to contact Pajitnov to secure the rights for the PC version, but before the deal was firmly settled, they had already sold the rights to Spectrum Holobyte. After failing to settle the deal with Pajitnov, Andromeda attempted to license it from the Hungarian programmers instead. Meanwhile, before any legal rights were settled, the Spectrum Holobyte IBM PC version of *Tetris* was released in the United States in 1986. The game's popularity was tremendous, and many players

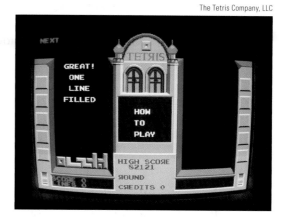

The Tetris Company, LLC

were instantly hooked—it was a software blockbuster. By 1989, half a dozen different companies claimed rights to create and distribute the *Tetris* software for home computers, game consoles, and handheld systems. Nintendo released their version of *Tetris* for both the Famicom and the Game Boy and sold more than three million copies. The lawsuits between Tengen and Nintendo over the Famicom/NES version continued until 1993. In 1996, Alexey Pajitnov and Henk Rogers formed The Tetris Company, LLC and Blue Planet Software in an effort to get royalties from the Tetris brand, with good success on game consoles but very little on the PC front. *Tetris* is now a registered trademark of The Tetris Company, LLC.

What eventually became a great rivalry between Sony and Nintendo began in 1986, when the two companies agreed to create a CD-ROM for the SNES. In 1991, Sony revealed its "PlayStation" console (an SNES with a built-in CD-ROM drive) at the Consumer Electronics Show. After this announcement, Nintendo turned to Philips to create a CD-ROM compatible with the Philips CD-i ("interactive") system. Concerned with Nintendo's move, Sony scrapped the old "PlayStation" developed for Nintendo and began developing a 32-bit CD-only game machine to compete aggressively with Nintendo both in Japan and in the United States.

I remember being six years old, and all I wanted for the holidays was an NES. I played *Duck Hunt* with my father every day after school. It was like our bonding time between school and work—and it became a routine as the years, and systems, went on. By the time my brother was three years old, he would join in on the fun, too!

—Lisa Hathaway (game art and design graduate)

Cheating with the Genie

In 1991, Galoob Toys released the Game Genie, which lets players cheat in NES games and win more easily. Nintendo attempted to prevent Game Genie sales—citing that it reduced the long-term value of its games.

Nintendo revolutionized the industry again with the Game Boy—a portable system that launched a new era of handhelds in 1989. The ever-popular *Tetris* was the flagship title for the monochrome system. The Game Boy was succeeded by the Game Boy Color (1998) and the Game Boy Advance (2001). The Game Boy Advance SP (2003)—which resembles a miniature laptop and has a backlit screen—is still in wide use. Its successor, the Game Boy Micro, was launched in 2005. Nintendo continues to play a major role in the newest era in portable (now "handheld") gaming with its DS series, first launched in 2004 and discussed later in this chapter.

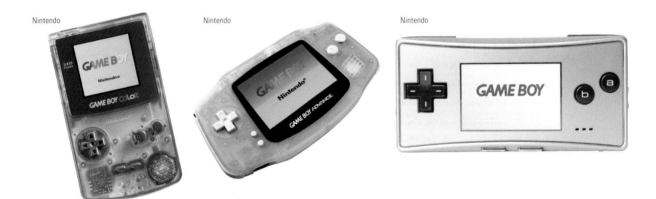

Nintendo's Game Boy (Game Boy Color, left)—followed by the Game Boy Advance, Game Boy Advance SP (middle), and Game Boy Micro (right)—kicked off a new era in portable gaming.

Tiger's Multipurpose Handhelds

In 1997, Tiger released a monochrome handheld system called "game.com" to compete with the Game Boy. Unlike Nintendo's special-purpose game system, Tiger's featured a built-in solitaire game, calculator, personal contacts database, and calendar. It also included a stylus and touch-screen technology, and it could hook up to a standard modem to access a text-based email service.

Sega

Following Nintendo's successful launch of the NES, Sega began releasing a slew of game systems in the 1980s and 1990s—including the Sega Master System (SMS), Genesis, Saturn, and Dreamcast. In 1991, Sega reinvented itself with *Sonic the Hedgehog*—a game that featured a fast-moving blue creature in red tennis shoes. The character of Sonic was so successful that it became Sega's mascot (and a serious challenger to Mario), giving Sega 55% of the 16-bit market. (The character's name was trademarked by Sega as "Sonic The Hedgehog" with a capital "T"; Sonic's middle name is officially "The"!) Although the Sega

The Sega Master System (SMS) was Sega's first entry into the console market.

Genesis outsold SuperNES in 1992, allowing Sega to effectively take control of the U.S. console market, Sega's follow-up releases did not fare as well and were both discontinued. By 1995, Sega of America was juggling seven separate and incompatible game platforms—Saturn, Genesis, Game Gear, Pico, Sega CD, 32X, and 32X CD.

:::::: Video Game Violence: Senate Hearings & the ESRB

In 1993, U.S. Senators Joseph Lieberman of Connecticut and Herbert Kohl of Wisconsin held hearings on violence in computer and video games. Shortly thereafter, the industry created the Entertainment Software Rating Board (ESRB) to provide parents and consumers with detailed information on game content so they can make appropriate purchasing decisions for their unique households. The ESRB independently assigns computer and video game content ratings, enforces industry-adopted advertising guidelines, and helps ensure responsible online privacy practices for the interactive entertainment software industry. The rating system is voluntary, although virtually all games that are sold at retail in the U.S. and Canada are rated by the ESRB. Many retailers, including most major chains, have policies to only stock or sell games that carry an ESRB rating, and most console manufacturers will only permit games that have been rated by the ESRB to be published for their systems. For more information on the ratings, visit http://www.esrb.org.

The ESRB rating icons are registered trademarks of the Entertainment Software Association.

ESRB ratings symbols include EC (Early Childhood), E (Everyone), E10+ (Everyone 10+), T (Teen), M (Mature), AO (Adults Only), and RP (Rating Pending).

In 1992, Electronic Arts founder Trip Hawkins started 3DO—a new company that received major backing from Panasonic, Time-Warner, and MCA—to release a 32-bit game console that they hoped would take over as the new industry leader. A year later, Panasonic marketed the console; although reviews were positive, the price (at $699) was not. Atari responded by jumping ahead to a 64-bit console system with the release of the Jaguar. Sega responded by releasing the 32X, a peripheral device that enabled the Genesis to run a new set of 32-bit cartridge games.

Since the Saturn was outselling Sony's PlayStation in Japan, it was assumed that the Saturn would also do well in the United States. After announcing that the system would be released in the United States on "Saturnday"—September 2—Sega released the system four months earlier than expected. Overall, sales were low and few titles were released—primarily because developers were caught off guard by the early release. Although the system continued to do well in Japan, sales remained disappointingly low in the United States. By 1996, rumors persisted that the company would stop developing hardware and focus on game software.

Sony Computer Entertainment America

The launch of Sony's original PlayStation started a new era in the console wars.

In 1997, Sega announced its merger with Japanese toy company Bandai— which, ironically, was developing software for the PlayStation. After Bandai's board approved of the merger, internal dissent ultimately caused Bandai to reverse its decision. In 1998, Sega launched the Dreamcast, which used Microsoft's Windows CE operating system—allowing for easier game conversions to and from the PC. Even with the success of this release, President Hayao Nakayama stepped down from his position and Sega ceased distribution of the Saturn in the United States.

The entry of Sony's PlayStation into the console market in 1995 launched a new era in the console wars. Even with the release of industry leader Nintendo's N64, the PlayStation kept its spot as the number one worldwide next-generation game console. In 1997, Sony and Nintendo continued competing with the PlayStation and N64.

The "Big Three" Console Wars

The console wars involving the "big three" (Sony, Microsoft, and Nintendo) emerged in 2000 with the launch of Sony's PlayStation 2 (PS2)—which became the fastest selling console in history, with over 100 million units shipped by 2006. Nintendo's GameCube and Microsoft's Xbox joined the new console war in 2001 and 2002, respectively. The GameCube focused on a younger (primarily early childhood and pre-teen) market, and the Xbox's emphasis on performance and features attracted the "hardcore" gamer population.

The PlayStation 2, GameCube, and Xbox consoles were manufactured by Sony, Nintendo, and Microsoft, respectively (the "Big Three").

A new generation of systems from the "big three" currently vie for attention in the marketplace—Microsoft's Xbox 360, Nintendo's Wii, and Sony's PlayStation 3 (PS3). We will explore these systems in more detail in Chapter 2.

FoxTrot by Bill Amend
Courtesy of Universal Press Syndicate

The Personal Computer Revolution

During the mid-1970s, another segment of the electronic gaming industry began to enter a new era. The personal computer revolution brought technology that was once the exclusive territory of programmers and hobbyists into the home. Games that had once been developed on a whim by university students could now be adapted for personal computers—and the general consumer would get to join in the fun. Already, arcade games were being repurposed into home game systems, taking some of the business away from video game arcades. The growth of computers in the home also contributed to the eventual decline of the arcade business—and it also represented a threat to the game console business. Several personal computers—such as the Apple II and Commodore 64—were created with gameplay in mind. (In fact, Steve Wozniak, who designed the Apple II, was an avid gamer.) As you read this section, think about the first personal computer your or your family owned and what games you liked to play on it.

Mainframes & Text Adventures

Colossal Cave (also known as *Adventure*—not to be confused with the Atari VCS game of the same name) was developed by assembly-language programmer William Crowther and influenced a generation of adventure game developers at colleges and defense contractors. Donald Woods expanded on it, resulting in Infocom's popular *Zork* in 1979. The two-word commands, which originally were developed by Crowther so that his young daughters would understand them—were immortalized in ZIL (Zork Interpretive Language)!

::::: *Colossal Cave*: Text Addiction

Will Crowther

Author Jeannie Novak's father, who was a mathematician for a defense contractor, often brought his work home with him; this sometimes included a terminal with a 300-baud modem attached to it, which is about 100 times slower than a sluggish modern dial-up connection! Playing *Colossal Cave* involved using two-word commands such as "go west" and "get inventory." As simple as this sounds, the game was highly addictive—and the lack of graphics allowed the imagination to run wild.

Other mainframe games included:

- Richard Greenblatt's *MacHack-6* (1966)—the first computerized chess program to enter a tournament (and beat a human player). The program was an expansion of Alan Kotok's BS project on the IBM 7090.
- John Horton Conway's *Life* (1970)—a cellular automata-artificial life program that allowed the "player" to set rules and watch what happened to computer-based "life-forms" as they evolved. Software Toolworks later released *Life* for personal computers.
- Don Daglow's *Trek* (1971)—a very popular *Star Trek*-like sci fi game that began on the Pomona College mainframe. Cygnus Software later released *Star Fleet I* (a "slick" version of *Trek*) for personal computers.
- Gregory Yob's *Hunt the Wumpus*—incorporated a maze based on a dodecahedron (12-sided polygon). Players explored this "map" and attempted to kill the Wumpus (an odorous beast who hid in caves surrounded by pits and superbats). The beast remained asleep until unwary adventurers awakened it by firing an arrow and missing. If the Wumpus ended up in the same room as the adventurer, it ate the adventurer. During the game, the adventurer received clues about how close in proximity the Wumpus was (based on the strength of the creature's odor).

IBM PC: the "Business Machine"

In 1981, IBM released the IBM PC using Intel's 8088 microprocessor. Although the system was not targeted toward the business and programming communities—and it was not designed for entertainment—it ended up capturing the market for computer programmers (including game developers) because IBM used an open system architecture and allowed itself to be cloned. Today, personal computers based on the original IBM technology are the standard hardware used by computer game developers and players.

Apple II

While at Hewlett-Packard, Steve Wozniak designed what eventually became known as the Apple I and demonstrated it at the Homebrew Computer Club—a popular computer hobbyists' hangout. Steve Jobs approached him at the meeting and suggested that they start a company together. The result was the first personal computer system—and the beginning of a revolution that threatened to compete with video arcades and home consoles alike. Computers were out of the exclusive realm of university and research engineering students and hobbyists, and into the home.

Steve Wozniak implemented the BASIC programming language into what he called "Game BASIC" to develop games for the Apple II. Consumers could program the system as well, or play games such as *Zork*, *Lode Runner*, *Wizardry*, and *Ultima*.

The first home computer games were played on the Apple II.

In 1984, Apple released the Macintosh—a system with superior graphics, sound, and an accessible, user-friendly interface. A year later, Microsoft released the Windows operating system to compete with the Macintosh. Although Windows eventually grabbed a majority of the market share, the initial releases of the operating system were weak.

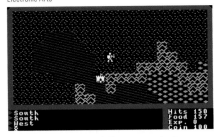
Electronic Arts

Ultima I is the first of nine games in the popular *Ultima* series.

::::: *Ultima*'s Origin

In 1979, Richard Garriott's California Pacific Computer (later Origin Systems) released *Akalabeth*—the precursor to the popular *Ultima* series. A year later, a tile-based graphics version of *Ultima* was released for the Apple II. After seven sequels, the highly successful adventure/role-playing game series continues with *Ultima Online*.

Electronic Arts: Star Power

Former Apple employee Trip Hawkins later started what became one of the largest game companies in the United States: Electronic Arts. Initially treating his designers and artists like "rock stars," he referred to game packaging as "album covers" and sent his developers on in-store game signing tours. Hawkins' later decision to focus his attention on celebrity advisors in the sports industry helped make sports the top-selling game genre in the United States—with titles such as *Dr. J and Larry Bird Go One-on-One* and the ever-popular *John Madden Football*. (EA's success was arguably built on the sports games it made for the Sega Genesis. The company's experience with the Amiga gave it a leg up when creating games for this console.)

Atari Interactive, Inc.

The Atari 400 was a hybrid computer-game system.

::::: From Console to Computer

Atari shifted its focus to compete directly with Apple by releasing the 400 (a game machine that was also a computer), 800 (with a real keyboard and internal expansion capability), and 5200 (a pure game machine—but it did not handle 400 or 800 cartridges). Coleco also tried to compete with Apple by releasing the unsuccessful Adam Computer. Not only did this effort detract from the ColecoVision console system, but 60 percent of all Adam Computers were returned defective.

CDTV: Commodore's Edutainment System

In 1990, when companies such as Davidson & Associates, the Learning Company, and others launched the "edutainment" computer software movement, Commodore released the CDTV (Commodore Dynamic Total Vision)—a home entertainment system that was basically a Commodore 64 without a keyboard. This "interactive" system was one of many released at the time that stressed educational software as well as games. The software was sold on CDs rather than cartridges.

Commodore 64

After releasing the PET (Personal Electronic Transactor) and the VIC-20 to compete with the Apple II (and failing to do so), Commodore Computer made another attempt to enter the personal computer market in 1982. This time, the company was successful beyond belief. The affordable Commodore 64 (C-64), released in 1982, was a formidable competitor to the more expensive Apple II. In fact, the C-64 was one of the most successful computers of all time. Its $300 price tag (equivalent to Intellivision) and programmability made personal computing affordable. Its color monitor and spacious memory made rival computer Texas Instruments' TI-99 look primitive. Software continued to be developed for the Commodore 64 into the next decade. Commodore also released the Amiga computer in 1986; designed to support high-end games, the Amiga was an exceptional platform but was marketed poorly.

Commodore Computers

The Commodore 64 made personal computing affordable.

Sierra On-Line: Leading the Pack in Computer Game Development

New game companies were launched that created software only for home computers instead of arcades and consoles. Inspired by *Colossal Cave*, Roberta Williams started Sierra On-Line with her husband Ken; most of the team's game development was done at the kitchen table! In 1984, Sierra released *King's Quest*—a graphical adventure/role-playing game targeted for IBM's PC Jr. The game became a successful and long-running series.

Sierra Entertainment

YOU ARE IN THE FRONT YARD OF A LARGE
ABANDONED VICTORIAN HOUSE. STONE STEPS
LEAD UP TO A WIDE PORCH
----------------- ENTER COMMAND?

One of the first graphical computer adventure games, *Mystery House* launched Sierra On-Line

Before the personal computer revolution even began heating up, innovations in the online world were going strong—among those fortunate enough to have access to the online world. It took the emergence of networked gaming—and especially the commercialization of the Internet—to break open this world for the consumer public. Until the introduction of the World Wide Web in 1993, playing personal computer games was mainly an isolated activity. Let's look at the evolution of online games—an industry segment that began with a small, elite market decades before personal computers took over home entertainment.

Multiplayer Meets the Online Elite

You might think that online games began when the Internet became commercial, attracting a wide market of consumers. In reality, online games pre-dated this era by several decades. In the early days of online gaming, players had access to technology that was not readily available to the public. As a result, networked games evolved away from the public eye—and they really did not get public attention until the World Wide Web came into consumer use.

The following are a few milestones in the history of online gaming. You might recognize some of the services that helped fuel this segment of the industry. In fact, you might even be using at least one of them today!

PLATO

It all started with PLATO (Programmed Logic for Automatic Teaching Operations), introduced in 1961 at the University of Illinois. The system was intended to be used for research in the area of computer-based education, but Rick Blomme turned it

Atari Interactive, Inc.

The mainframe game that started it all—
Spacewar!

into a multiplayer game network. Creating a two-player version of *Spacewar!*—Steve Russell's MIT mainframe game that started it all—Blomme catalyzed the growth of a new phenomenon in gaming. PLATO soon introduced a *Star Trek*-based game for 32 players (*Empire*), a flight-simulation game (*Airfight*), and a popular precursor to today's chat rooms known as *Talk-O-Matic*—foreshadowing the importance of social interaction in online games. In the 1970s, PLATO featured *Dungeons & Dragons*-inspired *Avatar* (origin of the *Wizardry* series) and *Oubliette*. This was the beginning of what became online role-playing games—which are now played on a "massive" scale, with thousands of simultaneous players. It was also the beginning of many educational games and interactive experiments.

MUDs

Roy Trubshaw and Richard Bartle at Essex University (U.K.) created what later was referred to as a Multi-User Dungeon (MUD) in 1978. As the Essex network became

Dr. Richard Bartle

MUD1, considered to be the oldest virtual world in existence, was created by Richard Bartle and Roy Trubshaw in 1978.

a part of ARPAnet—a worldwide computer network of academic institutions and the basis of what is now known as the Internet—students and researchers connected to the network began creating their own MUDs with the freely available code. Like *Talk-O-Matic* and future online chat rooms, MUDs focused heavily on the social aspects of games. This, and the ability for players to design their own environments, helped build social interaction and player design into the online game tradition.

CompuServe

CompuServe, the first Internet service provider (ISP), immediately recognized the monetary potential of allowing its customers to play games over a public network. Teaming up with developers John Taylor and Kelton Flinn of Kesmai Corporation, CompuServe released ASCII-text role-playing games such as *Islands of Kesmai* and *Megawars I*. Charging its customers a whopping $12 per hour (even more expensive primetime at $25–65) to play these games, CompuServe launched commercial online gaming.

CompuServe

The First Monthly Game Service

Marc Jacobs provided the first online gaming service for a monthly rate ($40) with the text-based role-playing game called *Aradath*. Jacobs' company, AUSI, was the predecessor to Mythic Entertainment—the developer of *Dark Age of Camelot*.

Quantum Link

America Online (AOL) actually started as a game company. The predecessor of today's AOL was launched in 1985 to directly compete with CompuServe's online multiplayer game services. The first graphics-based online service, Quantum Link, was initially available only to Commodore 64 users. The first game available on the service—developed by Randy Farmer and Chip Morningstar at LucasFilm—was *Habitat*, the first graphics-based MUD online environment that focused on social interaction. Richard Garriott of Origin Systems approached Quantum Link in 1991 to develop *Ultima Online*—an online version of the successful *Ultima* series.

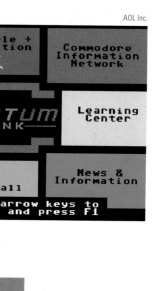

Why Not Play-By-Email?

Play-by-mail (PBM) games such as *Diplomacy* (which began in the 1960s) were developed as a way for geographically separated gamers to compete with each other. With the advent of online services such as GEnie and QuantumLink (AOL), pioneers Don Daglow and Jessica Mulligan launched the first commercial play-by-email (PBeM) games. Chat-based multiplayer space strategy game *Rim Worlds War* was developed by Jessica Mulligan for the GEnie online service. *Quantum Space* was designed and programmed by Don Daglow for QuantumLink (AOL).

GEnie

The GE Network for Information Exchange was an online service that competed directly with CompuServe and Quantum Link. Kelton Flinn of Kesmai Games developed *Air Warrior* for GEnie. *Air Warrior* was a groundbreaking World War II flight simulator that could be considered the first graphically based massively

During the late 1980s, GEnie established itself as the premier online service for multiplayer online games.

multiplayer online game. During the late 1980s, GEnie established itself as the premier online service for multiplayer online games—licensing game environments such as AUSI's *Galaxy II* and Simutronic's *Orb Wars*. The first commercial online 3D shooter, *A-Maze-ing*, was launched in 1989. (In 1974, Dave Lebling and Greg Thompson wrote a multiplayer first-person shooter called *Maze* for the Imlac PDS-1, with PDP-10 as a server. It supported up to eight players, chat, and bots.)

id Software: Revolutionizing Networked Gaming

In 1993, several events took place that helped accelerate the online multiplayer game segment. The first graphical web browser, NCSA Mosaic (created by Mark Andreessen while he was a student at the University of Illinois) marked the end of text-only communication on the Internet—opening up this global network to the commercial world, as well as to the general public. The commercial online service competed for subscribers. Then, in 1993, id Software released *Doom*—which allowed up to four players to connect over a LAN (local area network) and play against each other in a "death

Doom helped commercialize networked gaming.

match." The company's next title, *Quake*, featured built-in Internet capabilities so that geographically dispersed players could engage in death matches. Other computer game developers added modem and LAN functionality to games that allowed for simultaneous players. Yet another entirely new section of the computer game market was created, involving CD-ROM products being played over networks. Built-in, Internet-based multiplayer capability also became a requirement with games—rather than an option.

::::: The LAN Party Phenomenon

The 1990s saw major developments in computer graphics, processing speed, and sound—and computer games were raised to new standards. Networked multiplayer games such as *Doom*, *Quake*, *StarCraft* and *Diablo* spawned a new social trend among gamers. "LAN parties" involved friends networking their computers together in a room and playing in teams or against each other—in between bites of pizza and (root) beer.

PD

::::: The Saga Continues in the Online World

The rise of massively multiplayer online games (MMOs) in the United States began when Origin Systems launched *Ultima Online*—hitting the 50,000-subscriber mark within the first three months. Turbine Entertainment developed *Asheron's Call*, and Verant Interactive (later acquired by Sony) launched *EverQuest*—which became the largest massively multiplayer online role-playing game (MMORPG) in the United States, claiming to have over 500,000 simultaneous players. (MMOs are discussed in more detail in Chapter 3.)

Electronic Arts   Sony Online Entertainment

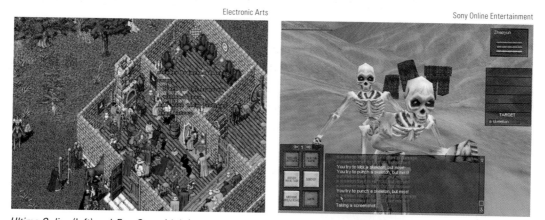

Ultima Online (left) and *EverQuest* (right) were two of the first massively multiplayer online games (MMOs).

As the information revolution, fueled by the World Wide Web, infused American culture in the mid 1990s, computer games became truly interactive—with the capacity for hundreds of thousands of people worldwide to play "massively multiplayer" games simultaneously. Players immersed themselves in a simulated, persistent fantasy world—customizing their own characters, forming collaborative teams or "guilds," and engaging in adventurous quests.

Mobile & Handheld Games: Nomadic Culture

Other segments of the industry are starting to experience growth. The portable game business—first seen in the 1970s with Mattel's sports-oriented handhelds—has evolved into a full-fledged mobile game market. Digital download services have also helped make games much more available to players worldwide.

Nintendo

Nintendo revolutionized the handheld industry with the Nintendo DS—a dual-screen system with Wi-Fi and local wireless capabilities. Past models in the series include (left to right) the original DS (2004), DS Lite (2006), DSi (2009), and DSi XL (2010).

Sony Computer Entertainment America

Sony's PlayStation Portable (PSP) was the first portable game console to launch with games supporting online play. Past models in the series include (left to right) the original PSP-1000 (2005), PSP-2000 (2007), PSP-3000 (2008), and PSPgo (2009).

David Carr (Wikipedia Commons)   Nokia, Inc.

The Nokia 6110, released in 1997 (left), was the first cell phone to include a pre-installed game (*Snake*). Nokia's N-Gage, released in 2003 (right), was an early attempt at a multi-purpose cell phone/game/MP3/Internet-based system.

Developers and hardware manufacturers are jumping on the bandwagon and putting together portable gaming development initiatives (Sony's PSP), creating innovative motion-sensing hardware (Microsoft's Kinect and Sony's Move)—and experimenting with techniques that address the graphics, memory, and screen size limitations (mobile and handheld devices). See Chapter 2 for a detailed discussion of current game platforms.

Convergence: Industry Segments Come Together

After decades of developing in parallel, the console and computer game segments began experiencing some technology convergence—where characteristics of once-separate industry segments intersect. This has been fueled by an unexpected development involving online games. The online world has become a popular place for communication and entertainment. Console game companies, in their desire to grab this market, now offer Internet connectivity through their systems: Xbox 360 (Microsoft), PlayStation 3 (Sony), and Wii (and its successor, the Wii U—from Nintendo).

Reprinted with permission from Microsoft Corporation   Sony Computer Entertainment America   Nintendo

The three current dominant console systems—Xbox 360, PlayStation 3 (PS3), and Wii—all offer online multiplayer games, browsing, and transactions through Internet connectivity.

Convergence is the theme for most newer portable and console systems—whether they connect to the Internet or incorporate cell phone technology. The current generation of console systems has pushed the notion of convergence to new levels. The Xbox 360, PS3, and Wii not only connect to the Internet (some through very usable browsers), but they allow players to connect to each other and purchase games and HD movies. (See Chapter 2 for more specs on current portable and console systems.)

Samsung   Apple   Apple   Nintendo   Sony Computer Entertainment America

Galaxy S2 (Android phone), iPhone, iPad, 3DS, and PlayStation Vita

Even arcade and online worlds are converging in the form of online arcade emulation programs—which duplicate the function of one system with a different system, so that the second system appears to behave like the first. For example, the MAME (Multiple Arcade Machine Emulator) software emulator allows computers to run arcade games on computer hardware. One of the more creative is a *Pac-Man* emulation that was programmed through an Excel spreadsheet! A popular use of emulators is to run games written for hardware that is no longer sold or readily available—not only arcade hardware, but console and computer hardware (such as Commodore 64 and Amiga). The Nintendo Wii has a Virtual Console functionality (NES, SNES, Genesis, and TG-16), and compilations are now common (such as the Sega Genesis Collection for PS2/PSP).

Into the Future

You have taken a brief look at major milestones in the history of electronic game development. Where do you think the industry will be 10 years from now? Do you sense another industry segment beginning to bubble under the surface? Will one particular segment experience a growth spurt? Will another touted segment fail? Will consumers choose portability over the cinematic experience of home theatre-style console gaming? As the mobile gaming industry continues its rapid climb, will developers start to focus overwhelmingly on the small screen? Will the social aspects of online multiplayer games become so compelling that players will spend more time in the virtual environment than in RL ("real life")—or will they integrate both worlds successfully through augmented reality or an as yet unknown technological breakthrough? Throughout the rest of the book, you'll have the opportunity to form your own opinion on these possibilities.

This chapter introduced you to the history of electronic game development—covering the companies, people, and games that helped this industry take shape. In the next chapter, we'll take a more thorough look at current game console, mobile, handheld, computer, and arcade systems. As you read the chapter, consider how these systems and the number of players using them simultaneously might affect the way a game is developed and played.

:::CHAPTER REVIEW EXERCISES:::

1. What are the key phases and milestones in the history of electronic game development? How has convergence played a role in connecting these phases?

2. Why have some game development companies succeeded while others have failed? How can you apply this knowledge to the current industry?

3. What electronic games helped attract a larger audience to the industry? Why did they succeed in doing so?

4. What traditions in early game development are still in existence? How are they appealing and useful to developers and players?

5. Several theories have been used to explain the decline of the arcade industry and associated video game slump of the early 1980s. Do you agree with any of these theories in particular? Do you have a theory of your own? Is there anything that could have been done to prevent this slump?

6. What was the first electronic game you ever played? Did it capture your attention? Why? What are some non-electronic games that were popular when you were a kid? Do you feel that the thrill of any of these games has been captured in digital form?

7. Choose a time in the history of electronic game development, and pretend you are a developer working in the industry. Knowing the limitations of the time, what type of game would you create?

8. You've read about the many eras and phases of the electronic game industry. Are we at the dawn of a new era? Can you predict the primary features of the next phase in game industry history?

2

Platforms & Player Modes

what is the framework?

Key Chapter Questions

- What *platforms* are available for games, and what specific elements are associated with each platform?

- How does choice of *hardware* affect the way a game is developed and played?

- How do *modes* based on number of players affect the way games are created?

- What types of platforms and modes are most appropriate for *cooperative* or *competitive* styles of play?

- What are time *interval* options, and how do they change the way a game is played?

Chapter 1 introduced you to some games that succeeded (or failed) during the brief history of electronic game development. Much of the industry's historical development has been fueled by advances in hardware—including progressive console generations and multi-purpose hardware such as smartphones. This chapter picks up where Chapter 1 left off—honing in on current and near future game systems. From there, the discussion moves to player modes and time intervals associated with the way games are played—and how choice of platform can affect both. The foundational elements introduced in this and the remaining chapters in Part I apply to all areas of game development. As you continue to read through this book, you will notice that these elements come up repeatedly in other contexts.

Platform

You are familiar with the evolution of arcade, console, computer, handheld, and online games from Chapter 1. All of these formats are known as game systems or *platforms*. Since each game platform has distinct characteristics, games developed for each platform differ in several important respects. Let's review the platforms, discuss their distinctions, and look at how this might affect game content.

Arcade

Arcade games are stand alone game systems found in public venues—such as video arcades, bowling alleys, amusement parks, and pizza parlors (a trend begun by Atari founder, Nolan Bushnell). Most games are played standing up—with player controls consisting of buttons, joysticks, or a combination.

Mach 3 arcade game being played during the Classic Gaming Expo at the Electronic Entertainment Expo (E3).

Two-person cocktail table arcade games were introduced in the mid-1980s and became popular items in diners and hotel lobbies. Some games use other types of controllers—such as pedals and steering wheels (sit-down driving simulators), guns (shooters), and foot pads (dancing, as in *Dance Dance Revolution*). These games evolved from black and white/grayscale to full-color displays. Since these games are usually coin-operated, it is important from a business perspective to get players to deposit as many coins as possible into the game—so arcade developers focus on creating fast-moving, time-limited games that do not involve detailed story or character development. During the height of the arcade craze, there were also many technical issues such as memory limitations that made it difficult to provide this complexity. Since time is limited in arcade games, action is one of the main elements of this platform. Arcade games gave birth to the *action* genre—which still focuses primarily on speed and certain types of skills (eye-hand coordination, aim, and navigation—as in shooting and racing games). Other elements, such as story and character, have been emphasized more in the action genre on other platforms.

Atari Interactive, Inc.

Crystal Castles is one example of a cocktail table arcade game—often seen in diners and hotel lobbies in the mid-1980s.

There are three main entities associated with arcade game development:

1. *Hardware manufacturer*—owns the rights to the hardware and has control over what content is played on it.

2. *Game (or content) developer*—often develops the game for the manufacturer, but is sometimes the same company as the manufacturer.

3. *Venue operator*—licenses or purchases the game from the manufacturer and collects revenue from the players.

Since the hardware manufacturer owns and controls the content, it is involved in the planning, development, and testing process. In cases where the developer and manufacturer are separate entities, the developer has to answer to the manufacturer—who has final approval over whether the game will be developed.

Console

Console systems are usually played in the home, hooked up to a television set. The systems support four controllers. Three proprietary console systems on the market are vying for audience attention: Microsoft's Xbox 360, Sony's PlayStation 3 (PS3), and Nintendo's Wii.

Reprinted with permission from Microsoft Corporation   Sony Computer Entertainment America   Nintendo

The Xbox 360, PS3, and Wii are the dominant console systems on the market.

Like the arcade platform, the console platform is proprietary—which means that hardware manufacturers such as Sony, Microsoft, and Nintendo have control over what software is developed for their respective platforms. An advantage of developing for a proprietary console system is that the hardware will not vary from player to player. (As you will see in the next section, this is a problem for the computer platform and for Android development.) When a game is developed for the Xbox 360, there's no doubt in the developer's mind that the game will work on *all* Xbox 360s (assuming the hardware is working correctly).

Another feature of game consoles is that (like arcade systems) they have traditionally been special-purpose devices that were created specifically for playing games. The hardware controllers, for example, were designed to provide an optimum game-playing experience. This is in contrast to computer platforms, which were not originally intended as game-specific machines.

Console systems are also moving away from their special-purpose roots; most are used for playing DVDs, MP3s, streaming movies, and television content—not just for playing games. Sony's PS3 has a Blu-ray drive, and the Xbox 360 originally had an HD-DVD add-on drive (which now only works as an external drive, since the HD-DVD format has been supplanted by Blu-ray). All three major console systems have Internet connectivity—such as browsers, online multiplayer networks, and marketplaces where players can download games, music, TV shows, and movies. The original PS3 model contained a 20, 40, 60, 80, or 160 GB hard drive. The re-designed, slimmer version (known as "PS3 Slim") is currently the only model in production—with an upgradeable 120, 160, 250, or 320 GB hard drive and 33% smaller than the original. Microsoft's Xbox 360 has gone through several configurations: 20 GB Pro/Premium and Core (both available at launch), Elite, Arcade (which replaced the Core), 60 GB Pro, and Xbox 360 S—with redesigned internal architecture featuring the Valhalla motherboard containing 30% more space, two additional USB ports, and a custom port for use with the Kinect sensor. Nintendo's Wii revolutionized the concept of the wireless controller, which can be used as a handheld pointing device and detects movement in three dimensions. All three major console platforms are used heavily for Netflix streaming.

:::::: Wii U: The Console with a Twist

After Nintendo unveiled the Wii U prototype during E3 2011, there was a rush of excitement – but amidst all the "oohs" and "aahs," there was also some confusion. Was the Wii U a new console, a new controller or a portable system? The truth is that the Wii U is "all of the above"—sort of. The Wii U controller resembles a portable system—but it interacts with a new console base. The prototype version features a six-inch touchscreen, built-in microphone, speakers, gyroscope, accelerometer, rumble, and a camera that supports video chat. By acting as an overlay (trivia, sniper scope) or extension (golf tee) of the game being played on the television screen, the controller allows for *augmented reality* games (where graphics are superimposed over a real-world environment in real time). Cooperative and competitive play experiences are enhanced by having one player use the new controller while another uses the original Wii remote; if the players solely use the Wii U controller's screen and television screen, respectively, their experiences are completely different. Although the controller looks like a standalone portable system, it actually depends on the console base for processing. The controller's touchscreen either supplements or replicates the gameplay displayed on the television screen—and it allows a player to continue a game session by displaying the game even when the television is turned off. The system, which outputs in HD (a nice step up from the original Wii) is fully backwards compatible with the Wii and its associated peripherals.

Nintendo

All this represents a dramatic move toward multi-purpose convergence; the flipside of convergence is known as *transmedia*—a way of telling stories and/or delivering content across multiple platforms, such as game platforms, televisions, radio, books, and film. Console systems are clearly destined to support *all* features associated with computers and providing all content viewed through our television sets.

Computer

Unlike the console and arcade platforms, the computer (or PC) platform is not proprietary. This frees the developer from having to answer to the manufacturer. However, there is so much variation in hardware setups between players that it is next to impossible to predict the average speed, hardware space, and memory allotment that players will be using. In the planning stages of creating a game, the development team needs to create prospective technical specifications for the game and try to develop the game around these requirements. Both *minimum* and *recommended* tech specs should also be available to the player. Minimum specs are those that are necessary to load and play the game from beginning to end (e.g., processing speed, memory, disk space). Recommended specs expand further on the minimum specs—also allowing for an enhanced game-playing experience (e.g., high-end sound and video cards). Many games have a variety of advanced graphics and sound options that a player can disable if the system is incapable of handling them. A computer traditionally has had sharper graphics than a console system due to higher resolution; even a computer's lowest resolution (640 × 480) has twice that of any 16-bit console and most 32-bit titles.

iStock Photo

The computer platform adds complexity to the development process due to non-standard setups and a variety of systems.

Console systems such as the Xbox 360 and PS3 arguably have as sharp (or even sharper) graphics than computers—at least given the resolution permitted by software. Both consoles have 1920 x 1080 as native resolutions (1080p), and the Wii has a resolution of 720 x 480 (480p). Computer resolution can conceivably go much higher (1600 × 1200) than next-gen consoles.

Online

Online games are played on a computer platform or through a console system connected to the Internet, but the technology behind online games differs greatly from games on other platforms. Players need an Internet connection to play, and game information might be stored on a *server.* The largest online games involve thousands of simultaneous players, which sometimes requires that the information for the game be stored on several servers. *Massively multiplayer online games* (*MMOs*; (discussed in more detail in Chapter 3) might even entertain thousands of players simultaneously. Due to the 24/7 nature of the Internet; MMOs are also ongoing *persistent worlds*—posing some unique development and maintenance problems. (The monthly subscription-based model that was initially associated with MMOs has given way to micropayments, virtual item sales, in-game economies, and premium services.)

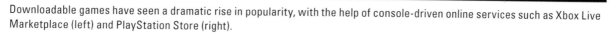

Downloadable games have seen a dramatic rise in popularity, with the help of console-driven online services such as Xbox Live Marketplace (left) and PlayStation Store (right).

Another technical issue related to online games includes connection speed, which is made up of bandwidth and latency. Bandwidth is how many bytes per second the connection can average, and latency is the time it takes for packets to be transferred to you (plus any delays from your own computer).

Live 24-hour customer service is essential for subscription-based MMOs. Players expect to get help immediately on a diverse set of issues. Customer service representatives must be trained to solve online-specific problems, including connectivity issues and player misbehavior. Customer service is of primary importance for any game that involves a subscription fee. Some customer service representatives are referred to as *Game Masters (GMs)* (see Role-Playing Games in Chapter 3 for the history of this term) and provide technical support, create new content (e.g., quests, events), and participate in online game-related discussions with players.

Bill Louden on the Role of Online Services :::::

BL

Bill Louden
(Director, International Business Institute at Austin Community College; online game industry pioneer)

Bill Louden is one of the early pioneers in the online, Internet, and computer massively multiplayer online game (MMOG) industries. He was a founding member of CompuServe and Founder and President of GEnie at the General Electric Company from 1985-1991. Bill designed and developed *MegaWars*, the first commercial multiplayer game, in 1982 while at CompuServe. *MegaWars* was a science fiction, space exploration game based on multiplayer teams. The game ran continuously for over 18 years until it was retired in 2000. Bill was also instrumental in the production, licensing, and publishing of over two dozen multiplayer games that helped to launch Mythic Entertainment, Kesmai, and Simutronics. Bill teaches game computer industry courses at Austin Community College, where he is department chair and professor in International Business. He also teaches graduate business courses in digital media at St. Edward's University in Austin.

In 1982, when I was in charge of games at CompuServe, I bought a copy of *DECWAR* on tape for $50 and soon discovered that it did not run as hoped. It also was laden with many Star Trek and other copyright violations and had to be extensively modified before it could ever become a commercial product. I took *DECWAR* and made some major changes designing the game for CompuServe's Fortran IV language. Working with the "Wizard of Dec-10," Russ Ranshaw, the *MegaWars* game was developed. I also had to remove *Star Trek* related copyright names (no more Romulans, etc.), and develop a new scenario/storyline to become the first commercial MMOG, *MegaWars*. It went up on CompuServe in late 1982 and ran continuously until 1998.

The biggest design changes included different ship classes and goals, offline strategy and world-building components, exploration strategy, planetary economics, live team combat, and extensive team collaboration. By the time that game launched in 1983, it was much more complex and a commercially stable product in comparison to *DECWARS*—very little like the original.

In 1985, I moved on from CompuServe and convinced GE's Information Services division to set up a public service similar to CompuServe—using the evening hours excess capacity on GEIS's mainframe computers. Named GEnie by my wife for "GE Network for Information Exchange," it was priced at $5 an hour for both 1200 and 300bps—making it half the price of CompuServe at 1200bps.

I also convinced GE that in order to make the service a success, GEnie would need online games. So in 1986, I hired Kesmai to rewrite *MegaWars* I and relaunched it on GEnie as *Stellar Warrior*. The game ran for years—dying only when GE threw in the towel and unplugged the entire GEnie service a few years after I had left.

Handheld

The small size of handheld devices makes it convenient for them to be taken with the player almost anywhere. Nintendo's Game Boy series initially focused on kids—but, with the release of the Game Boy Advance SP (GBA SP), this format has become much more popular with adults. The GBA SP is a significant improvement over the original GBA—with a backlit screen and fully rechargeable (and long-lasting) battery. Add-ons, such as Majesco's GBA video player software with a DVD-style interface, allow players to experience the GBA as a multipurpose device—watching movies as well as playing games. The Nintendo DS (a dual-screen portable) presents another innovative expansion of the handheld experience—as players experience simultaneous perspectives and points-of-view during a game.

Nintendo   Sony Computer Entertainment America

Nintendo's 3DS (left) and Sony's PlayStation Vita (right) currently dominate the handheld market.

In 2011, Nintendo released the 3DS—an *autostereoscopic* handheld system, which means that it can project stereoscopic 3D images without requiring additional accessories (such as goggles or glasses). *Stereoscopy* (discussed in more detail in Chapter 8) is a technique for creating a 3D image by by presenting two offset images separately to the left and right eye of the viewer; these 2D images are then combined in the brain to give the perception of 3D depth.

The 3DS contains a slider that adjusts the intensity of the 3D effect, a round analog input known as the "Circle Pad," an accelerometer, and a gyroscope; it also has two cameras that are capable of taking 3D photos, as well as a camera positioned above the top screen on the inside of the device that faces the player that is capable of taking 2D photos and capturing 2D video.

Sony's PlayStation Vita (also known as PSVita or PSV), also released in 2011, is the successor to the PSP; it includes two analog sticks, a five-inch OLED multi-touch screen, Bluetooth, Wi-Fi, and 3G support (in the 3G version), and LiveArea as its main user interface (succeeding the XrossMediaBar). Games are distributed on a proprietary flash card format known as NVG Cards rather than on the Universal Media Discs (UMDs) used by the original PSP.

Mobile

In addition to handhelds such as Nintendo's DS series and Sony's PSP and PSVita, which were created specifically for playing games, other portable devices such as mobile phones and PDAs have also been used as platforms for games. When first introduced at the tail end of the 20th century, these devices were more popular outside the United States and often contained puzzle or trivia games that didn't require a lot of time investment to play. Nokia made the first effort to combine a cell phone with a handheld platform with the release of its N-Gage in 2003. Although the N-Gage's initial launch did not meet expectations, the QD (its follow-up release) was an improvement—and Nokia's effort inspired other manufacturers to consider the possibilities of the mobile gaming market.

Greg Costikyan on Issues in Mobile Game Development : : : : :

GC

Greg Costikyan
(game industry
consultant and
freelance game
designer)

Greg Costikyan has designed more than 30 commercially published board, role-playing, computer, online, and mobile games—including five Origin Award-winning titles. Among his best-known titles are *Creature That Ate Sheboygan* (board game), *Paranoia* (tabletop RPG), *MadMaze* (first online game to attract more than one million players), and *Alien Rush* (mobile game). His games have been selected on more than a dozen occasions for inclusion in the Games 100, *Games Magazine's* annual roundup of the best 100 games in print. He is an inductee into the Adventure Gaming Hall of Fame for a lifetime of accomplishment in the field, and won the Maverick Award in 2007 for his tireless promotion of independent games. He also writes one of the most widely read blogs about games, game development, and the game industry (*www.costik.com/weblog*).

The spread of iOS devices and other smartphones has been a huge boost to the market for mobile games—but Apple's insistence on the best-sellers list as the main view into content and its gatekeeper role (along with the huge number of apps now available) make developing for its devices an increasingly chancy undertaking, especially for new entrants. There may actually be more opportunities for small developers in moving to Android or Meego (an open-source smartphone OS promulgated by Intel and Nokia). Unfortunately, Apple competitors have not yet provided functionality as robust as the iPhone store, meaning that finding customers and converting them to purchase on these platforms is as yet an unsolved problem.

Apple

Samsung

Apple

Samsung

Smartphones such as Apple's iPhone series (iPhone 4, shown; left) and a a variety of Android-based systems (Galaxy S2, shown; right) dominate the mobile market.

Tablet systems such as Apple's iPad series (iPad 2, shown; left) and a variety of Android-based tablets (Galaxy Tab 10.1, shown; right) are basically larger versions of their smartphone counterparts.

The mobile market has been undergoing rapid change since 2007, when developers and publishers began to recognize that the "always on/always connected" nature of the mobile platform could help widen the player market and make room for a new type of playing experience. Since then, the mobile platform (dominated by Apple's iPhone series and a whole slew of Android systems, such as Samsung's Galaxy S2) has become more sophisticated—threatening the single-purpose handhelds. Tablet devices such as Apple's iPad series and Android-based systems such as the Galaxy Tab 10.1 present an interesting hybrid—falling on the continuum between smartphones and netbooks. For example, as a larger-scale iPhone, the iPad's size allows for local multiplayer capabilities (see Player Modes in this chapter)—and it lends itself to other uses, such as an e-book reader rivaling Amazon's Kindle and a "bottomless" sheet music repository … a performing musician's dream!

Tabletop

A tabletop game refers to the traditional analog (rather than digital) game platform—including games that might be played on a tabletop. Examples of tabletop games include board, card, dice, tile, block … and even pen-and-paper games such as *Dungeons & Dragons (D&D)*, where the game pieces literally consist of pens (or pencils) and paper! Miniatures and battle maps (plasticgraph paper players can write on with erasable markers) are also common in games such as *D&D*. It's extremely important to study tabletop games to understand the underlying gameplay challenges and strategies behind

pearlgracehu (PhotoBucket)

A high-energy game of *Risk*—the popular "world domination" board game.

games in general. (See Chapter 6 for a discussion of gameplay.) Another important use of tabletop games is as prototypes for future electronic games (discussed in Chapter 11). Many game development companies create preliminary versions of their games in tabletop form to ensure that the gameplay is functioning properly.

Time Interval

Time intervals are time-dependent elements that affect the pacing of the game. This pacing affects whether the game is played *reflexively* or *reflectively*. Would you develop a game that allowed players to spend an unlimited amount of time responding to challenges—or one that encouraged them to react quickly to them? What about something between the two extremes: allowing each player a limited amount of time to make decisions? There are three basic time intervals used in games: turn-based, real-time, and time-limited.

Turn-Based

In traditional board and card games, each player takes a turn moving a token along the board or playing a card. Usually, the time allotted for each turn is unlimited (unless the player's opponents begin impatiently drumming their fingers on the table). In this case, players have as much time as they need to plan their moves and decide how to play their hands—allowing for reflective, deliberate thought. These games are *turn-based*—meaning that each player (whether artificially generated or human) may take a turn.

Getty Images

Pool and billiards are classic turn-based games.

Big Stock Photo

Soccer is a real-time sport.

Real-Time

The opposite of a turn-based game is known as a *real-time* game. In this case, there is no time interval between turns. In fact, there are no turns at all. Winning a real-time game requires having quick physical reflexes, as opposed to the reflective thought required for turn-based games. Real-time games are difficult to play online due to performance-related technology issues—including the speed of the player's connection, server load, and regional Internet traffic bottlenecks. However, these games are extremely popular online—partially due to the ability to communicate in real-time with other players.

Time-Limited

A *time-limited* game is a compromise between turn-based and real-time games. Time-limited games limit the time each player has for their turn. In the case of some single-player puzzle games (discussed in Chapter 3), a time limit is placed on the game itself. In timed games containing more than one player, each player can take their turns separately (as in chess) or at the same time (as in some online games). In the latter case, each player has the experience of taking a turn—but the game itself is happening in real time because neither player waits while the other player is taking a complete turn.

Big Stock Photo   Big Stock Photo

Boxing is a time-limited, real-time sport, while timed chess is a time-limited, turn-based game.

Deciding on an interval for your game is the first step in considering how the game will be played. How does the interval affect a player's involvement in the game? Do real-time games feel more real? If turn-based games encourage reflective thought, does this mean the game always appears to be slow paced? These are some questions to consider when considering time intervals.

Player Mode

There are several possible *player modes,* which directly correlate to the number of people playing a game. These modes range from single-player to massively multiplayer—involving thousands of players. Your choice of player mode—as well as the content—has a significant impact on how your game is played. What platforms might work better in certain modes? Can you combine a real-time interval with a single-player mode? Think of ways you could combine intervals and modes to create a unique game.

Silver Creek Entertainment

Solitaire (*Hardwood Solitaire IV,* shown) is a classic single-player card game.

Single-Player

Only one person can play a *single-player* game. Any additional players (usually opponents) in the game are known as *artificial intelligence (AI)* characters or *non-player characters (NPCs)*. (Player characters and NPCs are discussed in Chapter 5.) The limited amount of screen space (known as *screen real estate,* discussed further in Chapter 8) on handheld platforms such as Nintendo's Game Boy Advance SP and Sony's PSP makes these systems ideal for single-player games. If you were to create a single-player game, what platform might you avoid?

Two-Player

Two-player (also known as *head-to-head)* games initially evolved from single-player arcade games. Early in the industry, games weren't CPU-controlled because there wasn't enough computational power to drive the *artificial intelligence (AI)*; this meant that local two-player games such as *Tennis for Two* and *Pong* were were more common early on. The first two-player arcade consoles contained two start buttons—one for single-player mode, and one for two-player mode. Players took turns playing against the game itself. Each player's experience of playing the game was identical to what it would have been in single-player mode. The only difference was that the game kept track of both players' scores and compared the two to determine the winner. Players did not compete against each other onscreen, but they both knew that the game would declare only one of them the winner. This idea of player-to-player competition was akin to trying to beat a high score on the arcade console—but instead of a faceless set of initials on a screen, your opponent was standing right next to you.

Sega

In *Streets of Rage 2,* two players control characters such as Axel and Max to cooperatively defeat enemies simultaneously.

These early games were turn-based. It wasn't until *Double Dragon* that a two-player arcade game had a real-time interval. In this game, two players were able to share the console and play side-by-side at the same time—using buttons and joysticks to control the movements of their characters as they fought cooperatively against a common enemy. (*Double Dragon* might be one of the earliest examples of "coopetition," a term that will be discussed in Chapter 6. After playing cooperatively against common enemies and beating the "big boss" at the end of the game, both players play against each other for the final competition.)

Local Multiplayer

In *local* player mode, all players sit in the same space and play the game on the same machine—sharing the same screen using separate *input devices* (controllers). This is a common mode of play on console systems, which allow for local play of up to four players. Since all players share the same screen, each player can see what the other players are doing. Players cannot hide information from each other; this poses a problem when creating games that require players to make secret moves and decisions. Since consoles have introduced network capability, this pattern of local play might change or disappear. Players with Game Boy Advance systems can plug them into the GameCube console as controllers. This allows the players to hide information from each other.

DL

Getty Images

DDRMAX2 Dance Dance Revolution is a two-player, real-time game where players dance side by side and control the game with footpads.

Local console games allow 2–4 players to share the same screen and use separate input devices.

Players can also engage in local play on a personal computer—which involves not only sharing a screen, but input devices (in this case, a keyboard and mouse) as well. Needless to say, a real-time interval would be next to impossible in this case. (Some early computer games, such as *Rampage,* were developed for local play—requiring each player to use a different area of the keyboard.) It is interesting that local play has increased in recent years as parents play games with their children—who sit on their laps!

::::: "Co-op" Play

PD

Some two-player and multiplayer games are known as co-op two and co-op multiplayer. In these cooperative games, players team up to play against the game itself. An early co-op two game was *MicroSurgeon* for the Intellivision console—where one player would move a robot inside a human body and find viruses, while the other player would shoot antibodies at the viruses to heal the person. *Gauntlet* was an early co-op multiplayer local arcade game with four joysticks that involved up to four simultaneous players. Each player was either a wizard, warrior, valkyrie, or elf; all players cooperated with each other to kill monsters, ghosts, grunts, and demons.

Gauntlet's four joysticks enabled four players to cooperate simultaneously to fight a common enemy.

LAN-Based Multiplayer

LAN-based games allow players to share the game on a *local area network (LAN)* without sharing the screen or input device. In Chapter 1, you learned how LAN-based games represent an intersection between the personal computer and online multiplayer phases of electronic game history. With LAN-based games, it became possible to combine the networking capabilities of online mainframe games with personal computers that could be placed in one local area. A simple LAN can be created by linking 2–4 Game Boy Advance handheld systems together through gamelink cables. Unlike home console-based local play, the players *can* hide information from each other because they are not sharing the same screen—only the game itself. At a LAN party, players might bring their personal computers to one location (anywhere from a modest living room to a large convention hall), plug them into the LAN, and play games together as one large group. (Workplaces are also often on LANs, making LAN play popular as a lunchtime or after-work activity.)

Fragapalooza

LAN-based games allow several players to plug their machines into a local area network (LAN). Fragapalooza (shown), with about 1,000 players, is the biggest LAN party in Canada.

Online Multiplayer

Like LAN-based games, *online* games represent a form of *networked* play—where players connect their computers to a network and share the game. In the case of online games, the network is the global *Internet.* You've already learned that *online multiplayer* games can be played by thousands of players simultaneously. Although single-player and two-player games can be played online (and on a LAN, for that matter), it is the multiplayer mode that has become closely associated with online play.

Thousands of players interact while while playing the online multiplayer game, *Rift.*

When do online games become massively multiplayer? This mode is associated with games that persist 24 hours per day and maintain a subscription-based revenue model in which players pay a monthly fee to continue playing the game. The sheer number of players (who might or might not be playing at certain times of the day) greatly affects the way this sort of game is developed and maintained. These games often encourage team-based play, where players form groups and cooperatively defeat opponents or solve problems together. Since the game involves large numbers of players who could easily be playing from locations throughout the world, it's fairly easy for players to find other players at any time of the day or night.

:::::: Player vs. Player (PvP)

The player vs. player (PvP) mode specifically refers to instances in MMOs in which players compete against each other. The usual MMO mode involves players forming cooperative teams to defeat non-player characters (NPCs; discussed in more detail in Chapter 5). Many players prefer PvP because combat is more interesting if it occurs against another player. Some players in an MMORPG (massively multiplayer online role-playing game—an MMO sub-genre discussed in Chapter 3) would rather kill a member of a competing guild than kill a computer-generated monster.

NCsoft

PvP mode is a popular feature of *Guild Wars 2.*

MMO developers have learned that the society of the game (friends made while playing) is a primary incentive for many people to keep playing the game. By offering team-based play, the developers encourage friendships to form, thereby strengthening the game's society and increasing its player-retention rate. It is next to impossible to expect large numbers of people to play the game the way it was originally meant to be played. Instead, players drop in and out of the game and socialize with other players about topics unrelated to the game. Are massively multiplayer games really social communities? Is not the *player control* and a sense of freedom of choice important in almost every type of game? These ideas will be discussed in more detail in Chapters 5 and 6.

Game Elements: The Significance of Platforms, Intervals & Modes

This chapter is the first to focus on the basic elements necessary for the development of electronic games. The target platform is one of the first components that must be considered—and it can have a great effect on how a game is played due to everything from screen size, surrounding environment, online capabilities, portability, audio/video quality, processing speed, and storage capacity. Time interval and player mode interact with platform to provide a variety of playing experiences. All of these elements should be considered early on when planning a game project.

:::

Consider applying the basic game elements you learned in this chapter to the next chapter—which focuses on genres and goals associated with game development. You'll learn that platform and genre are interrelated, and the content of many games is closely associated with their target systems.

:::CHAPTER REVIEW EXERCISES:::

1. What is your favorite game platform, and why? Choose a game that you enjoy playing on that platform and discuss how the platform enhances the playing experience. How would that experience change if the game was only available on a completely different platform?

2. You've recently acquired the rights to port a computer game to the arcade, console, handheld, and tabletop platforms. Choose two of these other platforms and discuss how you would modify the game so that it is optimal for your chosen platforms.

3. Play *Scrabble* or *Words with Friends* on a smartphone or tablet system. Both of these games are turn-based, but the time between turns can last for days—allowing primarily nomadic players using portable systems all the time they need. This type of asynchronous play can be thought of as an extension of the turn-based time interval. Another feature of these games is that there can be several games running simultaneously—allowing players to jump from game to game at any point in time. Choose another game that might benefit from these features, and discuss why.

4. Local play is common on console systems, but it can be awkward on computer systems. Can you think of a situation in which it would be fairly comfortable for two players to share a keyboard and mouse? Your company has been asked to develop a local play game for the computer plat¬form. What type of game would you develop for this player mode—and why?

5. How do platform, time interval, and player mode affect the playing experience? You learned in this chapter that the chess tabletop game isn't always merely a turn-based game – but it has a time-limited version. Imagine what chess would be like if it were played in real time. Now change the player mode to multiplayer. How would the experience of playing chess change if it was a real-time, multiplayer game? Come up with a variation of one of your favorite electronic games by tweaking the time interval and player mode.

Goals & Genres

what are the possibilities?

Key Chapter Questions

- What are some non-entertainment *goals* associated with game development?

- What are the characteristics associated with popular game *genres*?

- Which goals and genres work particularly well together?

- Which particular game content is traditionally associated with certain genres?

- How are genre hybrids and new types of genres changing the way games are categorized?

Chapter 1 introduced you to some games that succeeded (or failed) during the brief history of electronic game development. Chapter 2 presented a closer look at the basic options that are available as you consider developing your own game. This chapter continues the discussion of game elements—focusing on goals and genres that are often part of the first step in the creative development of a game. You might be surprised at the wide variety of goals and genres that are in use today. As you read through this chapter, consider the types of games that you enjoy playing. Do most of them fit into a particular genre? There also might be a few genres described in this chapter that you never knew existed.

Goals

Why do you want to create a game? Do you want to entertain, educate, support, market, build a social community—or get players to work up a sweat? Games are developed for a variety of purposes—and pure entertainment is just one of them!

Entertainment

It is a common assumption that games should be developed purely to *entertain* the players. You will learn in Chapter 4 that many people play to escape from the stresses of daily life—or to relieve boredom. There are also those who play for the same reason they might watch a movie or read a book. It's a diversion that immerses them in an alternate world and engages them emotionally. Some games specifically allow players to become someone new—to role-play as characters, some of their own creation. Others keep them occupied by having to react quickly to physical reflex and mental problem-solving challenges. Notice that players are not just passively sitting and letting the entertainment unfold in front of them. Instead, they are involved in actions such as role play, physical movement, and problem-solving. This medium is uniquely interactive—allowing players to manipulate, modify, and sometimes even take part in creating the entertainment experience.

Sony Computer Entertainment America

Most games, such as *Uncharted 2: Among Thieves*, are created for entertainment purposes.

Social

In Chapter 4, you'll learn that one of the motivating factors for playing games is *social* interaction. Some multiplayer online games, discussed later in this chapter, are developed for this purpose. In these cases, entertainment in the traditional sense takes a backseat to community-building.

A non-game example of community-building include social networking sites and tools such as Facebook, Foursquare, and Twitter—or even a dating site such as Match.com, where people spend a lot of time browsing each other's profiles and communicating through secure email, IM, and chat. There are other types of multiplayer games (such as LAN-based and local, discussed in Chapter 2) that also result in a great deal of social interaction.

Social interaction as a focus can happen by accident. The original purpose of *The Sims Online* was to entertain players through scenarios that involved role-play and character maintenance. The ability to communicate through the game attracted players who preferred discussing non-game topics rather than playing the game. (Player communities within and outside of online games are so significant that an entire section of Chapter 12 focuses on this phenomenon.) Games developed for the specific purpose of creating communities need not be limited to online games with a large customer base. These games would be appropriate for support groups, membership associations, religious organizations—or even "family and friends" networks.

It has been argued by some that games focusing on social interaction (i.e., *social games*) could be more than just applications—but actual game genres (discussed later in this chapter). Social games have become incredibly popular due in no small part to the rise of Facebook. The immense popularity of games created for the social network helped kick off a resurgence in the casual player market (discussed in Chapter 4). Social games have also redefined the notion of "casual" as distinct from frequency of play; it's more about how the games are designed and played—rather than how often. Casual games played on Facebook might be in small spurts, and the difficulty level associated with many of them might be lower—but players tend to play them

Social games such as *My Empire* require players to interact with Facebook friends in order to build resources necessary to progress in the game.

quite frequently. At an International Game Developers Association – Los Angeles (IGDA-LA) event in 2010 focusing on the casual game "renaissance," Cynthia Woll of Cul de Sac Studios referred to *FarmVille* as a "stealth MMO"; this is not far from the truth! (MMOs will be discussed in more detail later in this chapter.)

Emmy Jonassen on the Shift to Casual & Social Games :::::

Emmy Jonassen is responsible for all communication efforts surrounding the 3DVIA Studio game engine—including positioning, messaging, promotion, acquisition/retention programs, advertising, public relations, and the development of demo/learning materials. From its collaboration with its community of game developers, 3DVIA has gained valuable insight into the state of game development, the hurdles faced by studios of various sizes, and how to develop tools to fit these needs.

Emmy Jonassen
(Marketing Manager,
3DVIA/Dassault
Systemes)

Through our interaction with various developers, we have seen quite a dramatic shift from the need for console development solutions to tools for building mobile, casual/social, and online applications. This most certainly stems from a consumer demand, since many studios have changed their entire workflow and business strategy to adapt and capitalize on this ever expanding market. The casual/social game community cannot be ignored; it's massive and viable. This has been proven by the enormous success of such companies such as Zynga, Playdom, and Playfish—along with our own community of developers.

Educational

Educational games are those created to teach while they entertain. In Chapter 1, you learned about the *edutainment* era in CD-ROM game development. These games were specifically developed for educational purposes, and they were all aimed at children. Examples include *Oregon Trail, Reader Rabbit,* and *Math Blaster* (from Sierra On-Line, The Learning Company, and Davidson & Associates, respectively). These games feature in-game knowledge acquisition—where knowledge of certain topics (such as geography, math, and reading) is taught or accessed within the game itself. In most edutainment games, the topics are taught overtly. All types of simulation games discussed later in this chapter allow players to acquire in-game knowledge about real-world objects (such as the controls in the cockpit of a jet) and to apply knowledge they have learned outside the game (such as how an economic system works).

Why were *edutainment* games designed mainly for children? There is a large market of adults in colleges, universities, research institutions, vocational schools—even in corporations—who would benefit from games that serve an educational purpose. As you will learn in Chapter 4, players are not just kids! An interesting educational application might be online distance learning. Most online classrooms consist of discussion threads—which enhances social interaction (as it does in online multiplayer games). Instead of posting only discussion threads—which greatly enhances lateral learning but does not involve constructivism (learning by doing)—students could be playing online multiplayer games that incorporate real-world simulations, such as economics, archaeology, auto mechanics, music, marketing…even surgery!

Houghton Mifflin Harcourt

Oregon Trail teaches American history as players journey into the West.

Even though education can be a specific goal when designing a game, it could be argued that all games are educational "by accident." Several motivating factors discussed in Chapter 4 have a lot to do with learning. In addition to gaining and applying knowledge about real-world events (the traditional definition of an educational game), there are other forms of learning that occur in most (if not all) games.

Recent "puzzle games" have started to deviate from the genre and, to the surprise of many, these games might be inconspicuously realizing the promise of edutainment. Puzzle games can be thought of as workouts for the brain. Nintendo's *Brain Age* and *Big Brain Academy* take this concept to the next level. Each of these games is loaded with math, logic, and visual exercises that score players based on their brain age and brain weight, respectively, making it clear whether the player's brain skills are up to par. (If not, some "brain-training" sessions can correct this!) While each title focuses on different sets of skills, both are based on research conducted by Professor Ryūta Kawashima and have been a huge success for the Nintendo DS.

For example, *mastering* the game is tied into a learning process. Players are not usually satisfied with investing time into playing a game, only to lose. Most people play to win. The game accommodates this by allowing the player to save the game at different intervals (discussed in more detail in Chapter 8), so that players can go back to a point in the game *before* they made decisions that might have resulted in losing the game. Winning is also accommodated by providing the player with feedback—which sometimes appears in the form of a score or even a letter grade! For example, Nintendo's *Advance Wars* involves a series of missions that a player must complete to eventually finish the game. At the end of each mission, the player receives a numerical score and letter grade

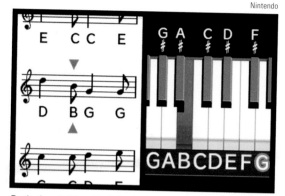

Brain Age 2: More Training in Minutes a Day challenges players in a wide variety of ways, including playing a piece on the piano.

("S" for "Superior," followed by A, B, C, etc.). If the player made a few mistakes while playing the mission and wants to start over, the player can exit out of the mission and start again at any time before completing it. The letter grades assigned to the missions provide a form of assessment for the player, who now has an idea of how well he or she is playing. It's like getting feedback from an instructor every time a student finishes a homework assignment! *Advance Wars* also offers a field training section—a tutorial that helps teach new players how to play the game, which can be a more entertaining alternative to reading the instruction manual for some players.

Serious Games

Games created for non-entertainment purposes are also known as serious games—used by business, medicine, education, and the government to educate, inform, recruit, persuade, or market to players. Serious games have captured the interest of a large portion of the developer market—as evidenced in events such as the Serious Games Summit, Games for Health, Games for Change, and Games, Learning & Society. The "serious games" category is considered by some as a specific game genre. Although genres are discussed later in this chapter, games created for non-entertainment purposes will be discussed here in the Goals section. Some categories discussed (including social and advergames) are not always included under the "serious" umbrella, but it could be argued that they belong in this category because the primary goals of these games are not entertainment-related.

Active Learning

Students tend to take more ownership of knowledge when they acquire it through a dynamic interactive experience. In a game setting, students receive immediate feedback on their performance in a problem-solving activity. This is an environment that inherently encourages active learning.

—Jan McWilliams (artist & Director of Interactive Design, Art Institute of California, Los Angeles)

KK

Karl Kapp, Ed.D.
(Professor of Instructional Technology &
Assistant Director
of the Institute for
Interactive Technologies,
Bloomsburg University)

Karl Kapp has been researching and studying 3D virtual immersive environments for a number of years, and the culmination of his efforts is the book he co-authored with Tony O'Driscoll titled *Learning in 3D: Adding a New Dimension to Enterprise Learning & Collaboration* published by Pfeiffer. A noted writer and expert on the convergence of learning, technology and education, Karl is author of four additional books—including the widely-read *Gadgets, Games & Gizmos for Learning.* Karl earned his doctoral degree at the University of Pittsburgh and has been a professor of instructional technology for over 12 years.

The serious games movement is significant and can have a real impact on education. Schools are just now opening up to the concept that students can learn through games if they are designed from an instructional perspective and focused on education as well as entertainment. These games require a balance between pedagogy and gameplay between learning and instruction. If done well, serious games can provide learning opportunities well beyond the classroom.

James Paul Gee is a theoretical linguist by training, but he has worked on issues in education for the last two decades. He has served as Professor of Linguistics at the University of Southern California (USC), Jacob Hiatt Professor of Urban Education at Clark University, Tashia Morgridge Professor of Reading in the School of Education at the University of Wisconsin-Madison, and Mary Lou Fulton Presidential Professor of Literacy Studies at Arizona State University. James was a founding member of the New London Group, an international group of scholars who have stressed the importance of design and design thinking for students in the modern world. He has been published widely on issues dealing with cross-cultural communication, literacy learning, and learning inside and outside schools and workplaces. Inspired by his then six-year-old son, he began playing and eventually researching computer and video games and has written short pieces for *Wired* and *Game Developer*, as well as several additional academic papers. His books include *The Social Mind, The New Work Order, What Video Games Have to Teach Us About Learning and Literacy,* and *Why Video Games Are Good for Your Soul.*

JPG

James Paul Gee, PhD
(Mary Lou Fulton
Presidential Professor
of Literacy Studies,
Arizona State
University).

Real learning is not about "facts"—but about having such deep experiences of the world ... that the facts become part of what it takes to "play the game" or take on the identity. Real learning means learners cannot just talk about what they have learned, but must actually do things with it. Real learning should be assessed by asking how the current experience has prepared learners for future learning. If the experience makes them do better on a later—perhaps even more important—learning task, who cares how many "facts" they get right or wrong today?

When adapting games for learning, developers should create:

- Strong identities that learners can create or inhabit (e.g., being a certain type of scientist).

- Immersive experiences that naturally cause people to learn important things by living through and actively thinking about the experience. Make the meanings of words, concepts, and symbols concrete through experiences and actions.

- Well-ordered problem spaces, which give meaningful practice that eventually makes skills routine, and then challenges that routinization with a new higher-level problem. Give learners plenty of opportunity to interact both within and outside the game.

Encourage learners to talk and think about their experiences outside the game (e.g., debrief them about their strategies).

Bill Shribman is responsible for all interactive media for kids within the WGBH Educational Foundation, including national PBS sites for *Arthur*, *Between the Lions*, *Zoom*, *Postcards from Buster*, *Curious George*, *Design Squad*, *Martha Speaks*, and *Fetch*—which have won several awards, including the first Prix Jeunesse given to a web site. Bill is the creator of several original broadband projects including the *Fin, Fur and Feather Bureau of Investigation*, *The Greens*, and a photographic news service for PBS KIDS called Beeswax. He has written and produced content for web, audio podcast, CD-ROM, interactive television, kiosk, radio, and television— and he is currently working on interactive content for emerging platforms including PSP, iPhone, interactive whiteboard, Wii, and surface tables. Bill has received Emmy nominations for his television and online work.

BS

Bill Shribman
(Senior Executive
Producer,
WGBH Educational
Foundation)

My team's work focuses almost exclusively on educational games for kids ages 4-12. Each project may involve creating games and supporting narrative on multiple platforms. Working in this age group requires a very keen focus on age-appropriate skills, and we'll narrow our target to within a year or two. Fine motor skills with a mouse or an iPhone will vary between a four- and five-year old, for example. We factor in typical cognitive skills such as reading level and prior knowledge. Generally speaking—whether we're trying to teach math, science, literacy, engineering, art history or nutrition—we'll always try to create compelling, "repeat-play" games to deliver our advisor-led curricula. Repeat-play is the key to building an investment in content and characters. Wherever possible, we will level up a game based on players' demonstrated progress, keeping them comfortably challenged. With a national footprint for our games, we also create, manage, and maintain massive communities of kids. They can share and publish their work, always in safe, pre-moderated ways: this is a huge editorial undertaking but one well worth the effort, since the investment in a brand is strengthened by including players not simply as consumers but as active producers of engaging and meaningful content.

Second Life as an Educational Tool

Author Jeannie Novak's research at the University of Southern California showed that massively multiplayer online games (MMOs) incorporate many elements associated with *constructivist* theory that provide a perfect framework for learning— including *active learning* (character customization and game world modification); *social interaction* (communication and interaction with other players); and *problem solving* (observing processes and applying real-world knowledge to simulations in the artificial game world). This led Jeannie to theorize that MMOs would be perfect online distance learning applications. Instead of joining an online class, students would join a game! Jeannie was producer and lead designer on a project that utilized *Second Life* (*http://www.secondlife.com*) as a learning system. (Although *Second Life* might be described more appropriately as a multi-user virtual environment, it has the capacity to exhibit features of an MMO.) The course behaved like a game; instead of logging into an online classroom (using a learning management system [LMS]), students would appear to be joining a game in progress. Jeannie first presented this concept at the Teaching, Learning & Technology Conference at the University of Southern California (USC) in 2003. "Now Loading: Classroom, Game … One & the Same," an updated version of this concept, was presented at the Game Education Summit, coincidentally also held at USC seven years later in 2010.

JN

Surveying construction of a "serious game" in *Second Life*.

Economic Missteps During the "Edutainment" Era

Over 10 years ago, the best educational games had similar budgets and quality to what you found on the game shelf. Then some of the educational game marketers set out on a campaign to "increase market share by cutting prices." Rival publishers struck back by combining what had been three to six different titles in one box for the same price. In the short term, consumers saved lots of money on software for their children. Then the chain reaction started. You could no longer charge full price for educational software, so budgets for innovative new titles shrank, often to 10% of their prior levels. The warring software publishers, drained by the loss of profitability on these titles, were often acquired or parted out through bankruptcy. Broderbund, one of the highest quality publishers, was acquired three times, then subdivided and sold again to different buyers. Parents and kids have joined the publishing company shareholders as the losers in this MBA-driven scheme. Only a broken publishing model separates us from a new generation of inspiring and impressive educational games.

—*Don Daglow (Chief Executive Officer & Creative Director, Daglow Entertainment LLC)*

Recruitment & Training

Games have also been used by the military, government, and even for-profit corporations for recruitment and training purposes. Simulation games (discussed later in this chapter), which replicate processes, environments, and objects that exist in the real world, have been used by government and military institutions such as NASA and the Air Force to train astronauts and pilots to adjust to changes in atmosphere and to navigate vehicles. *America's Army* (*www.americasarmy. com*)—the first online simulation game used as a military recruitment tool—was so popular when it was launched that the web-site was jammed with requests. Corporations have developed games to help build their employees' leadership and management skills.

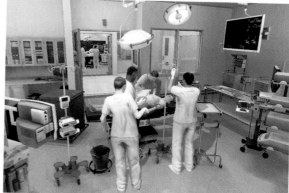
Applied Research Associates

In *HumanSim*, textbooks and lectures are replaced with interactivity and serious fun.

Health & Fitness

Games created for health and fitness include those used for psychological therapy, physical rehabilitation, and even exergames—a sub-category specifically related to fitness. Many exergames are commercial products such as *EA Sports Active* and *Wii Fit*; even some music and rhythm games such as *Dance Dance Revolution* and *Dance Central* (discussed later in this chapter) could be considered exergames. Medical games include *Re-Mission*, which gives children with cancer a sense of power and control over their disease by battling cancer cells.

Electronic Arts

EA Sports Active 2 uses motion-sensing to track a player's exercise progress.

Playing games has been known to improve the link between physical and mental skills ("mind-body connection")—providing unexpected training for the medical profession. A recent study found that surgeons who played games for three or more hours a week made 37% fewer mistakes than doctors who did not play games. Conducted by Boston's Beth Israel Medical Center and Iowa State University's National Institute on Media and the Family, the study also found that the surgeons who played games were also 27% faster than their counterparts. The next step? Surgery simulations! The realm of accessibility games—designed for players with physical and cognitive impairments (discussed in Chapter 8)—often falls into this category.

Goals & Genres: what are the possibilities chapter 3

Consciousness & Change

Games created for social consciousness and change (sometimes termed "games for change") might be created by non-profit, political, and/or religious groups to raise awareness of certain beliefs, attitudes, values, lifestyles, and causes. Examples of social issues covered by these games include poverty, human rights, global conflict, and climate change. Titles include *Darfur is Dying*, *The ReDistricting Game*, and *September 12: A Toy World*.

Newsgaming

September 12: A Toy World focuses on the civilian casualties of terror attacks.

Sony Computer Entertainment America

flOw was clearly developed with aesthetics and artistic expression in mind.

Aesthetics & Creativity

Some games are created to elicit creative expression or aesthetic appreciation from players or are developed to express or share artistic ideas. *WarioWare D.I.Y.* for the DSi XL allows players to make their own games, music, and comics. In *The Movies*, players are able to create animated sequences with special effects and custom camera angles. *Guitar Hero World Tour* allows players to create and share instrumentals via its GHTunes Service. Games such as thatgamecompany's *flOw* and *Flower* have often been considered works of art—and were clearly developed with aesthetics and artistic expression in mind.

Marketing & Advertising

Some games are created for the purpose of marketing a product or service to consumers. *Advergames* are specifically designed as advertising tools. Many of these games exist online and are created in Flash or Java—tools that are efficient for developers and players due to quick downloads and short development cycles; these tools will be discussed further in Chapter 10. Advergames are used as alternatives to other web-based advertising, such as banners. Advertisers pay sites to host these games, which usually feature the advertiser's brand. Another online form of game-related marketing is *advertainment*—in which sites developed for the purpose of showcasing a brand contain games and discussion forums, becoming a fun hangout for customers. An early example of advertainment is the *Joe Boxer* site (*http://www.joeboxer.*

com), which invited customers to download a virtual pair of underwear before entering a circus-themed site—complete with carnival games and a chat room.

Movie sites containing games, screensavers, and trailers focus on creating a fun experience for site visitors while marketing the film series. It could be argued that games based on movies and other forms of media are really types of advergames—but some of these games, such as *The Chronicles of Riddick*, *The Lord of the Rings: The Two Towers*, and the award-winning *Batman: Arkham Asylum* (based on the Batman comic franchise) stand on their own as rich playing experiences. More obvious examples of advergames are short, often Flash-based online games that appear on web sites created to help raise brand awareness or directly sell a product—such as movies (Disney's *Toy Story Mania*, distinct from the standalone *Toy Story* computer and console games), food (McDonald's *Hot Shot Pinball*), and even office supplies (Post-it's *Draw It*).

Many film and television shows have been used as vehicles for advertising products. For example, *Seinfeld* was notorious for its blatant advertising of Diet Coke—a supply of which was always available in Jerry Seinfeld's refrigerator. This form of advertising is known as *product placement*—and advertisers pay large sums of money for this. In-game product placement is becoming just as common. As you'll learn in Chapter 4, falling television ratings in the United States have caused some advertisers to turn to games to promote their products. Activision and the research organization Nielsen Entertainment reported that television viewing among men ages 18–34 in the United States has steadily decreased. In a study of 1,000 men, Nielsen found that 75% of the subjects owned a game console and watched less television. In 2010, Nielsen Games (a division focusing exclusively on video game research) found that nearly 25% of all Xbox 360 usage occurs during the prime time television block (7:00pm - 11:00pm).

Major corporations regularly utilize product placement in games as a significant part of their advertising budgets. Sports franchises such as *NBA Street* and *Tony Hawk* feature popular clothing labels and sports accessories. In *The Sims* franchise, players experience a wide range of product placement "activities"—including the use of Intel-branded computers in their virtual homes and offices and the ability to become McDonald's franchisees. The fast food giant was also added as a friend for one day in *FarmVille*; players who visited the McDonalds farm were given a free McDonalds blimp and a McCafe, which caused players to move very quickly (as in "caffeine buzz") for one session. Other companies have provided similar promotions within the game: Farmer's Insurance offered crop insurance, which yielded a blimp that players could fly over their farms to avoid crop wilting for weeks (until the promotion ended). Finally, the movie *Megamind* was added as everyone's friend the day of its theatrical launch. Players who visited the movie's farm would receive a *Megamind* blimp and a spray bottle of "mega grow," which made all crops immediately ready for harvesting.

Muskedunder Interactive

Pepsi Music Challenge is a Flash-based game with musical challenges that promotes the company's products.

Genres

Game *genres* are categories based on a combination of subject matter, setting, screen presentation/format, player perspective, and game-playing strategies. In looking at your target market, consider what genre these people play. In Chapter 4 you'll learn that some people focus on playing one particular genre. Certain genres are more playable on particular platforms. If you were to choose a mobile phone as your primary development platform, do you think a puzzle game or a role-playing game would be most appropriate? Which genres would be more appropriate for an MMO using a high-end, multiple server platform? As you learn more about game genres in this section, apply what you know about platforms, intervals, and player modes. What genres work best in single-player mode? Would it be better to develop a real-time game for a particular platform or genre? If you were developing a game for a handheld device, which genres might you choose?

Setting or Style?

Unlike genres in books and movies, current game-industry genres are not necessarily related to story, plot, and setting. Instead, they focus on how the game is played—its *style.* The traditional definition of genre relates more to what is known as the *setting* of a game. Some examples of setting include fantasy, sci-fi, horror, and crime. Setting will be discussed in more detail in Chapter 5.

Genre: A Double-Edged Sword

I tend to de-emphasize genre in my designing and thinking. I feel that genre is a bit of a double-edged sword for designers. On one hand, genres give designers and publishers a common language for describing styles of play. They form a shorthand for understanding what market a game is intended for, what platform the game will be best suited to, and who should be developing a particular title. On the other hand, genres tend to restrict the creative process and lead designers toward tried-and-true gameplay solutions. I encourage students to consider genre when thinking about their games from a business perspective, but not to allow it to stifle their imagination during the design process.

—*Tracy Fullerton (Associate Professor, USC School of Cinematic Arts; Director, Game Innovation Lab)*

Action

The *action* genre has been around since the arcade craze. In fact, almost every arcade game (such as *Pac-Man*, *Asteroids*, and even the comparatively slow-moving *Pong*) is an action game. The goal of most action games involves quickly destroying your enemies, while avoiding being destroyed yourself. These games tend to be simpler because they focus on player reaction time. Simplicity is necessary in action games because the average brain cannot process much additional information in a fast-paced environment. Eye-hand-coordination is necessary to excel in action games—also known as "twitch" games (a term that comes from the quick hand movements associated with using joysticks and pressing buttons repeatedly).

:::::: Music & Rhythm Games

Through its "Bemani" (music video game) division, Japan's Konami launched a series of games where players perform in some way (by either dancing, singing, or playing instrument-style controllers) to create music or rhythm patterns. The goal of play involves either completing a song, dance, drum pattern, guitar solo, or hand wave. Examples of Bemani games include *Dance Dance Revolution*, *Beatmania*, *Drummania*, *Guitar Freaks*, *Dance Maniax*, and *Karaoke Revolution*. These games have become so popular that they are quickly defining a new genre, especially with games such as Sony's *Singstar*, Activision's *Guitar Hero*, Electronic Arts' *Rock Band*, Ubisoft's *Just Dance*, and Microsoft's *Dance Central*.

HillsDan (Photobucket)   brattle (Photobucket)   DL

SingStar (left), *Rock Band 3* (center), and *Dance Dance Revolution Hottest Party 2* (right) in action.

The relentless fast-paced nature of these games means that they are always played in a real-time interval. People are motivated to play action games for the adrenaline rush involving quick reflexes and snap judgments—focusing on reflexive actions rather than reflective thought—while sometimes a much-needed reflective break can appear in the form of mini games (games within the larger meta game) that involve puzzle-solving or turn-based strategy. When the player solves the puzzle or finishes the game, it's back to the action of the larger game experience! The following are a few sub-genres in the action category that have taken on styles of their own.

Nintendo

From *Donkey Kong* to *Super Mario Galaxy 2* (shown), Nintendo's mascot—Mario—has been the star of countless platformers.

Activision

Call of Duty: Modern Warfare 2 is a popular first-person shooter.

Reprinted with permission from Microsoft Corporation

Gears of War 3 is an award-winning third-person shooter.

Platformers

The *platformer* action sub-genre focuses on players moving quickly through an environment—often jumping and dodging to avoid obstacles, and sometimes collecting items along the way. Examples of platformers include early arcade games such as *Donkey Kong* and *Sonic the Hedgehog,* and newer 3D console games such as *Ratchet & Clank* and *Jak & Daxter.* These games have clearly identifiable and memorable characters (such as Mario and Sonic) that often act as mascots for the companies that develop these games.

Shooters

The shooter action sub-genre focuses on combat between a player and the other characters in the game world—usually in the form of shooting with guns and other weapons controlled by the character's hands.

In *first-person shooters (FPSs),* the player has a first-person perspective and cannot see his or her character onscreen. The player can see the character's weapons, as well as the other characters in the game (usually a mix of team members and opponents). The action in an FPS is sometimes thought to seem more immediate because the perspective can provide the feeling of being thrown into the game world. Perspective is discussed in more detail in Chapter 7.

Third-person shooters allow players to see their characters, along with the rest of the game world. If you develop a third-person shooter, it's important to ensure that the player's character can be easily differentiated from the others on screen. An advantage of third-person shooters is that the player has a much wider perspective than in an FPS—which is limited to straight-ahead vision (without even the normal peripheral vision experienced in a real-life, first-person perspective).

Racing

Games in the *racing* sub-genre also use first-person or third-person perspective. The standard scenario involves the player's vehicle (usually a racecar) racing one or more opponents on a variety of roads or terrains. The player attempts to make the vehicle move as quickly as possible without losing control of it. Racing games in the action genre are often considered arcade racing games, while racing games that are part of the simulation genre are known as vehicle simulations (discussed later in this chapter). New console systems always launch with a racing game because it's one of the best genres to show off any advances in movement, response, graphics, and general performance.

Reprinted with permission from Microsoft Corporation

Forza Motorsport 3 is an innovative multiplayer racing game.

Fighting

Many *fighting* games are two-person games in which each player controls a figure on screen and uses a combination of moves to attack the opponent and to defend against the opponent's attacks. These games are often viewed from a side perspective, and each session lasts only an average of 90 seconds. The combination moves that have been a focus of the fighting sub-genre have been incorporated into larger action games.

THQ

UFC 2009 Undisputed is a recent installment in the popular fighting game franchise.

Adventure

In Chapter 1, you learned about the first text-adventure game known as *Adventure* (or *Colossal Cave*). In this game, the player was an explorer, wandering around an enormous cave filled with treasures and dangers. The goal of the game was to gather the treasures and bring them out of the cave. To find all the treasures, the player had to use objects to unlock areas that allowed deeper access to the cave. This game might have been the first to give the player an illusion of freedom of choice, which is still an important quality of adventure games. The game also gave feedback to the player in the form of human-like sentences, such as "I don't know how to do that" (instead of the "value too high" error messages exhibited by other mainframe games). The *adventure* genre was named after this game.

Replayability in Adventure Games

The idea of being able to replay a game is appealing to most players. Not only does this often more than double the hours of play, but it also provides a different perspective of the game's story (e.g., whether it involves playing the game from a different character's perspective, a different location, or a different time period). Unfortunately, most adventure games intrinsically are not replayable because they often consist of puzzles with a single solution. When the game is over, the player has solved the game's mystery—and there isn't an opportunity to "re-solve" the game in a different way. How can adventure games be modified so that they can be replayable?

Telltale Games

Sam & Max: The Devil's Playhouse is one in a series of episodic adventure games.

Colossal Cave spawned a series of text adventures that went beyond puzzle-solving and exploration—adding strong story elements. As graphics capabilities on game platforms increased, text adventures gave way to graphic-adventures—leading to titles such as *Myst*, a point-and-click graphic adventure that was the best-selling computer game of all time (until *The Sims* came along).

Currently, only a handful of adventure games are released each year—but there is still a niche group of adventure fans out there. Characteristics of adventure games include exploration, collecting, puzzle-solving, navigating mazes, and decoding messages. Unlike action games, adventure games are usually *turn-based*—allowing the player time for reflective thought. This key difference in the way the game is played is most likely the primary reason adventure gamers are not into action-adventures.

:::::: Survival-Horror: A New Trend in Story Genres?

A group of games with a dark, menacing theme—such as *Resident Evil, Silent Hill, Clock Tower, Fatal Frame* and *Alone in the Dark*—are known as survival-horror games. This trend in game classification incorporates story and content genres, rather than focusing on how games are played (e.g., first-person shooters), or gameplay (the focus of Chapter 6).

Valve

In *Left4Dead2*, players have horrific fun—assuming they survive.

Action-Adventure

The *action-adventure* genre is the only hybrid genre that has distinguished itself as an accepted genre in its own right. The action component allows for quick, reflexive movements as the character dodges and hunts down enemies—while the adventure component adds conceptual puzzles and story elements to the game. Pure adventure gamers aren't usually interested in action-adventures because they are used to the slower pace of adventure games. The action-adventure hybrid has attracted a new audience as well as some pure action players.

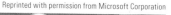

Sony Computer Entertainment America

God of War III is the third installment in the popular franchise, which has helped push the envelope of the third-person shooter genre by incorporating rich story elements.

Casino

In Chapter 4, you'll learn that addiction can be a motivation to play games. This is particularly apparent in *casino* games, which are often electronic versions of popular games—such as roulette, craps, poker, blackjack, and slot machines—found in on-ground casinos. The addiction motivation is closely tied to gambling, and many online versions of this genre are run by online gambling sites.

Reprinted with permission from Microsoft Corporation

Microsoft Casino: Mirage Resorts Edition duplicates the gambling experience—right down to the slot machine visuals.

Goals & Genres: what are the possibilities

chapter 3

Puzzle

Although puzzle elements appear in many game genres, a pure *puzzle* game focuses on the player solving a puzzle or series of puzzles without controlling a character. There is little or no story surrounding puzzle games, which can be either real-time or turn-based. The pattern-based puzzle game *Tetris*—one of the most popular puzzle games of all time—is played in real-time, involving a fast-paced game-playing experience. Many puzzle games (such as *Rocket Mania*) are timed—falling between real-time and turn-based intervals. Others, such as the *Scrabble*-esque *Bookworm*, are turn-based—giving the player all the time needed to form words out of adjacent scrambled letters. Handheld platforms—which can be played while standing in line or waiting in doctor's offices—are ideal for these games.

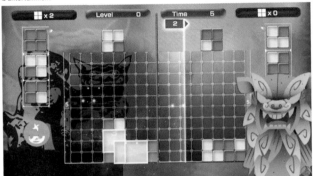

Q Entertainment

Lumines helped open the puzzle genre to a wider marketplace by being arguably the first "killer app" for the PSP.

Rarely, puzzle games involve more than one player or a non-player opponent. One example of a multiplayer puzzle game is *Puzzle Fighter,* in which players simultaneously solve puzzles. This game goes beyond just solving a puzzle and brings in elements characteristic of the *strategy* genre (see next section) because each player must also pay attention to what the other is doing.

Puzzles Everywhere

A great site for online puzzle games is PopCap Games (*www.popcap.com*), a Java-based game collection that includes all types of puzzle games—from the maze-like *Rocket Mania* to word-scrambling *Bookworm* to the color/pattern-matching *Alchemy*. Some games, such as *Insane Aquarium*, are fast-paced and incorporate reflex skills specific to action games.

PopCap Games

PopCap Games

Bejeweled (left) and *Peggle* (right) are just two of the many puzzle games that can be played at PopCap Games.

Role-Playing Games

Role-playing games (RPGs) originate from the tradition of the *Dungeons & Dragons* paper-and-pencil fantasy role-playing games that originated in the 1970s. In these games, players take on roles such as fighters, wizards, priests, elves, or thieves. Players also explore dungeons, kill monsters (such as dragons and ogres), and gather treasure. One player, the Dungeon Master (later known as a Game Master), sets up the game world and takes on the roles of the other (non-player) characters in the game.

The Game Master

The term *Game Master (GM),* which originated from paper-and-pencil role-playing games, is currently used in online multiplayer games to refer to those who play an important role in supporting players online.

Like adventure games, RPGs are characterized by containing strong storylines—but RPGs also contain player-characters that improve throughout the course of the game. Due to the strong emotional character development—and because winning is tied in with this character advancement—RPG players usually experience close emotional involvement with their characters. The genre's presentation is diverse, ranging from simpler arcade-style games such as *Dungeon Siege* to the graphically rich environments in *Final Fantasy.* Themes in RPGs are usually variations on "save the world"—such as finding the person responsible for a murder, rescuing someone who's been kidnapped, destroying a dangerous object, or killing monsters.

The characters in RPGs are often termed heroes because they engage in heroic quests—usually in a team, known as a guild in online multi-player versions of this genre. Combat is one way in which the heroes advance—gaining strength, experience, and money to buy new equipment. Chapter 5 goes into more depth on character development in all genres.

Electronic Arts

Dragon Age 2 is a huge role-playing game with a rich environment and in-depth characters.

Is an RPG Always Fantasy?

Why do most RPGs take place in fantasy worlds—and involve killing monsters, embarking on quests, and saving someone or something (usually the world)? Many RPGs such as *Star Wars Galaxies* allow for other goals (fame, wealth, and power) and roles (musician, smuggler, doctor, bounty hunter, storm trooper). What about creating a modern-day RPG? If you were to create an RPG, where would it take place—and what roles would exist?

Simulations

Simulations (sometimes referred to as *sims*) attempt to replicate systems, machines, and experiences using real-world rules. Earlier in this chapter, you learned that some simulations are used in military and government institutions for training and recruiting. Many simulations also have been created for sheer entertainment purposes. Types of simulation games include vehicle, participatory, and process sims. Rules associated with all simulation games are based on real-world situations and objects. Players familiar with the subject matter associated with a simulation game often enjoy applying these real-world rules to the game-playing experience.

Vehicle Simulations

Reprinted with permission from Microsoft Corporation

Flight Simulator X: Acceleration is a descendent of the first widely popular vehicle sim.

In *vehicle simulations,* the player usually operates complicated machinery (often vehicles such as jet fighters, ships, or tanks). Microsoft's *Flight Simulator* (discussed in Chapter 1) was the first widely popular vehicle simulator. Most of these games are highly accurate, right down to the equipment controls and user manual—which is often thick with text describing the intricate details of the machine. In addition to being developed for entertainment purposes, adaptations of these simulators have been used widely by the military for training and recruiting purposes. (Non-entertainment goals such as education, training, and recruitment are discussed earlier in this chapter.) Flight and racing simulators (both military and civilian) are popular applications of machine simulators.

Sports & Participatory Simulations

Take-Two Interactive

Sports games such as *MLB 2K11* rely on players' knowledge of real-world rules so they can master the game.

Participatory simulations engage the player to experience the simulation as a participant within it. The *sports* genre is a type of participatory sim because—like other sims—sports games often accurately reproduce real-world rules and strategies associated with the sport. Players vicariously participate in their favorite sport—as a player *and* often a coach. Why is the U.S. game-buying public so fascinated with this genre? Perhaps because it allows players to experience "wish fulfillment"—to become extraordinary athletes, and to accomplish things they might not be able to in real life. Wish fulfillment can apply to many other real-world experiences. What about the ability to play a musical instrument, become a master chef, or create a work of fine art? In *Project Rockstar*—where the player manages a rock band—it's a rock band instead of a football team. Perhaps other participatory simulations will begin surfacing as the game industry continues to mature.

Process Simulations (Construction & Management)

Process simulations involve real-world systems or processes. These games are also known as *construction and management sims (CMS), god*, or *toy* games. Examples of these games include *Rollercoaster Tycoon, Sim City*, and *Black & White*. Instead of focusing on operating machinery and understanding how to use controls, this type of sim focuses on the ongoing maintenance of a system, which could include anything from social to economic constructs involving people, creatures, objects, or whole worlds. Although some of these games are set in fantasy worlds complete with unusual creatures and rituals, all duplicate the rules of real-world socioeconomic systems. The goal in process sims is not to defeat an enemy or opponent, but to build something within a process. These games are considered *constructive*—involving building and creating—rather than destructive. To win these games, players need to understand and control these processes. The success of *Sim City* proved that games don't need high-speed action or violence to be popular. The game also appealed to a broad audience.

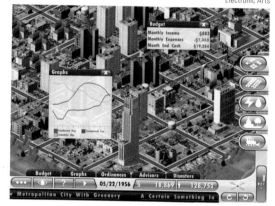

Electronic Arts

The goal of *SimCity Deluxe* is to develop and maintain a successful metropolis.

Playing in the Sandbox: Games Without Goals?

Many process sims have often been referred to as "sandbox" or "god" games in which there is no goal involved and players can do no wrong. However, the process of building and maintaining systems incorporates the ongoing goals of system balance—whether it's ensuring that your roller coaster does not malfunction, that your city does not go into deficit, or that your creature does not (or *does*) "misbehave." Peter Molyneux and Will Wright are considered the "gods of god games," with their innovative *Black & White* and *Sim City* franchises, respectively. Molyneux's *The Movies* (where players must successfully release films to maintain their movie mogul status) and Wright's *Spore* (where players evolve a single-celled organism into a space-faring race that explores the galaxy) continue in this trend.

Richard Wainess on Education Through Simulation :::::

Richard Wainess, PhD (Senior Research Associate, UCLA/CRESST)

Richard Wainess came to the game arena from a circuitous route—as a musician, graphic designer, programmer, 3D animator, interactive multimedia developer, video writer, producer, and director. Richard has also taught a wide range of media-related courses, including multimedia authoring, 3D modeling, character animation, digital media design, and media management. Along the way, he created board games and programmed arcade-style games. For eight years, Richard was on the faculty of the University of Southern California (USC), where he taught game design, level design, and 3D animation. He was involved in the development of two of the university's cross-disciplinary video game minors and the university's cross-disciplinary 3D animation minor. Now, with a Ph.D. in Educational Psychology and Technology from USC, Richard is a senior research associate at the National Center for Research on Evaluation, Standards, and Student Testing (CRESST) in the University of California, Los Angeles (UCLA) Graduate School of Education. His research centers around the use of games and simulations for training and assessment. Richard's most recent work focuses primarily on the assessment of problem-solving and decision-making using computer-based interactive tools. He has authored and co-authored numerous reports, articles, and book chapters and has presented at many conferences on the topic of games and simulations for learning—with a particular emphasis on instructional methods, cognitive load theory, metacognitive processes, motivation, and learning outcomes.

Games and simulations provide players with an opportunity for exposure beyond what is available in real life. They can visit inaccessible environments --those that are dangerous (inside an active volcano), microscopic (inside a molecule), or remote (visiting the surface of Mars). Through the combination of a game environment (goals, rewards, and realistic 3D visualization) and simulation (i.e., scientifically-based experimentation), students are given the opportunity to virtually visit unique locations to experience scientific concepts and conduct experiments *first-hand*—and to feel as if they are really there, all within the comfort and safety of the classroom.

Strategy

Strategy games have their origin in classic board games such as chess, where players are required to manage a limited set of resources to achieve a particular goal. Most strategy games take place in a military setting. Unlike RPGs, the player's character is relatively unimportant. (In fact, sometimes the player has no character.) Instead, the player's resources (e.g., troops, weapons) become central to the game experience. *Resource management* typically includes constructing a variety of buildings or units, and deciding how and when to put them into action. The strategy in these games is based on comparative resources and decisions between opponents. A sub-category of the strategy genre known as *grand strategy* resembles tabletop wargames; examples include *Axis & Allies*, *Making History*, *Storm Over the Pacific*, and *Romance of the Three Kingdoms*.

What's Wrong with a Detective Strategy Game?

Most strategy games take place in a military setting and involve traditional warfare. Of course, the elements of building units and expending resources can be applied to a variety of situations that don't involve warfare. How about criminal investigations? *Emergency Fire Response* is an example of a unique strategy game where players are firefighters who must defeat a natural enemy and put out fires. See if you can think of some other innovative ideas!

Turn-Based Strategy (TBS)

Until the early 1990s, almost all strategy games were turn-based. This interval lends itself nicely to strategy games because it encourages players to take time to think strategically before making decisions. In *turn-based strategy* (TBS) games, resource management involves discrete decisions such as what types of resources to create, when to deploy them, and how to use them to the best advantage. The player's ability to take the time to make these decisions is part of the game's appeal.

Take-Two Interactive

Sid Meier's Civilization V is a popular turn-based strategy game.

Real-Time Strategy

Real-time strategy (RTS) games incorporate a real-time interval. Although strategic thinking doesn't lend itself well to real-time action, it's surprising how popular RTS games have become. RTS players are under such constant time pressure that they don't have the opportunity to truly ponder a move. Multiplayer RTS games have to be played in one sitting. Another issue in RTS games is *micromanagement*—the process of rapidly balancing sets of resources (e.g., troops) containing a number of features. Since the game moves quickly in real-time, one set of resources might flourish while others fail because the player can't feasibly focus on all sets at once. A player might decide to concentrate on managing one set of troops, who might be engaging in combat to defend the player's territory. In the meantime, another set of the player's troops—left "helpless" without the player to control them—is defeated. (The player must employ a certain level of *multitasking* to avoid some of these disasters.) These games involve such a great deal of action and reaction time that the genre should really be referred to as an Action-Strategy hybrid!

Reprinted with permission from Microsoft Corporation

Halo Wars, part of the *Halo* franchise, is an Xbox 360 exclusive.

RTS Challenges

RTS games need a lot of time for two types of game balance—for the single-player campaign, and for the multiplayer experience. This isn't easy—and it occupies a lot of effort throughout the middle and end of development. RTS titles have borrowed bits and pieces of other game genres. This is a useful experiment…but some don't fit well.

—*Frank Gilson (Senior Producer, Kabam)*

Massively Multiplayer Online Games

In Chapter 2, you learned about technology issues related to *massively multiplayer online games* (MMOs). Now let's look at the content and genre characteristics of these games. Under the MMO umbrella, there are several variations on some genres we've already discussed—known as massively multiplayer online role-playing games (MMORPGs), massively multiplayer first-person shooters (MMOFPSs), and massively multiplayer real-time strategy games (MMORTSs).

Blizzard Entertainment

With millions of subscribers, *World of Warcraft* is the most popular MMO on the market.

One of the biggest issues in MMO development is balancing social interaction with *immersion*. This poses a problem for MMORPGs in particular. Traditional RPG players want to escape into a fantasy world and become involved in rich storylines and character development. If MMORPG players discuss real-world topics during the game or don't stay in character, other more traditional players might not enjoy the experience of playing. Does a developer try to enforce role-play, or do the players have to accept that the game cannot be fully immersive? Issues related to story and immersion are discussed further in Chapter 5.

::::: *Yohoho! Puzzle Pirates*:
The First MMOPG?

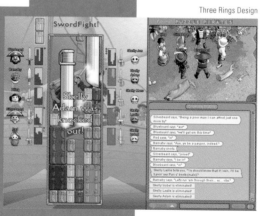

Three Rings Design

I created *Puzzle Pirates* because of my love of pirates—both as a concept and pretending to be a pirate—combined with the realization that puzzle games made the ideal gameplay backbone to an MMOG. My girlfriend at the time becoming pathologically addicted to *Bejeweled* was a tip-off. [Author's Note: Although *Puzzle Pirates* contains elements associated with MMORPGs, its incorporation of puzzles into the game could make it the first of its kind—an MMOPG (puzzle game)!]

—*Daniel James (Chief Executive Officer, Three Rings Design)*

Another related issue involves player misbehavior. Some players are simply rude—while others harass, cheat, or even commit fraud … providing a more serious threat to others' enjoyment of the game. The anonymity provided by the Internet is a primary reason this type of behavior is so prevalent. This could pose a threat to the trend in which parents and children play online games together (discussed in Chapter 4). Fortunately for young children, there are now some interesting MMORPGs created just for them—such as Nickelodeon's *Neopets* and *Monkey Quest*, Sony's *Wizard101* and *Clone Wars Adventures*—and Disney's *Club Penguin* and *Toontown Online*.

::::: *Shattered Galaxy*:
A Rewarding MMORTS

KRU Interactive

Unlike most other MMOs, *Shattered Galaxy* is based completely upon player vs. player combat. Every player belongs to a team, or faction, that competes with other factions for game resources. Since we wanted players to actively support their team, we made several changes to traditional RTS gameplay. For example, penalties for death are negligible, and we reward players for participating in battles whether they win or lose. When you're not afraid of dying, you're able to sacrifice yourself for teammates without hesitation.

—Kevin D. Saunders (Creative Director, Alelo)

Multiplayer Games: "Splashing in the Shallow End of the Communication Pool"

What hasn't been done yet in multiplayer games? Enabling people to communicate and connect on a deeper level. Why? Because life is about connecting with others, sharing ideas, and coming away richer for the experience. So far, we've been splashing in the shallow end of the communication pool. There's so much lost through a simple text chat. Still, I find this to be the single most compelling challenge in game design: How do you capture and convey the energy of a group playing together in a room when the people are spread out all over the globe?

—Patricia A. Pizer (Creative Director, ZeeGee Games)

::::: Chatting in Digital Space

One of the benefits of MMOs is the ability to "meet" new friends in a virtual world. In some ways, this is equivalent to what one of the first graphics-based chat rooms, *The Palace*, tried in the mid-1990s. *The Palace* became a very popular hangout for those who were using the Web at the time.

DigitalSpace Corp.

MMOs are sometimes referred to as *persistent-state worlds* (*PSWs*) because they are available 24-hours per day and do not end when a player logs out of the game—allowing the player's character to "persist" in time. This persistence can pose some interesting challenges. Since an MMO doesn't have a final endpoint, content for the game is produced on an ongoing basis—and it is expected to change periodically to keep players interested in the game.

Game Elements: The Significance of Goals & Genres

This chapter continued where the previous one left off—covering additional game elements that form the foundation of game development. Once you've determined the goal of your game, identify a subset of genres that might best address that goal. For example, if you're creating a game that is intended to educate players about a real-world process such as fixing a car, an obvious genre match would be a process simulation game—but is this the only possibility? A game that's developed to encourage consumers to purchase a product or service might not utilize the same genre as one designed to allow the players (or developers) to express themselves creatively—or perhaps both of these games could share the same genre. Think about it!

:::

Next, let's look at the players—who they are, where they are, and why they play. Although often overlooked by game developers, the player market must be understood to develop successful games. As you read Chapter 4, apply what you've learned about genres and goals to different player markets. You'll notice that there's often a direct relationship between players and the types of games they play!

:::CHAPTER REVIEW EXERCISES:::

1. In this chapter, you learned about several non-entertainment game goals. Choose five genres introduced in this chapter and discuss which particular goal might be a good match for each. Can you think of a goal not mentioned in this chapter that might inspire you to create a game?

2. How do game platforms influence game goals and genres? Web-based Facebook games—accessed initially through the computer platform, but now also through mobile devices—are often considered to be "social games." Although multiplayer online console games have always had a social component, the console platform did not give rise to the "social game" moniker. Why do you think this is the case? Choose two distinct platforms and discuss which game genres would be particularly relevant for them—as opposed to other platforms.

3. The ESRB has used a "T" rating on some MMOs. This rating is not necessarily accurate. Why is this? What do you feel motivates people to play MMOs? How does the structure of an MMO differ from LAN-based multiplayer and single-player games?

4. Choose one of your favorite games and change its genre. For example, what would *Halo* be like if it was a puzzle, simulation or RTS game instead of an FPS? Now, create a brand new game genre that is distinct from those discussed in this chapter. Tie this genre to what you learned about platforms in Chapter 2. What type of platform would be most appropriate for this genre, and why?

5. Combine two genres discussed in this chapter to create a new hybrid (mixed) genre. What type of game would you create for this new genre? List five unique features of the game.

6. Adventure games have declined in popularity in the last 15 years. Why do you think this is the case? What would you change about the content or structure in adventure games to incite new interest in this genre?

7. Strategy games don't always need a military backdrop. Discuss three settings or scenarios *not* related to the military that could be incorporated successfully into a strategy game.

8. Do you feel that all games are educational by accident? Why or why not? The "edutainment" movement of the 1980s and early 1990s focused on the early childhood market and players in the K-12 grades. What about games created specifically to educate beyond K-12 (post-secondary)? Create an idea for an educational game geared toward adults who are taking a college course. Now choose another type of "serious" (non-entertainment) game goal—such as corporate training, military recruitment, or health. How would you ensure that your game was still fun and engaging while retaining its purpose?

4

CHAPTER

Player Elements

who plays and why?

Key Chapter Questions

- What *motivates* people to play games, and how does this affect the types of games that are developed?

- What is the difference between *geographics*, *demographics*, and *psychographics*?

- How has the *player market* changed over time?

- What is the difference between the United States and other *geographic markets* such as South Korea, Japan, China, and Germany?

- What are the different *generations* of players in the United States?

Now that you understand how the game industry has evolved throughout history and all the basic elements that should be considered before developing a game, it is time to look at the players. There was a time when the profile of a "gamer" was a teenage boy—but that profile is now wildly inaccurate. The market for players has changed dramatically since the mid-1990s, due to the advent of the Web as a commercial medium. As the multimedia interface to the Internet, the Web fueled the growth of a new communications industry. Now, we've gone beyond just having our own personal web sites to creating personal blogs on Tumblr and Word Press; microblogging to our followers through Twitter; updating our status through Foursquare; and sharing our opinions (and photos of our family and pets) with our Facebook friends. Taking up where the Web left off, social networking has dramatically expanded the player market.

Game Market

If you plan to develop games, you need to understand the game *market*—the people who play games. Which portion of this market do you want to target? The answer to this question is *not* "everyone." You need to understand who *your* market is to create a compelling game that suits your market's needs.

With over half of all Americans playing electronic games, interactive entertainment is the entertainment choice of the 21st century. The Entertainment Software Association (ESA) conducts an annual market survey on Essential Facts of sales, demographics, and usage in the computer and video game industry. In 2010, the ESA poll found that 67% of United States households play games on a regular basis; adult gamers have been playing for approximately 12 years; just under half (49%) of all players are adults between 18 and 49 years of age; and 64% of gamers play games with others in the same room. Parental beliefs and involvement have undergone significant change: ESA results show that 64% of parents believe that games are a positive part of their children's lives, and 48% of parents play computer and video games with their children at least once a week.

Player Motivation

Why do people play games? Understanding this can help you develop games that will fulfill these needs. Some developers create games without considering why their audience would want to play them—and components of games that are most attractive to the players are not utilized enough by game developers to keep the players interested. Following are just a few factors that motivate players to keep on playing.

::::::Player Suits

In 1996, Richard Bartle published "Hearts, Clubs, Diamonds, Spades: Players Who Suit MUDs" (*Journal of MUD Research*), a paper in which he proposed that multi-user dungeon (MUD) players fall into four categories, depending on whether they enjoy acting on (manipulating, exploiting, controlling) or interacting with (learning, communicating, examining) the game world or players. Bartle originally came up with four player types, corresponding to the four suits in a deck of cards:

Hearts: These players are *socializers*—those who enjoy learning about or communicating with other players.

Clubs: These players are *killers*—those who enjoy manipulating other players.

Diamonds: These players are *achievers*—those who enjoy interacting with the game world.

Spades: These players are *explorers*—those who enjoy manipulating the game world.

Diagram by Per Olin

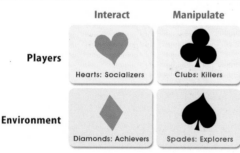

Hearts, clubs, diamonds, spades—types of players that "suit" MUDs.

Bartle theorized that a healthy MUD community requires a certain proportion of each type of player to sustain itself.

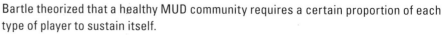

Richard Bartle on Player Types :::::

Dr. Richard Bartle co-wrote the first virtual world, *MUD* (multi-user dungeon), in 1978 and has thus been at the forefront of the online game industry from its inception. A former lecturer in artificial intelligence and current Visiting Professor in Computer Game Design at the University of Essex (U.K.), he is an influential writer on all aspects of virtual world design, development, and management. As an independent consultant, Richard has worked with most of the major online game companies in the United Kingdom and the United States for more than 20 years. His book, *Designing Virtual Worlds*, has established itself as a foundation text for researchers and developers of virtual worlds. Richard was the inaugural recipient of the Game Developers Choice Online Legend Award in 2010.

RB

Dr. Richard Bartle
(Visiting Professor
in Computer Game
Design, University
of Essex)

My theory has developed since I first proposed it. As it stood originally, it had four problematical elements to it:

1. There were two types of killer.

2. It didn't explain how players gradually changed type over time.

3. It didn't account for one of the oft-cited reasons that players give when asked to explain "fun," namely "I like immersion."

4. It was all observational, with no connection to existing theoretical works.

The two types of killer were "griefers" and "politicians": one who tries to dominate others slyly and selfishly, and the other who tries to do so openly and selflessly. I could also see, though, that there were subtle differences in other types, too. For example, explorers who explored to expand the breadth of their knowledge did so in a scientific fashion, yet those who explored to expand the depth of their knowledge were more like computer gurus who "just knew" how things should work. I added an extra dimension to capture this distinction, which I called implicit/explicit: implicit actions were not reasoned out in advance but were done unthinkingly; explicit actions were considered and thought through. Griefers do not think about why they do what they do (although they may think about how they do it); politicians do give thought to their motivations and rationalize them in terms of helping the game. Explorers working scientifically will consider what they're doing as if it were an experiment, testing the boundaries of their theories; gurus wouldn't bother, since they already know the world so well that they understand it implicitly.

Adding the extra dimension gave me eight types instead of four and solved one of the problems. I was then able to use the new 3D model to trace how players changed behavior over time. The most common development path I observed was evident in the four-type, 2D graph: killer to explorer to achiever to socializer. Some other paths seemed to oscillate between two types, though—for example, killer to socializer to killer to socializer. With the new model, I could place them in particular subtypes of killer or socializer or whatever and, as a result, I found that all four of the paths I'd observed empirically followed the same basic course of action: implicit to explicit to explicit to implicit, along a track the shape of a reversed Alpha.

With this, I was able to account for immersion—which is how far you are along the track at any one moment. The farther you are along, the more you understand the virtual world; therefore, the more a part of it you are able to feel, and (crucially) the closer you are to being yourself. Immersion is basically a reflection of how close to self-understanding you are playing in the world. Virtual worlds were always about freedom and identity (MUD1 was specifically designed for both), and a sense of immersion is how progress in this regard manifests itself.

Finally, I could link the theory to other, existing theories from other disciplines. The player development tracks that players of virtual worlds follow the "hero's journey" narrative that was discovered by Joseph Campbell in the 1940s. His theory was that all myths and folk tales followed the same basic pattern, because in understanding that pattern people were able to understand themselves and their place in the world. Players of virtual worlds follow the same journey, but instead of experiencing it secondhand through the eyes of a protagonist, they can undertake it themselves. This is why virtual worlds are so compelling: they enable people to be, and to become, themselves. The "hero's journey" links to many other areas of academic study, in particular psychology, so at last my player types model could be anchored in other work supported by other tried-and-trusted theories. *[Author Note: The hero's journey will be discussed in more detail in Chapter 5.]*

Basically, you play a virtual world to have "fun"—which is whatever you can do now that will advance you along your hero's journey. You can have a virtual world that can be relatively stable, attracting mainly players who are socializers or achievers —but they need a continuous stream of newbies to keep them going. Balanced worlds don't shed players as much, so they don't suffer so much if the newbie flow is reduced.

Social Interaction

When more than one person is playing a game, the players might be motivated to interact socially with their opponents or team members. This *social interaction* could exist in simple two-person games at an arcade or in massively multiplayer online games (MMOs), with thousands of people playing simultaneously. Players in MMOs are often allowed to communicate through the game itself—often discussing non game-related topics rather than "staying in character." Sometimes players who meet through games arrange to meet each other in real life at game conventions. Marriage ceremonies have even taken place in games!

Nintendo

Social interaction can be a motivating factor for some players. Although social interaction can take place in the immediate environment (shown), it can also occur in-game—especially in social games and MMOs.

Physical Seclusion

The idea of *seclusion* might seem to be the opposite of social interaction. However, players who want to be secluded are still interacting socially with people—but in the privacy of their own physical environments. This challenges the definition of "being social." Some would argue that people who prefer to stay home and play an MMO must be antisocial. Others would argue that these same people must be highly social, because they are most likely interacting with many more people than would be possible at a dinner party. Is email considered anti-social? Before it was accepted by the masses as a viable way to communicate, it certainly was viewed in this way. Now it is accepted as a way to broaden one's social network and now has the capacity to transcend geographical boundaries, becoming global. Players motivated by

iStock Photo

Physical seclusion can be a motivating factor for some players. Although physical seclusion can take place in the immediate environment (shown), it can also be part of the game experience—common in single-player puzzle games.

physical seclusion would probably prefer to play games in a private place—such as their homes. Other players could easily play games in public places, such as arcades—or almost anywhere, with their handhelds in tow!

Midway Games

Competition is the motivation behind playing many fighting games such as *Mortal Kombat vs. DC Universe*.

3 Blokes Studios

Educational games such as *Brainiversity 2* focus on providing knowledge.

Midway Games

Score summaries, shown in this "magazine article" from *Guitar Hero III*, are necessary for players who are motivated by mastery.

Competition

Some players enjoy the thrill of *competing* with other players. The competitive spirit has been associated with games throughout history—and it forms the basis of the tremendously successful sports industry. In Chapter 6, you will learn that competition can be combined with cooperation to make games more compelling and challenging.

Knowledge

Players can be motivated to gain *knowledge* of particular concepts, processes, and strategies by playing games—although this motivation often is unconscious. If players made it clear that they truly wanted to learn while playing, game developers might market their games as educational tools—providing "fun learning" for everyone. In Chapter 3, you saw that most games allow players to learn "by accident"! In Chapter 6, you will also learn that players apply knowledge within and outside of games to play them successfully.

Mastery

Some players are motivated to *master* the game itself—demonstrating their ability to dominate the game world and figure out how to become advanced players. Mastery is most obvious during games that depend on increasing character skills to "win." Players motivated by mastery focus on assessing their status in the game by attaining high scores and rankings.

Escapism

Players often indicate that they are motivated to play to *escape* from the ongoing stresses and challenges of real life. An imaginary game world follows its own rules, some of which are less restrictive than those in real life. Although people can escape into the "worlds" of other media such as books and movies, they do not directly participate in those worlds like they do in games. The next chapter introduces the concept of *immersion* and how it is particularly effective in games. Players' participation in games can even involve close bonds with characters within the games—especially if a character is "inhabited" by the player!

Take-Two Interactive

Game worlds such as the vast landscape in *Borderlands* provide escape for some players.

Electronic Arts

My most memorable experience working on a title was right after we shipped *Ultima Online*. We were having a terrifically hard time stabilizing and optimizing the game (i.e., it was crashing and lagging all the time). Despite our success in attracting the largest number of subscribers ever to an online game, we were a bit down on ourselves for the lack of quality in our product. About that time, we got a letter from a player who described what a wonderful time he was having in the game. In the somewhat lengthy letter, he talked about how *UO* allowed him to experience things he never had a chance to experience in real life. In *UO*, he was a strong leader with lots of friends—and he was able to explore the vastness of the land and destroy evil. At the end of the letter, he said how much he appreciated us for giving him a chance to run—which, since he was confined to a wheelchair, he could not do in his real life. That letter made all the pain and effort worth it. More importantly, it taught me that these games can be more than money-making entertainment. They can have real meaning and impact for our customers. I have never forgotten this lesson, and I still cherish that letter today.

—*Starr Long (Executive Producer, The Walt Disney Company)*

Addiction

Some players indicate that they are motivated by *addiction*—the tendency to focus on one activity at the expense of all others. A recent panel conducted by the International Game Developers Association (IGDA) indicated that one of the best compliments game developers receive is that their games are addictive. Unlike the comparatively

505 Games

Casino games such as Texas Hold 'em in *Playwize Poker & Casino* can be very addictive.

"passive" entertainment of television and film, games offer players the opportunity to take active roles in the entertainment experience—including making decisions and getting feedback. This can be highly rewarding for players, but it can also make them crave and indulge in continuous play to the point of ignoring other more important areas of their lives. Gambling has been shown to be addictive, and some game developers are considering incorporating gambling into more sophisticated electronic games. However, it can be argued that many worthwhile hobbies might be addictive—and that it is the player's responsibility to maintain some balance!

In addition to the motivating factors already discussed—social interaction, physical seclusion, competition, knowledge, mastery, escapism, and addiction—there are many other reasons people play. Some feel it is a form of *therapy*—a chance to work out troubling issues in a "safe" environment separate from (but sometimes eerily similar to) the real world. Konami's *Dance Dance Revolution* launched a new type of fan base that played to *exercise* and work on new dance moves. *DDR*'s popularity influenced the release of several other dance-oriented franchises—including *Dance Central* and *Just Dance*. With the advent of motion control and motion sensing devices (Nintendo Wii, Sony Move, Microsoft Kinect), physical/rhythm games have taken on a life of their own. The immensely popular *Guitar Hero* and *Rock Band* franchises take onscreen pattern matching to another level through singing and "playing" controllers that resemble musical instruments. A game's *playability* (discussed in more detail in Chapters 10 and 11) is related to player motivation. If the game satisfies a player's particular motivation, it is more likely to be fun, engrossing, and worthwhile to that player.

> A game is often the key that sets my imagination free. I can't put on a cape and go flying around the city for obvious reasons. Playing games gives me a chance to do the things I dream of, to a certain extent.
>
> —Chris Lenhart
> (game art and design graduate)

Geographics

Geographics relate to the players' geographic locations—which could include various countries or even regions within those countries. The U.S. game industry alone does over $10.5 billion worth of business annually (NPD Group), and the industry's value added to the U.S. GDP (gross national product) was $4.95 billion in 2009.

When NCsoft, now the largest game developer in South Korea, launched the *Lineage* MMO in September 1998, the country was experiencing an economic crisis that had resulted in a dramatic devaluation of Korean currency and an unprecedented increase in unemployment. "Refugees" from the high-tech industry, mostly middle managers, became entrepreneurs overnight—starting PC game rooms (Baangs) in their living rooms. A profitable industry had begun, with hourly fees of $1 (U.S. equivalent) paid by the unemployed gamers—a low price to pay to conquer foes in "virtual worlds" and escape the real economic catastrophes in the offline world, without having to own a personal computer.

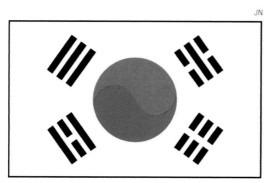

JN

South Korea—still a world leader in household broadband penetration —boasts the largest subscriber base to online multiplayer games.

As South Korea's financial situation began to improve, and the total households with broadband service increased rapidly, the number of personal accounts on home PCs also rose. In addition to playing at PC Baangs, gamers can now download game software onto their home PCs and pay using micro-transactions rather than paying monthly subscription fees. Baangs have also grown in popularity—making a dramatic transformation from entrepreneurs' living rooms to full-blown entertainment centers, some of which are as ritzy as Las Vegas casinos. It is commonplace to see men and women gamers in Baangs—which often provide "his" and "hers" chairs so that couples can play online games together. Online gaming has also grown beyond being just a pastime into a competitive national sport—with many game competitions now being televised regularly. Currently, South Korea's online game market is expected to reach $2 billion during 2011 (Pearl Research/Gamasutra). South Korea represents the world's most developed online game market.

> I play games to escape the life that most of us live and live the life that most of us want.
>
> —*Arash John Sammander*
> *(Game Art & Design student)*

Cyrus Kanga

Mark Terrano (Design
Director, Hidden Path
Entertainment)

Mark Terrano is the Design Director at Hidden Path Entertainment—an indie game development company founded with friends who were former members of the Xbox Advanced Technology Group. His focus is on social, character, and storytelling games that "feel different." At Xbox, he consulted with developers around the world to help them launch best-in-class titles on the Xbox and Xbox 360. At Ensemble Studios, he worked on the *Age of Empires* series as a designer and programmer. His free time is spent enjoying Seattle's natural beauty, photography, playing music, and, of course, playing all kinds of games.

When people ask where I think games are going in the near future, I always refer to South Korea. Game parlors are on every block and apartment complex, the professional gamers are on billboards and television, and everyone you meet has a favorite *StarCraft* story. Games are not just accepted in popular culture; they are integrated, and nearly everyone plays.

"Professional gamer" is a recognized career, and it is well-respected; tournament competition is fierce and followed in the media on par with any other sport. The government is a strong proponent of game developers in Korea as well—providing services, resources, information, and tools to start-ups. The students just moving into their first jobs now have grown up with games, and they understand games as an interactive medium. Even a little-known new game can easily attract 100,000 beta players—and the rate of introduction and evolution of multiplayer titles is staggering.

Competition and tournament play are also important in popularizing gameplay. The World Cyber Games started in South Korea; this is an Olympics-style event with players competing from all over the world and converging for the world finals, which lasts a week in the host country. Professional gamers work their way up through the competitive ranks and represent their neighborhoods, schools, and companies. Large tournaments and local heroes create media attention that follows the professionals and builds a fan base. The commercial sponsorships and endorsements follow the fans, which leads to more competition and tournament play. Full-color weekly magazines are thick with strategies, tactics, and interviews with the pro gamers and developers. Fashion, gadgets, accessories, and other media are also influenced by games.

Mark Terrano

Arcade (Seoul)

Korean developers are bringing new perspectives, stories, mythologies, and even completely new social structures to online game design. In the game *Lineage*, players gather to defend their castle from a siege which has been scheduled to take place. A group of players actually commandeer a game room for the siege; it transforms into a base of operations, and defenders quickly organize and change strategies as orders are shouted around the room. This completely new kind of game and social experience has not been available before in any medium. While the physical and social properties of the PC game room don't always translate worldwide, the use of voice, command structure, team tactics, group balance, and shared risks and rewards are powerful gameplay devices that will shape the next generation of games.

Mark Terrano

WCG Competition (Seoul)

Initially, Japan did not even appear on the list of most wired countries due to being dominated by NTT DoCoMo, a wireless service that has a telecommunications monopoly in the country. NTT's presence was so strong that it was financially prohibitive for Japanese citizens—who were charged by the minute for Internet use—to order broadband service. The game industry has thus revolved more around video game consoles—and not online games. The wireless network was primary, while the Internet was secondary.

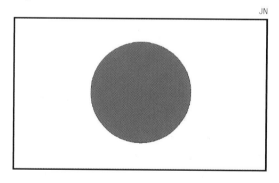

Japan's game industry has historically revolved around video consoles and wireless games, but broadband penetration is now growing.

It is interesting that Japan and Korea—countries that traditionally led the way in mobile gaming—have been somewhat eclipsed by the United States and European markets, which now account for over 50% of mobile game revenues (*Screen Digest*). By 2010, the worldwide mobile gaming market could grow to over $6 billion in revenue, with 134 million average users per month (a threefold increase from 2005).

Troy Dunniway on the Chinese Market :::::

TD

Troy Dunniway
(Vice President &
General Manager;
Globex Studios)

Troy Dunniway's time at Globex Studios China is creating and publishing massively multiplayer online role-playing games for worldwide release—with a strong emphasis on the Chinese market. Prior to Globex, Troy held senior management roles at Electronic Arts, Microsoft, Ubisoft, and many other top companies for the last 20 years. He is also primary author of Gameplay Mechanics (part of the Game Development Essentials series) and is a regular columnist on Gamasutra.

Building games for each market can affect the direction of the game in a major or minor way. Many games only localize the text and voiceover for a game for foreign markets -- but in some large markets such as China, this is usually not enough. For example, in China, there is no console game market—and everyone only plays massively multiplayer online role-playing games (MMORPGs) and online casual games that cannot be pirated. All MMORPGs in China are also free to play, and not subscription-based like many in the US (and in much of the rest of the world). This changes the core of many games. China also has a very different cultural history, many elements that might be found in a story or game in the US may not be understood by most of the Chinese market. As an example, the science fiction genre is not really liked or understood in China, and it isn't popular at all. Even major movies such as Star Wars were not well received in China. The direction of a game for some markets can be very challenging, to say the least. The Chinese market is beginning to be more interested in new types of games, and new features within the MMO space—but developers must very slowly introduce these new features. For example, action MMORPGs are starting to become popular in China—but all of the features of most traditional MMOs are there, but pace of the combat is increased. However, this is dangerous in China – since the average player here actually sees games as a way to socialize. If you increase the rate of play, thinking you will make it more fun minute to minute, you can actually turn off the average player who likes a slower-paced game that allows them to chat while they play.

littlebig (Photobucket)

Internet cafe (Shanghai)

However, largely because of Softbank, Japan is catching up in the broadband arena with ADSL technology in its fixed-line telephone networks. Once an extremely expensive alternative, Japan's broadband service is now one of the most affordable and most advanced, according to its Ministry of Internal Affairs and Communications (MIC). Consoles (a major Japanese export) have not been as popular in South Korea. Historical conflicts between Korea and Japan—especially related to the World War II occupation—also affect online gameplay. Korean players, who have more experience playing in the online arena and can easily organize into powerful teams, often seek retribution for past grievances through *player kill (PK)* targeted toward Japanese players. ("Player kill" refers to characters who are killed in a game by other characters—where both characters are controlled by players. The term "offline PK" became used by South Korean authorities when PK was taken out of the game and into the PC Baang—resulting in some real-world violence between players.)

China boasts a growing market for MMORPGs and online casual games—but there is no console market.

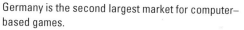

Germany is the second largest market for computer-based games.

Using licensed properties has become a content issue in Japan (also in France and the Scandinavian countries)—where properties such as *Star Trek* are not nearly as popular as they are in the United States, Germany, and the United Kingdom. Another content issue in market geographics includes the depiction of violence in games. *Quake II* did not have a retail launch in Germany—the second largest computer game market in the world—due to the game's level of violence. In order to sell *Command & Conquer: Generals – Zero Hour* in the German market, the game's graphics had to be modified so that all military units were robots—not people—ensuring that no humans were killed in the game. In Germany, games must avoid showing blood, shooting humans, and anything that glorifies Hitler, the Nazis, or the Third Reich. Other countries, including Australia and Korea, have also banned titles that are identified as being too violent.

Markets can differ widely—even on a national level. In the United States, certain pastimes such as hunting and fishing are popular in certain regions—such as the Midwest. This might affect the sales of a game such as *Bass Fishing* or the *Deer Hunter* series. Similarly, games associated with sports that are particularly popular on the East Coast (such as squash, lacrosse, and fencing) might have a much larger market there than on the West Coast.

Kate Edwards on the Importance of Localization :::::

KE

Kate Edwards
(Principal Consultant,
Englobe Inc.)

As the founder and principal consultant of Englobe Inc., a Seattle-based niche consultancy for cultural content management, Kate is a gamer who is also a unique hybrid of an academic geographer, writer, and geocultural content strategist—all coexisting with a passion for cultures, technology, and games. Formerly as Microsoft's senior geopolitical strategist in the Geopolitical Strategy team (a position and team she created and managed), Kate was responsible for protecting against political and cultural content errors across all MS products and locales. She implemented a geopolitical quality review process at Microsoft Game Studios and was personally responsible for reviewing potential sensitivities in all first-party games. Since leaving Microsoft, she has worked on numerous titles—including *Dragon Age 1* and *2*, *Star Wars: The Old Republic*, *Ninja Gaiden II*, and *Dance Central*. Kate is also the founder of the IGDA Game Localization SIG and is a regular columnist for *MultiLingual Computing*.

My function is to help game designers and developers create content that won't be considered offensive, sensitive, or otherwise problematic in overseas locales. I do this by advising them early in the game development cycle on potential issues with their concepts and then help review specific pieces of content as they're developed throughout the cycle. In short, my job is to maximize the number of players across as many locales as possible by ensuring there won't be problems that obstruct sales in a specific market or region.

The game industry needs to embrace the concept of global game development. Localization, which accounts for about 50% of the industry's total revenue, is still an afterthought in many game development cycles. Yet localization and culturalization are just as important as other considerations that occur during the inception of the game idea (e.g., dev, audio, writing). Instead of making a game for one market and then localizing, game developers need to think of it as developing one title for the world—and then consider how this changes their assumptions.

Psychographics

Psychographics consist of people's values, attitudes, and lifestyles. How do they like to spend their time? How do they see the world? Are they social people? Are they ambitious? How do they feel about money, religion, culture—themselves? Are they cynical or optimistic? Do they participate in social and environmental causes?

The Gamer Brain

Rob Beeson—a biologist and learning scientist whose fascination with how *infographics* (visual representations of information, data or knowledge) can help aid in learning—pieced together pre-existing research on the brain's reward centers and came up with a graphic showing how these centers map to different areas of the brain. Calling his infographic *The Gamer Brain: The Science & Stories Behind a Gamer's Brain*, Beeson came up with seven types of players: conqueror, socializer, mastermind, seeker, daredevil, survivor, and achiever.

VALS Psychotypes

The VALS™ Survey was developed by the Stanford Research Institute and is currently run by Strategic Business Insights. VALS analyzes the consumer market based on eight segments associated with ideals, achievement, and self-expression. Take the survey at *http://www.strategicbusinessinsights.com/vals/surveynew.shtml* and find out if you are an innovator, thinker, achiever, experiencer, believer, striver, maker, or survivor.

The VALS survey analyzes consumers based on psychographic dimensions related to motivation and resources.

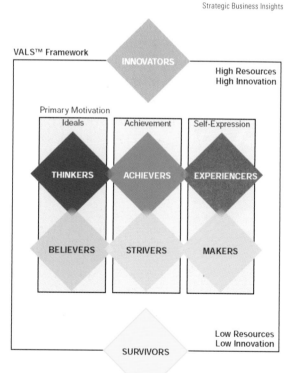

Strategic Business Insights

VALS™ Framework

INNOVATORS

High Resources
High Innovation

Primary Motivation

Ideals — Achievement — Self-Expression

THINKERS — ACHIEVERS — EXPERIENCERS

BELIEVERS — STRIVERS — MAKERS

Low Resources
Low Innovation

SURVIVORS

One of the primary ways the game development community has segmented the player market has been by frequency. Traditionally, a "casual" player was one who played only occasionally—focusing on games that took a relatively short amount of time to play (or that could be stopped and started at any time) such as Web and cell phone games. These games are designed with the casual player in mind—they are short, easy-to-learn, entertaining ways to pass the time. Today, the word "casual" usually describes the game rather than the player demographic. "Hardcore" (sometimes referred to as "core") players are still more likely to immerse themselves in a game that might last weeks or months (rather than hours or minutes). Games that might require a lot of social interaction or detailed storylines with complex character development are often ideal for these players. These definitions, however, are just extremes that focus on frequency of play. The game development community should consider much more than this when researching their target audience.

Myers-Briggs Type Indicator (MBTI)

In 1943, Isabel Briggs Myers and her mother, Katharine Briggs, developed a model to measure personality types. The model, known as the Myers-Briggs Type Indicator (MBTI®), is based on the work of psychologist Carl Jung—whose character archetypes will be discussed further in Chapter 5. The Myers-Briggs personality types contain four letters, each corresponding to one of two opposing personality characteristics:

- **Extrovert (E) vs. Introvert (I):** Energy is more outer- or inner-directed.

- **Sensing (S) vs. Intuitive (N):** Perception is more present- or future-oriented.

- **Thinking (T) vs. Feeling (F):** Judgment-formation is more objective or subjective.

- **Judging (J) vs. Perceiving (P):** Approach to world is more structured or spontaneous.

Diagram by Per Olin

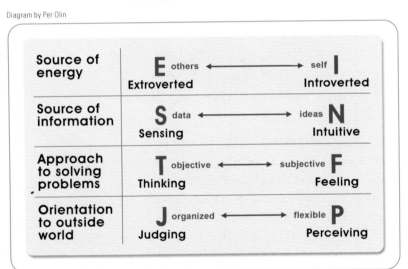

Preferences on each scale of the MBTI instrument combine to yield a four-letter psychological type [e.g., ISFJ, ENTP]. (Source: Myers & Briggs Foundation, Inc.)

Linking Players to the Experience

During the early years of the computer game industry, developers paid little attention to who its customers were. Most game concepts were based upon the personal preferences and opinions of the developers. In more recent years, some game companies have employed demographics to consider our target populations. Most game industry efforts to profile customers and potential customers are limited to the demographics of age, gender, and gaming preference (hardcore vs. casual). These parameters are of limited usefulness because they do not directly tell us how to best entertain these players. The more directly any demographic information can be linked to how the game is played, the more readily we can apply it to our design. Studying player personalities and motivations brings us one step closer to the real question: What makes a game fun for a certain type of person?

—*Kevin D. Saunders (Creative Director, Alelo)*

Beyond Demographics

Knowing your target player market isn't just an issue of pure marketing; it has huge significance to the design of a game. Knowing your audience means more than simply knowing age, gender, and spending habits; it means understanding the way your game fits into your players' lives. Do your players think of gaming as a time waster or a dedicated hobby? Do your players view games as a medium for self-expression, personal growth, socializing, escapism, or something else entirely? Knowing the answers to these questions should fundamentally shape the way your games are designed.

Brandii Grace (Game Designer, Engaging Designs)

Some members of the game industry have taken notice of psychographics such as MBTI®. International Hobo—a company founded by game developer and author Ernest Adams—developed a research study that applies the Myers-Briggs personality test to the player population.

Behavior patterns can also be seen as part of psychographics. As U.S. citizens continue to play more games, they are clearly spending less time on other activities. According to the Entertainment Software Association (ESA), 52% of players who spend more time playing games report watching less television as a result. In addition, 47% of gamers are going to fewer movies—and 41% watch movies at home less often. The decline in television viewing is becoming such an issue that advertisers are now considering in-game advertising as a more viable way of reaching much of their market. The ESA also reported in 2010 that 72% of U.S. homes own a console and/or PC used to play games; this might have further contributed to the decline of other traditional entertainment pastimes.

Demographics

The *demographics* of players include statistical information such as gender, age, income level, education level, marital status, ethnicity, and religion. Let us take a close look at a few of these demographics with regard to online game playing to see how they have changed over the years.

Courtesy of Skate Estate and RJ Vending & Amusement

Early arcades were populated more by boys than girls.

Gender

As discussed in Chapter 1, public arcades reached a market of kids who played after school and on weekends. The atmosphere and marketing strategies did not attract the adult population—so this player demographic was ignored. Although these arcades could have easily reached young girls as much as boys, that did not happen. Even with games such as *Pac-Man*—which were specifically designed to reach a wider market—the arcades continued to be dominated by teenage boys.

:::::: Gender Role Representation in Toy Commercials

Toy commercials aimed toward girls focus on toys that encourage nurturing play (e.g., domestic items such as baby dolls and toy ovens), while those targeted toward boys focus on toys that encourage aggressive play (e.g., military items such as guns and tanks). Author Jeannie Novak theorized that this is the result of childhood socialization by parents and the media—which has been perpetuated by many game developers.

iStock Photo   iStock Photo

Domestic toys such as baby dolls are marketed toward girls (left), while aggressive toys such as guns are marketed toward boys (right).

This theory comes from a content analysis study conducted in 1992 at UCLA on gender role representation in toy commercials. Jeannie analyzed over 300 toy commercials for type of toy, gender of children depicted in the ad, cooperative vs. competitive behavior—and features such as camera movement, music tempo, cuts, and pans. Among other results, she found that girls in the ads cooperatively played with dolls and other domestic toys, while boys played competitively with vehicles or war-themed action figures (e.g., GI Joe). Very rarely did both genders appear together in the ads. Toys depicted in ads with both genders were board games—and all but one ad showed boys teaming up against girls and winning the games. Jeannie concluded that children are socialized at a young age by the media to play with certain toys (in certain ways) based on their gender. This socialization is most likely perpetuated by parents, who often begin their children's lives decorating and clothing their children in pink or blue. If girls are taught to play nicely and cooperatively with baby dolls and Barbies, they will most likely feel "out of place" walking into a noisy, dark arcade—where most games involve shooting or destroying creatures and spaceships.

Jumping ahead to the dawn of the home console era, arcade gamers encouraged their parents to buy the games so they could play at home with their friends, using their television sets as monitors. Although there were plenty of female siblings around, their more experienced arcade-going brothers (and their friends) might have initially dominated these games.

In Chapter 1, you learned about the computer segment of the game industry—including home personal computers and mainframes. This industry was also male-dominated. It was not until the advent of the commercial Internet—fueled by its multimedia interface, the World Wide Web—that electronic games became more gender-balanced.

Since 2003, the ESA has found that adult women make up a larger percentage of players than boys ages 6–17—dispelling the age-old stereotype that games are for boys. Females of all ages now make up 40% of the game-playing population.

Getty Images   jn2k108 (Photobucket)

Early personal computer gaming was dominated by boys (left), but adult women gamers (including the Frag Dolls, right) now outnumber male gamers ages 6-17.

::::: Games Aren't Just For Kids Anymore!

An Entertainment Software Association survey showed that men and women over 18 make up 75% of the gaming population—and that the average age of players is now 34 years old. A full 26% of players are over age 50.

Generation

Another age-related demographic borders on a psychographic. Its importance cannot be overlooked in any industry. *Generations* are considered part of both demographics and psychographics. Although associated with a discrete age range, members of each generation as a group have experienced particular historical events and climates—including economic, cultural, social, and political shifts—during their lifetimes. Therefore, they likely have developed a particular set of beliefs, attitudes, and values. This assumption is based on what is known as *cohort analysis*—which suggests that people of a certain group do not necessarily change over time (e.g., if people were "liberal" when they were younger, they continue to be liberal as they grow older). Life stage analysis, on the other hand, assumes that people's beliefs change over time (e.g., that people get more conservative as they get older). Generational analysis is based on the idea of cohort analysis. If you assume that people as a group retain generally the same values over time, those people might continue to like the same types of entertainment over time.

There are four *generations* of players currently in the United States:

1. Silent Generation (~70–90 years of age)
2. Boomer Generation (~50–70 years of age)
3. Generation X (~30–50 years of age)
4. Millennial Generation (~10–30 years of age)
5. Homelander Generation (~ 10 years of age and younger; this group has also been referred to as the "New Silents," and its name is still tentative)

A *generation* is composed of people whose common location in history lends them a collective persona. The span of one generation is roughly the length of a phase of life. William Strauss and Neil Howe—authors of *Millennials Rising*, *The Fourth Turning*, and *Generations*—have provided an extensive analysis of generations throughout U.S. history. Their theories form the basis of the discussion on generational player demographics.

Diagram by Per Olin

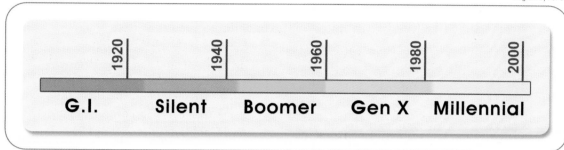

Generation birth years in the United States since 1900 (based on information from William Strauss and Neil Howe).

Silent Generation (Born 1924–1943)

The Silent Generation grew up staying at home under the secure wing of over-protective parents, while older siblings (GI generation) fought in World War II and joined the Civilian Conservation Corps. Upon entering the workforce, this generation donned nondescript "gray flannel suits" and opted for the job security offered by large, faceless corporations. Sandwiched between two active generations—the civic-minded group of GIs who fought in World War II and rebuilt America after the Great Depression, and the inner-focused group of Boomers who questioned authority and ushered in a major cultural shift in music and politics—the Silent Generation was like a "middle child," taking cues from others. Preferring to reap the benefits of America's unprecedented post-war prosperity, this passive generation consumed more than it created. As the first mass consumer audience, they used credit cards, cooked in space-age designer kitchens, and managed to escape the isolation of suburban life through the medium of television—which offered a superficial connection to the outside world. Not until adulthood did this generation finally break its silence—initiating a "midlife crisis" that resulted in the splintering of the very nuclear family system they had helped strengthen during the 1950s.

If you were to create a game that focuses on the Silent Generation, what type of content would you include? Perhaps a game that made order out of chaos would work for this generation. Other than games based on traditional Silent heroes—such as James Bond—no contemporary games come to mind that target this group. Games with heroes who are clean and cold—but who are not motivated by cynicism or revenge—might connect with this generation. An ideal example might be a combination of the slick sophistication of James Bond and the intricate, romantic, yet uptight nature of Thomas Crown. (According to exit interviews conducted by Cinema Score, even the 1999 remake of *The Thomas Crown Affair* appealed to an older demographic and did not prove sufficiently engaging to a younger audience.)

Boom Generation (Born 1943–1961)

The Boom Generation (also known as the "Baby Boomers") grew up sheltered in the suburbs during post–World War II economic prosperity—with their parents following the permissive child-rearing philosophies of Dr. Spock and working to keep the nuclear family intact. Death rates, drunk driving, suicide, illegitimate births, unemployment, and crime doubled or tripled as this generation came of age. The Boomers rebelled strongly against their parents, creating what is known as the "generation gap." They also participated in an "awakening" that their families could not understand—establishing an unprecedented counter culture involving music, drugs, and sexual promiscuity. As this generation grew into adulthood, they became "yuppies" with mainstream careers, immersed themselves in New Age enlightenment, and took up yoga—realizing that their "sexual revolution" and once-dominant liberal lifestyle had come to an end because of the realities of AIDS and conservative Reaganomics.

If you were to create a game that focused on the Boom Generation, what type of content would you include? Perhaps a game with a social, spiritual, or political message would be ideal. Famed game designer Richard "Lord British" Garriott continues to tap into the worldview of this generation—most recently with *Tabula Rasa*, a sci-fi game of epic salvation that distinguishes itself from other games of its kind with its spiritual focus. Characters in *Tabula Rasa* are built around three attributes: mind, body, and spirit. This premise is similar to that of Garriott's earlier *Ultima IV: Quest of the Avatar*. In that game, players must master eight moral virtues (honesty, honor, humility, spirituality, sacrifice, compassion, justice, and valor)—which, in turn, are composed of the three principles: truth, love, and courage.

MagiTam

With its spiritual focus, *The Journey to Wild Divine* is an appropriate game for the Boom generation.

::::: Millennial Trends Quiz

Before you read the Generation X and Milliennial Generation sections, take this quiz and discover some surprising statistics from the U.S. Census Bureau, Gallup Poll, and other national surveys. No cheating!

Do you think that the following trends have gone UP or DOWN since the early 1990s for teenagers aged 12–17?

		Up	Down
1.	School shootings	☐	☐
2.	Crime	☐	☐
3.	Sexual activity among boys	☐	☐
4.	Abortion rate	☐	☐
5.	Out of wedlock pregnancies	☐	☐
6.	Non-alcohol drug use	☐	☐
7.	Academic performance	☐	☐
8.	Closeness to parents	☐	☐
9.	Time spent with fathers	☐	☐
10.	Divorce rate of parents	☐	☐
11.	Time spent studying	☐	☐
12.	Time spent watching TV	☐	☐
13.	Time spent playing organized sports	☐	☐
14.	Hours spent in community service	☐	☐
15.	Suicide rate	☐	☐
16.	Importance of religion	☐	☐
17.	Trust of the police, government, and teachers	☐	☐
18.	Respect for celebrities and athletes	☐	☐

Answers on next page :::::

::::: Millennial Trends Quiz (Answers)

Most people get almost every one of these answers wrong. How did you do? Are you surprised by the correct answers? If you are, there is a good chance that you are making the assumption that kids today are exactly the way kids were 20 years ago. You also might be influenced by the media, which currently focuses a lot more energy on reporting news related to teenagers. The media did not focus on teens 20 years ago. Why?

1. DOWN by 20%

2. DOWN—comparable to 1960s levels

3. DOWN by 30%

4. DOWN—now the lowest ever recorded

5. DOWN—now the lowest ever recorded

6. DOWN—all types of drugs

7. UP—particularly in math and science

8. UP by over 80%—highest ever recorded

9. UP—5 hours per week more than in the 1980s

10. DOWN 20%

11. UP—3 times more homework since the 1980s

12. DOWN—has been dropping steadily since 1997

13. UP—coincides with the "soccer mom" trend

14. UP since the 1980s

15. DOWN for the first time since World War II

16. UP—teen interest in religion has risen significantly

17. UP—even before September 11

18. DOWN—is this the end of the "cult of celebrity"?

Sources:
U.S. Census (1990–2002); Gallup Polls (1990–2002); UCLA Annual poll of Incoming College Freshmen (1967–2002); University of Michigan, Institute of Social Research (1999); ZOOM and Applied Research & Consulting LLC; 2001 survey of nearly 10,000 kids ages 9–13 for PBS; Horatio Alger Association (1999); U.S. Department of Justice Statistics/Juvenile Statistics (2001); National School Safety Center (2001); ChildTrends DataBank (2002); Alan Guttmacher Institute (2001); CDC Youth Behavior Surveillance Survey (2002); U.S. Substance Abuse and Mental Health Services Administration (1999); SAMSHA–Substance Abuse and Mental Health Services Administration (U.S. Department of Health and Human Services); University of Michigan MTF (Monitoring the Future); SAT College Board; University of California Berkeley Survey Research Center, as part of the center's Public Agendas and Citizen Engagement Survey (PACES) project, 2002.

Thanks to Pete Markiewicz, PhD for providing the statistics for this quiz.

Generation X (Born 1962–1981)

Does the following description of Generation X correspond to the answers you provided on the Millennial Trends Quiz? If so, you most likely got most of the answers wrong; this is because you are assuming that Generation X and Millennials are one and the same.

Members of Generation X grew up in an era when America experienced its lowest birthrate ever, and when it was commonplace for families to be torn apart by divorce—only to be stitched back together, patchwork-style, by remarriage, step-siblings, and half-siblings. As teens, many Xers were independent "latchkey kids" who worked at odd jobs or fast food restaurants instead of receiving an allowance. These kids came home to *After School Specials*, *Sesame Street*, *Electric Company*, and *Mister Roger's Neighborhood* on television, which became a de facto babysitter (instead of having after-school activities monitored by teachers or parents). During this era, suicide, murder, and incarceration rates skyrocketed. Growing into young adults, members of this generation have continued to assert their independence. They have expressed their cynicism and angst creatively through their art, while using their entrepreneurial tendencies to innovate do-it-yourself small businesses. Known as "Generation X," they were not given a descriptive name—although "X" has now come to mean "Xtreme" (a term that captures this generation's risk-taking, cutting-edge spirit).

Eidos   Valve

Tomb Raider's Lara Croft and *Half-Life*'s Gordon Freeman are both depicted as lone heroes.

If you were to create a game that focused on Generation X, what type of content would you include? Perhaps a game that focuses on an independent, nomadic character who is "on the edge" and takes risks would be ideal. Sound familiar? Since the Generation X age group makes up most of the game developers these days, games like this are pretty easy to find!

Millennial Generation (Born 1982–2002)

Does the following description of the Millennial Generation correspond to the answers you provided on the Millennial Trends Quiz? If so, you probably got most of the answers right; this means that you are in touch with the newest generation known as the Millennials—and you have not confused this group with Generation X.

Millennials were born in an era when parents proudly displayed "baby on board" placards on their minivans. As these kids grew older, their soccer moms helped organize their team sports and other activities, while their dads spent more time with them than fathers of any other living generation. Movies popular during this generation's childhood included *ET: The Extra Terrestrial*, *Parenthood*, and *Spy Kids*. From a combination of parenting patterns, interviews, and cultural depictions, the following are what appear to be the main characteristics of Millennials:

■ **Networked peer-to-peer communication:** This phenomenon is not surprising, considering that the Millennial Generation is the first to grow up using Internet technology for communication in their daily lives. Millennials make heavy use of email and social networks (such as Facebook)—and 91% of them have cell phones that they use primarily to text friends and family, keeping tabs on them 24/7.

■ **Collectivist team-players:** Think of how Millennials might make music, film, literature, and art more collaborative. Many such collaborations of these forms of popular culture are already happening, often through use of the Web as a communication medium. Could this mean that Millennials also like to be more active audience members—rather than engaging in more passive activities, such as watching television?

■ **Special:** Millennials are considered "golden children" and are depicted in the media as "power kids" (e.g., the *Spy Kids* film series, in which children help out and save their spy parents).

■ **Sheltered:** As opposed to the "latchkey" Gen Xers, Millennials grew up with overprotective parents. With the emphasis on national security, this theme will probably continue in their lifetime. Although teens feel "pressure" from their parents, they get along with them.

■ **Confident:** This generation displays a confidence that exceeds that of the Boomers in the 1960s.

■ **Open:** Millennial confidence seems to transcend into privacy issues. Millennials are so used to sharing everything with their parents that the notion of privacy does not seem to concern them. Since the first crisis faced by the Millennials was as children during the September 11th terrorist attacks, it has been speculated that Millennials have grown up in a national (as well as familial) atmosphere of concern over security at the expense of privacy. Millennials are not uncomfortable sharing their personal lives with the world—as shown in their use of MySpace and YouTube.

- **Female-dominated:** "Girls rule" in the Millennial generation. More girls than boys are enrolled in college, and girls are getting better grades in both elementary and secondary school.

- **Structured:** Millennials believe that rules have value. The results of the Millennial Trends Quiz informed you that Millennials generally trust the government but do not necessarily respect celebrities. This generation appears to follow the rules of society, rather than rebel against society. Will entertainment lose its "edge" when the Millennials begin contributing to the culture?

Pete Markiewicz on the Personality Characteristics of Generations :::::

Daniel Hayes Uppendahl

Pete Markiewicz received his doctorate in Theoretical Biology from the University of Chicago. After a decade of research in molecular biology (where he helped developed a powerful method for protein engineering), he entered the brave new world of the Internet in 1993. He is co-author of three nationally distributed books on the Internet revolution and co-founded Indiespace in 1994. Recently, Pete has developed futurist theories based on an analysis of rising U.S. generations and their impact on technology—robotics in particular. He currently teaches interactive media design at the Art Institute of California-Los Angeles, and provides development services within the Internet virtual world of *Second Life*.

Pete Markiewicz, PhD (Instructor, Interactive Media Design, Art Institute of California–Los Angeles)

Understanding generational personality characteristics requires familiarity with the events, trends, and changes in culture during a generation's childhood and young adult years. It is also necessary to remember that a generational personality is an averaged aggregate; it describes traits of large populations of similar ages and does not predict the behavior of individuals in the generation:

Silents: "90% of life is just showing up" (Woody Allen): Members of this generation experienced the Great Depression and World War II as small children—and came of age during the 1950s as the United States postwar economy boomed. As children, they were sheltered and protected—and as young adults they displayed a conformist, adaptive mentality. Their media entertainment featured subtle images of rebellion, "lonely crowd" attitudes (seen in movies like Hitchcock's *Vertigo*), irony, and emotional sensitivity—as opposed to the stoic hero of 1940s G.I. culture. Silents tend to compromise rather than divide, and see more shades of gray than Boomers in terms of cultural behavior. Their media show two sides to every issue, and tend toward the personal rather than ideological. In the 1960s and 1970s, they experienced a "midlife crisis" and turned away from their earlier "gray flannel" conformity, leading feminism and the sexual revolution in particular. Gender differences are great within this generation (relative to younger ones). Their archetypal hero is seen in James Bond—the ultra-cool, behind-the-scenes agent who nevertheless works "within the system" to maintain the balance of power. Relations with their children (mostly Generation X) are relatively distant. As they have aged, they have redefined the former image of senior citizens from quiet retirement to a "grandma drives a sports car" mentality. Throughout their lives, they have reaped society's benefits; the economic boom of the 1950s appeared when they started work, and numerous senior entitlements support their lifestyle today.

Boomers: "The times, they are a-changing" (Bob Dylan): Members of this generation were small children during the postwar boom. While young, they experienced a relatively safe but confined social climate based on material well-being. In reaction to this, they started a society-wide, values-oriented "spiritual" revolution in their famous coming-of-age during the 1960s and 1970s. As young adults, they sought to recast the moral underpinnings of society and have done their greatest work in the "culture and values" arena. More divisive and confrontational than Silents, they tend toward a more black/white ideology (ignoring shades of gray) and are responsible for the "culture wars" of the 1990s and 2000s. Their politics focus on grand, sweeping solutions rather than adjustment and compromise. Their media heroes tend to be a lone voice rising up against a faceless system, denouncing it prophet-style, and leading the masses to a new "spiritual" utopia. Instead of compromise, their heroes convert the unbeliever. Boomers led the rise in "bad" behavior in teens and young adults—and teen crime, drug use, and other negative social indicators peaked in their generation during the 1970s. Boomers were responsible for the huge (positive) shift in attitudes toward children during the 1980s and 1990s. Increasingly successful outside the home, Boomer women have managed to "have it all"—while Boomer fathers play a greater role in the lives of their kids than in earlier generations. Rejecting their own parents during their youth, they have surprisingly close relationships with their mostly Millennial children. As their children leave home, they are entering a new stage in their lives—one in which some expect their old radicalism to intensify as they seize political and cultural power from earlier generations.

Generation X: "There can be only one" (*Highlander*): Members of this generation were children during the social turmoil of the 1960s and 1970s—and were the targets of an anti-child cultural bias difficult for younger generations to understand. In their youth, they experienced the divorce epidemic, hands-off parenting, "latchkey" self-reliance, falling fertility, and declining investment in children. Many Xer media workers today mock the crude, low-budget animation and slasher/devil child programming that they experienced as kids. As young adults during the 1980s, they were often seen as a "disappointing" generation and were characterized as the "New Lost"—alienated, poorly educated slackers. Despite this, Generation X reversed many negative social trends (e.g. drug use) associated with Boomers, has started more businesses than any generation in history, and was the first generation to be comfortable with personal computing technology. Compared to older groups, gender relationships moved to equality within this generation. Their media "heroes" emphasize survival rather than rebellion; they are not out to change the world—just to keep their place within it. Politics and ideology hold far less interest for them than older generations, and they are more conservative on social issues than Boomers or Silents. Possibly due to their latchkey upbringing, they are drawn to media depicting edgy, "gladiator-style" death matches—everything from the lone girl left alive at the end of slasher movies to the ruthless voting of television's *Survivor*. Where Boomers might endlessly discuss the meaning of a conflict, Xers just make sure they win. Xers push the boundaries; being "X-treme" is primary. As they enter middle age, older Xers are showing surprisingly strong parent/family orientation, continuing the pro-child trend started by Boomers.

Millennials: "Wizards in training" (*Harry Potter*): Members of this generation grew up during the 1982–2000 economic boom—the greatest in history and one fueled by high-technology. A "wanted" generation, they enjoyed parents who deliberately sought to conceive and raise them, resulting in an "echo boom" in the 1980s and 1990s. Compared to Xers, Millennials have benefited from increased spending by their parents and rising standards in education. However, these benefits include a close, controlled, ultra-organized, "soccer Mom" parenting style and ideologically driven teaching. Compared to the "hands-off" childhoods GenX members experienced, Millennials have had a very "hands-on" life—ranging from standards-based tests and "zero-tolerance" classrooms to school uniforms. This has resulted in a generation that has successfully reversed many of the negative social trends long associated with youth; compared to Boomers and Xers, Millennials commit fewer crimes, use fewer drugs, get pregnant less often, and score higher on their SATs. Less concerned about "identity politics" of race and gender, they may be more class-conscious. Girls lead the way in leadership and education, while boys are doing worse in school, often rejecting college or dropping out. Despite this, gender relations are good. With ideologically driven parents, Millennials may ultimately become a "hero" generation—achieving great things in the exterior world and thereby supporting the expectations of their parents.

Homelanders: No movie yet. The first birth year for the post-Millennial generation falls sometime between 2001 and 2004. This generation has never known a world without a "war on terror", the Internet, 3D consoles, virtual worlds, and smartphones such as the iPhone and Android systems. Their parents are more "Slacker Mom" than "Soccer Mom," and they are already changing the emphasis of their education away from objective, standardized testing to "social skills." Games will be an integral part of their education, as well as entertainment. With the rise of augmented reality and lifelogging, the real world will seem ever-more like a game as they mature. The Strauss and Howe theory predicts this generation will be most like the Silent generation.

Activision Blizzard

Players cooperate in teams in both *Call of Duty: Modern Warfare 2* (playing as either Axis or Allies) and *World of Warcraft*.

If you were to create a game that focused on the Millennial generation, what type of content would you include? Perhaps an online game involving a lot of communication and cooperation between players would be ideal. You learned in Chapter 1 that MMOs involve a lot of collective, teamwork behavior. This sounds like a great form of entertainment for the Millennial Generation, does it not?

If Millennials are so focused on collective, team-based behavior, then why is the United States dominated by consoles and not online multiplayer games? As you learned earlier in this chapter, the player market no longer consists of one (youngest) generation, but at least three generations. That is a market spanning a 60-year age range. Generation Xers and Baby Boomers gravitate toward a certain type of entertainment—and they also have a great influence on their Millennial children, many of whom still live at home and have a close relationship with their parents. Since Millennials are too young to have an impact on the creation of popular culture, they are consuming the culture of the generation just before them. Could the fact that Generation X makes up the bulk of current game developers have something to do with the lone hero, single-player console focus of the U.S. game industry?

Playfish Three Rings Design, Inc.

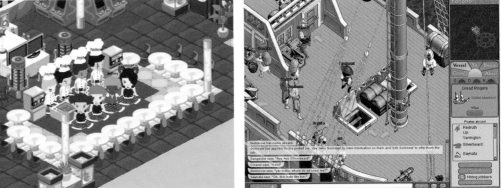

Games that incorporate cooperation—such as *Restaurant City* and *Puzzle Pirates*—might be ideal for the Millennial Generation.

You might wonder why the Millennial Generation is significant when over half of the game-playing population is over 18. At 85 million people, the Millennial Generation is even larger than the Boomer Generation (60 million)—and it dwarfs Generation X (35 million). Now that the Millennials have come of age, they're creating more of our entertainment. From what you know of Millennials, the enormous rise of social and mobile games should not come as a surprise!

TIME Magazine © 2000 Time Inc. Reprinted by permission.

Newsweek, Inc

Generation X and Millennials have been depicted very differently by the media. A 1990 *Time* cover referred to Generation X as: "Laid back, late blooming or just lost? Overshadowed by the baby boomers, America's next generation has a hard act to follow." A 2000 *Newsweek* cover referred to Millennials very differently: "God, sex, race and the future: What teens believe."

From our discussion of the Millennial Generation, you might have a particular idea of what games this age group might be interested in playing. If you wanted to create a game that provided the opportunity for this group to engage in teamwork behavior, you would most likely choose a multiplayer mode. Age might also correspond to the genre. Gen Xers might prefer horror-themed games or single-player games that concentrate on a lone hero who overcomes incredible odds to vanquish a series of foes.

Rating

In Chapter 1, you learned about the establishment of the Entertainment Software Rating Board (ESRB)—the industry's reaction to the Senate hearings on game violence. Like the film ratings established by the Motion Picture Association of America (MPAA), the ESRB ratings are tied into the age group of the target market. Ratings include:

- EC (Early Childhood)
- E (Everyone)
- E10+ (Everyone 10+)
- T (Teen)
- M (Mature—17+)
- AO (Adults Only)
- RP (Rating Pending)

Content descriptors are found on the back of a game's packaging. These descriptors indicate elements in a game that may have triggered a particular rating and/or may be of interest or concern.

What rating would you propose for a game you'd like to create? Many EC-rated games are educational because certain developmental skills (such as learning to read) are stressed at that age. It is interesting that many MMOGs are rated T. This rating is based on the game itself before it is played by multiple players. Online games that include user-generated content (e.g., chat, maps, skins) carry the notice "Game Experience May Change During Online Play" to warn consumers that content created by players of the game has not been rated by the ESRB.

Reprinted with permission from Microsoft Corporation

Every game released in the United States is given a rating by the Entertainment Software Rating Board. *Fable II* is rated M, for Mature.

Applying Player Markets to Platforms, Genres & Goals

In this chapter, you learned that there are many different types of people who enjoy playing games. Who do you want to reach? This set of players is your target market. Are you interested in developing a game that attracts a wider market of teens (without being gender-specific) or an even wider market consisting of teens and young adults? Now tie the market into goals, genres, and platforms. How about focusing only on women who enjoy playing MMOs? Or perhaps creating an educational game for adult students attending a nationwide culinary school? In this case, you'd probably be marketing to the school itself instead of (or in addition to) the students. You could also concentrate on developing games for a particular platform—such as an iPad tablet or an online social game played on Facebook. (Now that over 55% of the player population regularly plays games on mobile devices, you might want to consider at least porting your game to a mobile platform.) How might you apply player characteristics—including motivation, generation, and other demographics and psychographics—to platforms, genres, and goals? Use the knowledge you have gained from this chapter to help you decide which game elements are right for your player market.

::

All of the foundational elements described in Part I should help form the beginning of your game concept. It's important to understand how these elements work together to give your game a strong foundation. A complete concept also includes the areas covered in Part II, which focuses on creating compelling content—including storytelling, character, gameplay, levels, interface, and audio. As you read through the chapters in Part II, try to apply the basic historical, player, and game elements to content development. Later, in Chapter 11, you will also learn to incorporate some of the basic elements in this chapter into game documentation such as the concept document (which will include your target market, genre, and platform).

:::CHAPTER REVIEW EXERCISES:::

1. What motivates people to play games? Discuss three different motivational factors and provide examples of games that address these factors. Motivations such as exercise took game developers by surprise, and they might lead to a new series of games that address this player motivation. Come up with a new motivation that game developers might have overlooked, and discuss which types of new games might address this player motivation.

2. Why do *you* play games? What elements in your favorite games make you want to continue playing? If you were to test one of your favorite games for the "fun factor," why would it pass the test?

3. How does the market for games in the United States differ from other countries such as South Korea, China, Japan, and Germany? What are the most popular genres, platforms, and trends in these respective countries—and what are the associated driving factors?

4. What is the importance of psychographics such as values, attitudes, and lifestyles in player markets? Discuss three games that incorporate a distinct belief system. If you were to create a game based on your own psychographics, on what features would you focus?

5. How have age and gender demographics in the player market changed over time? How might these changes affect the way games continue to be developed? Can you envision any particular trends in game content or structure that would help continue to broaden the player market?

6. Discuss the difference between Boomers, Gen Xers, and Millennials. If you were creating a game specifically targeted toward one of these groups, what features would be present in the game? (How did you do on the Millennial Trends Quiz?)

7. Violence in our society continues to be blamed on the influence of entertainment content such as explicit films and song lyrics. Some games have been blamed for violent outbreaks. Provide a real-world example of a violent incident for which an electronic game was held responsible. Do you agree with this view, or do you believe that there is not a distinct correlation between real-world violence and the "fantasy" violence in games?

8. Which of Richard Bartle's player suits best describes you as a player? What types of games naturally cater to your player suit? Take the questionnaires associated with VALS (*http://www.strategicbusinessinsights.com/vals/presurvey.shtml*) or MBTI (*http://similarminds.com/jung.html*). Do your results correspond to your player suit self-evaluation?

Part II:
Scenarios

creating compelling content

CHAPTER

5

Story & Character Development

creating the narrative

Key Chapter Questions

■ How do *story elements* in games differ from those in films and other entertainment media?

■ What are some traditional *story structures* and *character archetypes*?

■ What is *interactivity* and how can it be applied to storytelling?

■ What are some dramatic storytelling devices used in games, and how do they affect *immersion*?

■ What are the different forms of *character development*, and how do they specifically apply to game characters??

Where do game ideas come from? Why do these ideas seem compelling enough to get produced? Why do they succeed or fail? This chapter focuses on the process of putting story ideas into practice—applying traditional storytelling structure and character archetypes to game-specific devices. What sort of impact can game characters have on the player? The importance of characters in a game environment can add a personal dimension to a player's experience. Unlike characters in other entertainment media, game characters can interact directly with the player—who might also play a character role. This chapter also introduces all aspects of game character development—including how characters look, act, move, feel, and communicate. It's important to note that the most powerful storytelling device involves what the player experiences while playing the game. This is the gameplay itself, discussed in detail in Chapter 6.

Storytelling Traditions

Cave paintings were flat, 2D images that told simple stories without words or sound. This was the beginning of the visual storytelling tradition, which has evolved into the visual media of today—including film, television, art, and interactive entertainment. Games form a significant proportion of the highly visual medium of interactive entertainment; this medium incorporates the visual storytelling tradition, but it has also revolutionized the way stories are told. Other storytelling traditions (including oral, audio, and text) have also been folded into the game medium—as music, sound effects, voiceover narration and dialogue, player-to-player chat, and onscreen text dialogue.

Valroe (Wikipedia Commons)

Cave paintings (Lascaux, France, shown) are considered the first examples of visual storytelling.

Story is Primal

"We tell each other stories in order to live." This memorable quote has guided me through many years of educational game and simulation development. Without storytelling, it is hard to inspire and excite. There are clearly game experiences that work without story—but my sense is that storytelling will continue to become a much larger component of game design, and this will broaden the target audience for all types of games significantly.

—*Bjorn Billhardt (Founder & Chief Executive Officer, Enspire Learning)*

Story is primal in nature. It is one of the most innate characteristics that we as humans possess. We are compelled to tell them and are captivated while listening. Story is what allows us to empathize with a character; and without empathy, we could not find the allure to care about them.

—*Bill Buckley (Animator, Neversoft Entertainment)*

Generating Ideas

Without reading further into this chapter and delving into story structure and unique features of the game storytelling process, consider how story ideas are generated. You've heard the phrase "write what you know." That's a start. But if we all wrote what we knew, there would not be anything but stories based on real-world events—and there certainly would not be fantasy, science fiction, or horror stories! How would we ever experience the fantastic or the surreal: aliens taking over the earth, superheroes that can fly "faster than a speeding bullet," time machines, parallel universes?

Writers often get ideas from thoughts that just come to them throughout the day. These ideas could be anything from observations of the people and the environment around them to portions of dreams they remember from the previous night. Direct personal experience is another common idea generator. Have you ever been in a difficult situation and had to do some clever problem solving to "escape" from it? Do you know anyone who's unusual or eccentric (and you caught yourself thinking, "This person would make a great character in a story!")? What was it like for you growing up?

In *Spider: The Secret of Bryce Manor,* the player is a spider who must "play detective" to uncover a mystery surrounding an abandon mansion while frequently spinning webs in order to capture enough food to survive.

You can also be inspired from stories that already exist. What are your favorite movies, television programs, plays, and books? What was it about these stories that involved you emotionally? Have you come upon interesting news stories? You might be inspired by a television situation comedy, such as *Seinfeld,* to create a game that involves ordinary characters in ordinary situations. Or you might be inspired by a musical, such as *Moulin Rouge,* to create a game in which the characters sing!

Adaptations

Existing movies, books, plays, and television shows can inspire you to create original games. But if you decide to do a direct adaptation of a pre-existing work, you need to clear the subsidiary rights with the copyright owner and make a licensing deal. This can be rather expensive—and these rights are often already taken. For example, Electronic Arts and Vivendi Universal have made deals with New Line Cinema and the estate of J. R. R. Tolkien, respectively, to create games based on the *Lord of the Rings* trilogy.

Ghostbusters: The Video Game is a game adaptation of the *Ghostbusters* film.

Start carrying a notebook with you at all times so that you can jot down any ideas that come to mind throughout the day. Make sure you use the notebook only for this purpose—not for writing down "to do" lists or contact information. If you get into this habit, you'll start to notice that you have many creative ideas. The tough part will be transforming them into good game storylines.

Marianne Krawczyk on the Challenge of Writing for Games :::::

MK

Marianne Krawczyk
(Writer, Monkeyshines
Entertainment)

After writing professionally for several years, Marianne Krawczyk got her break when her first feature, *Popular Myth*, was quickly optioned. Moving onto the hit Saturday morning show *Sweet Valley High*, she learned the ins and outs of the writers' room. Marianne focused even more of her attention on writing for children and was hired to write and develop the animated project *Swamp & Tad* for Wild Brain Studios. Later that same year, she wrote *Caffeine* (a pilot based on the comic book series of the same name) for Studios USA/Universal Television and, in January 2005, she wrote a story for the animated series *Bratz*. Taking the knowledge and experience from her career in traditional storytelling, Marianne has successfully made the transition into the world of video games, using her understanding of the delicate relationship between story and gameplay. She wrote the story for Sony's highly acclaimed first-party AAA title *God of War* and was tapped again for *God of War 2*. Since her foray into video games, Marianne has written and story-designed for several games, including *Untold Legends: The Warrior's Code*, *Field Commander*, *The Sopranos: Road to Respect*, and *Area 51*. Marianne is first author of *Game Story & Character Development*, part of the *Game Development Essentials* series.

Good writing is always challenging. You need interesting twists, truthful characters who drive stories, and compelling worlds. If writing were easy, every film would be a blockbuster, every TV show a hit, every game a 500,000-unit seller. Obviously, this isn't the case.

Introducing game design into how stories are told is a whole new challenge. To further complicate matters, good stories are linear, while games are not. A common mistake is to start out with something complicated that will only get more so throughout the process of creating a game. Negotiating a simple, direct story in a world that is designed to drift sideways is difficult—but, ironically, it's probably a better metaphor for life itself than the medium of film.

Classic Character Archetypes

Why do we tell stories? Noted psychologist Carl Jung explains the reason for storytelling in terms of the *collective unconscious*: a knowledge we are all born with and yet can never be directly conscious of. Within this collective unconscious are universal themes and *archetypes*, which appear in our culture in the form of stories and character types in art, literature, music, film, and games. Jung's collective unconscious forms the basis for our connection to certain universal character types. These archetypes are used in all entertainment media to heighten the audience's connection to the story.

Hero

The *hero* archetype is the central character in a single-player game. When you create a hero character, keep in mind that the hero will be the player's avatar—and the player must identify and bond with this character. Later in this chapter, you'll learn about Campbell's "hero's journey" *monomyth* and the process by which the hero transforms during this classical story form. The hero is always presented with a problem toward the beginning of the story and embarks on a physical or emotional journey to eventually solve this problem. The hero performs most of the action in a story and assumes the majority of risk and responsibility. Luke Skywalker is a classic example of a hero character.

Nintendo

Link is the hero in *The Legend of Zelda: Skyward Sword.*

Shadow

The *shadow* is an extremely important character—representing the hero's opposite, often the ultimate evil character in a story. The shadow could be the adversary who is responsible for the hero's problem. Sometimes this character remains hidden until the story's climax, which can add to the story's dramatic tension. Sometimes the shadow represents the dark side of the hero. This was explored symbolically in Robert Louis Stevenson's classic, *Dr. Jekyll & Mr. Hyde.* Darth Vader is another example of a shadow character—someone who has gone completely over to the dark side.

Eidos

The Joker (from *Batman: Arkham Asylum*) is a shadow character.

Mentor

Albus Dumbledore in *Harry Potter and the Order of the Phoenix* is a mentor who trains the player character.

The *mentor* is a character who often guides the hero toward some action. In this chapter, you'll learn that the mentor character provides the hero with the information needed to embark on the hero's journey. The mentor is often an older advisor character—someone who might have been in the hero's shoes at one time, who can provide the hero with wisdom learned from that experience of making a similar journey. Obi-Wan Kenobi and Yoda are examples of mentor characters. In the *Civilization* series, the advisors (military, domestic, culture, science) provide warnings and hints to the player. Sometimes a mentor character gives bad advice to the hero—deliberately leading the hero down the wrong path. In the tutorial for *Black & White*, a devilish advisor gives only evil advice to the player.

Ally

An *ally* is a character who helps the hero progress on the journey and may also assist the hero with tasks that might be difficult or impossible to accomplish alone. Han Solo and Chewbacca from the *Star Wars* franchise are examples of allies.

Sheva Alomar is an ally in *Resident Evil 5*.

A guardian (the Inquisitor) in *Sacred 2: Fallen Angel* attempts to block the player character from reaching a goal.

Guardian

The *guardian* blocks the progress of the hero by whatever means necessary—until the hero has proven his or her worth. A classic guardian character is the sphinx who guards the gates of Thebes in the Greek play *Oedipus*. For the hero (Oedipus) to gain access to Thebes, he must answer the famous riddle posed by the sphinx. The guardian character tests the hero. By answering the riddle correctly, the hero has proven worthy of continuing on the journey. Sometimes the guardian character is the shadow's henchman. The guardian could also be a "block" that exists within the hero's mind—such as self-doubt, fear, discomfort—that makes the character hesitate to continue on the journey.

Trickster

The *trickster* is a neutral character who enjoys making mischief. Trickster characters can either cause severe damage through their pranks—which can stop the hero from progressing along the journey—but they are more often simply jesters who provide comic relief for the story. Examples of these characters include C3PO and R2D2. These characters can be the hero's sidekicks or even a shadow character.

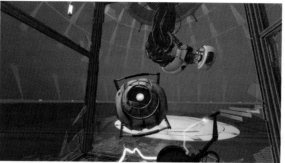

Glados is a trickster character in *Portal 2*.

Herald

The *herald* facilitates change in the story and provides the hero with direction. An example of a herald character is Princess Leia, whose call for help motivates Luke Skywalker to take action toward a specific goal.

Princess Zelda repeatedly triggers Link's actions in the *The Legend of Zelda* series (*The Legend of Zelda: Twilight Princess*, shown).

Protagonist

In addition to Jungian archetypes, there are other classic character types that are associated with every story. The first of these is the *protagonist*—who is often equated with the Jungian hero archetype. The protagonist is the main character. A single-player game centers around this character, and the game's story is told from this character's point of view—even if the game is not played in first-person perspective. The protagonist in *Half-Life*—Gordon Freeman—is central to the action that takes place in the story.

The protagonist must always drive the story forward—*acting* instead of reacting, *making things happen* instead of waiting for them to happen. Any *reaction* on the part of the protagonist is out of the character's control—and the immediate goal in the story then becomes regaining control. For example, a character could be goaded by bullies and lose control—reacting to their taunts by taking physical action (such as throwing a punch at one of the bullies).

Lara Croft (*Tomb Raider*) and Ezio Auditore da Firenze (*Assassin's Creed II*) are two classic protagonists.

The protagonist is unusually strong physically or morally—but not always "good." In fact, the protagonist often has a fatal (or tragic) flaw—which is universal and reflects vulnerability. This makes the character likable and human—allowing the audience to identify and empathize with this otherwise larger-than-life character. The flaw could be in physical form (e.g., paralysis, scarring, stuttering) or appear as a personality characteristic (e.g., greed, stubbornness, envy). Consider any classic Greek or Shakespearian tragedy. In Sophocles' *Oedipus Rex,* the protagonist loses his temper and kills a man (who turns out to be his father). In *Othello,* the flaw is jealousy—as the protagonist is led to believe that his wife has been unfaithful, Othello's jealousy is so powerful that it drives him to murder. Even Superman is greatly weakened when exposed to kryptonite. Your goal is to develop a protagonist who is believable, likable, and flawed—with the ability to grow and transform throughout the story.

Antagonist

A story's *antagonist* is the opposite of the protagonist. The Jungian archetype conforming to the antagonist is known as the *shadow* (or opposite). This does not mean that the antagonist is "bad." The protagonist and antagonist could simply have opposing views—political (liberal vs. conservative), ethical (privacy vs. security), or lifestyle preferences (business vs. family). In this chapter, you'll learn that stories derive dramatic tension from conflict—and this opposition between the protagonist and antagonist is one form of conflict.

BioWare　　　　　　　　　　　　　　　　　　　　　　　Warner Bros.

The Archdemon (*Dragon Age: Origins*) and Alma (*F.E.A.R. 3*) are both antagonists.

When the protagonist and antagonist want the exact same things (e.g., love interest, precious stone, or leadership of a clan), they become linked together in the story. This device is known as the *unity of opposites,* and it makes any conflict or competition more relevant. Interestingly, players can sometimes become attracted to an evil force in a game—which is why some player characters are antagonists. There are several types of evil antagonists that often appear in stories—including transformational, mistaken, exaggerated, and realistic.

Transformational

A *transformational* antagonist is an *anti-hero* character who could have been a protagonist. This antagonist receives punishment at the end of the story to satisfy the audience's need for justice. Stephen King's *Carrie* is a great example of this: As a reaction to being victimized by her classmates, the protagonist uses her tele-kinetic power to destroy. Although the anger and humiliation faced by this character might stir up feelings of empathy in the audience, her power causes the deaths of innocent people. In the process of destroying others, she is killed— and the audience feels some sense of relief. (The ending, however, suggests she might come back from the grave. Stay tuned!)

Nintendo   Nintendo

The greedy Wario (right) is the antagonist of the joyful protagonist, Mario (left). Wario's upside-down "M" could be seen as a clue to Wario's transformational nature.

Mistaken

Mistaken antagonists are characters who the audience initially thinks are villains— but they turn out to be innocent. These characters are popular in murder mysteries and crime dramas. In the *Prince of Persia* series, the Empress of Time is a mistaken antagonist who is killed by the Prince—with her remains forming the Sands of Time. After realizing the Empress is not a villain, the Prince attempts to save her by resetting the timeline prior to when he killed her. Sometimes a mistaken antagonist might turn out to be the protagonist! However, don't confuse a mistaken antagonist with a protagonist who might have "villainous" tendencies, such as the serial killer protagonist in the Showtime series, *Dexter*.

Exaggerated

Exaggerated antagonists are those who are larger-than-life, bizarre, and sometimes even comedic villains who might even dominate the story because they are often more interesting than the protagonist. Examples of these exaggerated antagonists include Dr. Evil in *Austin Powers*—and most of the villains in *Batman* (e.g., Joker, Riddler, Cat Woman).

Realistic

Realistic antagonists are the opposite of exaggerated—and the toughest to create. They are mild-mannered, fairly "normal" characters (which can sometimes make them seem a bit creepy—especially if it is revealed that he or she is the "killer next door"). Stories containing realistic antagonists usually also have more colorful protagonists.

Co-Protagonists

Pals Ratchet & Clank (left) and Jak & Daxter (right) are examples of co-protagonists.

Co-protagonists join forces with the protagonist in a story. These characters often appear in games such as massively multiplayer online games (MMOs) that require teams. Sometimes these characters do not start out as co-protagonists, but as antagonists. For example, some characters compete with each other for resources. If a natural disaster strikes or a major villain shows up, and threatens to deplete everyone's resources, co-protagonists often band together to defeat the larger evil (a common enemy). In Chapter 6, you will learn that competitors can sometimes cooperate as well as compete in order to win the game. This can be applied to the roles of protagonist, antagonist, and co-protagonist.

Supporting Characters

In the next section of this chapter, you'll learn how Act I in a three-act structure introduces a problem to the main character. *Supporting* characters—also known as *pivotal* characters—exist primarily to prevent the protagonist from walking away

Troops in *Call of Duty: Black Ops* act as supporting characters.

from this problem. An example of a supporting character is the mentor in Joseph Campbell's *hero's journey monomyth*. The supporting characters often jump-start the action in the story—sometimes even through carrying out the bidding of the antagonist. Think of supporting characters as sets of troops under both your (the protagonist) command *and* your enemy's (the antagonist) command during a military strategy game. These characters bring a variety of viewpoints to the story. They can be your sidekicks or the antagonist's henchmen.

Now that you've taken a quick look at some classic character archetypes, you'll be able to apply what you've learned to the next section on traditional story structure. Characters are essential components of storytelling traditions; in fact, you'll see that approaches such as Joseph Campbell's *The Hero's Journey* depend on strong characters to move a story forward.

Traditional Story Structure

Story structure has been the topic of Hollywood screenwriting classes for decades. It is seen as a formula that, when applied correctly, can ensure an audience's emotional involvement in a film. The most common structure is known as the three-act plot structure. Other story structure formulas are considered more universal and philosophical, such as Joseph Campbell's *Hero's Journey,* and, in turn, Christopher Vogler's *Writer's Journey.* Let's take a look at these approaches.

Hollywood Three-Act

The *three-act* structure touted in the Hollywood screenwriting community emphasizes the simple idea that a good story has a beginning, a middle, and an end. The beginning introduces the main character's *problem;* the middle focuses on *obstacles* that prevent the problem from being solved; and the end illustrates a *resolution* of the problem, following the ordeal of having to remove or defeat the obstacles.

1. **Beginning (Act I):** The most interesting stories begin by placing the audience into the action or drama of the story. The backstory and any background events leading up to this moment can be introduced later. The goal is to capture the audience's attention. Act I focuses on the character's problem. The story should introduce this problem immediately.

2. **Middle (Act II):** The middle of the story focuses on the obstacles that stand in the way of the character's ability to solve the problem introduced in Act I. There are usually a series of obstacles in Act II that the character must overcome. This act comprises the bulk of the dramatic tension in the story.

3. **End (Act III):** The story ends when the problem introduced in Act I has been solved. The character often has to systematically face and remove each obstacle in Act II to reach this resolution.

Diagram by Per Olin

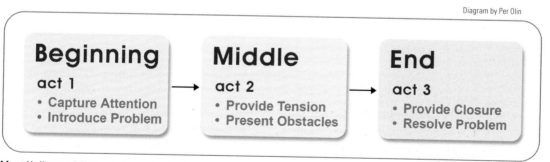

Most Hollywood films employ a simple three-act story structure.

Screenwriters are encouraged to begin their stories in the middle of the action (e.g., the main character is chased by the police), which allows the immediate introduction of a problem. In a game, it has been argued that players need to learn how to use the game and bond with the character before the problem is introduced. This is especially important in games that allow the player to take on the role of the character.

In film, all scenes in the middle of the story should advance the plot or reveal an important aspect of a character's personality. This is related to the closed nature of linear media. In addition to being limited by time (usually no more than two-and-a half hours), movies are not meant to be vast worlds for the audience to explore. In a game, there's all the time in the world for an unrelated storyline, twists and turns, and other tricks, which help create the illusion of freedom for the player as well as a more realistic game world with endless experiences. Players are also given the option of taking any number of paths in the game, which can further allow for a rich game-playing experience.

Linear stories include tragic endings (and sometimes even non endings) that leave the audience guessing what will happen to the character. One or more main characters could even meet with disaster, such as *Romeo & Juliet*–inspired *Moulin Rouge* and *Westside Story,* as the story ends. However, games can have numerous endings that are specifically related to the many paths available for the players to take in the game. Each of these endings should make sense to the player and correspond to the actions chosen. These endings should range from total success to complete failure.

Monomyth & Hero's Journey

In *The Hero With a Thousand Faces,* Joseph Campbell introduced the concept of the *monomyth*—a specific story pattern that legends and myths of all world cultures share. Campbell calls this monomyth "hero's journey," where a fictional hero must leave his community and go on a dangerous journey—usually to recover something (or someone) of value. Campbell attributed George Lucas' success with the original *Star Wars* trilogy to a story structure that made use of this monomyth. The path taken by the hero is marked by various characters, which often represent Carl Jung's archetypes. Some examples from *Star Wars* include the hero (Luke Skywalker), the nomad (Han Solo), the mentor (Obi Wan Kenobi—and, later, Yoda), and the shadow (Darth Vader).

In *The Writer's Journey,* Christopher Vogler applied Joseph Campbell's "hero's journey" to screenwriting. Vogler's steps are used as a framework below. The 12 steps of the hero's journey change the hero irrevocably before he or she can return home:

1. **Ordinary World**: The hero's ordinary world is established. Everyday life and surroundings are introduced. In *Final Fantasy*, the ordinary world is alluded to with the introductory slogan, "It was a day like any other."

Illustration by Ben Bourbon

Joseph Campbell's *The Hero's Journey* is a monomyth that can be found in all legends and myths.

2. **Call to Adventure**: The hero is introduced to an alternate world and is asked to go on a quest or journey. In this section, the alternate (or special) world is introduced to the main character. Usually, elements in the alternate world somehow intersect with those in the ordinary world—and the main character is asked to enter this alternate reality and embark on a quest or journey.

3. **Refusal of the Call**: The call is refused because the hero is not willing to sacrifice his or her comfortable and ordinary surroundings. The hero is uncomfortable, however, with this refusal.

4. **Meeting with the Mentor**: The hero receives information that is relevant to the quest and the hero's personal need to go on the quest.

5. **Crossing the First Threshold**: The hero has abandoned his or her initial refusal because of the information received. The hero embarks on the journey, commits to the adventure, and enters the special world. This section usually marks the end of the traditional Act I in a story.

6. **Tests, Allies, and Enemies**: The hero's mettle is tested through a series of challenges. Through this period, the hero meets allies and enemies. This step makes up the main action of most stories. This is where the hero must solve problems, face fears, rescue others, and defeat foes. This section usually marks the beginning of Act II in a story.

7. **Approach to the Inmost Cave**: More tests and a period of supreme wonder or terror. Preparations are made for the ordeal.

8. **Ordeal**: The biggest challenge the hero faces thus far. The hero must defeat the "big" villain. In this phase, the hero displays vulnerability (e.g., Superman and kryptonite), and it isn't clear whether the hero will succeed or fail.

9. **Reward (Seizing the Sword):** The hero receives a reward. It feels like the end of the story, but it usually is not! This section usually marks the end of Act II in a story.

10. **The Road Back**: Once the ordeal is over, the hero has the choice to stay in the special world or return to the ordinary world. Most choose to return. This section usually marks the beginning of Act III in a story.

11. **Resurrection**: The hero must face death one more time in another ordeal known as the climax. It is here where the hero demonstrates that he or she has been changed by the journey and resurrected into a fully realized person. During this step, the villain may resurface briefly. (This is the moment in a horror film when the audience shouts at the main character, "Turn around! He's not dead yet!") This is also the place where a storyteller might include an unexpected "trick ending." Perhaps the villain really isn't a villain at all. Maybe the mentor was an imposter. (Could Yoda have been evil? Hmmm.)

12. **Return with the Elixir**: The hero finally returns home but is forever changed from the experience—returning with an elixir from the special world that will help those whom the hero originally left behind. The structure is circular, with the hero returning back to the beginning. This makes it easy for the audience to draw "before and after" comparisons and notice how the hero has been transformed. The circular structure also leaves room for open-endedness. Could the hero be called upon again in the future? Has the enemy really been defeated? Is another threat on the horizon? Will the hero ever really be at rest? Leaving questions like these open—instead of opting for a neatly tied-up ending—not only intrigues the audience but leaves room for a sequel. What if the hero is unexpectedly transported back into the artificial world right at the end of the story? The main character in *Back to the Future,* Marty McFly, finds out right at the end of the film that his journey into the past has caused some major changes in the future. He must answer another call and travel into the future to save his family from disaster. In *Half-Life's* last-minute plot twist, main character Gordon Freeman is just about to escape when he is approached by the "man in black" and is offered a difficult choice.

Although it is important to have a framework for traditional storytelling, using rigid storytelling structures could result in tired, overused stories. Instead, try to see these as guidelines and expand on them. These structures also do not account for scenarios involving multiple main characters who all share equal importance in the story. As discussed in Chapter 2, there are several player modes (ranging from one to thousands of simultaneous players) that allow for groups of characters to go on journeys together. How would you incorporate some of this structure into MMOs where players need to cooperate with each other?

::::: Generational Storytelling

You learned about generations of players in recent U.S. history in Chapter 4. What types of stories do you think would work well for games that were created for the Millennial generation? Knowing that the Millennials are more team-oriented and collective, perhaps games involving cooperation, communication, and heroic teamwork will appeal to them. What types of games work for Generation X? Knowing that this generation is more independent, cutting-edge, and entrepreneurial, is it any wonder that *The Legend of Zelda, Tomb Raider, Half-Life, Metal Gear Solid,* and other games involving the lone nomadic hero are so appealing? If you are a member of this generation, do you find yourself wanting to develop a storyline like this?

iStock Photo   iStock Photo

Generation X is thought of as a more independently minded generation, while the Millennial generation is thought of as a more team-oriented generation.

Valve   NCsoft

Are *Half-Life* and *City of Heroes* examples of generational storytelling?

How about games that can be played only in teams made up of heroes? Going further, each hero could have a unique power that is potent only when combined with the powers of the rest of the team. Can you think of some comic book series and Saturday morning cartoons that fit this description? *City of Heroes* takes this tradition and brings it into a massively multiplayer environment. Players take on the roles of heroes to defend Paragon City from "super-powered villains, alien invaders, and underground monsters." Superhero statistics, skills, powers, and costumes can be customized by the players.

Story Elements

In traditional entertainment media such as film, literature, television, and radio, it is conventional for writers to produce stories—complete with compelling characters and specific settings—that form the basis of the content. Although storylines also exist in many games, they are not necessary for a satisfying game-playing experience. In Chapter 3, you learned that puzzle games often do not incorporate stories. Consider *Tetris*, an extremely popular puzzle game without a storyline that has captivated players since the mid-1980s. On the other side of the spectrum, some role-playing games (RPGs) rely heavily on story. In fact, an RPG is most like a movie for some players—where the game can become merely a delivery vehicle for the story.

The following story elements—premise, backstory, synopsis, theme, and setting—will help you begin to take your rough ideas and structure them into a preliminary form.

Chris Klug on the Importance of Dramatic Form :::::

CK

Chris Klug
(Faculty, Entertainment
Technology Center,
Carnegie Mellon
University)

Starting his game industry career in 1981 with Simulations Publications, Inc., Chris Klug assisted with the design of *Universe*, the second edition of *DragonQuest* (winner of a Game of the Year Award), *Horror Hotel*, and *Damocles Mission*. When TSR bought SPI in 1982, Chris and the rest of the SPI staff moved on to form Victory Games—where Chris headed up the role-playing games group, designed the *James Bond 007* role-playing game (also a winner of a Game of the Year award), and oversaw the entire Bond product line. Chris also worked as Creative Director for Electronic Arts' MMORPG *Earth & Beyond*. A leading proponent of making the game industry realize its full potential, Chris was a keynote speaker at the Second International Conference on Entertainment Computing hosted by Carnegie Mellon University in May 2003. He also serves on the advisory board of Indiana University of Pennsylvania's Applied Media and Simulation Games Center and is a Program Advisory Committee Member for Game Art & Design for the Art Institute of Pittsburgh. In addition, Chris has taught Game Design and Production at Carnegie Mellon University's Entertainment Technology Center.

The best writers I've worked with are not novelists, but playwrights—who understand dramatic form: that scenes have to turn; that dialogue must be written with subtext, allowing room for the actor; and that the theme has to be delivered and visible in every scene and beat … like the best movies and plays.

Premise

The *premise* or *high concept* is a summary (consisting of 1-2 sentences or a short paragraph) of the game's purpose and overall theme, and it often appears on packaging associated with the game. It is intended to intrigue customers, enticing them to purchase the game. A premise can be written from any point of view, but I suggest focusing on a second-person perspective so that you address the player directly. Here are just a few examples:

NovaLogic, Inc.

Does the premise of *Devastation* entice you to play the game?

- *Devastation:* "As the leader of a group of Resistance fighters in a future devastated Earth, you must assemble your army and travel the globe, restoring peace and sanity in a very dangerous world."

- *Wolverine's Revenge:* "You have just 48 hours to find the antidote for the virus that was implanted in Wolverine. Along the way, you'll face some of the greatest X-Men villains, including Sabretooth, Juggernaut, and Magneto."

- *Driver:* "Drive a getaway car for the mob in this action-packed street-racing game."

- *Metal Gear Solid 2: Sons of Liberty:* "Assume the role of Solid Snake, a one-man army determined to stop a deadly high-tech weapon from falling into the hands of the wrong people. Snake must utilize his skills in stealth, weaponry, and counter-terrorism to fight off the competing powers and destroy the gigantic killing machine, Metal Gear Ray."

- *Half-Life:* "Take on the role of Gordon Freeman, an ordinary technician who is forced to battle trans-dimensional monsters after an accident at a secret research facility."

- *Spider: The Secret of Bryce Manor:* "You are a spider. One afternoon, you discover an abandoned mansion. Where is the family who lived here? What happened, and why did they leave? Search for clues as you adventure from room to room on the hunt for your next meal."

This summary should focus on what is unique about your game. In addressing the player directly, you also might want to indicate the game's genre. For example, if one of the unique features of the game is that it is played in a massively multiplayer context, try to incorporate this into the summary. As you come up with your high concept, you need to think like a "marketer"—understanding that this is one element used to sell the game to the public and potential investors.

Let us say you have decided to explore the world of archeology in a game. Within this world, you have the opportunity to go on an archaeological dig in five different locations (volcano, underwater, desert, jungle, and polar). You could build an interesting story to go with each of these settings. However, this card game (*Lost Cities*) focuses on the mechanics of playing the game (gameplay—discussed further in Chapter 6) rather than a storyline. Although there's a premise (you and your opponent are archaeologists competing for the most funding and return for your respective digs), there is no focus on story synopsis. The goal is to build cards that represent a particular dig in a certain sequence. You could play the game without knowing anything about the setting. When playing games such as these, players either keep the game abstract or imagine a story going along with the gameplay. While playing *Bohnanza*—a highly addictive card game that focuses on bean farming—players might find themselves discussing their bean fields and the process of planting, nurturing, and harvesting the beans. After a while, it is easy to imagine taking a game like this and integrating it with more story. The next time you play a card or board game, imagine creating a digital version of the game and expanding the game's premise into a meaningful storyline.

Backstory

A *backstory* provides information that leads up to where the game begins. It usually consists of a short paragraph in the game instruction manual, or it appears as text (usually accompanied by a voice-over) at the beginning of the game. This helps orient the player to the purpose and action involved in the game, and it allows the player to sometimes establish initial bonds for certain characters.

Cyan Worlds

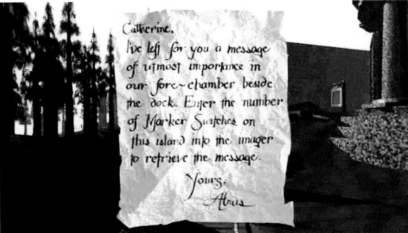

Myst has a strong backstory that is referred to throughout the game as the character solves mysteries related to events that happened in the past.

Synopsis

A *synopsis* or *storyline* can also exist throughout the game itself. In this case, the player might be involved in the setting and actions that take place in the game. A running storyline can also help a player escape from reality and become immersed in the "artificial" game world, during which the player can become emotionally involved with the game's characters. (See "Parasocial Interaction" note below.)

Trion Worlds

Players experience the storyline associated with the MMO, *Rift*, differently depending on their chosen faction (Guardian or Defiant).

Parasocial Interaction

An interesting effect known as *parasocial interaction* can occur when an audience becomes so attached to characters that they actually believe the characters are real people. This effect has occurred with audience members who bond strongly with characters and the make-believe world they observe week after week on television series. "Evil" characters are hated by these audience members, who often send threatening letters addressed to the characters (not the actors). Parasocial interaction is extremely powerful—even though these audience members do not take on the roles of any of the show's characters and are only passive viewers. Couldn't this type of character bonding be even stronger in games?

Theme

The *theme* represents what the story is truly about—even if it's not shared explicitly with the player. Themes usually relate to a primary obstacle in the story faced by the main character(s). Is the obstacle an enemy (villain), nature, society, fate—or the characters themselves? What is the philosophical idea behind the story? The theme could be a defining question—such as "Is murder justified?" or "Can love triumph?" What theme do you want to explore in a story?

Take-Two Interactive

In *Bioshock 2*, players must decide whether to harvest Little Sister (for a big ADAM boost) or rescue her (for a modest boost and the possibility of beneficial gifts later). This tension suggests a number of themes—including redemption, ambition, and remorse.

Setting

The *setting* or *backdrop* represents the world that is being explored by the audience, characters, or player. In creating a game story, think of the world in which your characters will live and interact. Think beyond the stereotypes. Will it be a real-world location (e.g., Sahara Desert, Alaskan tundra), or a specific time period (e.g., Victorian era, Roaring '20s)? Will it take place in the world of organized crime, behind the scenes of network news, or amid the uncomplicated lifestyle of the Amish? What is the history and geography of the world? (Elements of the game environment are discussed in Chapter 7.) How about settings associated with traditional media genres such as science fiction (space), horror (haunted house), or mystery (crime scene)? The setting is often tied in with the game's genre. Many puzzle games do not have a real setting (or story)—but exist in an *abstract* world—and most RPGs take place in a fantasy world.

Reprinted with permission from Microsoft Corporation   Ubisoft

Shadow Complex (left) takes place in a dark, modern industrial interior, while *Assassin's Creed II* (right) takes place primarily in a Medieval exterior setting.

Plot

Plot is more about *how* the story unfolds rather than *what* the story is about. Earlier in this chapter, you learned about story structure. Each of the structures contained plot elements that guided the story along. In Vogler's *Writer's Journey,* the hero's initial refusal to heed the call to adventure and the appearance of the mentor (who supplies

Naughty Dog

Nathan Drake is gradually drawn into the plot of *Uncharted 2: Among Thieves.*

important information to the hero) are both plot elements. Game plotting can be part of the game's story structure—but it can also be dictated by how the game is played. In Chapter 6, you'll learn about *gameplay*—which involves how a player might react to challenges faced in the game. Doesn't this sound similar to the classic hero, who must make decisions related to tests and obstacles along a journey? In this way, plot and gameplay are interconnected. The key to making these challenges and obstacles interesting to a player is to relate them to the story with the use of various plot devices that optimize dramatic tension.

Balancing Conflict

Dramatic tension in a story is maximized when the player often seems to be on the brink of disaster but is able to escape repeatedly from this situation by just the narrowest of margins—a plot device known as *balancing conflict*. In a multiplayer game, this same balance also must be maintained between the players. (More on game balance is discussed in Chapter 6.)

Shifting Focus

Even though players make choices and have apparent freedom while playing the game, players can be drawn back to the main storyline. This effective storytelling technique can be accomplished by *shifting focus* while capturing the player's interest—such as widening the scope of the game by providing more subquests or by introducing new characters or objects that lead the player into other unexplored areas.

Foreshadowing Events

Foreshadowing events is a device that ominously alerts the audience about an important event or change that will happen in the future. In *Half-Life*, main character Gordon Freeman catches glimpses of strange alien landscapes that feature heavily in later parts of the game. Neither the character nor the player is aware of this as they are introduced to these powerful images.

Suspension of Disbelief

With *suspension of disbelief*, your story must somehow cause the players to forget real life and accept the artificial reality you've created. This is related to immersion, but it more specifically refers to the players' acceptance of rules and experiences that might not make sense in the real world. Any film or book set in the future—or any story involving monsters or aliens—has to convince the players to believe that what is happening in the story is important ... and "real." What if people in a game could fly without the aid of air transport? What if the game world included a rule indicating that all characters who resembled humans were evil, while the horrific-looking demons were good? If you are caught up in the story behind the game, you will disregard the real world while you are playing it and adopt the artificial world as yours for a while.

Sony Computer Entertainment America

In *Flower*, the player must suspend disbelief and play as the wind—controlling petals.

Realism

Realism, in contrast to the suspension of disbelief device, can be used in games to mimic the real world as closely as possible. In the discussion of simulation games in Chapter 3, you learned that the application of real-world rules to these games is often the most significant element for the players. In this case, players want reality and authenticity. Such stories might include the visual realism of a contemporary real-world setting—such as Luxoflux/Activision's *True Crime: Streets of LA,* in which LA streets are replicated in the environment, right down to signs on the surrounding buildings. Related to realism is *harmony.* To ensure that a game is harmonious, nothing should seem out of place or inconsistent. For example, characters in a story set in medieval times should not wear watches. These types of temporal inconsistencies are known as *anachronisms.*

Electronic Arts

Although it's set in a fictional city, *Skate 3* takes place in an architecturally-rich environment with hyperreal graphics.

::::: *Call of Duty:*
    Realism & Ratings

Activision

When game characters end up looking like real people, others might want to stop people from seeing graphic things happen to them. We experienced this a bit during the ratings process for *Call of Duty.* Because of the level of immersion provided by the experience, it was almost rated a mature game.

—*Grant Collier (former President, Infinity Ward)*

Many military games employ realism to appeal to their fanbase. *Call of Duty* (which takes place during World War II) contains authentic weapons used during that time, along with realistic depictions of wartime violence.

David Brin on
What Drives Storytelling :::::

David Brin's 15 novels—including *New York Times* bestsellers and winners of the Hugo and Nebula awards—have been translated into more than 20 languages. His 1989 ecological thriller, *Earth,* foreshadowed global warming, cyberwarfare, and the World Wide Web. *Kiln People* explored a near future when people might be able to be in two places at once. *The Life Eaters* rocked the world of graphic novels with a stunning and heroic portrayal of an alternate World War II. A 1998 movie directed by Kevin Costner was loosely based on *The Postman.* David wrote the scenario and introduction for the highly touted video game *ECCO the Dolphin.* His "Uplift Universe" was adapted by Steve Jackson Games as *GURPS Uplift* and features a unique system for creating new alien life forms. The simulation game *Tribes* allows players to strive for survival and reproductive success in the Neolithic Age. David is also a scientist and commentator on public policy. His nonfiction book *The Transparent Society: Will Technology Make Us Choose Between Freedom and Privacy?*—which deals with issues of openness and liberty in the new wired age—won the Freedom of Speech Award of the American Library Association.

DB

David Brin
(science fiction author and futurist;
Owner, Epocene)

In the world of electronic games, story is driven by two things—game-playing procedure and depiction technology. You might expect a storyteller like me to resent this, but I don't. As a science fiction author, I have always felt that the constraints of a fictional world—its science and technology background—should play a role in constraining the plot. So when Sega asked me to write the story for *ECCO,* I studied their gameplay and images first before putting down a single word. Games tell stories in much the same way that movies do—with far more attention to gloss and surface than background or character. In a book, the point-of-view character thinks, and shares those thoughts with the reader. In a movie or a game, the hero or heroine is supposed to snarl "Oh yeah?" at the villain and then blow up 100 henchmen. That may change as multi-user dungeons (MUDs) start lacing their worlds with greater layerings of texture and meaning.

Many people think that sci-fi is driven by science—but the real driver is *history*: the long, horrible saga of nasty existence under brutal chieftains and kings and mystics. I look around at a new civilization that is at last based on a principle of personal choice by educated and fiercely independent people. I am awed that we live in an era when, at last, we can all choose to find some way to be creative … or at least to have fun.

Chris Swain on Games as the New Storytellers :::::

CS

Chris Swain
(Associate Research
Professor, USC School
of Cinematic Arts;
Director, USC Games
Institute)

Chris Swain is a game designer, entrepreneur, and co-author of the textbook *Game Design Workshop*. Chris also co-directs the EA Game Innovation Lab at USC. His serious game-lab projects include *Immune Attack*, *The New New Deal*, *ELECT-BiLat*, and *The Redistricting Game*. Prior to coming to USC, Chris worked on games for Microsoft, Sony, Disney, Activision, Acclaim, and many others. He was a founding member of the New York design firm R/GA Interactive. At R/GA, he led over 150 interactive products for clients such as America Online, Warner Brothers, PBS, Intel, IBM, Kodak, Ticketmaster, Children's Television Workshop, and many others. At R/GA, he led the team that created *NetWits* (for the Microsoft Network)—the world's first massively multiplayer online game show. Some of his other notable projects include *Multiplayer Wheel of Fortune* and *Multiplayer Jeopardy!* for Sony Online Entertainment, and *webRIOT*—a mass audience interactive television show—for MTV. Chris was a co-founder of the technology start-up Spiderdance, Inc. He served on the Board of Directors of the Academy of Television Arts and Sciences from 2000–2004. He started his career at the pioneering interactive firm Synapse Technologies.

When thinking about story, I like to draw an analogy between games today and films from the early 20th century. Back in the 1910s, films were silent and black-and-white—and the stories were told almost exclusively using techniques borrowed from theater. Those films really didn't make much of an emotional connection with people. If you could have told someone back then that film would become the literature of the 20th century, they would have laughed you out of the room. However, film evolved and became transformed through technical (sound, color) and creative breakthroughs (close-ups, flashbacks, camera movement) to become the most influential storytelling medium that we've ever known. I think of games today like films from 1910—crude from a storytelling perspective, not able to make real emotional connections with people—and I see them becoming transformed through technical and creative breakthroughs into an incredibly powerful storytelling medium.

It's an exciting time to be a game designer because there are many technical and creative avenues for breakthroughs, innovation, and original thought. I may get laughed out of the room today, but I'll go on the record to say that games will become the literature of the 21st century.

Game Story Devices

There are several game-specific story devices—many of which differ from traditional story devices. These devices include interactivity, non-linearity, player control, collaboration, and immersion.

Interactivity

Games have a higher level of interactivity than other media. If consumers only want a story, they would watch a movie or read a book. In Chapter 6, you will learn that games depend even more on *gameplay* than story for player satisfaction. By nature, stories are not interactive. They come out of the storyteller's mind and are meant only to be received by the audience passively (and not actively manipulated by the audience in any way). In games, players are not limited to playing the role of the traditional audience. They can also be co-storytellers—and sometimes, they can even be the *only* storytellers.

Electronic Arts

In *The Sims 3*, the player takes on the role of storyteller.

Traditional Storyteller Backlash

After the Web became commercial in the mid-1990s, several well-known authors attacked the medium publicly. "I don't want feedback from my readers!" one exclaimed in an interview—appalled at the online forums, in which his fans discussed details of one of his recent novels. Some traditional storytellers such as authors and filmmakers still have a problem with online forums regarding their work. How would they react if their stories were made into games that allowed players to take part in the storytelling process?

Non-Linearity

Linear stories follow a physical and temporal straight line—beginning with the most distant events and ending with the most recent. Games do not have to follow a linear storyline. This is tied to the apparent freedom of choice attributed to the players, who might take any number of paths through the game.

Square Enix

Deus Ex: Human Revolution allows players to choose different paths within one storyline.

For a simple example of a non-linear story, consider the *Choose Your Own Adventure* book series—which provides the reader with several choices (represented by page numbers) in the book at certain moments in the story. The reader could take any combination of paths and experience the story differently each time. This idea most closely resembles an interactive game experience.

Non-Linearity in Film

Filmmakers and authors have played with non-linearity. The structure of Quentin Tarantino's *Pulp Fiction*—in which several interconnecting storylines (each related to a specific set of characters) are presented out of sequence—gives the impression that time is not running in a straight line. Tom Tykwer's *Run Lola Run* provides three different possible paths the main character could take in the story—one right after another; the film also pauses on characters and shows images of how their lives differ, depending on the particular path taken by the main character. The screen in Mike Figgis' *Timecode* is divided into four quadrants, each of which represents parallel storylines. All four storylines can be followed by the audience visually, but only one audio track can be emphasized at a time. Director Figgis performed live remixes of the audio tracks during some screenings to give audiences varying storytelling experiences. Christopher Nolan's *Memento* is composed of two separate, alternating narratives. Black and white scenes appear in chronological order, while color sequences are told in reverse order—telling the story of a character whose memory does not exist. In *Inception*, Nolan uses non-linear storytelling to show characters traversing through the human mind by invading several levels of dream states. Even though some filmmakers have provided the audience with unique non-linear experiences, there is no way for individuals in the audience to choose which paths to take within the film itself. Therefore, the audience is still engaging in a passive experience. This is due to the linear medium of film—which must run from beginning to end on film, tape or disc. The DVD and Blu-ray formats allow for interactivity—but this has so far been utilized for the bonus features associated with the film, and not the film itself.

Player Control

Players have the ability to manipulate the game in some way—in sharp contrast to an audience watching a movie or a television show. The game's story can change based on who is playing the game. In this way, players can be storytellers in games—something they cannot do in books and movies.

A common form of player control involves *character customization*, where players create their own characters with personalized features. In RPGs that feature a single character, the protagonist is often left deliberately undefined because the character is the player's alter-ego in the game world. The character creation process in RPGs gives the player the freedom to personalize the avatar. In this case, the character becomes

Nexon

MMOs such as *Dungeon Fighter Online* allow for player control—including the ability to customize player characters.

the player. In first-person games with a story, the player must become the character—taking on the role of a character such as *No One Lives Forever*'s Cate Archer, in a process similar to acting. Unlike many strategy games and process simulations, first-person games allow you to become the protagonist and get right in the middle of the action.

Players are also given the ability to choose *paths* to take in the story. Although there are a finite number of possible story paths within a game, the mere fact that the player can make choices in the game means that the player is involved in creating a custom plot. Players can also often build their own versions of a game using *world-building* tools—which allow them to take on the role of game developer as well as storyteller. Finally, multiplayer games often allow players to *communicate* within the game itself—which adds unpredictable behavior patterns and dialogue to the game. (See the "Verbal Character Development" section, later in this chapter, for a more detailed discussion of character dialogue.)

Story in the traditional sense can be seen as the backdrop or framework associated with the game, while all the details are supplied by the players. This idea becomes more obvious when the game is replayed. Games often have replayability—which means that they can be played to the end, replayed (usually many times), and still provide an enjoyable (and unique) experience each time around. The adventure genre, discussed in Chapter 3, has little replay value—in part because it is heavily focused on traditional storylines and puzzle-solving (where there can be only one solution). But most games are developed with replay value in mind. Players get more play time for their money, and they get to experience different story angles every time they play.

In games, the storyteller role is not always filled by those who create the game. The players themselves play an important role in the storytelling process. Knowing this, it is important for game developers to avoiding overwriting the story. For example, players do not need extraneous dialogue or narrative that holds up the game and takes players away from truly participating in the story themselves.

Warren Spector on the Player as Storyteller :::::

WS

Warren Spector (Vice President & Creative Director, Junction Point - Disney Interactive Studios)

Warren Spector received a BS in Speech from Northwestern University and an MA in Radio-TV-Film from the University of Texas. In 1983, just shy of receiving his PhD in Communication, Warren worked on a variety of board games, RPGs, choose-your-own-adventure books, and novels with Steve Jackson Games (where he became Editor-in-Chief). He also worked at TSR, which he joined in 1987. Warren entered the world of electronic games with Origin Systems in 1989, as co-producer of *Ultima VI* and *Wing Commander* and producer of *Ultima Underworld 1* and *2*, *Ultima VII: Serpent Isle*, *System Shock*, *Wings of Glory*, *Bad Blood*, *Martian Dreams*, and others. In 1997, after a year as General Manager of LookingGlass Austin and producer on *Thief: The Dark Project*, Warren started Ion Storm Austin. He was project director on Ion's award-winning action/RPG, *Deus Ex*—first published in June 2000, reissued in a 2001 Game-of-the-Year edition, and re-released in 2002 as *Deus Ex: The Conspiracy* on PS2. As Studio Director, he oversaw development of *Deus Ex: Invisible War*, released in December 2003, and *Thief: Deadly Shadows*, released in June 2004. He left Ion Storm in November 2004 to start Junction Point Studios, Inc.—an independent game development company. In 2007, Junction Point was acquired by Disney Interactive Studios. The first game from Junction Point and Disney was *Disney Epic Mickey*, released in November 2010.

The biggest stumbling block for people thinking about story and games is failing to recognize the centrality of the player. Most narrative forms are vehicles of expression for authors. Games, at their best, are different, allowing a level of collaboration between creator and consumer that's completely unprecedented. Everything in a game story is driven by player choice, by player action. If what you want to do is impose a narrative on your players, you might as well write a novel or make a movie. What that means is that you have to focus on the consequences of player decisions. You have to think in terms of active verbs, rather than passive ones (i.e., the player *does* things; the game doesn't do things *to* players). You should focus on story as it contributes to player experience rather than on story as a vehicle for communicating ideas to players. It's easy to lose sight of this kind of thing when you're working out a game story with your team; paradoxically, players often get lost in the shuffle of creativity.

Stephen Jacobs on Components of Good Game Writing :::::

Stephen Jacobs teaches courses in computer game design, history and analysis, interactive narrative, and writing for the Web. He currently also serves as Visiting Scholar for the International Center for the History of Electronic Games. Stephen's Lab for Technological Literacy is actively involved in the development of serious games for One Laptop Per Child and Sugar Labs.

A. Sue Weisler

Stephen Jacobs
(Associate Professor
of Interactive Games
& Media, Rochester
Institute of Technology)

To be a good game writer, you have to be a master of saying a lot with a little. Writers are often told, "Show, don't tell." In the case of games, this is especially true; the more time you spend telling, the less time there is for playing. While it's true that good film writers become especially talented at letting the camera's eye tell much of the story, those talents are not enough to let most screenwriters make the leap to games. The game writer must allow the player to take control (or at least appear to take control) of the direction of the story and the relationships and actions of the characters within the story. Authors used to working in linear media often have trouble putting authorship in the hands of the players.

Collaboration

The multiplayer game mode introduced in Chapter 3 makes it possible for players to engage in *collaborative* storytelling. This is most pronounced in massively multiplayer games in which thousands of players could conceivably personalize their character roles, introduce new plot points, and modify the environment itself, all while playing the game. Collaboration is similar to interactive theatre—where the players are performers improvising with each other and with the audience. As character and game-world customization become more sophisticated, developers might play an even more hands-off role in these games—and the players might take over as the primary storytellers. A collaborative storyline could be initiated by the game development team, and the paths of the story might be added by the players. As players become more involved in the storyteller role, the line could blur between developers and players. This phenomenon is much like a *prosumer* effect (a term coined by futurist Alvin Toffler), where consumers (players) and producers (developers) become one and the same.

Diagram by Per Olin

Beth turned and chased after him.

Beth shook her head derisively and reached for the crypt door.

They paused for a moment, then Beth slowly entered. Jim followed her closely.

Jim panicked and ran.

Before they could react, a gruesome arm reached out, grabbing Jim and pulling him into the darkness.

Just as they reached it, the crypt door creaked open slightly.

The dark crypt loomed before them. They nervously approached, wondering if the legends were true.

A story tree is used in collaborative storytelling to map out different possible paths in a scene.

A simple model for collaborative fiction is a *story tree*. You can experiment with this model easily. Let us say Author A writes a few paragraphs of a story. Authors B and C pick up where Author A left off and write the continuation of the story (with or without knowing what the other is writing). Authors D and E write the continuation of B, and so on. Multiple paths are created, and the authors have engaged in a collaborative writing experience. In a more sophisticated and organized model, a theme and set of characters are created before the writing process starts. The online world is a great place to find countless examples of collaborative storytelling—including art (virtual graffiti walls), music (jams, remixes), and stories (hypertext trees, blog entries).

> The most challenging aspect of the storytelling process is *consistency:* tying myriad threads together so that they all make sense, and doing this at the right moment in the plot.
>
> —*David Brin* (science fiction author and futurist; Owner, Epocene)

Why not create collaborative games? In a possible collaborative game scenario, players could develop plots that make up possible paths in the game—much like a story tree. A very basic example would involve starting off with a story (just like Author A does with the tree). Authors B and C (and more) consider all possible decisions a player character could make in the game—and so on. This could be done for all possible player characters in the game—who may be introduced at the very beginning. Take an adventure-style opening and a hero-player character as an example: A soldier has been left for dead on a battlefield in the middle of a vast desert wasteland. The soldier awakens, unable to remember anything that has happened. There are several objects lying nearby (weapon, rope, canteen, satchel) and some sounds in the distance. At this point, Authors B and C (and maybe others) decide for each object what will happen if the soldier either picks it up, uses it (fires weapon, drinks from canteen, etc.), throws it, combines it with another object, and so forth. Other authors might decide to focus on other aspects of the environment (sounds in the distance, surroundings) to anticipate what a player might want to do. Notice that the idea of collaborative storytelling is connected to the characters in the story. Most game storytelling is *character-driven,* in which the stories revolve around the characters' actions. This is because players often inhabit the role of the game characters, and the decisions they make through these characters enable them to play the game.

"It's Not Your World Any Longer"

In social and massively multiplayer online games (MMOs), the key is to realize that at the moment you ship, it's not your world any longer: it's the player's. Embrace the players' decisions and support them in how they want to play. Don't force your story in the direction you think it should go; build it around what your players do.

—*James Portnow (Chief Executive Officer, Rainmaker Games; Professor, DigiPen Institute of Technology)*

Quest Storytelling in MMOs

In a massively multiplayer online game (MMO) with a quest system, there is a lot of thought put into the lore and consistency of storytelling associated with quests. Colleagues of mine have come up with some really interesting tales, but they had a hard time telling them in the context of the game. It really boils down to the fact that no matter what you write to create the backdrop for a quest, some player out there is going to skip it. Our job is then to create a situation that tells the story as well as or better than the text that introduced it (and the follow-up text at the end).

—*James Owen Lowe (Content Designer, ZeniMax Online Studios)*

Immersion

Game storylines play a significant role in what is known as game *immersion*—in which the story, characters, and gameplay are so powerful and engaging that the players find themselves deeply caught up in the game world. Valve's *Half-Life* and Square Enix's *Final Fantasy* both have strong, emotional storylines. Infocom's text-

Eidos

adventure *Zork* (inspired by *Colossal Cave*) and the graphically rich *Myst* are also extremely immersive games because they create an atmosphere and a mood that is rich and consistent. The experience of roaming through the graphically rich yet uninhabited environment in *Myst*—while putting together the missing details of a mysterious story—can elicit feelings of dread and anticipation. Developing effective game environments is discussed further in Chapter 7.

Batman: Arkham Asylum has a strong storyline that helps immerse players in the game.

The concept of immersion was originally introduced in Chapter 3 with regard to MMOs. In massively multiplayer mode, the social interaction between players (which sometimes can involve discussions of nongame-related topics such as the news headlines of the day or movies that have just been released) can take the

Three Rings

players out of character and out of the game world itself. In this case, player *immersion* is compromised. If indeed players often feel that the storylines in RPGs are of highest importance, then this can be a big problem in MMORPGs (which are the most popular type of MMO).

In *Puzzle Pirates,* players stay in character by maintaining "pirate-speak" during in-game chats.

Cinematics

Another way immersion can be compromised in a game might be surprising to the film industry because it is a device that is borrowed from linear media. In Chapter 1, you learned that cinematics were introduced in the arcade era as mini-movies that were created to reward the player for completing difficulty levels in *Ms. Pac-Man*. *Cinematics* are sequences that run like movies, usually at the beginning or end of a game. *Cut-scenes* are mini-movies that run within the game. The goal of a cut-scene is to either develop characters, introduce new environments, advance the plot, or set out goals for a new section in the game. The assumption in the film business is that these cinematic scenes allow players to become immersed in the game, just like an audience might get emotionally involved in a film. However, this is not necessarily the case. If players have been actively playing the game—making decisions, solving problems, communicating with characters, or engaging in some game-related action—a cut-scene introduced at the wrong time (e.g., right in the middle of real-time combat) could be a disaster for the player's enjoyment of the game. Instead of providing the total emotional involvement this same scene might provide during a film, it could ironically have the opposite effect.

Square Enix

Valve

The introductory cinematic in *Final Fantasy XIII* (top) and the end-game cinematic in *Portal* (bottom) help create immersion.

Take-Two Interactive

Electronic Arts

The cut-scenes in *Red Dead Redemption* and *Command & Conquer Red Alert 2: Yuri's Revenge* are like mini-movies within the games.

Cinematic Inconsistency

Imagine the contrast of being able to make decisions—only to have those decisions taken away from you as you watch your own character act in a specific way. The contrast could actually result in unintended laughter. When author Jeannie Novak played *Grand Theft Auto: Vice City* for the first time, she was having difficulty controlling the motorcycle driven by Tommy Vercetti (the main character), and the poor guy was bumping into poles and flying off the cycle half the time, only to bravely get back up and try again. But when he walked into various buildings and met with the seedy drug dealers, the cut-scenes took over—and he became cool and composed (not the bumbling character Jeannie had created)! Not only was Jeannie eager to get back to playing the game instead of watching a movie, she was laughing uncontrollably during the cut-scenes because of the apparent split-personality disorder of the character! The key to the cut-scene problem is that it is a non-interactive sequence. If a game is a form of interactive entertainment, the introduction of elements that do not allow for interaction (as defined earlier in this chapter) might no longer feel like a game at all to the player.

Scripted Event

Another storytelling device is a *scripted event*—a brief sequence that is either time-based or triggered by a player's actions. These contain either small portions of dialogue or action, and their purpose is to either build character, convey backstory, or redirect the player toward a new goal.

What movies remind the audience that it is "just a movie"? If you have ever seen unintentional bad acting, you were probably reminded of this. However, some movies specifically reference the real world—often through popular culture and expressions of the time. The *Scream* series references other horror movies and contains inside jokes for those who are familiar with these films. There are other examples of entertainment that purposely remove the "fourth wall," which is when characters in a story talk directly to the audience (also called an *aside*).

::::: Machinima: Storytelling Convergence?

Machinima is a blend of "machine" and "cinema." The machine in this case is a game engine (discussed further in Chapter 10) that is used by filmmakers to create an animated movie instead of a game. From the film industry side, machinima can be seen as an example of technology convergence—adopting a tool originally created for game development to make movies. From a game-industry perspective, machinima takes cinematics and cut-scenes even further away from the game experience itself and toward linear storytelling. The low development costs associated with using game engines to make animated movies adds machinima to DV technology as another revolution in independent filmmaking. Compared to a computer-generated animated film such as *Toy Story* or *Final Fantasy*, it costs next to nothing to produce a full-length machinima feature.

Strange Company founder and artistic director Hugh Hancock was inspired to blend game engines with cinema after being involved in player communities that modified the original *Quake* game by developing in-game mini-movies. (Player communities and game mods [modifications] are discussed in Chapter 12.) According to Hancock, "Machinima is important because it opens up a third way of creating films. Steering a course between digital video (quick to produce, but restricted) and animation (unlimited, but extremely slow), Machinima opens up entire genres of filmmaking to hobbyists and low-budget filmmakers. Now, rather than just making *Clerks*, upcoming Kevin Smiths can cut their teeth on making films with the scope of *Star Wars* or *The Matrix*."

Timgie4tw (Photobucket)

teapotbeaver (Photobucket)

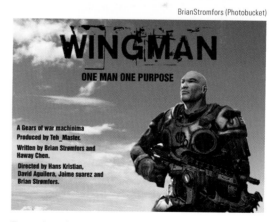

BrianStromfors (Photobucket)

Examples of machinima include *Isolation* (from *Halo*), *Teapot Elephant* (from *Sims 2*), and *Wingman* (from *Gears of War*).

"I'm Clicking on a Cow. Why?"

Back in the '90s, you could get by with "Monster! Shoot it! And don't ask questions!" Now, story is so important. Reviewers will crush a game for "being pretty but shallow," and users expect a reason for what they're doing. Of course, casual and social games such as *FarmVille* don't really need story. "I'm clicking on a cow. Why? So that I might have a sheep pop out of it." Not exactly Pulitzer work, but it's not needed either. Take story to heart when designing—but if a rich narrative isn't needed, just keep it in the back of your mind and let the users get it through osmosis.

Mark Chuberka (Director of Business Development, GameSalad)

Games Need More Than Story

Like a film, a game is a powerfully dramatic medium—one that requires ideas and vision in order to move the audience, whether they are players or viewers, emotionally and intellectually. Growing up, we are not really taught how to communicate ideas using dynamic systems in the same way that we are taught to write essays or tell stories. But there is a lot we understand about the world that can't be told using linear media. Game systems offer us a new way of making stories and communicating this type of knowledge. One thing that I find over and over with the games I play, and with the games I've worked on—including student games—is how difficult it is, and yet how important it is, that the *mechanics* (associated with gameplay) drive the storytelling. The mechanics provide structure—objectives, procedures, and rules; these create the action and the play. But there needs to be dramatic elements that give context and meaning to that play, overlaying and integrating these structural elements. A gratuitous story, not supported by the mechanics, won't add to the experience; that's pretty clear. But when dramatic elements are completely integrated into the mechanics, the player's connection to the game can be extreme. I'm thinking of my own obsession with a particular *Sims* family. I could tell you their story, but it would take too long. Suffice it to say that it was epic and tragic, and other than some custom skins and my own imagination, they emerged completely from the dynamics of the system in play.

—Tracy Fullerton (Associate Professor, USC School of Cinematic Arts;
Director, Game Innovation Lab)

Game Characters

Game characters are either player characters or non-player characters (also known as NPCs). Sometimes one player can control several player characters (often in a group, such as sports teams or military troops). Of course, some games do not contain any characters. This is the case with most puzzle games—in which the player only interacts with the puzzle and does not take on the role of a character. As discussed in this chapter, these games also often do not have stories. Many games, however, contain characters that are controlled by the players or the game itself.

Player Characters & Avatars

Player characters are characters or other entities in a game world that are controlled by the players. When a player controls only one character, that character is called an *avatar*. The direct connection between the player and the avatar can sometimes result in a player assigning personal identity to the avatar. This can be more pronounced if the avatar displays realistic features and actions. When you play games, do you feel that you have actually taken on the role of the character in the game? Do you sometimes see some of yourself in the character?

Electronic Arts

Eddie Riggs is a player character in *Brütal Legend*.

A player can control several characters. This is common in strategy games and process simulations, in which players often manage sets of resources that include several characters. Most of the time, these characters are all fairly distant from the player—and no emotional bonding occurs. Some of the time, one particular character stands out as a main character—becoming the player's avatar. There are also a few games in which the player bonds with all of their characters. This happens most often in role-playing games (RPGs) involving guilds, in which every member of the group might connect with the player emotionally. Intelligent Systems' *Fire Emblem* is a strategy RPG in which all units have a distinct history and personality. Death is permanent, so a player is emotionally encouraged to take care in combat to prevent fatalities.

Non-Player Characters

Non-player characters (NPCs) are those characters in a game world not controlled by players. Instead, these characters are created and controlled by the game's *artificial intelligence (AI)* engine (discussed in more detail in Chapter 10). An NPC can range from a merchant who sells you food to a monster you must defeat.

Nintendo

Wii Sports Resort has plenty of non-player characters.

:::: *X-COM*: Emotional Attachment to Non-Player Characters

Take-Two Interactive

It's especially difficult to get players to care about non-player characters (NPCs). If you want to make a player care about characters, do your best to make them rely more on NPCs, and make the player character more vulnerable and less omnipotent. In the classic strategy game, *X-COM*, there is no formal "story" other than a premise: aliens are attacking earth and you run the organization defending the planet. You recruit soldiers (who are procedurally generated and have random names) to do your fighting, but they never speak and there are never any formal dramatic moments. Yet whenever my injury-prone recruit "Hans Hafner" would somehow get himself shot 12 times and *still* survive the mission, I imagined the commander visiting him in the infirmary and placing a medal on his neck. When he eventually recovered, I imagined him having a beer with his comrades in the mess hall and recounting his many scrapes with death. I was just the faceless commander. He was the man in the trenches. I *needed* Hans to survive that mission. I cared more about Hans, who was a randomly generated "disposable" character than I ever did about every pink-haired space princess in every Japanese RPG I've ever played.

—*Lars Doucet (educational game designer)*

Character Types

There are five common character types used in games: animal, fantasy, historical, licensed, and mythic:

- **Animal:** Sonic The Hedgehog is an example of an *animal* character. Common in games that are marketed toward families or children, animal characters are often given human characteristics (e.g., Sonic's sneakers) to allow for more identification between player and character. Animal protagonists were popularized in animated cartoons that catered to children—with characters such as Bugs Bunny and Mickey Mouse. Not all games featuring animal protagonists are family-oriented. (See the discussion of adult-oriented *Conker's Bad Fur Day* later in this chapter.)

- **Fantasy:** Characters who do not have counterparts in the real world fit into the *fantasy* category. Examples include Mario, Luigi, Wario (Mario's nemesis), Lara Croft, Duke Nukem, and Pac-Man. This category covers any character who was specifically created for a game—and not licensed from a pre-existing source.

- **Historical:** Characters that are *historical* have distinct counterparts in the real world—but often from past history. Political and military games focusing on real-world events contain historical characters—including Benjamin Franklin, General Lee, Cleopatra, William the Conqueror, and William Wallace in games such as *Ally's Adventure* and *Medieval: Total War*.

- **Licensed:** A *licensed* character also already exists in the real world—but in a pre-existing medium. These characters are usually fantasy-based, but already have established recognition in literature, comic books, films, and television. James Bond, Frodo (*Lord of the Rings*), Neo (*The Matrix*), Harry Potter, and Bart Simpson are examples of licensed characters. It's important to note that licensed characters can appear in games only with the permission of the license holder (which normally involves a large sum of money)! When licensing pre-existing characters, game developers do not have to start from scratch on character development—whether visual, personality, or verbal.

- **Mythic:** Characters in the *mythic* category have counterparts in mythology from all over the world. Many role-playing games such as *Neverwinter Nights* and *EverQuest* use standard mythic characters—including orcs and trolls. *Age of Mythology*—a mythology-specific strategy game—contains the Cyclops, Medusa, and other characters from Greek, Egyptian, and Norse mythology.

These character types can be either player characters or NPCs. Have you noticed that you gravitate toward games that focus on a certain character type? In addition to these broad character types, there are classic, specific character types that are often used in games and other media. Let's look at these types of characters in detail.

Character Development Elements

Basic character development in a story involves the relationships among characters and the changes they might undergo throughout a story. The elements of the *character triangle* and *character arc* play a significant role in development of character relationships and character change.

Character Triangle

A *character triangle* forms a powerful three-way relationship among characters in a story. In this relationship, contrasting characters (usually the protagonist, antagonist, and supporting) are connected in threes. The most common example of this is a love triangle in which the protagonist and antagonist both vie for the attention of the same love interest (supporting character). There can be many triangles in a story, and the character's role can change based on each of these triangles. For example, the same protagonist who's involved in a love triangle might also be involved in a career triangle—where the protagonist and antagonist compete for the same position at a company. Each of these triangles represents subplots in a story and must be connected in some way.

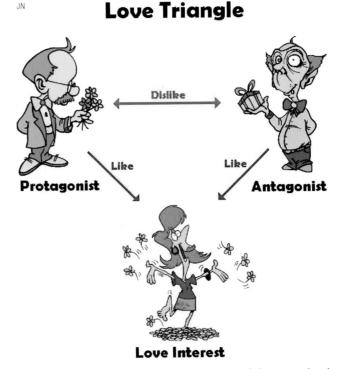

A twist on the love triangle—the most common type of character triangle.

Cocktail Party Character Quotations

I was at a cocktail party shortly after *The Space Bar* shipped. The woman I was chatting with started telling me about a game she'd been playing and how much she was enjoying it. Then she began to quote characters in the game—*my* game! Hearing my writing being repeated was astounding. All those hours of sitting at a computer, writing, rewriting, wondering if it worked, all melted away. I had reached her, given her a meaningful experience, and she wanted to share that with someone else. It's magic.

—*Patricia A. Pizer (Creative Director, ZeeGee Games)*

Positive Effects on the Player

Compelling storylines increase player immersion in a game—while memorable, entertaining characters give the player someone to relate to and make the game experience more enjoyable.

—*Deborah Baxtrom (screenwriter and filmmaker;*
Full-Time Faculty Member, Game Art & Design, Art Institute of Pittsburgh Online)

Character Arc

A protagonist rarely changes during the course of a story—but the character always *grows*. Even a passive protagonist learns how to turn the tables on an antagonist and become strong enough to reach a specified goal—growing as a result of the events in the story. The process of character growth and development is called the *character arc*. This arc consists of several levels and is illustrated through a character's behavior rather than monologue or dialogue. Understanding a character's value system is the core of character development. The following character development levels are based on sociologist Abraham Maslow's *hierarchy of needs* model. The levels begin with the smallest unit, the self, and expand to the largest (and most abstract) unit, humanity.

Diagram by Per Olin

Based on Abraham Maslow's model, the *social hierarchy of needs* can be used to map a character arc in a story.

Level 1: Intrapersonal

In the *intrapersonal* level, the protagonist is concerned only with his or her own needs and thoughts.

Level 2: Interpersonal

In the *interpersonal* level, the protagonist bonds with another character in a one-on-one relationship. This other character could be a lover, friend, colleague, or family member. The protagonist is no longer just looking out for himself or herself, but another character as well.

Level 3: Team

In the *team* level, the protagonist bonds with a small group of characters who have common interests. These characters could be members of the protagonist's circle of friends, family, sports team, or activity club. The need to *belong* is fulfilled at this level. An example of this level occurs in many MMOGs that involve the formation of guilds with other players.

Level 4: Community

In the *community* level, the smaller team becomes part of a larger organized network, which could include a neighborhood, city, school, or company.

Level 5: Humanity

In the *humanity* level, the protagonist often goes through what Maslow calls *self-actualization*—spiritual growth that can occur now that the protagonist has achieved comfort, love, and acceptance among a larger community.

Sometimes protagonists can start at a higher level and move down the ladder. Michael Corleone in *The Godfather* is one example. These characters are really anti-heroes or transformational antagonists. The character arc illustrates that the protagonist is either better or worse off from experiences in the story.

Eidos

Reprinted with permission from Microsoft Corporation

The protagonist in *Hitman: Blood Money* fights for his own selfish needs.

Master Chief in the *Halo* series fights for all of humanity.

Point-of-View

Games usually have specific player *points-of-view (POV)*. Some POVs are seen through the eyes of the player's avatar in first-person perspective, and some allow the player to observe the avatar in third-person perspective.

First-Person

In a *first-person point-of-view (POV)*, the player sees through the eyes of the avatar. In a *first-person shooter (FPS)*, the player also sees the avatar's hand holding a weapon in the lower portion of the screen. This POV can sometimes enable the player to bond with the character, because the player steps into the character role physically and cannot observe the avatar separately. However, this POV makes it more difficult for the player to form a mental image of the avatar because the character cannot be seen onscreen. Some developers use cut-scenes and in-game scripted

First-person point-of-view (POV) in *Borderlands*.

sequences to address this—shifting the perspective of the game so that the avatar can be seen in third-person POV. These sequences can sometimes feel like interruptions and take the player out of the game world. This can be avoided by creating a cinematic sequence as an introduction to the game, and by including images of the avatar in the game interface menu system (discussed further in Chapter 8). Packaging and poster art associated with the game (and usually handled by the marketing department) can also depict images of the avatar. First-person games can also use reflective surfaces (e.g., mirrors) to show the character to the player.

First-Person Identity in Film

Assuming that a first-person POV could help the audience identify with the protagonist, several filmmakers in the 1950s tried this technique. The first and only film shot in first-person POV was *The Lady in the Lake*. Although innovative at the time, audiences didn't relate to the character—partially because they were never able to form a mental image of him. In *Dark Passage*, starring Humphrey Bogart, the film begins with first-person POV (as Bogart, hiding in a garbage can, is dumped out of a truck and rolls down an embankment). The transition is made to third-person POV as we see Bogart's character—but we don't see his face because it is wrapped in bandages. As the bandages are removed, the POV shifts again to first-person—and then permanently shifts back to third-person after the bandages have been completely removed, revealing a new identity. We never see the character's "original" face.

Third-Person

In *third-person POV*, the player can see the avatar onscreen. This allows the player to retain a mental image of the avatar, but it does not provide the feeling of truly inhabiting the body of a character and seeing the world through the character's eyes. The

Electronic Arts

Third-person POV in *Dante's Inferno*.

ability to see the avatar at all times could put the player in the role of *observer* rather than *player character*. However, players often allow themselves to eventually bond with the character onscreen as the game continues. When you create an avatar who will be seen onscreen, it's especially important to ensure that the avatar's look (including color scheme) can be easily differentiated from the rest of the characters onscreen. In third-person action-adventure games, players can often see the game by looking over the character's shoulder.

Since movies are rarely shot in first-person POV, third-person games such as the award-winning *Uncharted 2* and *Batman: Arkham Asylum* often has a cinematic feel. The main characters of a third-person game are often marketed as movie stars; in fact, the character of Lara Croft might be considered the first attempt at creating a game icon. Cinematic suspense is created by allowing the protagonist to be seen onscreen, especially when players can see a threat—such as an enemy approaching—before the character does. It could be argued that there is also more emotional connection to a character that the player can see onscreen (third-person POV), rather than one that can only be seen periodically in a mirror or represented as a disembodied hand holding a gun or other object (first-person POV).

Uncharted Series: Nathan Drake as "Everyman"

Sony Computer Entertainment America

Uncharted 3: Drake's Deception

Story and characters have great potential to drive games and help them become a really cinematic experience. A good example is the *Uncharted* series on the PlayStation 3, which revolves around the protagonist Nathan Drake. The personal background story and relationship of the protagonist to Sir Francis Drake provide a credible frame for the adventure story in the first game. The character artists also went to great lengths to make the character a naturally attractive "everyman" persona to whom both men and women can easily relate.

—Dr. Lennart E. Nacke (Assistant Professor, Faculty of Business and Information Technology, University of Ontario Institute of Technology)

:::::: What's in a Name?

Each of your characters (especially your protagonist) should have a strong, distinctive, and memorable name, which might even reflect the character's personality traits. Here are some examples:

Gordon Freeman (*Half-Life*): The last name indicates a hero character—someone who wants or fights for freedom. This has universal appeal.

Max Payne: The possible translation of this name into "maximum pain" suggests someone who is in pain—and might give a great deal of pain to others. Since this character is motivated by revenge over the death of his wife, this name is particularly fitting.

Duke Nuke'Em: This name suggests that the character is the "duke" of "nuking" or killing people.

Cate Archer (*No One Lives Forever*): The last name suggests the character is precise and on target, just like an archer.

Leisure Suit Larry: This name suggest a bachelor character who might have a Vegas lounge-lizard style.

Kate Walker (*Syberia*): This is an appropriate name for an adventure character who spends much of the game walking into various buildings, exploring strange rooms, and uncovering hidden secrets.

Fox McCloud (*Star Fox*): This name suggests that this character is clever (as a fox), and spends most of his time in the air rather than on ground.

Master Hand (*Super Smash Bros.*): It's no accident that this character consists of a white glove that is larger than any of the other fighters in the game. Master Hand's moves range from flicking, poking, slamming, swatting, punching, and throwing.

Protoman (*Megaman III*): This name suggests the "first" of its kind—and it is! Protoman was the first robot created by Drs. Light and Wiley together: the prototype of what was to become the Megaman cyborg.

Sam Fisher (*Splinter Cell*): This undercover cop is good at "fishing"—baiting enemies and performing stealthy operations.

Sonic The Hedgehog: The sonic moniker is related to the speed of the character, who's faster than the speed of sound!

Viewtiful Joe: Normally an ordinary Joe, this character can transform into the larger-than-life Viewtiful Joe—a virtual superhero who can slow down or speed up time.

LucasArts

Guybrush Threepwood from the *Secret of Monkey Island* series.

Capcom

Dante from the *Devil May Cry* series.

Visual Character Development

The physical characteristics of game characters are art-driven, but they also need to correlate with the character's role in the story. For this reason, you need to develop a character's personality before you create the character's appearance. If you were creating a *hero* character, how would you indicate strength while hinting at vulnerability? You might make the character tall and muscular, but you might make the character appear sad. If your character is a trickster who starts off as an *ally* but becomes a *shadow,* how would you provide a subtle visual hint that this character is not quite what he or she seems? You could have the character's hands clench into fists periodically, or make their eyes dart around occasionally.

Blizzard Entertainment   NCsoft

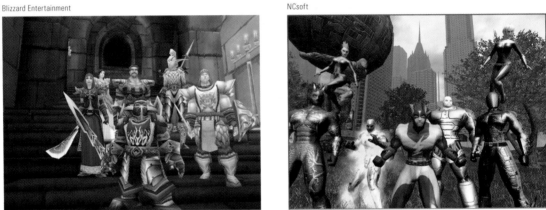

Characters from *World of Warcraft* (left) and *City of Heroes* (right).

Aspects of a character's physical appearance include gender, age, facial features (including hair and eye color), body type (tall, short, large, small, muscular, flabby, angular, round), skin color, health, and abnormalities or distinctive physical characteristics (moles, acne, nervous ticks). Your character should also have an identifiable pose that differentiates the character from the others. Would players be able to pick out your characters if they were all in shadow?

You should also consider each character's costume—including clothing, armor, and accessories such as shoes, glasses, hats, gloves, and watches. What is the color scheme of the character's costume? If the character is a protagonist and the game is viewed in a third-person perspective, make sure that the character's colors stand out against the environment and are differentiated from the colors worn by other characters in the game.

Are there any props associated with this character? Consider weapons, bags, briefcases, and any other items the character might be carrying. Make sure your character's prop can be identified with the character. A great example of a character prop is the hat belonging to Odd Job in *James Bond;* the hat is worn only by the character and is also used as a weapon.

Techniques

There are several art techniques used in games that help to convey the physical characteristics of game characters. Software associated with these techniques and phases of game art production are discussed in Chapter 10.

Concept Art

Concept art involves creating several views of a character (front, sides, back) using pencil sketches or 2D digital renderings. A strong profile or silhouette is essential for your character to be instantly recognizable. The color scheme of your character's costume should not be too busy nor contain more than three or four colors. A character should also have distinctive features, which could include particular facial characteristics (Mario's moustache), accessories (Harry Potter's spectacles), or even a hairstyle (Lara Croft's braids).

Mark Soderwall

Character concept drawings from art director Mark Soderwall.

Modeling

Modeling involves creating a character's size and stature in 3D (from 2D assets). The modeling process begins with the creation of a 3D wire mesh, to which 2D textures related to the character's skin and costumes are applied.

The majority of 3D programs use polygons as building blocks because these shapes provide the illusion of 3D on the 2D surface of a screen. The artist starts with a 3D space of infinite size within the computer, defined by its center (or origin). From this point, distance is measured along three axes: X (side to side, or horizontal), Y (up and down, or vertical), and Z (toward and away). A point in space can be defined by providing figures for X, Y, and Z. When three points are defined, the computer software joins them together and fills in the space—creating a polygon. Models are constructed by joining several polygons to the initial polygon.

Unlike film and television animation, 3D models in games must work in real time. Although computer graphics systems are getting more powerful, they still have limits to the number of polygons they can move around. Modelers attempt to build efficient, low-polygon models. As the hardware becomes faster, artists will be able to work with more polygons, allowing characters to have less angular curves and more detail.

Sony Computer Entertainment America

Sony Computer Entertainment America

Wireframe and flat shaded models of Kratos from *God of War*.

Craig Ferguson

Texture skins are applied to 3D model meshes.

Texturing

Texturing involves creating 2D surface textures (e.g., skin, costumes) known as *texture maps* that modelers apply to 3D wire meshes. Texture maps give depth to the character's physical appearance. Applying texture maps involves cutting apart, peeling, and spreading a model's parts flat for painting. Some programs contain an integrated painting program that allows the artist to paint directly onto the model in 3D. In addition to texture maps, other maps can be applied to models—isolating areas of the model that contain the map's property, such as reflection, transparency, glow—and even bumps!

Animation

Character movement is conveyed through *animation*. Initially, *rotoscoped animation* photographed and traced an actor's movements to add realism to character movement. In most 2D games, animation is restricted to small areas of the screen that are controlled by the player or respond to commands given by the player. These small areas are often referred to as *sprites,* and might contain a character or object that moves over a static or scrolling background. These sprites are animated in short sequences, which isolate an individual action made by a character. The process of 3D animation is similar to stop-frame animation. Using the *keyframing* technique, an animator creates each pose of a movement and sets sequential keyframes to generate animation files. *Motion-capture*—where an animator captures the motions of real people, placing markers on joints of the person to track movement and create motion data—is becoming more popular. All of these techniques will be discussed further in Chapter 10.

Style

The characters in the game world are often created in a style that fits with the look and feel of the game environment. (The environment is discussed in more detail in Chapter 7.) A consistent character style helps maintain the game's harmony. In many children's games, for example, the character style might be referred to as "cute." In *Conker's Bad Fur Day,* cute characters were transplanted into an adult-oriented game—complete with vulgar dialogue. The irony worked for the adult audience. If this had been reversed and a villain in a children's game appeared as an HR Giger-esque alien, this might terrify a young audience! Many artists feel that they must copy popular styles to get noticed. This myth occurs in all areas of entertainment—music, screenwriting, filmmaking—and it couldn't be further from the truth. Exposing yourself to game-art styles is a valid way to learn your craft, but the important thing about style is to make it your own. Art styles used in game worlds are discussed in more detail in Chapter 7.

Amanita Design

Machinarium has a distinctive visual style.

Verbal Character Development

Narration, monologue, and *dialogue* refer to verbal commentary, discussions, or interactions among any number of characters in a game. The use of verbal communication in a game can occur through voiceover audio (discussed further in Chapter 9) or onscreen text.

Narration

Narration specifically refers to verbal commentary made by the narrator in a game. The narrator could be one of the NPCs in the game, or a special narrator character whose role is only to inform the player about the game's backstory or provide unbiased comments on events that are happening in the game. The narrator might or might not appear visually onscreen.

Reprinted with permission from Microsoft Corporation

Portal: Still Alive offers a good example of first-person narrative.

Monologue

A *monologue* is usually a lengthy speech given by one of the characters in a game for the purposes of illustrating the character's emotions or personality characteristics— or to reveal that character's inner thoughts. Shakespeare's soliloquies—including Hamlet's angst-ridden "to be, or not to be" speech—are examples of monologue.

Dialogue

Dialogue technically refers to two-person verbal interaction. However, it is used in games to refer to verbal interactions among any number of characters. Keep in mind that characters are a *part* of the story and should not talk *about* the story. The events that occur in your story are much more important than what the characters say. The purpose of dialogue is not just conversation. Go to a public place and eavesdrop on a conversation. It will most likely take at least a few moments for you to understand what is being discussed. This is because conversation is *context-specific*—depending almost entirely on the relationships, backgrounds, personalities, and motivations of the speakers. In multiplayer games that allow the players to interact through their characters, the dialogue is often more context-specific (and realistic) because the characters are real people. However, this sort of dialogue often does not move the game forward. In fact, in-game conversations sometimes do not have anything to do with the game at all. Dialogue created for non-player characters (NPCs), on the other hand, should fulfill the purposes discussed in the following sections.

Storyboards from *Batman: Vengeance.*

Reveal Character

The dialogue should reveal the character's background—including personality, physical, and social characteristics. (See the end of this chapter for a discussion of incorporating these characteristics into a character synopsis.) Text dialogue must reflect any specific vocabulary and choice of words. Each of your characters will have a certain way of talking, so any voice-over dialogue also must reflect certain audio speech patterns—such as tone, volume, pace, accent, and any speech abnormalities (such as a stutter or lisp). If one of your NPCs is an impatient person, you might want the voice-over artist to speak at a hurried pace and use an irritated tone.

Reveal Emotion

Dialogue can reflect any emotion—anger, sadness, happiness, disappointment, excitement. Understand how each character might express any of these emotions. If an impatient character is always impatient, how would you change the character's tone if he or she became angry or *extremely* impatient?

Advance the Plot

The game story's plot can be advanced through conversations among characters, but this method often sounds forced. Narration is the preferred method of advancing the plot. Some games become tiresome when players have to scroll through endless dialogue among the characters explaining what's going on in the story. Perhaps this could be handled better by having a text-based or voiceover narrator fill players in on the plot. Some well-written character dialogue can advance the plot brilliantly, but this takes a great deal of subtlety and a lot of practice.

Reveal Conflict

A dialogue exchange can reveal that there's conflict happening between the characters in a game. However, a much better way to handle conflict is through the actions of the characters. This will be discussed in more detail in Chapter 6.

Establish Relationships

Dialogue can help establish relationships between the characters. If not written well, this can also be very awkward. You've probably noticed forced dialogue in games where characters say things like, "Remember—you're my brother!" or "Brother John, …" to make it clear to the player that the characters are siblings.

Comment on Action

Some dialogue exists so that characters can comment on or react to the action in the game. Again, this must be written subtly to avoid throw-away dialogue such as "Ouch—that hurt!" (unless this is a comedic moment) or "Why do you think Mary hit Bill?"

::::: Dialogue in *Earth & Beyond*

The sample dialogue on the following page from Loric (an NPC) shows specifically how game dialogue differs from screenwriting. Game designers must anticipate all possible dialogue choices a player could make. Note that the following excerpt reads more like a "map" of these possible choices (similar to the story tree discussed in this chapter). Loric's dialogue is much more extensive, revealing the character's personality and mood, while advancing the story. The player dialogue, on the other hand, is terse—representing choices rather than revealing the player's personality (which cannot be assumed by the designer). The script reads like a flowchart—with "if/then" statements involving the player dialogue.

Electronic Arts

LORIC   005T

Never mind. Why imitate the Ancients and their celestial
example when you can hang around Earth Station, have a Coke,
and bore yourself into a daze? Why dream when you can phase
out? You know? You think deWinter is doing something to the
air here?

[If the Player responds:]

PLAYER

I don't know.

LORIC   006T

Breathe in. Go on. It's like there's something in it. It's
like she's desperate to have us think it's wonderful. She
owns the air, you know.

[Continue after 005]

[If the Player responds:]

PLAYER

Yes.

LORIC   007T

I think so, too. I think she's changing things. Things most
people take for granted—like the air. Know how long it's
been since I had a breath of independent air? Know how long?

LORIC   008T

Aw, never mind. I need some money to get to Deneb. Ten
credits is all I ask. Will you help me or not?

[If the Player responds:]

PLAYER

Forget it.

LORIC   009T

I just want to stand where everything in sight hasn't been
bought and sold and already owned by somebody else. What's
ten credits to you?

[Continue after 008]

[If the Player responds:]

PLAYER

I guess I can spare ten credits…

LORIC   010T

You made the right choice. Be generous to the adventurers.
You never know when you might be one yourself.

LORIC   011T

When I get there, I'll remember you. You and the ordinary
people just like you. It'll be different there. Better. I'm
sure of it.

[Continue after 009]

Movement

There are several forms of movement that should be considered for all characters—such as signature gestures, idle movements, and walking cycles.

Signature

A *signature* movement is an action move (usually a gesture) that showcases a character's personality and character type. If an antagonist character (such as a sharp-clawed monster) is supposed to instill fear in the player, you might want to include a signature move that appears foreboding—such as having the monster slice through all objects in its path with its claws.

Konami

Sega

Solid Snake's signature pose reflects the character's alert readiness (*Metal Gear Solid 4: Guns of the Patriots*, shown).

Idle

An *idle* movement takes place when the character is "waiting" for something to happen—usually for the player to make a decision that involves that character. Sometimes these idle movements can be humorous. Leisure Suit Larry, for example, holds his breath and changes colors accordingly while waiting for the player to resume control over him.

Sonic The Hedgehog shows impatience through his idle movement by tapping his foot.

Walking Cycle

The *walking cycle* is the most basic of character actions, and it reveals much about a character's personality. For example, Mario's comfortable yet energetic walking cycle illustrates his easygoing nature. The importance of reflecting character attributes through movement cannot be overlooked. As discussed earlier, motion capture is one way of accomplishing this.

Nintendo

A wide range of movements is used for the player character, Link, in *The Legend of Zelda: Four Swords Adventures.*

Background, History & Advancement

Aspects of a character's social background include race, religion, class, home life, education, occupation, skills, relationships with other characters, political views, and hobbies. The concept of character advancement is integral to a game's story, a character's history, and the concept of player control.

Becoming Somebody Else

Many MMOs allow players to create customized character profiles. This is a set of attributes associated with the character, such as name, gender, age, clothing, and skin/eye/hair color. Gender swapping has become a common practice in these games, enabling players to assume identities they do not get the opportunity to explore in the real world.

Class & Race

In many games, character attributes such as *class* and *race* can be chosen by the player. The MMO *EverQuest,* for example, allows players to choose from over 14 different attributes—each of which is tied to a unique skill level. Here are some examples of online games and their associated classes or races:

NetDragon Websoft Inc.

Class selection options in *Conquer Online*

- *World of Warcraft:* human, orc, or tauren (minotaur)
- *Allegiance:* Iron Coalition, Gigacorp, Bios, Belters, or Rixian Unity
- *Starcraft:* Terran, Zerg, or Protoss
- *Return to Castle Wolfenstein:* soldier, medic, engineer, or lieutenant

Skill

Character advancement is usually accomplished through an increase in statistics—such as strength, experience, and skill. Characters in particular classes or races are often further divided into various skill levels. One fighter might be skilled with a sword and another with a bow. Most game characters have at least one special skill or power that is identified with them. If your character fulfills the hero archetype, create a skill that fulfills a fantasy. Look at some classic superheroes for examples: Superman has x-ray vision and can fly "faster than a speeding bullet." Spiderman can climb walls and has unusually strong intuition (spider sense).

Frogster Interactive Pictures AG

Skill choices in *Runes of Magic*.

Subversive Games

I think most games are political in nature, even if the politics are implied. Tom Clancy's Rainbow 6 is a "political game," just as much as *Deus Ex* is—in that the player is submitting to a patriarchal, conservative figure (or organization), accepting the values and context placed upon the situation: Good people follow orders, the goal is to follow orders, violence is a means of implementing a government's will, anyone not aligned with the government is "bad" by definition, the player is a part of a hierarchy, etc. That's all highly political, but somehow we just accept this. It's only when a game is subversive that people call it out as "political." In my view, this medium can prompt interesting questions about the role we play in the world, much more actively than in film. We need more subversive games.

—*Harvey Smith (Co-Creative Director, Arkane Studios)*

Character Description

To get started with character development, you need to write a *character description* (also known as a *character synopsis*) for each major character. A character description represents a brief summary of a character's life. The purpose of putting together a character description is to explore each of your characters in depth—to understand where they come from and who they are. Think of your characters as real people. (Even if they're fantasy creatures or monsters, try to give them some human characteristics.) How will they react or respond to situations that might have absolutely nothing to do with your story? How will they relate to others in the real world? Elements of a good character synopsis include all the elements discussed in this chapter, such as the following:

- Name
- Type (class, race, archetype, fantasy/mythic/historical)
- Gender/age
- Physical appearance (body type, height, hair color/style, eye color, skin tone, costume, color scheme, signature pose, profile, gestures, facial expressions, distinguishing marks)
- Background and history
- Personality characteristics (reflect these back onto the character's physical appearance; mood, motivation, nervous ticks, idle moves)
- Vocal characteristics (vocal tone and pace)
- Relevance to story synopsis

The following is a character description of Ariad from *Earth & Beyond*:

> *Ariad: Leader of the Jenquai Traders. Young and appears a bit flighty at times—but this is a cover for a shrewd negotiator. Ariad might be described physically as light, airy, flowing, almost elfin. In typical Jenquai fashion, she has spent her life in low-G, and she is unnaturally tall and thin, with long, precise fingers and fragile limbs. She possesses an unearthly grace. Less a trader than an artisan, she sees trade as a vehicle leading to truth, order, and beauty. Typically dresses simply but elegantly, adorning herself with one or two exotic baubles of unsurpassed beauty. She is in her late 20s.*

After you complete your character synopsis, summarize each character's physical appearance, personality traits, and relationship to the story in just a few sentences. Use one paragraph per character and identify each character by name. Character synopses and summaries can be incorporated into documentation as part of the planning process. This will be discussed in detail in Chapter 11.

Game Storytelling & Documentation

Once you have come up with a game story, you need to incorporate components of the story into several game documents (discussed in more detail in Chapter 10). These documents help organize your ideas and clearly convey them to others. The *concept* document is intended to express the basic vision of the game, and it includes the game's premise. Sometimes this document is expanded into a proposal—which provides more detail on the game's story and characters. The *story treatment* is usually a one- to two-page summary of the game's overall storyline. It should not be a detailed discussion of all the possible paths that characters can take in the game. Instead, it should incorporate the story's theme, structure, and a few significant plot elements. A standard script containing dialogue might be created for cinematics and cut-scene producers/dialogue sessions, while a story tree or flowchart might be created to map out the story's structure. Finally, the *game design document* provides a reference for the development team and includes plot elements related to gameplay.

:::

You have learned how to tell stories in the traditional sense, and you have learned how stories can be very different when applied to games. This difference is tied directly to *gameplay*—the subject of the next chapter. It could be argued that gameplay is the essential storytelling component in games; it is a non-traditional device that allows the player to take on the role of storyteller. As you read through Chapter 6, consider how the game story and character development elements you've learned in Chapter 5 apply directly to gameplay. Your goal is to successfully blend story and gameplay elements together into a rich game-playing experience.

:::CHAPTER REVIEW EXERCISES:::

1. Create a premise, backstory, and synopsis for an original game idea that targets either Boomers, Xers, or Millennials. Describe your target market in detail, and outline why you chose to create this sort of content for this group.

2. What role do *cut-scenes* play in a game, and how can they sometimes compromise *immersion*? Choose a cut-scene from a pre-existing game and identify three reasons you think it is being used. Is the cut-scene necessary? If you were on the game development team and were told that the scene had to be removed, what would you do to ensure that the reasons for the cut-scene were still being fulfilled? Create a synopsis for an original cut-scene and discuss why it is essential to the game experience.

3. Choose a tabletop game with a distinct setting or premise. (If you want to see some cleverly designed tabletop games, go to Funagain Games at *http://www.funagain.com*.) After familiarizing yourself with the game, discuss how you would adapt it to electronic form. What story elements would you expand on to create a more enriching, immersive experience for the player?

4. If you were to create a customized character based on yourself, what would it be like? Describe yourself in terms of a game character. What are your physical and personality characteristics, goals, strengths and weaknesses, likes and dislikes, general mood? Discuss other characters that might also appear in the game. (*Note*: These characters might not necessarily be helpful but could represent obstacles that prevent you from reaching your goals.)

5. Write descriptions for three characters associated with an original game idea. At least one character should be a player character. What elements will you include in your character descriptions, and how will the player and non-player characters differ?

6. How do you distinguish the main player character from the game environment? Choose one of your original characters and discuss three specific ways you could ensure that players can always easily detect where the player character is and what the character is doing.

7. How do the visual features of a game character reflect the character's personality? Discuss how you would utilize profile, facial expressions, gestures, poses, costume, character movement, color scheme, and even associated objects to reflect the personality of one of the original characters you created.

8. Using the original game story you created, construct a five-page scene involving at least two of the characters you described in the previous exercise. Make sure one of your characters is a player character and one is a non-player character. How will you distinguish between the dialogue written for the player characters and NPCs? (*Note*: You are not writing a linear cut-scene, but one in which the player still has control of the avatar.)

CHAPTER

6

Gameplay
creating the experience

Key Chapter Questions

- How are a game's *challenges* and *strategies* associated with gameplay?

- What are *interactivity modes* and how do they relate to gameplay?

- What is the relationship between *gameplay* and *story*?

- What is the difference between *static* and *dynamic* balance?

- How can the *Prisoner's Dilemma* and the *tragedy of the commons* be applied to cooperative gameplay?

What makes games different from other forms of media? It can be argued that games allow for more interactivity than other media. In Chapter 4, you learned about what motivates people to play games. Did you notice that most (if not all) of the reasons had something to do with the process of actually *playing* the game? Players seem to tie in their motivations with *doing,* or engaging in, some activity. In Chapter 5, you learned that *gameplay* is actually a storytelling device that is unique to game development. The *experience* of playing the game is really what allows the story to unfold.

Rules of Play

For further reading on this topic, please see *Gameplay Mechanics* (Dunniway/Novak)—part of the *Game Development Essentials* series.

Gameplay can be defined as choices, challenges, or consequences that players face while navigating a virtual environment. Now that you understand some of the basic elements of story structure and character development, apply these to gameplay. Think about how challenges in a game are often linked together—almost as if they represent plot points in a story. For each challenge (or plot point), consider the many strategies that can be used by a player (or character in a story) to overcome it. It can be argued that the gameplay is what truly makes a game compelling.

All games contain rules. Even the first popular arcade game, *Pong,* was equipped with the simple instructions, "use your paddle to avoid missing ball for high score." Many games contain rules that are much more complicated. These rules are documented in an instruction manual (and also often onscreen) to aid play. For more complicated games, strategy guides that provide gameplay tips are available for players to purchase. Players gravitate toward in-game tutorials most often, though—and developers have found clever ways of including immersive tutorial modes that involve the game's storyline and characters to help "train" new players. The rules of a game define the actions or moves that the players may make in the game (and also those that they cannot make). To formulate rules for a game, it's important to first understand the *conditions* or terms of the game. The rules of the game should be communicated to the players. Although this can be accomplished through in-game tutorials and hints, an instruction manual often accompanies the game.

Victory Conditions

A game's *victory conditions* correspond to how players win the game. Is there only one winner, or can there be several? What does a player have to do to win? Does the player have to rescue a kidnapped family member, slay a dragon, save the community from a disease outbreak, defeat an alien race, or solve the mystery of a friend's death? At what point in the game can it be said that this victory condition has been met? In the classic two-person game, *Battleship,* you know you've won when your opponent says, "You've sunk my battleship!"

Gameplay and story are the same. The best game systems tell a story through the system itself. We really hit home runs when gameplay goals and story emotional goals intersect.

—*Chris Klug (Faculty, Entertainment Technology Center, Carnegie Mellon University)*

Many puzzle games have no victory condition. In *Tetris,* the game just gets increasingly difficult until the player decides to stop. Any notion of victory stems from comparing your game score to others. (This is like the high score technique used in arcade games.) Process sims usually don't have any explicit victory conditions, but the ability to help your resources improve through the game is most certainly a type of ongoing victory. In *The Sims,* you maintain a victory condition as long as your Sim doesn't die. Multiple victory conditions can be incorporated into a game for replayability and to appeal to different playing styles. For example, in *Civilization IV,* two of the victory conditions are conquering the world (which appeals to players who prefer strategic warfare) and achieving a dominant culture (which appeals to players who prefer construction and management activities).

Nintendo

Victory exclamation in *Wii Fit Plus*.

Allen Varney on the Importance of Gameplay :::::

AV

Allen Varney (designer & writer)

Allen Varney is a freelance writer and game designer in Austin, Texas. In addition to his computer game design work for Origin Systems, Looking Glass, and Interplay, Allen designed an online business leadership simulation—*Executive Challenge*—which has been utilized by major companies and business schools nationwide. In the paper-and-dice role-playing arena, Allen is best known as the designer of the 2004 edition of the classic satirical science-fiction role-playing game, *Paranoia.*

A good game design defines and explores an unstable boundary between decision spaces. Now, whole categories of computer games—seduced by 3D graphics—minimize interesting gameplay decisions in favor of environmental exploration or minimally interactive narrative. These are fine recreations, but not really games. Although many players in online role-playing games enjoy the standard level grind in the same recreational way outdoorsy folks enjoy whittling (as Raph Koster observed), that "gameplay" doesn't contribute much to the game design discipline.

Using Tabletop Games in Gameplay Design

Trying to understand the nature of a gameplay experience directly from a video game is akin to trying to understand an internal combustion engine while it's running at 60mph! A tabletop game allows you to break down all the components of the game and see how all sections (mechanics, rules, characterization, player risk/reward structures, psychological paradigms) interrelate. Good designers understand instinctively that the platform must always fit the task at hand. When constructing a gameplay experience, it is crucial to select a way of depicting it so that you can "see" how the elements work in the best context. Just as some stories are best told in the form of a novel and others are best told in the language of film, certain game elements fit best into different modes. This allows you to shift the gameplay fluidly from platform to platform as the situation demands. Good design is like kendo: When the object is to win, the weapon you use should be the one that will best accomplish that goal.

—Mike Pondsmith (Founder, Owner & Lead Designer, R. Talsorian Games; Senior Lecturer,
Game Software Design & Production, DigiPen Institute of Technology)

FluidPlay

Loss indicator in *Torment.*

Loss Conditions

A game's *loss conditions* specify how players lose the game. Two types of loss conditions are *implicit* and *explicit*. Losing because you're not the first to achieve victory is an *implicit* loss condition—common in games that require competition between the player and other players or non-player characters (NPCs). Losing because your character dies or runs out of vital resources is an *explicit* loss condition—common in construction and management games such as process sims.

The Dynamic Language of Games

Only the active contribution of the players can determine the actual outcome of the game, the specificity of the experience. I have noticed that it is very hard for students to get past this aspect of game design; the fact that the player input will intrinsically change the nature of what they've created. But once they do understand this, and start thinking about games as a dynamic language, rather than trying to force a particular experience on the players, they realize just how exciting this type of entertainment can be—both for players and designers.

—Tracy Fullerton (Associate Professor, USC School of Cinematic Arts;
Director, Game Innovation Lab)

Emotional Gameplay

Create mechanics that can attain the sweet spot of challenge and reward as well as accommodate multiple play styles. Then wrap those mechanics up in a blanket of story, character development, and/or emotional ties. Story provides a comforting security blanket as the player mentally traverses the rules and mechanics of the game. And, with any security blanket, players form an emotional attachment -- and when the rules and mechanics either fail to amuse/stimulate or reach a plateau (think grind), the player can always latch on to this blanket until they get to the next gameplay challenge.

— *Jennifer F. Estaris (Senior Game Designer, Nickelodeon Virtual Worlds)*

Story and character development interact on a very deep level. The more connected players feel to a character, the more invested they are in the gameplay. When this relationship is created effectively, developers can really pull at certain strings to create certain emotions in the player. When there isn't a relationship to the character, the gameplay can feel stale; it can still be fun, but players will be less invested – and less likely to share their experiences with others.

— *Nathan Madsen (Composer & Sound Designer, Madsen Studios LLC)*

From a ludological perspective, experiencing gameplay includes interacting with game designs to perform cognitive or motor tasks that can trigger various emotions. The interesting part is how these emotions arise, since they can be triggered by player motivations, performance of the game task or by closure through completion of tasks. I would argue that the most significant and most memorable gameplay elements are therefore those that have a strong emotional impact on us. This can be the addition of a new skill or weapon or the pure joy of performing wall jumps with a lively animated character.

— *Dr. Lennart E. Nacke (Assistant Professor, Faculty of Business and Information Technology, University of Ontario Institute of Technology)*

::::: *Final Fantasy VII:*
Gameplay as an Emotional Device

Sony Computer Entertainment America

In games, *players* are very different from *readers* when it comes to how they care about characters. In a written story, how much we care about a character generally involves how sympathetic they are, how much we can relate to them personally, and how much time we've spent investing seeing the world through their eyes. This is less so with games—where we primarily care more about characters the more *useful* they are to us in the game. The reason so many gamers cited the death of Aeris in *Final Fantasy VII* as the first time a game made them cry has as much or more to do with losing an *essential healer* as it did with losing a cherished love interest in the story. Players are still moved by the standard literary hooks, but you have to get the gameplay hooks in first or they just aren't going to care in the same way.

—*Lars Doucet (educational game designer)*

Interactivity Modes

The concept of *interactivity* was introduced in Chapter 5 as an element of game storytelling. There are several types of interactivity that affect the gameplay. In each of these modes, the interactive element originates with the player—which illustrates how important the player's decisions are in the gameplaying process.

Player-to-Game

In Chapter 2, you learned about player modes associated with the number of people playing the game. In single-player mode, the player is interacting only with the game itself and the platform. Even though the non-player characters (NPCs) might exhibit

Namco Bandai Games America Inc.

Player-to-game interactivity includes how the player interacts with the game's computer-generated characters (such as in *Tekken 6*).

many human characteristics (and the player might sometimes think they *are* human!), they are still generated by an artificial intelligence (AI) system. *Player-to-game* interactivity is a very common form of interactivity, especially when it involves single-player mode. Player-to-game interactivity involves issues such as the game's spatial representation, mapping, environment, atmosphere, and content. Multiplayer games utilizing the player-to-game interactivity mode are really expanded single-player games, since the players do not interact with each other (e.g., *Bingo*).

Player-to-Player

In multiplayer mode, players are not only interacting with the game, but with each other. *Player-to-player* interactivity is the connection between players: how they communicate with each other and ways in which they play the game together (which could include cooperative and/or competitive behavior). As you've learned with massively multiplayer online games (MMOs), developers can only create the *potential* of player-to-player interactivity, but cannot easily predict how players will actually interact during the game. Competition between players can be structured in several ways. One-on-one player competition is common in fighting games and classic tabletop games such as chess. *Unilateral* competition involves two or more players competing against one player (e.g., tag, dodgeball). In the board game, *Scotland Yard* one player is the criminal, while the other players are detectives. The game maintains a balance between the criminal and the group of detectives; the criminal has all the information associated with the game, while the detectives cooperate with each other as a group to catch the criminal. *Multilateral* competition involves three or more players directly competing with each other (e.g., *Monopoly*). This pattern reflects most multiplayer games. However, many MMOs allow players to *cooperate* with each other by forming teams or guilds while competing against non-player characters (NPCs). (The tension between cooperation and competition will be explored later in this chapter.) Traditional team sports such as soccer, football, and baseball involve *team* competition, with equal groups of players competing against each other.

Cryptic Studios

Team player-to-player interactivity occurs in games such as *Star Trek Online*.

Player-to-Developer

It is also possible for players to interact with those who have actually developed the game. *Player-to-developer* interactivity is most commonly illustrated in chat rooms and discussion forums available on the game's website. Many developers take great care to read comments and concerns from the players, and they will often participate in the conversations directly.

Electronic Arts

Player-to-developer interactivity occurs in official player forums, as shown in *The Sims 3*.

Player-to-Platform

The *player-to-platform* interactivity mode is the connection between a player and the game platform's hardware and software. Issues involved in player-to-platform interactivity include the system's graphics or sound capabilities, input devices, memory, battery, and storage.

Nintendo

Players interact with their Wii remotes (input devices) while playing games such as *Wii Sports*.

Kevin D. Saunders on Gameplay Mechanics in Quest Design::::::

KS

Kevin D. Saunders
(Creative Director,
Alelo)

Kevin D. Saunders programmed his first game, a port of Intellivision's *Astrosmash*, on a ZX81 at the age of six. His interest in programming (and games) continued through college, where he worked on developing artificial intelligence systems for natural language processing. His official career as a game designer evolved from his graduate research in environmental engineering. This research included lab experiments that required hourly monitoring over two- to three-day periods. These lengthy experiments gave Kevin the time to explore the world of online games and led to an opportunity to work on Nexon's *Nexus: The Kingdom of the Winds*, which launched in 1998 and became one of the world's earliest massively multiplayer online games. Kevin subsequently designed and produced *Shattered Galaxy*, the world's first massively multiplayer online real-time strategy game and winner of the Best Multiplayer Strategy Game and Most Innovative Game awards from GameSpot in 2001. Kevin worked on real-time strategy games at Electronic Arts before joining Obsidian Entertainment in 2004. While at Obsidian, he transitioned from game design to production and led the development of several role-playing games. He has been credited on seven titles, five with composite review scores of at least 80%. In 2009, Kevin joined Alelo, a serious games company, as Creative Director. Kevin earned his Bachelor of Science and Master of Engineering degrees from Cornell University.

Quests are powerful tools in the game designer's arsenal. They can provide the player with short- and long-term goals, both of which are important motivators that keep the player playing. They can enrich the game world by expanding and communicating its story to the player. They lure and guide the player into experiencing the world we've created for them, in terms of both visuals and gameplay.

The first priority in a quest's design is that it needs to be rewarding for the player. The player should be given a good reason to undertake the quest. The magnitude of the rewards should generally be aligned with the quest's difficulty and duration. Because different players are motivated by different things, the ideal quest should incorporate as many types of incentives as possible. Some sort of material reward is generally a necessity, such as an item that is likely to be an improvement for the player and an appropriate amount of experience points. Through completing quests, players should feel as though they are advancing through the game.

Other incentives are less tangible, such as learning more about the game world or exploring and seeing the visual beauty of a new environment. Exposure to a new type of gameplay or a new feature is another possibility. For example, if interactive environment objects (such as levers) are added to a game that didn't previously have this feature, a quest could be used to encourage the player to experience this improvement, which both makes the quest more interesting and advertises the new feature.

In considering a quest's rewards, I would ask myself the following question: "What about this quest is going to cause the player to want to tell his friends about what they just experienced?" A good quest would provide at least one obvious answer to this question.

A second important consideration is the quest's clarity. Quests serve to give the player direction. While many players enjoy having an open world to play in, most also want structure – they want to be told what they should be doing. A quest should make clear to the player what actions they can take to make progress toward completing it. For example, if a quest involves slaying a particular enemy, the player should be told where to find them. (Note that game interface features, such as markers on mini-maps, messages about quest progress, and a well-organized list of current quests, can aid in this goal.)

A third priority in quest design is feasibility. Any design, quests included, must be kept within the scope of the project. A quest's design should be consistent with the design of the region to which it belongs and the direction of the game in general. For example, a quest shouldn't call for the creation of a new creature or a new gameplay feature unless those aspects are part of the overall vision for the design. While it is possible for a quest idea to motivate other elements of the design, in general quests should be designed to work within the confines that have been set.

Game Theory

Much of gameplay applies elements of classical *game theory*—which focuses on the types of conflicts that exist in games, and how players might respond to these conflicts. Game theory applies to games that contain two or more opponents. (One of the opponents could be an NPC that is not controlled by a player, but by the game itself.) Understanding some of the basic elements of game theory can help you ensure that the player is challenged when playing the game. These challenges are closely tied to the story's plot, and both heighten the dramatic tension in the game.

Getty Images

Chess is a classic example of a zero-sum game.

Zero-Sum

Zero-sum (ZS) games involve situations where players have completely opposing interests. In chess, for example, each player's goal is to win the game. Since there can be only one winner, it is impossible for both players to ultimately get what they want. Therefore, ZS games can only involve *competitive* behavior.

Non Zero-Sum

Non zero-sum (NZS) games involve situations in which players do *not* have completely opposing interests. These types of games are common in MMOGs where players form teams or guilds to compete against NPCs. In this case, the players are *cooperating* with each other (while *competing* against common enemies). This scenario gets more complicated when players are considered enemies, but they must cooperate with each other to ultimately win.

Activision

Games that involve cooperation such as *Guitar Hero 5* are non zero-sum games.

Although this might at first sound highly unusual, this situation is quite common in real life. For example, competing businesses often cooperate with each other to achieve their respective goals. Why do malls contain more than one department store? A combination of cooperation and competition (known as *coopetition*) describes this type of behavior.

In designer Reiner Knizia's *Lord of the Rings* board game, players (as Hobbits) compete and cooperate with each other simultaneously. Although only one Hobbit can win the game, no player wins if Sauron (represented by a black token with a menacing red "eye") gets close enough to any of the Hobbits to steal the ring. The structure of this game allows for a tension between cooperation and competition.

Prisoner's Dilemma

The classic game theory example known as the *Prisoner's Dilemma* illustrates what happens when all players try to compete with each other in an NZS situation. As you will see, the result can be disastrous for all:

In the *Prisoner's Dilemma,* there are two players involved. You and your partner in crime are arrested on suspicion of theft, but the authorities have no proof. You are each placed in a cell and questioned. You are each offered a deal: squeal on your partner, and you will be released. If you don't squeal, the authorities threaten to put you in prison for five years. Since you are separated from your partner, you have no idea what deal has been offered to him—if any.

You have two choices: cooperate with your partner and keep your mouth shut, or compete with your partner and squeal. Not given any additional information, which option would you choose? What happens if you both decide to squeal on each other? Would you both go free? That doesn't make much sense to the authorities. What if you both decide to cooperate by keeping silent? Does this mean that both of you will be put in prison for five years? But neither of you really confessed to the crime, so how could this be? There are four possible outcomes to this dilemma, based on how you and your partner decide to respond:

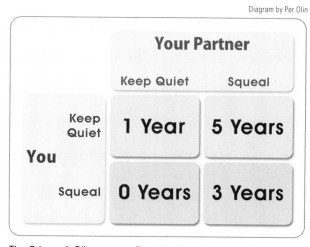

Diagram by Per Olin

The *Prisoner's Dilemma* payoff matrix shows four possible outcomes.

- ■ **Reward:** You are both rewarded for cooperating with each other. (Neither of you confessed to the theft, and the authorities can't prove that either of you were involved in the crime.) You are hounded by the authorities for a year until they finally give up (or you are kept in jail as long as possible before your lawyers come to get you!). You both earn 3 points and spend only 1 year in jail.

- ■ **Punishment**: You are both punished for squealing on each other. (The authorities now know that both of you were involved.) You don't have to stay in jail for five years, but three is bad enough! You both earn only 1 point and must spend 3 years in jail.

- ■ **Temptation:** You decide to squeal, but your partner keeps quiet. (The authorities have what they need on your partner.) This is the best possible outcome for you personally, but your partner suffers. You earn 5 points and are free to go.

- ■ **Defeat:** You decide to keep quiet, but your partner squeals on you. (The authorities have what they need on you.) This is the worst possible outcome for you, but your partner is home free. You don't earn any points and must spend 5 years in jail.

Each player has two choices [cooperate/keep quiet (C) or defect/squeal (D)], but each must make the choice without knowing what the other will decide. If a player chooses D, that player will either earn 1 or 5 points. If a player chooses C, that player will either earn 0 or 3 points. If both players choose D, they will both do worse than if they both had chosen C.

The preceding scenario illustrates one "turn" in a game that could have many possible turns. A game like this could also be played in real time, where both players lodge their decisions simultaneously. What do you think would happen initially? What if one player gets betrayed by the other on the first turn? Perhaps the player who just lost five years might think, 'I'm certainly not going to cooperate next time!' When a player decides to make the same decision the other player did on the previous turn, that player is engaging in a strategy known as *tit for tat*. This strategy could continue endlessly until both players are consistently competing with each other (losing 3 points per turn). The reverse could also happen: A player could risk cooperating with the other player, who might follow suit and cooperate.

A variation on the *tit for tat* strategy is known as *tit for two tats*. In this variation, a player would copy the other player's strategy only if that player used it twice in a row. Let's say Player A cooperated the first time, but B defected. Player A might initially think, 'I'm not going to get fooled again!' However, Player A might reconsider—giving Player B one more chance to cooperate. If Player B defects again (twice in a row—or "two tats"), Player A will subsequently copy Player B's strategy—and defect the third time. If Player B cooperated, however, then Player A would continue to cooperate.

Tragedy of the Commons

A related problem in game theory is known as the *tragedy of the commons*. This is a social trap in which a rational decision based on resources leads to an irrational result. As a real-world example, you might see an accident cleanup at the side of the freeway and slow down to take a closer look. This decision is rational in that it satisfies your curiosity and doesn't hurt anybody. However, to catch a glimpse of the accident, you have to slow down and drive under the speed limit. By doing this, you alert other cars behind you to do the same—changing the flow of traffic. If *everyone* behind you followed your lead and did the same thing, this could cause a collective "disaster" (a major traffic jam).

Similarly, the rational decision to not vote during an election won't hurt anybody. What could one vote possibly do to change things? However, if *everyone* made this same rational decision, there would be no election. In games involving closed systems with limited resources, players could hoard all the resources for themselves—which could result in inflation and an imbalanced economy.

Illustration by Ben Bourbon

iStock Photo

A *tragedy of the commons* will occur if everyone in a Viking ship stops rowing—since the ship would never reach its destination. Similarly, if everyone stops to look at an accident cleanup at the side of the freeway, a traffic jam will result.

Bjorn Billhardt on "Serious" Gameplay :::::

Bjorn Billhardt is the founder and CEO of Enspire Learning, an educational simulation development company based in Austin, Texas. Bjorn previously worked as a consultant and corporate trainer at Dutch software company, BAAN— where he conducted training classes in Europe and the United States—and at McKinsey & Company, a strategic management consulting firm. A native of Hamburg, Germany, Bjorn holds an MBA from Harvard Business School and dual undergraduate degrees (Bachelor of Arts and Bachelor of Business Administration) from the University of Texas.

BB

Bjorn Billhardt
(Founder & Chief
Executive Officer,
Enspire Learning)

Some important gameplay components in educational games (a subset of the "serious" games genre) include:

a) creating team-based competition among learners

b) providing challenging decisions and trade-offs around learning objectives

c) allowing learners [players] to 'build' and 'level-up' in the context of learning experience; and

d) designing an experience that one doesn't need to play multiple times in order to become proficient (e.g., educational games for adults are often played only once).

Gameplay: creating the experience   chapter 6

Challenges

Gameplay involves a series of *challenges* that are linked together. The types of challenges that occur in a game are often related to the game's genre. In fact, players who focus on playing particular genres have come to expect certain challenges to occur in these games, and they might deem a game inappropriate if the challenges don't match the genre.

Implicit & Explicit

An *explicit* challenge is intentional, immediate—and often intense. In an action game, an explicit challenge might involve the exact timing required to jump over rolling barrels or onto a moving platform. In an adventure game, the appearance of a locked door always suggests the challenge of unlocking it.

An *implicit* challenge is not specifically added to the game but is an emergent feature of the game itself. Examples include determining how to divide resources or deciding which units to deploy first in a strategy game.

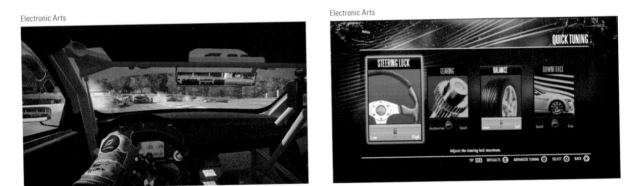

Electronic Arts

Electronic Arts

Challenges in *Need for Speed: Shift* are both explicit (win races, beat others) and implicit (tune your car to optimize it for each race).

Perfect & Imperfect Information

When *perfect* information is provided, the complete state of play is known to the players at all times. Perfect information yields *logical* challenges, where players assimilate the information and use it to decide on the best course of action. In chess, both players are always aware of the state of the board and the position of all the pieces. This allows players to come up with strategies that will yield the maximum benefit.

With *imperfect* information, players are provided with only a fraction of the information needed to make the best decision. In contrast to the logical challenges in games with perfect information, the challenges in these games also require *inference* (or the ability to make a guess about the nature of the missing information).

Illustration by Ben Bourbon Illustration by Ben Bourbon

Board games such as backgammon provide perfect information to the players, while card games such as poker provide imperfect information to the players.

In closed-hand card games, all players are provided with incomplete information—since no player can see any other player's hand. *Mastermind* centers around this idea. Player A hides information (order of four pegs with six possible colors) from Player B, who spends each turn making inferences about the hidden information as Player A provides feedback after each of B's turns. Sometimes, the game platform can affect the amount of information supplied. In Chapter 2, you learned that console games involving *local* play cannot display complete information due to the limitations of sharing one screen.

A standard way to graphically represent incomplete information in a strategy game is through a *fog of war*—in which each player cannot see enemy units that are beyond the sight range of their own units. The player uses inference to estimate the location of the enemy units. The tension in the Prisoner's Dilemma game theory example results from imperfect information given to the two players about each of their decisions.

Imperfect information is commonly used in games because it challenges players to interact with and participate more in the game world. It also ties in with story components to create an element of mystery in the game. With perfect information, there wouldn't be any detective stories, spy thrillers, soap operas—or any stories with unexpected plot twists (think *The Sixth Sense* or *The Usual Suspects*). Imperfect information draws players into the game through human nature—appealing to our curiosity!

Firaxis

Fog of war is a common way of graphically representing incomplete information in a strategy game such as *Civilization V*.

Intrinsic & Extrinsic Knowledge

Hothead Games

Platformers such as *Braid* typically require intrinsic knowledge and skills to achieve success.

Mojang AB

In *Minecraft*, players apply extrinsic knowledge (e.g., wood burns, ore melts) in order to build anything they can imagine—including shelters that protect them from the monsters that come out at night!

Koonsolo

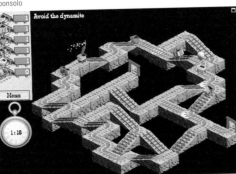

Players navigate through mineshafts in *Mystic Mine*.

Intrinsic knowledge is gained from within the game world. For example, a player could discover the purpose of a magical machine after getting some information from an alchemist NPC in the game. The memory of spells, combination moves, maze layouts, and character personalities throughout the game is also a form of intrinsic knowledge. Games that completely rely on memory include the *Simon* musical imitation game discussed in Chapter 1.

Extrinsic knowledge is gained outside the game world and applied to the game. This type of knowledge can add an element of reality to the game and often involves facts such as "wood floats," "ice melts," "paper burns," "diamonds cut glass," and "a magnifying glass focuses light." These common sense facts can be used to solve various puzzles or meet challenges in the game. If your character possesses a magnifying glass or lens and some paper, you could direct sunlight onto the paper with the lens and start a fire. Similarly, if you are trapped in a glass room, you might use a diamond amulet to cut through the glass. Players must rely on this type of knowledge completely to play trivia games. Another form of extrinsic knowledge involves a player's understanding of legends referred to in the game. For example, a mirror could be used in a game to detect a vampire.

Spatial Awareness

In *spatial* challenges, players usually have to navigate through environments. These challenges are very common in puzzle games and vehicle sims—where the entire gameplay experience depends on the ability to understand spatial relationships to reach a destination.

> **M**inecraft is not a game but a genre that embraces creativity, cares more about experience than rules, and lets people experience the joy of collaboration. If you apply this to every game you play, think of the worlds and experiences that are possible.
>
> —*Mark Terrano (Design Director, Hidden Path Entertainment)*

Pattern Recognition & Matching

Pattern recognition and matching challenges are common in puzzle games such as *Tetris,* where the blocks fall too fast for players to make conscious decisions about where to put them. The process by which we subconsciously match or recognize patterns is related to learning theory. This behavior is common in a lot of action games, where players simply don't have time for reflective thought and must rely on *automatic thinking* to master the game. It's no wonder that players fall into trances while playing these games!

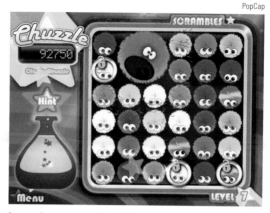

PopCap

In puzzle games such as *Chuzzle,* players match patterns based on colors and sequences.

Resource Management

Many games allow players to manage settings and actions associated with their resources or characters. This *resource management* (referred to as *micromanagement* in games that involve a high level of detail) is one way to allow the player to have many options in the game. For example, let's say a player's character is being threatened by several opponents. The player must decide how the character will respond to this threat. If the character has a series of powers and types of weapons, and can target only one opponent at a time, the player must choose which power to use, which weapon to use, and which opponent to target.

Resource management can get particularly exhausting when it's combined with *multitasking,* in which players must make these choices simultaneously. This is often found in real-time games, such as real-time strategy (RTS) games and first-person shooters (FPS), which involve reaction challenges. In *Warcraft 3,* hero units have many abilities; this requires a player to micromanage them in battle if they want to maximize their effectiveness. However, only one hero can be controlled directly at a time—forcing the player to multitask. In an FPS, multitasking might involve players having to steer vehicles while shooting at targets that are moving quickly around the game environment. In *Halo,* this multitasking is removed—since the driver can only drive, while another player rides "shotgun" and shoots. This way, neither player is driving and shooting simultaneously.

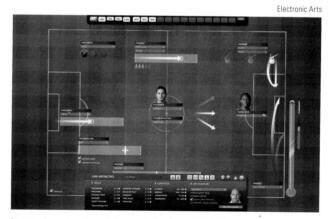

Electronic Arts

In sports management games such as *FIFA Manager 11,* players must carefully manage resources (e.g., team members) in order to progress.

Ubisoft

In *Prince of Persia: Warrior Within,* players must react quickly in response to challenges.

Reaction Time

Action games challenge a player's *reaction time.* This is especially significant when the speed at which a player responds to a challenge is directly related to the speed at which the player's character reacts in the game. This could mean life or death for the character if slow reaction time results in a missed opportunity to defeat the enemy or take the treasure before it vanishes.

Challenges & Game Goals

All the challenges discussed can be applied to specific goals within the game itself:

1. **Advancement:** Reaching a higher level in the game. Each successive level might increase in difficulty—as in many arcade and puzzle games. "Leveling up" could also allow your character to be more powerful, as in many RPGs.

2. **Race:** Accomplishing something before another player does; this is a reaction-time challenge associated with some action and multiplayer puzzle games.

3. **Analysis:** Applying mental processes to solving riddles and cryptic codes. This is a mental challenge that involves almost every other type of challenge—and it's used most widely in puzzle and adventure games.

4. **Exploration:** Moving into new areas and seeing new things; satisfies the curiosity of the player, and it's popular in adventure games and RPGs.

5. **Conflict:** Disagreements or combat between characters; used in almost all game genres to provide dramatic tension.

6. **Capture:** Taking or destroying something belonging to an opponent without being captured or killed in return; remains one of the most overarching game goals across all genres (including action and RTS games).

7. **Chase:** Catching or eluding an opponent—often by utilizing either quick reflexes or stealth strategies; popular in action and stealth games.

8. **Organization:** Arranging items in a game in a particular order—often by utilizing spatial and pattern-matching strategies; common in most puzzle games (e.g., *Bejeweled, Tetris*) and in strategy games with a great deal of resource management tasks.

9. **Escape:** Rescuing items or players and taking them to safety—often involving analytical reasoning and resource management.

10. **Taboo:** Getting the competition to "break the rules"—often involving physical or emotional stamina (e.g., *Twister, Don't Break the Ice*).

11. **Construction:** Building and maintaining objects—common in process simulations; involve resource management and trade.

12. **Solution:** Solving a problem or puzzle before or more accurately than the competition does—involving analytical reasoning and knowledge application. This goal is common in adventure games, which incorporate a lot of detective work.

13. **Outwit:** Applying intrinsic or extrinsic knowledge to defeat the competition.

Escapism & Challenge

Different genres of games emphasize either escapism or challenge over the other, but every game is ultimately judged by how well it delivers each of them. Escapism is the power to transport the player into a narrative—whether it's driving a race car, napalming hostile aliens, or being a make-believe mayor of a town named after your cat. Graphics, sound, story, and writing are essential to good escapism. Challenge is self-explanatory, but where many games go wrong is their failure to comprehend what kind of challenge best matches the product. Hardcore players are a vocal minority, and a game that is too challenging stops being good escapism and starts becoming work.

—*Matt MacLean (Lead Systems Designer, Obsidian Entertainment)*

Emergent Gameplay

Designing for emergence is like building a sandbox. If you give players a set of tools (mechanics) and a big area to play in (the game), they will figure out what they'll build in the "sandbox"—and how they'll play the game. [*Note:* In philosophy and systems theory, "emergence" refers to the way complex systems and patterns arise out of relatively simple interactions. Emergent gameplay is a creative use of a game in ways that were anticipated or planned by the game's development team.]

—*Troy Dunniway (Vice President & General Manager, Globex Studios)*

Balance

A game is *balanced* if players perceive that it is consistent, fair, and fun! The ease of winning the game also increases as the players' skills increase. Random events (e.g., a meteor hitting the area, destroying a player's resources) can still occur in the game that might decrease a skilled player's chance of winning. However, a better player should be more successful in general at the game than a less-skilled player—unless the game is based purely on *luck* instead of *skill*. To implement this balance, a game often has to be tweaked during the *testing* process (discussed in Chapter 11). To set up a balanced system for players, the gameplay needs to provide:

1. **Consistent challenges:** Players should experience gradually more difficult challenges.
2. **Perceivably fair playing experiences:** Players shouldn't be doomed from the start through their "mistakes."
3. **Lack of stagnation:** Players should never get stuck with no way to go on.
4. **Lack of trivial decisions:** Players should be *required* to make only important decisions in the game, even in games that incorporate micromanagement.
5. **Difficulty levels:** Players should have a choice of difficulty or the level should adjust to the player's ability throughout the game.

Static Balance

Static balance is associated with the rules of the game and how they interact with each other. This type of balance does not depend on time and exists before the game is played. For example, the rules might indicate the relative strengths of units in a war-strategy game. Players might use this information as a reference when deciding what units to deploy during the game. Static balance can be ensured by applying obvious strategies, symmetry, trade-offs, resource combination or feedback.

Obvious Strategies

A game should contain one or more *obvious strategies,* which are superior to other possibilities under many circumstances. In *Advance Wars,* each character has specific strengths and weaknesses. When a player is controlling a certain character, part of that player's strategy is to make decisions that correspond to that character's strengths. One of the game characters, Max, has powers that give his tanks more firepower—while his indirect-damage artillery vehicles are comparatively weak. When given the option to deploy tanks, those who are playing "Max" will attempt to do so—unless other circumstances arise that make this an unwelcome decision.

THQ

In *Warhammer 40,000: Dawn of War II*, units have more strength than others in certain situations.

Creating Meaningful Choices

The most important task for any game designer is to create meaningful and interesting choices for players. The nature of what makes a choice meaningful is something that varies widely from game to game. Is it a meaningful choice when I decide how to dress my character in a role-playing game? When I choose how many units to create for production and how many for combat in a real-time strategy game? When I determine how to use my roll in backgammon? All of these examples present good, interesting choices for players. Yet they don't offer us easy solutions for designing such choices in our own games. Studying how other games create choice is one way to learn; another way is to design by setting *player-experience* goals, rather then *feature-driven* goals (e.g., "the game will encourage shifting alliances between groups of trading partners," rather than "players will be able to trade resources"). With this goal in mind, the game can be tested to see when the player experience works as described (e.g., when players are making interesting choices about who to trade with and when to break an alliance with a partner). Learning how to create choices like this means getting inside the head of the player—not focusing on the game as you designed it. When you're just beginning to design games, one of the hardest things to do is to see beyond the game you envisioned to the actual game the players are playing. What are they thinking as they make choices in your game? How are they feeling? Are the choices you've offered as rich and interesting as they can be? Asking these types of questions means opening up your design process to player feedback—and this is a difficult, emotional process for most designers.

—*Tracy Fullerton*
(Associate Professor, USC School of Cinematic Arts; Director, Game Innovation Lab)

Symmetry

Symmetry, the simplest way to balance a game, involves providing each player and NPC with the same starting conditions and abilities. This ensures that the outcome of the game will depend only on the relative skill levels of the players. This often works well in abstract puzzle games, but it would be difficult to achieve successfully in a real combat simulation. It's neither natural nor realistic for opposing armies to have the same exact troops and abilities—and it can make the game much less exciting. However, symmetry is used often in RTSs such as *Age of Empires*—and it could work quite well in a participatory sim such as a team sports game. In the real world, teams do start with more or less the same external resources (although the skill level of each team member differs).

THQ

In *Age of Empires Mythologies,* players begin the game with the same resources.

Symmetry is associated with the relationships between resources. There are two types of symmetric relationships: transitive and intransitive.

A *transitive relationship* is a one-way relationship between two or more resources. For example, you could construct a set of characters (A, B, and C) in which A is more powerful than B, who is more powerful than C, who is not more powerful than anyone. Since this relationship is hierarchical, you can easily apply this relationship to a world with a caste system in which the royalty (A), merchants (B), and peasants (C) interact.

One way to utilize this relationship is to have all characters begin as Cs (or to initially give the players access to C-level units or abilities). As a player's skill level increases during play, the player graduates to a B, and so on. In this case, all players start with the same conditions (symmetry)—but some variation occurs in the game if players advance up the food chain at varying speeds. This is a form of character *advancement* discussed in Chapter 5.

Game theorists often refer to an *intransitive relationship* as "rock paper scissors" (RPS)—from the game of the same name. In RPS, rock beats scissors, which beats paper—which, in turn, beats rock. This relationship differs from the transitive in that it is circular rather than linear—with each resource having the ability to defeat and be defeated by another. This relationship can't be hierarchical in the classic sense, since the weakest characters are able to beat the strongest.

However, story elements can work with gameplay in this case. For example, the transitive caste system we set up could be turned into an RPS (intransitive) relationship if the peasants (C) were given special powers, abilities, or knowledge that would enable them to defeat the royalty (A). For example, they could storm the castle unnoticed! In this example, A beats B, B beats C, and C beats A. This gameplay device works better if the relationships between the resources varies throughout the game. For example, what if the peasants (C) were no longer able to defeat royalty (A)—but they somehow developed the ability to defeat the merchants (B)? To keep the intransitive relationship, the abilities of the other characters would have to change as well—so that A beats C, C beats B, and B beats A. (Be careful: This could result in some serious story continuity problems!) Intransitive relationships can also be defined by the actual abilities of the resources. For example, archers (A) might defeat infantry (B) because they are quicker; infantry (B) might defeat cavalry (C) because they have heavy armor; and cavalry (C) might defeat archers (A) because they can get to them before they have a chance to fire their bows enough times.

Trade-Offs

Not all relationships involve transitions between inferior and superior characters or resources. In fact, it's more common for some to be better than others in some ways. For example, in *The Sims,* expensive furniture is more aesthetic—but cheap furniture is more comfortable. To make a decision on which furniture your character will purchase, you have to weigh *trade-offs.* When players are provided with options that aren't entirely positive or negative, they face a decision-making puzzle.

A hierarchical caste system is a type of linear, transitive relationship—whereas a rock-paper-scissors system is a type of circular, intransitive relationship.

Electronic Arts / Crytek

In *Crysis 2,* players can shift between three modes: power (more power and ability to move quickly—but less protection and no invisibility), cloak (less power but ability to become temporarily invisible), and armor (shown—less power but more protection).

Combination

Players can sometimes *combine* resources or characters to meet a challenge. For example, in *Advance Wars*, players can join two sets of troops that might have been weakened by combat. Combining these troops adds the power of both so that the new entity is stronger.

Nintendo

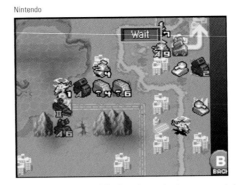

In the *Advance Wars* series (*Advance Wars: Dual Strike*, shown), players can join two resources (such as tanks) that have been weakened by combat and form a "new" unit that contained their combined strength.

Feedback

As a game progresses, it can get out of balance and fall back into balance. The tension between players can be increased with the aid of *feedback*. If one player is ahead in the game, for example, the game could get more difficult for that player—which would be *negative feedback*. This player could be advanced enough to be able to get resources from the other player—but there could be a high price for these resources.

On the other hand, if a player is behind in the game, challenges could get easier for that player—which would be *positive feedback*. An application of positive feedback involves ending the game once it's clear that the game has been won. In some games, players can get to the point when they know they're going to win—but they still have to play until the victory conditions are met. (For example, if a player has defeated all but one of the 1,001 monsters, that player will clearly win the game. However, if that one monster is hiding somewhere, the player could spend hours trying to find and defeat the creature.)

Completely *random events* should also occur in the game to keep it unpredictable, but these could throw a game off balance. For example, a volcano could erupt near one of the underdog player's characters—which could severely affect this player's ability to catch up.

Electronic Arts

In *SimCity Deluxe*, random events such as alien attacks can affect the game's balance.

> **W**riting good characters and story that fit in well with the gameplay you want to create is the hardest—and the most audience engaging—part of game development.
>
> — *Frank Gilson (Senior Producer, Kabam)*

Dynamic

Games begin with static balance—but once they're set in motion by the players, a *dynamic* balance emerges. It is this *dynamic* balance that allows players to truly interact with the game. Players can interact with dynamic balance through destruction, maintenance, and restoration.

Destruction

In a *destruction* scenario, the game is initially balanced. However, instead of maintaining this balance, the player(s) act as the opposing forces and attempt to throw the game off balance.

Maintenance

In the case of *maintenance*, the game is initially balanced. Once the player(s) interact with the game, opposing forces emerge that threaten to throw the game out of balance. The object of the game is to prevent these forces from overrunning the system.

Restoration

A *restoration* game is initially unbalanced and perhaps even chaotic. The object of the game is for the player(s) to move the system back into equilibrium—cleaning it up and making it orderly.

THQ

In *Red Faction: Guerrilla*, players wreak havoc across Mars.

Slashkey

In *Farm Town*, the precursor to *FarmVille*, players maintain balance of their resources.

Take-Two Interactive

In *BioShock*, players must take control of a world in anarchy.

Developing Rich Characters Through Gameplay

The best game stories grow out of the gameplay itself. What defines a character is what actions he or she takes, so the gameplay is a great way to develop rich characters over time. At the same time, a great story can add context and meaning for gameplay actions the player take. Ideally, story and gameplay play off each other to create a rich and entertaining experience for the player.

— *Anne Toole (Writer, The Write Toole)*

Economies

Game *economies* are systems in which resources move around—either physically (from place to place) or conceptually (from owner to owner). Resources can be money, troops, characters, weapons, property, skills—anything that players can "own" in the game (information, too!). In an FPS, a primary resource is often ammunition that can be found or obtained by stealing it from dead opponents. This resource is consumed by firing weapons. Health points are other resources that are consumed by being hit—and are restored with medical kits. Since resources interact with each other, players can't produce too much or too little of them—or the economy will be thrown out of balance. In process sims such as *Black & White* and *The Sims Online,* the game economy is balanced by nurturing and caretaking resources (characters); the focus in these games is on the characters and their needs.

In persistent-state world (PSW) economies, players can collect and trade items of value. Since thousands of people can react in ways the developer can't possibly anticipate, it's difficult to design and adjust (fine-tune) a PSW. *Ultima Online* was originally designed to have a completely self-contained, closed economy with a fixed number of resources. Players, acting in a way that had not been anticipated by the developers, hoarded objects without using them. Resources were depleted, which caused an inflation in the game economy (in which the hoarders could charge ridiculously high fees for these objects). Developers eventually had to do away with the closed system and adopted an open economy in which new resources were spawned.

Titus Levi on the Flexibility of Multiplayer Economies :::::

Kathleen Pittman

Titus Levi
(Associate Professor, United International College)

Titus Levi is an economist working as a consultant for individuals and organizations working in the arts and media industries. His clients include Interep, Susquehanna, and the Durfee Foundation. Titus has been a faculty member at the University of Southern California's Annenberg School for Communication—where he taught classes in business strategies and conducted research on the economics of the radio industry. His work in radio has spanned more than a decade, including serving as program host and producer for KUSC-FM and KPFK-FM. Titus also worked as a freelance journalist, most significantly writing for *Keyboard Magazine's* new talent column, "Discoveries." He has also been an arts administrator, organizing and producing concerts for the California Outside Music Association and the Los Angeles Festival.

Game economies add *flexibility* to the game experience. By adding in side bargains and incentives to create new systems, players, and so on, the game continues to change and adapt. Economies also give players more reasons or *incentives* to continue playing the game—due to their *dynamic* nature, providing novelty and discovery. This means that you don't get bored!

In MMOs, characters gain skills and objects they can trade with other players using the game's currency. In 2001, some *EverQuest* players decided to take the economy outside the game and began selling their assets for real money through auction and trading sites such as eBay. Economist Edward Castronova studied thousands of *EverQuest* transactions initiated through eBay to determine the real-world economic value generated by the inhabitants of Norrath—the fantasy world of *EverQuest*. The verdict? In 2002, Norrath's gross national product (GNP) was $135 million ($2,266 per capita). (If Norrath were a real country, it would have been the 77th richest in the world—just behind Russia!)

Edward Castronova on MMO Game Economies :::::

EC

Edward Castronova obtained a BS in International Affairs from Georgetown University in 1985 and a PhD in Economics from the University of Wisconsin–Madison in 1991. During this time, he spent 18 months studying German postwar reconstruction and social policy at universities and research institutes in Mannheim, Frankfurt, and Berlin. After graduating, he held professorships in political science, public policy, and economics at the University of Rochester and at California State University, Fullerton. Since the fall of 2003, Edward has been an Associate Professor of Telecommunications at Indiana University. He is the author of *Synthetic Worlds: The Business & Culture of Online Games* (University of Chicago Press.) His paper, "Virtual Worlds," is the most downloaded economics paper at the Social Science Research Network.

Edward Castronova, PhD (Associate Professor of Telecommunications, Indiana University)

In the multiplayer context, *all* economic theories can be effectively applied to games. Economics is about the interactions of human beings—so if human beings meet up in a game world, economics takes place. Economies are critical elements of immersion. Designed well, they sit in the background unnoticed and give a constant sense of value—and hence, reality—to every object in the game. Designed poorly, they are obvious at every turn—and make worthless items seem valuable (and make valuable items seem worthless).

The laws of game economics are the same as in the real world—just under rather unusual circumstances. There are thousands of real-world economic situations that could be adapted well into game environments: different monetary institutions; auctions under different rules; population response to shortages; production teams; income redistribution effects; tax effects; location decisions and urban development—and on and on!

Gameplay: creating the experience   **chapter 6**

Gameplay & Documentation

Now that you've learned about gameplay elements, you have everything you need to create a concept document, proposal or game design document (discussed in more detail in Chapter 11). You'll want to blend both story (Chapter 5) and gameplay elements together—identifying points in your storyline where challenges might occur, and creating a variety of strategies that player characters can use to address each challenge. Consider interaction modes, game theory, and ways to keep your game balanced. Do you see gameplay as a game element that is distinct from story, or do you see an integration of these two components? Analyze a few existing games for story and gameplay elements to determine whether they're separate or interdependent. Whether you separate or integrate gameplay with story, it's important to understand the value of gameplay as the core design component of your game. Without strong gameplay design, a game cannot fully engage the players in the experience.

:::

The gameplay elements discussed in this chapter exist in the game world—the environment of the game which contains the structures, terrain, objects, textures, and style of the game itself. Level design, discussed in the next chapter, focuses on creating the game world and incorporating gameplay into it. Gameplay and level design are closely related—and some aspects of the latter incorporate important game theory elements.

Expanded assignments and projects based on the material in this chapter are available on the Instructor Resources DVD.

211

:::CHAPTER REVIEW EXERCISES:::

1. What is the difference between *gameplay* and story? Choose one game and discuss its story and gameplay elements separately. How do these two elements intersect?

2. Contrast the static and dynamic elements of an existing game. How do players modify the game to make it dynamic, and what does this have to do with game balance?

3. What are the players' goals in a non-zero sum game (NZS)? How can the prisoner's dilemma and the tragedy of the commons be applied to gameplay? Create a scenario around one of these theories and discuss how a game involving both cooperation and competition could be compelling and interesting.

4. Play a card or board game (either a classic game like *Monopoly* or a modern tabletop game that can be found at *Funagain Games* [*http://funagain.com*]). Analyze the rules—including victory conditions, loss conditions, gameplay process, and game goals. What steps would you take to create a digital version of this game? (Consider expanding on the game's story as one strategy.)

5. How do game goals relate to challenges in a game—and what strategies can be utilized to overcome these challenges? Choose one game goal and write a high concept (premise) that incorporates that goal. List three plot points that incorporate challenges associated with the game goal you chose. Discuss several strategies that a player might utilize to overcome each challenge. By doing this, how are you integrating gameplay with story?

6. You create an original game in which you and other players must escape from a deserted island. There are three objects that could be built that might help players leave the island: boat, raft, and lifesaver. The boat is the most difficult to build, but it is the most stable escape object; the lifesaver is the easiest to build; and the less stable raft falls in the middle. The relationship between these objects is linear, or transitive. How would you revise this rela¬tionship (or alter the objects) so that it becomes intransitive?

7. A game's premise indicates "You are given immunity from a deadly disease that causes humans to age rapidly. It is up to you alone to find the cure. Use your powers of deduction to uncover the mysterious origins of this disease and find an antidote—before it's too late!" Discuss the specific victory and loss conditions for this game. Giving the game a genre of your choice, make up a set of rules for this game.

8. There are plenty of games that focus on the application of either *intrinsic* or *extrinsic* knowledge, but it's not as common to combine both in one game. Create an original game idea that makes use of both forms of knowledge as strategy elements.

9. *Unilateral* player-to-player interactivity is not common in electronic games. Create an original idea for an electronic game that involves this form of interactivity. How would you incorporate the idea of cooperation and competition into the game?

Levels

creating the world

Key Chapter Questions

■ What is *level design* and how is it related to gameplay?

■ What is the importance of the *structural* features of game worlds—such as duration, availability, relationship, and progression?

■ What is the importance of the *temporal* features of game worlds—such as authentic, variable, player-adjusted, and altered?

■ What is the importance of the *spatial* features of game worlds—such as perspective, scale, and boundaries?

■ How are *reality* and *style* achieved in a game environment?

The process of creating game worlds is often focused on *level design*—an area of game design that is wrought with confusion. Some are under the impression that level designers are members of art teams and primarily focus on 3D modeling. Others believe that level designers are programmers and focus heavily on scripting gameplay events. This chapter takes a physics or "space-time" approach to discuss level design—focusing on how designers construct the architecture and visuals of the physical game environment, and how they divide the basic structure of the world into different sections (levels). (Gameplay—which involves events that might occur in each level—is closely associated with level design. Please be sure to read or review Chapter 6 so that you have a solid understanding of the relationship between these two game design components.

Level Design

For further reading on this topic, please see *Game Level Design* (Castillo/Novak)—part of the *Game Development Essentials* series.

Level design is defined as the creation of environments, scenarios, or missions in an electronic game. A level designer usually utilizes level design tools (or level editors), such as Valve Hammer Editor (Valve Software), UnrealEd (Epic Games), World Builder (Electronic Arts), or the Aurora Toolset (Bioware)—and/or 3D graphics editing software, such as 3ds Max, Maya, or Softimage. Level designers might also use game engines and authoring tools such as Unity 3D, Torque 3D, and GameSalad. (Modeling/animation software, level editors, and game engines are discussed in more detail in Chapter 10.) Traditionally, *level design* involved the creation of game worlds for real-time strategy (RTS) or first-person shooter (FPS) genres. However, this form of design is now necessary in all but the simplest of games.

Consider what function the level fulfills in the game. The level could introduce a new character or object, focus on a plot point (such as discovering a secret or preventing an attack), or create a mood through visuals or storyline. The level's function should center around an idea that becomes a unifying theme.

Structure

Levels can be used to structure a game into effective subdivisions, organize progression, and enhance gameplay. When designing levels, consider their goal, flow, duration, availability, relationships, and difficulty.

Objectives

Each level should have a set of *objectives* that the player understands. Otherwise, the players are simply moving, shooting, puzzle-solving, and collecting until a signal appears indicating that the level is complete or that a new level is loading. Sometimes developers ensure that players understand the objectives for each level by creating a briefing in the form of a cut-scene or interactive tutorial at the beginning of each level, and by providing access to a status screen during the course of the game. The players might also be immediately thrown into the game's action, engaging in tasks that are fairly easy to solve and situations that immediately illustrate the rules of the game in the context of the game's environment. You should let the players know where they stand in relation to their goals by giving them progress reports—preventing a surprise defeat. This applies to a single-player mode. In multiplayer mode, the focus is on balance and strategic/tactical options presented to the player in FPS or RTS games.

Sony Online Entertainment

Free Realms uses tutorial quests to teach new players.

Flow

There are two main issues with game *flow* that you should address while designing a level. You first want to make sure that a player stays in a particular area of a level until he has accomplished necessary objectives. For example, in open world levels, there are not any natural barriers to the player's movements. A player can then run past opponents rather than engage them in battle (which is sometimes a strategy in itself). This problem can be solved by creating natural barriers that are destroyed as a by-product of the player's progress in the level. You also might want to prevent the player from returning to a particular area once the objectives associated with that area have been met. A method for doing this is to close off the area after the player has completed it (creating a one-way barrier, such as a door that locks after the player walks through it), which lets the player know that he is making progress.

Sony Computer Entertainment America

In many action games, such as *God of War III*, players must remain on a particular level until they complete a specific goal.

Duration

How much time should be spent on each level? One universal rule seems to be that a player must complete at least one level of any game in a single session. For computer games, level *duration* should be fairly short, 15-minute spurts for children, to approximately two hours of continuous concentration for hardcore gamers. Console game levels usually run about 45 minutes. If you'd prefer to develop a game with much longer sessions (e.g., strategy games such as *Age of Mythology* or *Civilization III*), make sure you provide milestones of achievement, such as advancement or task completion, on a regular basis.

Nintendo

The duration of levels in puzzle games such as *Wario Land: Shake It!* is fairly short.

Nintendo

In *Wii Sports Resort,* players can choose from several different games at the resort.

Hi-Rez Studios

Players choose levels from all over the world in the mission selection screen of *Global Agenda* (above), including desert and water missions (below).

Hi-Rez Studios

Hi-Rez Studios

Availability

How many levels will you include in the game? You will need to consider the various gameplay goals in the game and ensure that each level covers one primary goal. A greater issue is how many levels should be *available* to a player at once. If you were to allow only one level to be available at a time, this would work for games that require first-person immersion. If you were to allow only a small number of open levels at a time, this could alleviate frustration for many role-playing game (RPG) players, who might have several quests to fulfill and need to shift their focus. If you were to allow many open levels at a time, many players might become confused—but these levels would work well in process sims and RTS games.

Relationship

What are the *relationships* between levels in the game? Think of each level as a scene or even an episode within a larger story. From Chapters 5 and 6, you learned that story and gameplay are intertwined—and that story structure often consists of several acts or plot points. Levels in puzzle games are often related only through some increase in difficulty. Some levels are related through storylines—similar to traditional media such as television. In this episodic relationship, each level is self-contained, with its own internal plot line and conclusion. For example, many strategy games use the term *campaign* to describe a series of levels (known as *missions*) that need to be completed to finish the game. Some games contain several campaigns that are all separate from one another. Each time players complete a mission, they are closer to completing a campaign.

Progression

How do you pace the game's *progression* through level design? As discussed in Chapter 6, you want to make sure that a game's difficulty slowly increases as it continues. Just like story and character development structures discussed in Chapter 5, you need to make sure that each level builds conflict in a series of arcs. Vary the pace of your levels—allowing the player to alternately struggle to stay alive, systematically explore the environment, and reflectively solve challenging puzzles. Always keep the player occupied with things to do. Do not make your level a ghost town! Challenge is a good thing, but do not make your levels so difficult that only experts can survive, while other players die again and again.

A game does not have to be *linear*—consisting of challenges that steadily increase in difficulty as the game continues. It could also be *flat*—where difficulty does not vary from one level to the next. There is also the *s-curve* model, a combination of the linear and flat models that begins with a flat section consisting of a tutorial during which the player learns the game. After this training period, the difficulty level rises steadily throughout the game, and then flattens again a few hours before the game ends so that the players who get through most of the game will eventually be able to finish it.

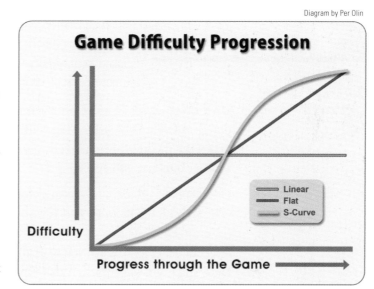

Diagram by Per Olin

Comparison of linear, flat, and s-curve progressions.

Depending on the goals of the level, you might want to warn players of impending danger, such as a monster behind a door or a sniper on a rooftop. One way of doing this is through audio (which will be discussed further in Chapter 9). It is also debatable whether developers should pit players against powerful enemies with only one weakness that the player must discover while trying to defeat the enemy. Although sometimes frustrating for the player, this is done in most platform-style console games. To challenge expert players, you can either build more difficult versions of your levels that can be accessed separately by the expert players—or you can build different levels of challenges within the level. There should also be several ways in which a player can meet each challenge and complete a level. Ideally, the different methods of success will appeal to different playing styles.

> Level structure gives players a sense of progression and a mental map of where they stand against the rules and storyline of the game.
>
> —Jennifer F. Estaris (Senior Game Designer, Nickelodeon Virtual Worlds).

James Portnow on the Practical & Theoretical Sides of Level Design :::::

JP

James Portnow
(Chief Executive Officer,
Rainmaker Games;
Professor, DigiPen
Institute of Technology)

After receiving his master's degree from Carnegie Mellon University's Entertainment Technology Center, James Portnow worked for Activision as a designer on the *Call of Duty* series. He then founded Divide by Zero Games and launched Rainmaker Games —a design and narrative consulting firm that has worked with partners from Warner Bros. to Zynga. James has written for major trade publications including *Gamasutra*, *The Escapist*, and *Edge*. He is currently the writer on *Extra Credits*, the hit consumer series focusing on game design. James is known for his theories on socially positive design and has spoken at universities and companies worldwide. He is the co-author of a book on invented languages.

Level design is made up of two parts: the practical and the theoretical. The practical side involves assessing your tool and deciding what is efficient to make; the theoretical side involves understanding how your mechanics and systems interact with space.

On the practical side, simply learn your system inside and out, then find where you can push the bounds. This is really where a lot of the great level design happens, by experimenting with the limits of what a particular scripting engine or level builder can do. Once you have all the tricks down, just take a moment, sit back, and think to yourself: 'What types of levels give us the most bang for our buck?' 'What types of interactions allow me to build the coolest levels in the shortest amount of time?' To an even greater degree than most other areas of design, level design requires iteration. You have to get it out in front of an audience to understand how to improve it, and this takes time—so the quicker you can construct it, the more iteration you'll be able to do … and the better levels you'll create.

On the theoretical side, you need to have a very deep understanding of your mechanics and how they relate to your space. This involves everything from player mechanics (e.g., how far can your player jump?) to AI (e.g., how many units wide does a gap have to be for enemies not to get stuck in a chokepoint?) to spawning (do enemy units spawn on triggers? on a timer? how does the player stop them from spawning?). A good level designer understands how all these elements interconnect and how they connect with the space in order to set up pacing, challenge, and novel experiences.

Jack Snowden on Level Design as the Foundation of Gameplay :::::

Prior to working at the Art Institute of Seattle, Jack Snowden spent nearly 10 years at Nintendo as a Lead 3D Artist working on such titles as *Machinex* (Wii), *1080 Avalanche* (Game Cube), *Bionic Commando* (Game Boy), *Pokemon Attack* (N64), and many others. Jack has also worked as a Lead Artist at Riverdeep and Electronic Arts—as well as at his own company, Laughing Mountain Productions. In addition to the Art Institute of Seattle, Jack's academic experience includes several years of service on the faculty of Washington State University (Pullman, Washington), where he was an Assistant Professor in the Interior Design department. Jack holds a M.F.A degree in Painting, Graphic Design, and Sculpture from Washington State University, and a B.F.A. from Fort Wright College in Spokane, Washington. He is also a graduate of the Cornish School of Allied Arts in Seattle, Washington.

Jack Snowden
(Academic Director,
Game Art & Design,
Art Institute of Seattle)

The "level structure" of a game is the foundation to gameplay. Level design incorporates and reflects the psychology and interaction all players have from their daily life (with "life" being *macro* and game levels being *micro*). At the micro level, players soon lose interest if the design doesn't provide mini adventures or distractions. The level designer is sending messages to the player through form, psychology of color, and historical image references. Through subtle messages, the levels are set up to control the journey and information the player will need to interact with the game. I call this *harnessing* the players to do, or *directing* what I want them to see, feel or discover. The game designer is the "Master of Ceremonies" for the good (or bad) experience had by the player.

Elements of Level Design

Level design is the process of creating a world filled with goals, sub-goals, and lots of obstacles between the player and those goals. The level designer is responsible for designing the level's world; determining which enemies, weapons, and power-ups appear in the level; how and when the enemies appear or spawn; and the overall balance of the level (so the level is neither too easy nor too hard). A level designer may also be expected to build the 3D environment or at least some of its elements, using 3D programs such as Maya or 3D Studio Max, and even program some of the triggers or other interactions, using scripting languages. While the level designer is constrained by the rules and mechanics envisioned by the lead designer, the level designer is also in the position to offer changes to those rules, if those changes (a) will result in a more engaging game and (b) do not alter the world or the game to the point that it does not match the overall vision intended for the game.

—*Richard Wainess, PhD (Senior Research Associate, UCLA/CRESST)*

Levels: creating the world   **chapter 7**

Time

The concept of time was introduced in Chapter 2 in the discussion of time intervals (turn-based, time-limited, and real-time). Time can also be thought of with respect to real-world time. "Game time" can move slower, faster, or not any differently from real-world time. In many turn-based and action games, there is no concept of time passing at all. Everything idles or runs in a continuous loop until the player interacts with it in some way.

Authentic

Some games try to portray time *authentically* and use the passage of time as a gameplay characteristic. The cartridge for *Boktai*, developed for the Game Boy Advance, contains a sensor that detects the amount of light where the game is being played.

Blizzard

The object of the game is to drag vampires out of the darkness into the sunlight. The game must be played outside during the day, and weak sunlight negatively affects your character's energy level. You must enter the correct time of day to configure the game before playing. Lionhead Studios' *Dimitri* provides a variant of authentic time through its characters, who progressively age as the game continues. In Wide Games' *Prisoner of War*, the player character must participate in both morning and evening roll calls. If the player is absent during any call, the POW camp officers conduct a search. In the game *Shrek*, the player can control time of day to accomplish different tasks. *Animal Crossing* also uses the date to trigger special events.

World of Warcraft has a 24-hour day, with different servers set to different time zones.

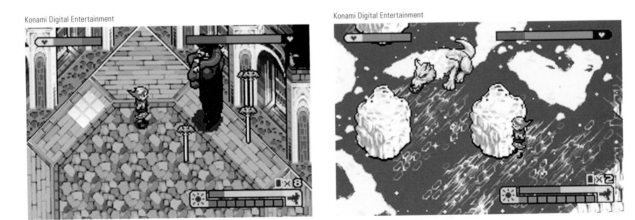

Konami Digital Entertainment   Konami Digital Entertainment

Boktai uses a sensor to detect the presence of daylight.

Limited

Time is sometimes implemented as a part of the setting of the game but not of the gameplay itself. Time creates an atmosphere and provides some variety, but it does not alter gameplay. Game time can feel artificial because players can do the same things at night that they can do in the daytime. However, there are a few games in which time is meaningful. Sometimes a player is put under pressure by being given a *limited* amount of real-world time to accomplish something. In *Baldur's Gate,* the shops are closed at night and characters run an increased risk of being attacked by monsters (because it's dark, and the monsters are harder to see).

XxSugarLovexX (Photobucket)

Time is crucial in *FarmVille,* where a few hours can mean the difference between a bountiful harvest (above) and a field of wilted crops.

Variable

If time is significant, the virtual time in a game is variable—running out much faster than in reality, jumping around, and skipping over periods when nothing interesting is happening. War games generally do not bother to implement a night time or require that soldiers sleep. Since players often want to play continuously without having to pause and wait for "morning," the night time portions of the game are not missed. *The Sims* depicts days and nights because the game is a process simulation and the characters require rest and sleep for health. However, time speeds up when the characters go to sleep.

Electronic Arts

Time is variable in *Ultima Online*: nights are always shorter than days.

Player-Adjusted

In many sports games, players may modify the time associated with game levels—known as *player-adjusted* time. Players can sometimes play shorter (5–10 minute) quarters instead of the standard 15-minute quarters in a football game. It's important to provide time options to players when possible. Many players do not want to devote a whole hour to playing a simulated football game. In some flight simulators, there can be long periods where nothing interesting is happening during the flight. In these cases, players might have the option of speeding up the time.

Electronic Arts

Players can adjust the time interval in sports games such as *Madden NFL 11.*

Altered

Several games incorporate *altered* time as an effect. *Max Payne* was the first game to use *bullet time*—the technique of going into slow motion while retaining the ability to move the camera's viewpoint at normal speed. (This technique was introduced in the film, *The Matrix*—and it was later used in games based on the franchise.) Since the game models bullets as real objects, it is possible to see a bullet in flight while this feature is activated. This same effect is seen in action movies such as *The Matrix* and *Crouching Tiger, Hidden Dragon.* In *Blinx,* the player can rewind time—and in *Prince of Persia: The Sands of Time,* the main character has the power to stop time during the game so that he can avoid being defeated by opponents.

Ubisoft

Players can stop time in *Prince of Persia: The Forgotten Sands.*

Space

Space incorporates the physical environment of the game—including its perspective, scale, boundaries, structures, terrain, objects, and style (color, texture, look, and feel). In Chapter 5, you were introduced to some visual character creation techniques—including concept drawing, modeling, texturing, and animation.

Environmental art is created using many of the same techniques as in character art—although it often is not animated specifically but utilizes some special environmental effects. Concept artists often sketch out a scene related to a game, which can reflect a particular level's style. After a sketch has been completed, you might use a level editor to build a 3D version of the level. Software for level design is discussed in more detail in Chapter 11. The editor should allow you to view the world in multiple perspectives (including the player view); modify geometry while you place characters in the world; and navigate through a level as you are building it.

Perspective & Camera

In Chapter 5, you learned about the importance of both first-person and third-person *point-of-view (POV)* with regard to characters in a game. POV is related to the *perspective* of the game world—or how the player views the game environment.

Omnipresent

In the *omnipresent* perspective, the player has the ability to view different parts of the game world and can take actions in many different locations of the world (even if parts are hidden at times). The omnipresent perspective allows players to look down at the game world from above. In Chapter 3, you learned about process simulations and god (or toy) games. *Populous* and *Black & White* were coined "god games" by the press because they not only utilized the omnipresent POV, but also allowed other characters to view the player as if he was above the game world—akin to a god looking down on the other characters.

Reprinted with permission from Microsoft Corporation

Halo Wars uses an omnipresent perspective.

Aerial (Top-Down)

The *aerial* (or *top-down*) perspective shows the player the game as seen from above—a bird's-eye view. This view is popular for games such as the original *Legend of Zelda* and *Pac-Man*.

Take-Two Interactive

Ubisoft

Railroad Tycoon 3 has an aerial (top-down) perspective.

Anno 1404 uses an isometric perspective.

Isometric

In the *isometric* perspective, the player can look slightly across the landscape at a 30- to 45-degree angle. In an isometric world, you can create many different angles of objects, and then place those objects on the screen. This allows you to create reusable objects rather than having to render them in real time. This perspective also makes the player feel closer and more involved with events than a top-down or aerial view. However, the fact that artists must create several (usually four) different versions of all objects from each angle can cause the process to get a bit tedious if the camera rotates. (Many RTS and strategy games were created in 3D isometric view without camera rotation.) Early versions of *Sim City* and *Civilization* were almost entirely aerial views—mainly because the hardware at the time did not support enough detail for any other view. Eventually, these games adopted an isometric view using 2D technology to create a pseudo-3D world—creating the effect of playing with scale models, appropriate for process simulations!

Height Maps

A popular technique for generating landscapes, a *height map* is a contour picture depicting the elevations of intersecting points on a 3D grid. Height maps translate quite well to 3D landscapes and are created by using grayscale to represent height.

Side-Scrolling (or Flat/Side-View)

In 2D space, characters can run only from left to right or jump up and down. They cannot run toward the player or away from the player. Working around these limitations, classic 2D arcade games used *side-scrolling* navigation to create the illusion of space. The player character would travel from left to right horizontally across the screen as the background moved from right to left. In a technique known as *parallax scrolling*, the camera moves vertically or horizontally, with different layers moving at different speeds—which gives the feeling of depth.

Take-Two Interactive

Nintendo

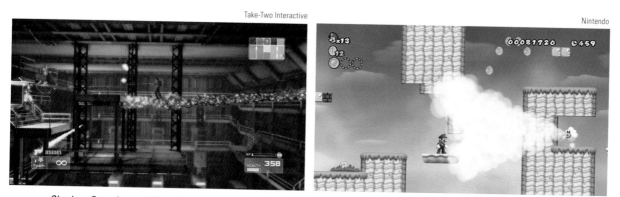

Shadow Complex and *New Super Mario Bros. Wii* are very different games, but both use side-scrolling navigation.

Designing Levels for Role-Playing Games

There are really not a lot of specific design issues—as long as you: stick to the role-playing game (RPG) formula (explore – kill – loot – sell/power up – level-up – repeat); make sure you space out your carrots along the level (here's a unique item, here's an area where the player can gain a bonus feat, here's a part of the level where a new part of a story mystery is solved, here's a nice vista in the level for the player to look at); and then, if you can, try to give players options to pursue their goals depending on how they made their characters (like rogues being able to sneak into situations, diplomats talking their way out of situations, or gunmen slaughtering their way to the end). A game should stroke the players' egos, and there's no better way to do this than to present them with levels and situations that allow them to flex the skills and abilities in they spent the most points.

—*Chris Avellone (Creative Director & Co-Owner, Obsidian Entertainment)*

Terrain & Materials

Environmental *materials*—such as metal, glass, sand, gravel, sky, and clouds—directly influence the look and feel of the game. A shading model defines how materials behave when they are lit. It combines the attributes of each material—such as texture, color, shininess, and translucency—with the attributes of light sources, including color and direction. Materials can then be shaded differently depending on their physical attributes. Terrain refers to textures that appear on ground surfaces—such as dirt, grass, tile, and pavement.

Sony Computer Entertainment America   Nintendo

Interiors made of steel, chrome, and wood textures in *Killzone 2* contrast with park-like exterior textures in *The Legend of Zelda: Skyward Sword.*

Normal Mapping

The technique of normal mapping is used a great deal in level and environmental design—enhancing the appearance of low poly models by adding details to shading without using more polygons. Normal mapping is an application of bump mapping, which simulates rough textures by creating irregularities in shading. While bump mapping perturbs the existing normal of a model, normal mapping replaces the normal entirely.

Consistency, Realism & Imagination

A level serves as the medium through which all game systems travel. If a game has shooting, acrobatics, and explosions, it better have levels that present a variety of shooting situations, scenery that can be navigated with grace, and plenty of reasons to blow up people and property. While levels need to showcase the systems, they also need to mesh with the story and setting. If an alien hive looks like a series of square rooms and long hallways—or if it looks suspiciously like a warehouse with some creepy textures on the wall—the game will be a disaster. Players pick up on poor level design, and it sours their view of every other feature in the game.

—*Matt MacLean (Lead Systems Designer, Obsidian Entertainment)*

Radiosity & Effects

Radiosity or *lighting* is just one effect that is used on game environments. Without the proper application of radiosity, players will not be able to navigate through the game environment— nor will they be able to see and interact with details that might determine whether they can progress through the game. Radiosity can also be used to give the effect of reflection (on water, glass, and other elements). Other environmental game effects include climate (rain, snow, lightning) and other natural movements (waves, wind, flotation) created through animation.

Rake In Grass Games

Radiosity makes this screen come alive in *Jets 'N' Guns Gold*.

Evoking an Accidental Mood

In developing the environment for a game in an archeological setting, I was challenged by the need to match the surroundings of the time (e.g., wind, no windows, no electricity)— ensuring it wasn't too creepy so that younger students wouldn't be frightened. I addressed the issue by first trying to identify all the environmental conditions that would have had an impact on the people who used the area. For example, windy spaces due to the lack of glass in the holes built into the sides of buildings to admit light meant that I needed to build in various degrees of "draftiness"—but I also needed the wind to interact with: (a) the monks' robes and hair; and (b) the oil lamps and other light sources. This resulted in the need to create shadows that reacted dynamically with the objects in each scene—which ironically made the eeriness unavoidable after all!

—*Virginia R. Hetrick, PhD (Game Architecture & Programming Consultant)*

Game Environments: Creating the Illusion

Most often, when you think of game art, it is the characters and creatures that come to mind—even though it is the environments those creatures inhabit that really create the illusion of a world. You want your game to be convincingly real to truly inspire mood and drama—and yet you have to be inventive, without straining credulity. It's a matter of combining and synthesizing, keeping the aspirations in your head, but looking for new ways to fit it all together.

—*Marc Taro Holmes (art director, concept artist, and illustrator)*

Scale

The *scale* of the game space includes the total size of physical space and relative sizes of the objects in the game. Since simulation games try to emulate reality, the space and objects within this genre should be scaled to relative size. In games involving a first-person perspective, the view is usually only contained within a few hundred feet of space—so scale is not a major issue. However, important objects such as keys, weapons, and ammunition should be exaggerated so that the player can easily spot them. Scale exaggeration is used in *Civilization III* to represent character units as larger in scale than structures so that players can easily manage and select the units. In games with an aerial or isometric perspective, the scale might need to be distorted. For example, buildings are often just a little taller than the characters in the game (making the height of the characters appear to be exaggerated). This allows players to see the roofs of buildings or the landscape without being unable to see the characters—and it allows units to be shown that otherwise would be behind a building.

Muzzy Lane

Troops, tanks, and planes are all the same size in *Making History II: The War of the World.*

Sony Online Entertainment

Griffons in *EverQuest II* offer rapid transit throughout the world.

The size of the physical space in the game might also be distorted to accommodate the player. The scale of the space needs to be small enough so that a character only takes a few minutes to get from one end of the game world to another (unless the object of the game is to explore a detailed environment). In contrast, the game's scale loses its distortion when a character walks into a building and interacts with objects within it. In this case, the interior space in the game is not distorted, while the exterior space is distorted. A great example of this is *Grand Theft Auto,* in which the player navigates the character quickly from place to place in the city—yet may take time to explore interiors of the surrounding buildings that seem much larger by contrast.

Tile-Based Worlds

A *tile*—also known as a *cell*—is a rectangular or square area of a map. (In isometric worlds, tiles are almost always diamond-shaped.) A tile can be any size, but it is often approximately the size of the character you are using—or at least the size of the part of the character that touches the ground (such as feet). Tile-based worlds (TBWs) are common in strategy games such as *Advance Wars* and the *Civilization* series.

Boundaries

In Chapter 5, you learned how game developers attempt to maintain a player's suspension of disbelief through immersive storylines. Many games do not explicitly reveal that the game world has *boundaries*—and that the world is limited. Since no game has yet to contain a limitless, infinite world, developers have come up with some solutions for dealing with the boundaries while keeping the player immersed in the game. Some games can explicitly reveal their limited worlds—such as football stadiums, racing tracks, or theme parks. Underground or indoor settings also help create artificial boundaries. Other games, such as flight simulators, allow the flat game world to wrap around itself—creating the impression of a spherical world. Another common tool for accomplishing this is terrain that the player will view as impassable—such as mountain ranges or thick vegetation. In many RTS games, the edge of the world is simply a black void!

Reprinted with permission from Microsoft Corporation

Flight Simulator X: Acceleration uses arbitrary environmental boundaries in the air.

Cultural Context

The cultural context of the game includes the beliefs, attitudes, and values held by the characters in the game world. This culture is reflected in the items that appear in the game environment—such as clothing, furniture, architecture, art, emblems, religious/magic items, decorations, and surroundings. What objects and structures should exist in this particular world—and how should they look? What rules apply to your game's culture? Consistency is important here. The same rules should apply to both the players and NPCs (including enemies).

Realism

Actual photographic and land-height data is used to create a realistic model for most flight simulators (such as *Flight Simulator 2002*). Extra details such as trees, buildings, and other traffic are created procedurally, and even the weather is realistic. In Chapter 5, you learned that miles of Los Angeles streets were re-created for *True Crime: Streets of LA*; this realistic environment enabled the designers to focus story elements on real-world events that have happened—or could occur—in present-day urban Los Angeles.

Consider how much detail you want to include in your game. As you add detail, you often must subtract speed and efficiency. Many simulation games attempt to model the real world—and players often rely on real-world common sense when playing them. But all games represent some abstraction and simplification of the real world. How real do you want your game world to be? In *The Getaway*, 40 square kilometers of London were re-created using over 20,000 digital photographs—incorporating everything from tourist hot spots to back alleys to overcast skies. All of these provide an instantly recognizable simulation of everyday life in their respective cities. In *Prisoner of War*, structures associated with different levels (such as the Colditz Castle level) are photographed hundreds of times. The structure is then modeled to scale, and then rescaled to provide an effective game arena while also maintaining authenticity.

Take-Two Interactive

Major League Baseball 2K11 uses familiar details to portray the game world realistically.

Hyperreality

Sometimes exaggerating visual reality can make a game more dramatic. If actual weather patterns were followed to a tee in a flight simulator, the lightning would probably not appear so close and threatening. In extreme sports games, such as *Transworld Snowboarding,* the drops are steeper than they would be in reality.

Style

The *style* of the game world influences everything from the character, interface, manual, and packaging. Although Western game art tends to be fairly conservative, students graduating from game art and design programs at universities appear to be pushing style boundaries—getting inspired by more cutting edge games from Japan, such as *Rez, Freak Out, Vib Ribbon,* and *Space Channel 5.* The physical appearance of the characters in Lionhead Studios' *Fable* transforms as they age, engage in battle, exercise, and drink—resulting in wrinkles, scars, muscles, and beer bellies! The environments in the game also incorporate vivid detail.

Flower's style evokes the beauty of nature, while *Resident Evil 5* reflects a much darker vision.

Cel-Shading

Cel-shading is the art of rendering objects to look like hand-drawn cartoons—in contrast to photorealistic renderings. The most simplistic algorithms simply fill the object with a solid color and then overlay lines on the edges of the objects. More complex algorithms engage in shading; take into account light sources and shadows; or attempt to mimic a more stylistic cartoon style—such as charcoal, watercolors, or etching.

Borderlands uses cel-shading to give a 2D look to a 3D world.

Sony Computer Entertainment America

The crafted Monkey King in *Little Big Planet* is an example of the game's unique style..

There are two main style forms that need to work together in the game: the style of the objects in the world, and the style of the artwork that will depict the world. For example, the neighborhood in the game could consist of Spanish-style homes, while the style of the art could be anime. As long as each style is consistently used for its purpose throughout the game, it will not detract from the gameplay.

Many styles have been overused in games. Do not borrow a style or setting from another game, but instead try something new. Forget the same old villains and environments. Think about the emotion you would like the world to bring out in the player: awe, fear, excitement, amusement? This will help you formulate your style.

Space & Time: Levels, Gameplay & Story

You probably noticed that level design draws upon both gameplay and story elements. The game environment acts as a setting for a story—and the elements within it tell us a lot about the characters. Consider the environment's spatial elements—natural resources, structures, vehicles, props, and other objects; all of these elements are utilized by the environment's inhabitants. The environment also informs us about time by giving us clues to its origins, climate, and place in history (past, present, future). The structural elements of game levels are closely related to all gameplay elements—including balance, progression, challenges/strategies, and victory/loss conditions. Creating a game that has a clear level structure will allow you to take full advantage of a wide variety of game mechanics and aid in replayability.

In this chapter, you learned the importance of temporal and spatial environments—including various ways that games can be structured using level design within the game world. In the next chapter, we move from the game world to the direct connection between the player and the game through physical and visual interfaces.

Expanded assignments and projects based on the material in this chapter are available on the Instructor Resources DVD.

233

:::CHAPTER REVIEW EXERCISES:::

1. What is level design and how does it relate to gameplay, story, and character development?

2. What are some unique ways games have utilized time—both real-world and game-world—to make a game more compelling? Create an original game concept around one of these methods. Can you think of another method that has not been used?

3. What are some spatial perspective tricks used in level design that sometimes overcome the limitations of the game environment? Which of these tricks might you incorporate into your original game?

4. How can a game retain authenticity through environmental design? Discuss some features you might use in developing a game centered around real-world rules.

5. Play a game in any genre and analyze how the game handles structure. Is the game split into levels? Does each subsequent level increase in difficulty? Does the game follow a linear, flat, or s-curve progression?

6. How does a game's style relate to its mood? Describe the mood of your original game. Then describe a particular scene in terms of setting and environmental atmosphere—incorporating that mood in your description.

7. Design an environment for your original game idea, First, go location scouting and take pictures of some unusual objects, textures, and scenes. Then, incorporate these textures into concept sketches of an original environment. What materials or terrain will you use in your design? What sorts of objects and structures will you add to the environment?

8. How does a game's cultural context affect its environment? Create a culture around your original game idea, and discuss how this culture might determine the look of interiors, exteriors, objects, vehicles, and structures, and the rules of the game world.

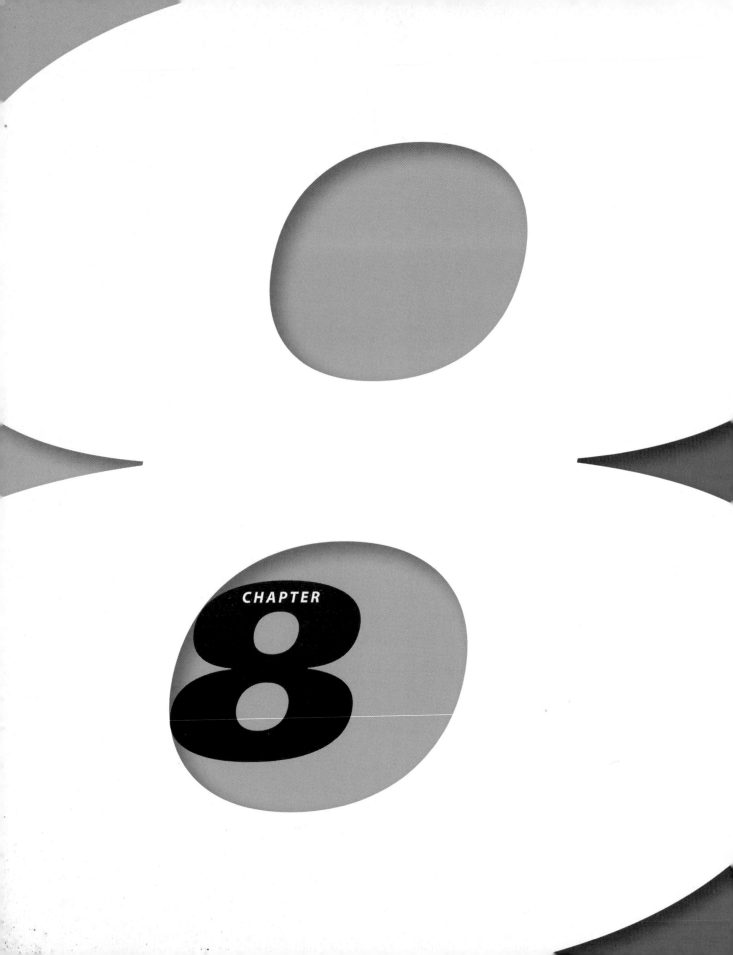

CHAPTER

8

Interface

creating the connection

Key Chapter Questions

- How do game interfaces relate to *player-centered* design?

- What are the *components* of game interfaces?

- What is the difference between a *physical* and a *visual* interface?

- What is the difference between a *passive* and an *active* interface?

- Why is *usability* important in game interface design?

A game-specific interface is the connection between the player and the game itself. The primary function of this interface is to help the player make choices to achieve certain goals within the game. The interface is the closest connection players can have to the game without being able to jump right into the game itself, like characters in the movie *Tron*! Game interfaces differ from other interfaces because their purpose is tied to a more immersive experience than surfing the Web or even talking on the phone. Even games that involve only one player must allow for an intensely high level of interactivity between the player and the game itself. The player must be able to focus solely on the game experience without external (environmental) or internal (mental) distractions. In addition to providing this connection and immersion, a game interface still must fulfill its general function: to help the player actually *play* the game. To ensure this, interface designers must understand the many tasks, actions, needs, and challenges the player must deal with throughout the game.

Player-Centered Design

For further reading on this topic, please see *Game Interface Design* (Saunders/Novak)—part of the *Game Development Essentials* series.

The importance of interface design—the connection between the player and the game—is often overlooked. For player activity to exist, there has to be a connection between the player and the game itself. In this way, interface design is closely linked to the idea of player control.

Interface design is traditionally known as user interface design. A user is someone who makes use of a certain technology—such as a web site, computer, or cell phone—to achieve a certain result. The term was coined during the advent of the home computer revolution, and it traditionally characterizes the user as an expert who fully understands the technology that they are utilizing. In Web design, the term user is commonly changed to customer because this better represents the role of the person who is utilizing the interface. In the same way, a user can be referred to as a player in game design.

Let's look at the concept of player-centered design. Who is the audience for your game? Are you designing the game for yourself, your company, or the players? Who will actually interact with the game? In all aspects of game design, constant focus must be on the player's needs, tasks, and choices. If you lose sight of the player, the game will be unplayable. The most important and obvious feature of a game that allows for player-centered design is the interface itself. When you catch yourself thinking of how to design an interface so that it's cool, complex, cutting-edge, and flashy, pretend that you're the player for a moment and see if your great idea will help the player play the game without getting frustrated! The interface should always be helpful and functional.

:::::: What's Wrong with This Picture?

American Cybercast

This ad (for American Cybercast, circa 1995) is missing a connection between the "audience" and the "content"—causing the content to resemble a television-style broadcast model rather than interactive entertainment. Can you describe the missing connection?

The interface allows the player to take control of game characters, navigate the game environment, and make decisions throughout the game. Without an interface, a game would be no more than a presentation, animation sequence, or a static environment—an unplayable game!

Interface & Game Features

You've already learned that the primary purpose of a player interface is to allow players to actually play the game, and that there are many player tasks, choices, and needs that must be addressed by the interface design. Let's split these tasks, choices, and needs into two categories: actions and information. During a game, each player will need to access information that might not be available from game characters or the environment. This information might include player status—such as lives remaining, power depleted, and skills attained. This information often changes based on where the player is in the game, or on what the player decides to do during the course of the game. All of this information must be available through the player interface. The player also takes various actions during the course of a game. These actions might involve navigating the game world, picking up an object, or firing a weapon. Each of these actions need to be accounted for in the player interface. You've already learned about some basic game features—such as gameplay, story, character, and the game world (which is often structured in levels). How do these features interact with the game interface?

Gameplay

The connection between the player interface and *gameplay* is what truly allows for the game's interactivity. As you learned in Chapter 6, gameplay is the core of the game experience. It involves all actions the player takes during the game. If a player chooses to take a certain path down a fork in the road or attempts to crack a code in a safe, the player needs to carry out those actions through the game interface. Designing an interface for a particular game involves understanding and allowing for all possible player actions in that game.

Reprinted with permission from Microsoft Corporation

The gameplay element of resource management is used extensively in real-time strategy games such as *Age of Empires III.*

Story

The game interface must reflect the game's *story.* The visual style of the interface should incorporate the setting, mood, time period, environment, and culture of the game. If the interface is created separately without knowledge of the game world, its presence will take the player out of the game, instead of allowing the player to become even more immersed in the experience.

Take-Two Interactive

Some games contain rich storylines—such as *Red Dead Redemption*'s gritty tale set in the Wild West.

Character

Just as a game interface must incorporate the story, it also must incorporate aspects of the story's *characters*. A player who takes on the role of a player character will have specific needs and goals, all of which should be addressed by the interface. It may be essential that a character have access to certain weapons, clothing, powers, vehicles, and even personality traits. Access to these items, characteristics, and abilities can often be found through the game interface, or a specialized character interface. When choosing or creating a character, players could utilize a character selection or customization screen, which is a specialized type of interface. Even non-player characters (NPCs) have information associated with them that often must be accessed by the player. For example, a player might want to look at what types of skills and abilities are associated with his or her NPC opponent in order to choose a character with matching (or complementary) skills and abilities.

Role-playing games focus heavily on character interfaces. *The Lord of the Rings Online* utilizes a character journal—which provides information on a character's equipment, stats, biography, war status, skills, traits, and titles.

Audio

Some game developers consider audio part of the player interface itself. *Audio* works with the visual or physical interface to bring a feeling of reality or tactile feeling to the experience. Types of audio include music, sound effects, and spoken dialogue/narration. In addition to providing a soundtrack to the game, music can also provide information—for example, warning the player of trouble ahead by becoming more dramatic right before an enemy appears onscreen. In this case, audio could be seen as being part of the information component of an interface. Sound effects and music can be triggered when a player accesses areas of a game interface. When a player decides to fire a weapon, the sound of that weapon firing will often occur in response to the player's action. When a player opens a jewelry box, music within the box could be triggered by the action. A spoken word option could be available within the interface itself for players with visual impairments. If a player wants to find out what items are in his or her character's inventory, these items could be "read" to the player by the voiceover in addition to being seen. Audio will be discussed in more detail in Chapter 9.

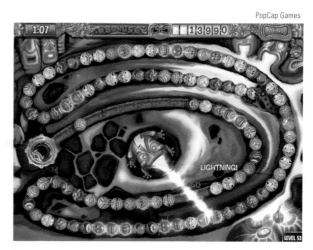

In puzzle games such as *Zuma's Revenge!*, audio provides both ambience and tactile enhancement.

World

In Chapter 7, you learned about how the game *world* might be structured in many ways. In addition to specific environments (interiors and exteriors) that reflect the condition and focus of the world, a game could contain parallel worlds or a series of worlds that become more or less complex depending on where they appear in a sequence. Sometimes a player interface is modified based on which portion or type of world is being accessed—and more or fewer components might appear in the interface. One of the most common ways of dealing with level design structure is through the use of maps that can be accessed through the game interface. These maps might appear on the periphery of the game playing field or be accessed separately through a menu system.

The interface in *Black & White 2*, which is simple and almost buttonless, is used to interact with different areas of the game world—including a Greek city devastated by an Aztec army.

As you can see, interface design is related to all other aspects of game development—including gameplay, story, character, audio, and world—and it helps bridge the gap between the game and the player. Now, let's take a look at the types of interface and their associated purposes and design components.

Interface Types

Chapter 1 discussed the history of game development in the context of the dominant hardware platforms associated with particular eras. Each of these platforms had distinct physical (hardware-based input devices) and visual (software-based onscreen displays) interfaces.

Arcade games did not achieve a standard interface style for either physical or visual interfaces. (A more detailed discussion of both types of interfaces appears in the next few sections.) Before a player deposited coins into these games, the screen would display the title along with instructions or a set of screens that also included a list of players' high scores and (later) a demo sequence from the game itself. The physical interface usually consisted of a start button and direction buttons or a joystick. *Centipede* was one of the few arcade games to use a trackball—which became a fairly popular physical interface (possibly because it was more durable than a joystick). Other interfaces, often associated with arcade simulation games such as driving and shooting, mimicked real-life objects (such as a rifle, periscope, or steering wheel/gas pedal). Visual interfaces in arcade games were fairly straightforward—consisting of score, level, and "lives remaining" displays. Due to the relative simplicity of the technology at the time and the coin-op business model, the interfaces had to focus on functionality rather than aesthetics. Arcade-goers would not take time out to read complicated user interface instruction manuals; they had to be able to understand how to play the game almost immediately, with a minimum of text instruction (which usually needed to fit on one screen).

Elements of a Game Interface

The interface is one of the least understood yet most critical elements in the game. The interface is the connection between the player and the game world. The invisible [physical] interface elements include the control triggers, keys, and mouse, which are used to select and use weapons, move around the world, and communicate with both NPCs and other players. The visible elements are the on-screen features that can let the player know his or her health, available weapons and their status, locations of enemies, distance to targets, position within the world, and any other information that is considered critical to gameplay, both in terms of what the player can do and what the player may not want to do (such as not attacking a powerful enemy when health is low). What makes a good game is intuitive, what makes a good interface is largely dependent upon a vast number of cognitive issues that are generally unknown to interface designers, yet are slowly beginning to make their way into the game industry. Understanding these issues can greatly advance the quality and usability of game interfaces, and, ultimately, of gameplay.

—*Richard Wainess, PhD*
(Senior Research Associate, UCLA/CRESST)

In Chapter 1, you also learned about the evolution of *computer* games, beginning with text adventures, which relied on two-word commands from the player to navigate through the game. In these games, the physical interface consisted of the computer's keyboard (pre-mouse), and there was no visual interface. Players simply had to look up the various commands to know how to move through the game.

When computer games evolved to contain graphics, the visual interface was still virtually nonexistent. Much of the time, the visuals depicted what was going on in the game world—but did not illustrate how the player could interface with that world. The introduction of the graphical *point-and-click* interface allowed games to be much more accessible to players—attracting a much larger consumer base.

Physical Interfaces

Physical or *manual* interfaces are the hardware-based controllers, keyboard-mouse combinations, and other input devices that players interact with physically to play the game. These interfaces are closely associated with the game's hardware platform.

Sega   Konami

Physical interfaces for *Samba de Amigo* and *Dance Dance Revolution* show that players don't always need to use their hands to control their game experience.

Arcade

Physical *arcade* interfaces are usually integrated into an arcade game's cabinet and consist of items such as buttons, joysticks, and sliders. Driving games often use steering wheel/pedal combinations. Specialized physical interfaces have been developed for particular games—including *Silent Scope* (gun), *Karaoke Revolution* (microphone), and *Periscope* (periscope—surprise!).

Sega

Brave Firefighters uses a fire hose as a physical interface.

Computer

Physical interfaces for *computer* games almost always consist of a keyboard-mouse combination. Players often navigate through the game environment on computers using the keyboard (sometimes W-A-S-D or arrow keys), the mouse, or both.

Big Stock Photo

Keyboard combinations can sometimes be used to open onscreen menus or take quick action in a game. Peripheral devices used in arcade games are seldom packaged with computer games. Even though there are many other input devices for computers (e.g., joysticks, steering wheel/pedal kits, flight yoke systems), developers can *only* assume a player will use a mouse/keyboard combination.

Computer physical interfaces usually consist solely of a keyboard-mouse combination.

Console

Console controllers often consist of navigation and action controls—handling action games much better than the keyboard-mouse combination, since they were specifically designed to enable simple, quick reflexes. Like arcade games (and unlike most computer games), console games also incorporate peripheral physical devices—such as dance pads (*Dance Dance Revolution*), fishing rods (*Bass Fishing*), maracas (*Samba di Amigo*), and microphones (*Karaoke Revolution*).

Each of the current primary console systems has a unique controller—with several variations manufactured by third-party companies. Features of each standard controller include the following:

- *Wii*: Three innovative controllers: classic, remote (Wiimote), and nunchuk. Classic contains four shoulder buttons, one D-pad, four action buttons (A, B, X, Y), two analog sticks—and Start, Select, and Home buttons. Wiimote contains a D-pad, B trigger, A, 1 and 2 buttons—and Home, plus (+) and minus (–) buttons. Nunchuk contains one analog stick, one trigger, and a C button.

- *PS3*: Two analog sticks, one D-pad, four action buttons, four triggers (two on the left side and two on the right side), Start and Select buttons, and an Analog button. (*Note:* The PS3 does not have rumble.)

- *Xbox 360*: Two analog sticks, one D-pad, four action buttons (X, Y, A, B), two triggers, Start and Select buttons, and two auxiliary buttons (black and white). For the Xbox 360, the auxiliary buttons have been removed and two additional triggers have been added.

Compare these specs to the old Atari 2600 joystick! Most controllers now also have rumble and vibrational feedback—providing a more tactile game experience.

Nintendo

Wiimote and Nunchuk (left), Classic controller (above), and Wii U (right)

Sony Computer Entertainment America

PlayStation 3 Controller (above) and Move motion controller (right)

Reprinted with permission from Microsoft Corporation

XBox 360 Transforming Controller (left) and Kinect motion sensor (above)

::::: Motion-Sensing: A Console Controller Revolution?

In Chapters 1 and 2, you learned about the fusion of remote control and motion-sensing technology—allowing players to control actions in the game through physical movement. Nintendo started this "motion-sensing revolution" through the launch of the Wii in 2006. The remaining "Big Three" hardware manufacturers eventually launched their own motion-sensing systems in 2010: Microsoft's Kinect and Sony's Move. What type of game might be ideal for these types of physical interfaces (or in the case of the Kinect, lack thereof)?

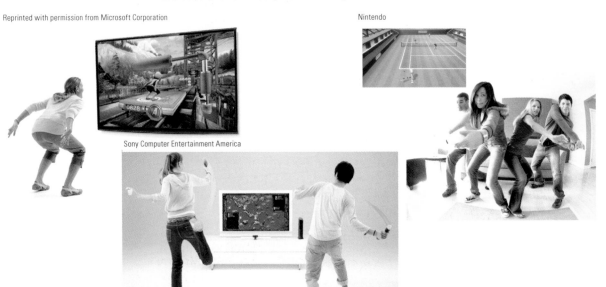

Reprinted with permission from Microsoft Corporation

Nintendo

Sony Computer Entertainment America

Microsoft's Kinect (left), Nintendo's Wii (right), and Sony's Move (bottom) are all motion-sensing systems.

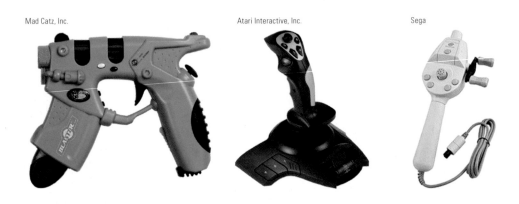

Mad Catz, Inc.

Atari Interactive, Inc.

Sega

Physical controllers can come in many shapes (Mad Blaster, left; joystick, center; fishing rod from *Bass Fishing*, right).

More complex input is required in other genres (such as RPGs, RTSs, and adventure games). The *point-and-click* interface style came out of computer platform necessity. RTS games are well-suited to a keyboard-mouse interface and have not yet been well-adapted to a console control scheme. In a computer RTS, a player drags a selection box over several units to select them. This has traditionally been awkward on a console system. However, a selection convention has been developed (initially popularized in Shigero Miyamoto's *Pikmin*) that allows players to press or hold a button to make a selection box larger. *Goblin Commander* and *The Lord of the Rings: The Battle for Middle-Earth II* are RTS games that have been successful on console systems. Online multiplayer games played through console systems often make use of a headset with microphone—a physical interface that is growing in popularity.

Interface Design for Consoles vs. Computers

The controller is one factor (without a mouse and keyboard, you have to be careful about the options and navigation through options in a console game), and screen resolution is another (you have to be careful about color usage and resolution—what looks great on a PC isn't going to hold true for what you see on a TV). Otherwise, the general interface rules apply: try to make it unobtrusive, keep the steps to select similar options logical and consistent throughout, try to provide the player with customizable controller options, and try to make sure it doesn't take more than a little d-pad [directional pad] switching or one or two button presses to get to what you need.

—Chris Avellone (Chief Creative Officer & Co-Owner, Obsidian Entertainment)

Handheld

Many *handheld* systems are like miniature console systems that contain their own screens and also have their own built-in specialized controllers. Although mobile devices such as smartphones (discussed in the next section) are also considered handheld devices, the initial definition of "handheld" in the game industry was "handheld console"—in essence, a miniature version of a console system. As such, handheld systems such as the 3DS and PS Vita are single-purpose—reserved only for games.

Nintendo

Sony Computer Entertainment America

Interface design handheld systems such as the PS Vita (left) and 3DS (right) pose certain challenges.

Mobile

Multipurpose mobile devices consist of two sub-categories: smartphones such as the iPhone and Android-based systems—and tablets (which emerged out of smartphone development), such as the iPad and Galaxy Tab. Like handheld game systems, mobile devices contain their own screens and controllers—although the latter may double as physical interface elements associated with non-game uses (e.g., entering phone numbers, texting, web browsing).

Apple

Samsung

Apple

Samsung

Mobile devices include smartphones (Galaxy S2, upper left; iPhone 4, upper right) and tablets (iPad 2, lower left; Galaxy Tab 10.1, lower right).

Visual Interfaces

Visual interfaces are either displayed onscreen at all times, or can be easily accessed by the player through the manual interface. There are two types of visual game interfaces: passive and active.

Active

Players can interact with an *active* interface—usually by clicking items displayed in the interface. This is because these items are meant to be manipulated in some way by the player as part of the gameplay process. One type of active interface includes a *menu system*, which is usually easily accessible throughout the game—even if it isn't always visible. A menu system often contains items that allow the player to make general decisions related to the game, including:

Sony Onine Entertainment

Active in-game interface from *Free Realms*.

- ■ Start a new game and reset
- ■ Save the game
- ■ Play a saved game
- ■ Access a tutorial
- ■ Configure the game
- ■ Navigate the game
- ■ Customize their character
- ■ Choose a player mode (such as single or multiplayer)
- ■ Get help/customer support

Another common active interface is the *action* (also known as communication or interaction) system, which contains player choices related to gameplay. The *action* interface accepts player input (or commands) and is related to the extent of player control available in the game. Choices available in this interface all contain action words (such as attack, talk, or retrieve), which allow the player to engage in combat, exploration, communication, and other gameplay elements (discussed in Chapter 6). Some action interfaces, such as in *The Sims Online,* are *radial*—appearing around the character or target object. Since many of these actions are related to movement, some of them are handled by the physical interface. The primary purpose of an active interface is to allow for *player control.* An active interface's control scheme might consist of selection buttons, action buttons, text input, and scroll bars.

Passive

Players cannot interact with the items displayed in a *passive* interface. This is because the items are unchangeable and cannot be directly manipulated by the player without compromising gameplay. This interface displays the player's (or character's) *status*—such as score, lives, energy, time remaining, or strength. This information could be displayed in one area of the screen, or the items could be spread out across the screen. For example, arcade games often display status items such as the score, lives, and time remaining in different areas of the screen (usually in separate corners).

Onscreen interfaces include *heads-up displays (HUDs),* which overlay the interface onto the entire game action screen—and *wrappers,* which display the interface in a smaller area of the screen (usually in the corner). *Return to Castle Wolfenstein* utilizes a HUD that provides information on the player's power, ammunition, compass, and health at all times. When the voice command menu is accessed, it appears as a wrapper in a small box at the corner of the screen. Sometimes the status menu is not displayed on the main screen, often due to space considerations. Instead, the information is accessed through a menu or submenu. The primary purpose of a passive interface is to inform or provide *feedback* to the player. A passive interface's feedback scheme might consist of information that the player needs to play, understand, and enjoy the game—such as player status (location, health), abilities, and goals.

Capcom Starwraith

Street Fighter IV (left) utilizes a wrapper interface, while *Evochron Legemds* (right) has a heads-up display.

Testing Gameplay Through Interface Design

Interface design is an excellent proving ground for gameplay features. After you have an idea for a new feature (or an improvement upon an existing one), consider how the interface will work. If you can't come up with a seamless interface, you should seriously consider abandoning or redesigning the feature.

—*Kevin D. Saunders*
(Creative Director, Alelo)

Platform-Specific Features

Interestingly, a visual interface is tied to a game's hardware platform. Here are just a few guidelines for incorporating platform-specific features into a visual interface:

Arcade

Visual interfaces for *arcade* games are generally simple—partially because these games are designed for quick play (maximizing the amount of quarters that are deposited into the game). Usually an arcade game contains an instruction screen—followed by a series of in-game screens that often contain passive interface displays. Therefore, it isn't surprising that early arcade games such as *Pac-Man* and *Donkey Kong* never contained active interfaces—but only passive displays showing lives remaining, score, and time remaining in the game.

Computer

Visual interfaces for *computers* range from heads-up displays (HUDs) to a series of menu systems that can be accessed by clicking buttons using a mouse or accessing menus using the keyboard. Some games employ a point-and-click style, where players click various objects to access them. As discussed in Chapter 2, LAN-based games (using a local area network) allow a number of players to hide information from one another—since players do not share a screen. Interface design for smaller screen sizes really comes into play for netbooks—which contain much smaller screens than the more traditional desktop PCs. (Netbook screen sizes range from below 5 inches diagonal to 12 inches—compared to up to around 24 inches for a desktop and up to 17 inches for a laptop.)

Console

Visual interfaces associated with most *console* systems are tied to the way these games are played. Initially similar to the computer platform, many console games provided a combination of visual displays and active menu systems. However, as discussed in Chapter 2, local console play involves 2-4 players sharing the same screen. This means that no "hidden" information can be displayed to particular players. In contrast, a multiplayer computer game interface could reveal information to a player that might be unavailable to an opponent. This concept is readily seen in traditional card games—where players don't share what's in each other's hands. Another feature of visual console interfaces is that many players like to hook up their systems to very large television screens. It's not as common for consumers to purchase large computer screens (such as cinematic displays)—partially because of the focus on computers as multi-purpose (business as well as entertainment) devices, rather than the single-purpose (games only) emphasis of console systems.

The possibility of a very large screen often affects the design of console games in terms of scale and detail—although the resolution of a computer screen is higher than that of a television monitor! Visual interfaces for the Xbox 360 and PS3 consist of the "dashboard" and the XMB (XrossMediaBar; pronounced "cross media bar"), respectively. (It should be noted that character creation in the form of user avatars is an integral part of the Xbox 360 dashboard interface. Character creation as a game interface element is discussed in the "Components" section.)

Handheld

The key feature of *handheld* systems is that the screen size is much, much smaller than that of consoles or even computers. This size drastically affects the way player interfaces are designed for these platforms. Visual interface components that might normally be displayed at the bottom of the screen, for example, will often be accessed through a series of menus. All handhelds within the Nintendo DS "family" (including the DSi and 3DS) have dual-screen displays—allowing for twice the amount of room. Some designers utilize one screen for the game's interface. Others use two screens for dual perspectives (such as simultaneous first- and third-person) and game views (such as simultaneous overall and close-up displays—macro and micro). Creating interfaces for handheld devices can be challenging—especially for designers who are used to the various "freedoms" associated with console and computer systems. The obvious challenge is the reduced screen size associated with handheld devices—but there are also issues related to the variety of input (stylus point, button click, touch, voice, tilt) and information (visual, auditory, vibration) modalities, portability, real-world environmental conditions (light, glare), touch accuracy, and color contrast.

Mobile

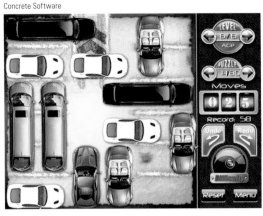

Concrete Software

Interface design for smaller screens constrains design choices (*Aces Traffic Pack* for iPhone, shown).

Like handheld devices and netbooks, mobile devices such as smartphones and tablets have reduced screen sizes compared to desktop computers and console systems (which are often connected to large-screen living room televisions). The original iPad screen size is 9.7 inches, and the original iPhone screen size is 3.5 inches. Unlike early cell phones, today's mobile devices are taking on the functionality of computers—and game applications are playing a large part in this transformation. All of the interface design challenges mentioned in the handheld section apply here—with the addition of addressing the "on-the-go," multitasking nature of mobile device users.

::::: "Auto" 3DS

Normal stereoscopy (*Half-Life*, above) vs. Nintendo 3DS's autostereoscopy (*The Sims 3 for 3DS*, right).

The Nintendo 3DS produces 3D effects without the use of accessories or add-ons. The handheld device uses autostereoscopy or Auto 3D (top screen only) to create the illusion of depth by presenting two offset images separately to the left and right eye of the viewer. Both of these 2D offset images are then combined in the brain to give the perception of 3D depth. Unlike stereoscopy, which requires the viewer to wear eyeglasses to combine the images, autostereoscopy occurs "automatically." In the case of the 3DS, the "3D" screen is capable of movement parallax—where the movement of a scene changes with the movement of the head. Unlike self-contained systems such as handheld devices, consoles are dependent on the user's display (often a television screen) for any 3D game experience.

Online

When games are played *online*—whether the hardware consists of a computer or a console system—player interfaces are affected by how many people are playing a game simultaneously. Interfaces for single-player online games are often identical to those created for the associated hardware platforms. In massively multiplayer online games (MMOs), in which player characters often interact with each other by forming teams (or guilds), it becomes necessary for the interfaces to allow players to access information associated with each member of the team. These interfaces should also enable communication between players (often involving chat windows or discussion boards—whether private or public). Games played on social networks such as Facebook usually exhibit interface elements representing a player's friends who might also be playing the game.

Blizzard Entertainment

Interface design components in *World of Warcraft* are extensive, yet they do not detract from the game's immersive experience.

Components

There are several components used in the visual interface of a game, regardless of whether the interface is active or passive. These components consist of either *information* that players access or *actions* that the players must take to complete tasks during the game. Here are just a few examples of some widely used visual interface components:

Score

The *score* is a numeric indicator that measures the player's success in the game. A high-score indicator keeps track of past scores and gives players a standard by which to measure themselves. This is the simplest of all basic score indicators and can be shown onscreen at all times, especially if score is a primary concern in the game.

Some games might display scores only after a player completes a section of a game—such as a mission in a strategy game. At that point, the game might reveal whether the player not only attained a particular numerical score, but a grade. At the end of

Omniverse Games

A score display is a common visual interface element (*Beach Volleyball Online*, shown).

each mission in *Advance Wars*, players discover whether they received a traditional letter grade (such as an A, B or C) or a "superior" grade (designated by S)—which is even better than an A! This display appears onscreen after the end of a mission—but it does not appear onscreen as a passive display while the game is being played.

Many games do not rely on ongoing scoring to assess how a player is doing. Instead, players can access their "score" based on where they've been able to go in the game environment, the number of levels they've been able to access, and how many obstacles they've been able to overcome.

Lives & Power

Lives remaining used to be shown with the score indicator. It reflects how many chances a player has remaining—often visualized in a number of mini-icons (usually representing the player's avatar) or a numerical display. Current games often do away with the remaining lives display and allow players to re-spawn (come back to life) infinitely. If a player can save the game at any point, the concept of "remaining lives" is no longer relevant. (Issues related to saving the game are discussed later in this chapter.) Often, lives remaining displays indicate both the number of lives (represented by a number—such as 3) and a graphical representation (such as three stick figures representing the player character). Early arcade games often displayed "lives remaining" to the player onscreen at all times. This is essential information needed by players to assess their status in the game. It also provides a feeling of how much time might be left in the game if the player goes along at the same pace (and doesn't necessarily improve their skill levels).

Lives remaining (red dots) and percentage damage taken in *Super Smash Bros. Brawl* (above), and health meters in *Tekken 6* (below).

A related component, known as the *power* (or health) bar indicator, is used in many games. This indicator consists of a horizontal bar colored in full. A power bar might appear in a corner of the screen, showing how much power the player has left. This bar is usually color coded as well as spatial—illustrated in the form of a bar with "0" on the left and "100" (as a percentage) on the right. If a player has full power, the bar will be full of color. As power depletes, the color drains from right to left—like a thermometer—down toward "0." Sometimes a "happy" color such as yellow is used toward the right. As the power decreases, the color might darken—becoming red when the player is in danger of losing all power. The player then has only one life (that can be re-spawned), but a limited amount of power. Once the color has drained from the bar, the player dies. Some simulation games use dials—a variation on the power bar—or bubbles (as in *Diablo* and *Dungeon Siege*).

Sega

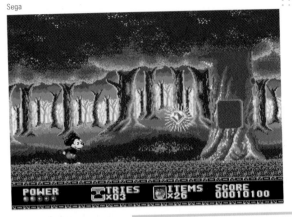

:::::: "Tries" in *Castle of Illusion*

The idea of a player character "dying" (or having more than one "life") might be disturbing to children. Several game companies have come up with alternatives to "lives" in order to address this issue. Disney in particular has been a vigorous proponent of replacing "lives" with "tries" in many of its games—such as the 1990 Sega release, *Castle of Illusion Starring Mickey Mouse.*

Map

For players to get a larger view of the game world and find their way around it, a map is often necessary. Many strategy games—such as the *Civilization* and *The Age of Empires* series—display a map as part of the game interface located at the bottom of the screen. A game map allows for macro and micro views of the game. In a macro view, a player is able to oversee all aspects of the game world, while a micro view of the game involves a close-up of one tiny portion of the map.

D3Publisher   TurnOut Ventures

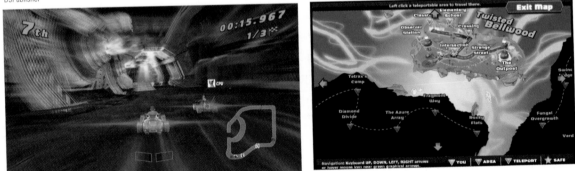

Maps can be effective interface elements, whether they appear passively outside the game's "playing field" (*Ben 10 Galactic Racing*, left) or are accessed actively as their own menu systems (*Ben 10 Omniverse*, right).

Usually, this closer micro view is displayed onscreen in the main game area—while a macro view is displayed as part of the interface. However, some games allow a player to toggle between the macro and micro view during the game. This option might be necessary to see what might be happening in far-off areas of the game world and to help players answer questions, such as, "What if a natural disaster or an enemy's troops are heading in my direction?"

Character

A *character creation* interface can sometimes be a highly complex series of screens that allow players to create and customize their own characters. Everything from physical appearance (including clothing, hair/eye/skin color, gender, ethnicity, height, and body type), sound of voice, personality, accessories, race, class, and even history/biography can be selected and combined through this interface. This type of selection is most popular among games that involve a lot of character advancement, such as RPGs. Usually accessed during the initial setup of the game, this interface might also be available at any point during the course of the game—allowing the players to go back to the interface during play and modify characteristics as needed.

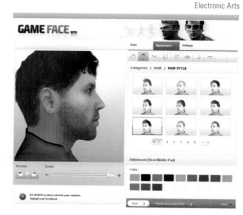

EA Gameface (in several EA Sports games) even allows you to start from a photo of your own face.

Player characters often have a certain set of *skills and attributes* that are either intrinsic to the type of character selected or that can be attained during the course of a game. This sort of information is essential for games that involve character advancement—such as RPGs. Skill and attribute information is provided during the character selection or customization process—but it can also be accessed throughout the game. Since the amount of skills and attributes can sometimes be extensive, a full-screen window might need to be accessed through the manual interface for players to see the amount. Constantly displaying this sort of information onscreen as the game is played can cause the game to look cluttered. Therefore, some games have an action button in a corner or at the bottom of the screen that triggers a skill and attribute display.

Associated with a player character, *inventory* is also an important game interface component. It helps players keep track of the items that are available to their characters, especially in games that involve collecting and gathering items (such as adventure games and RPGs). Some of these items might be weapons that can be used only in certain circumstances or spells that need to be cast at certain points in the game. The ability to manage this inventory and keep track of what items are available to the player character greatly helps the player make certain decisions during the game. The inventory might be part of a screen that contains other character information (such as skills and attributes). It could even stand on its own. In either case, a player character's inventory often needs space to be displayed. Therefore, it often will need to be accessed through a menu or a physical interface—just like a skills and attributes display.

Nexon

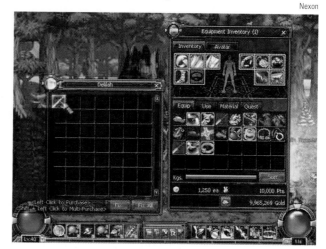

Player character inventory interface from *Dungeon Fighter Online*.

Start Screen

Early arcade games often employed *start screens* that would contain the title of the game, credits, instructions, and the ability to choose player mode (usually one or two players). Similar screens are used in online puzzle and other quick, action-oriented games. Other more extensive games might either use a simplified start screen that contains a high-end graphic representation of the game (often an exact replica of the game's box art) with just a start button—or a more detailed screen containing a menu of buttons with some of the following functions:

- Play Game
- Multiplayer Mode
- Setup
- Load Saved Game
- Select Character
- Instructions
- Tutorial
- Quit

Sega

The *Football Manager Handheld 2010* start screen utilizes a simple interface consisting primarily of five options on the left.

Depending on how the game is designed, the start screen can provide an introduction to the mood and style of the game in addition to the player interface. It can also allow players to customize controls and get help before starting or resuming play.

Genre-Specific Features

Most current game genres have very specific content structures and expected interface styles. What distinguishes these interface styles? What purpose do they serve? To understand why certain interface styles are used with particular genres, it's important to analyze the gameplay goals associated with each genre. Let's look at some popular game genres covered in Chapter 3 and discuss interface elements that are often associated with each.

Codemasters

Heads-up displays (HUDs) are common in action games such as *Colin McRae: DiRT 2.*

Action

Since *action* games are fast-paced—requiring eye-hand coordination, reflexive movement, and quick decision making—players don't have time to interact with a complex interface. Passive heads-up displays (HUDs) are best; players cannot pause the game to open a set of menus. A status panel—one of the most straightforward passive interface displays—allows players to check status indicators (lives, energy, time remaining, score) associated with their characters throughout the game.

Adventure

More than most other genres, *adventure* games try to hide the fact that the player is using hardware to navigate the environment. Player goals include moving through the world, communicating with other characters, and collecting objects in a way that will not interfere with the sense of immersion. Navigating adventure games is often accomplished through *point-and-click* or *direct control* interfaces. In a point-and-click interface, the player clicks somewhere on the screen, causing the player's avatar to move to that location. In a direct control interface, the player steers the avatar around the screen. Inventory is often shown as a pop-up box containing icons representing all items the player is carrying.

In adventure games such as *Heavy Rain,* character movement is controlled through a point-and-click interface.

Role-Playing

A *role-playing game (RPG)* interface is often split into three segments—character management, navigation control, and inventory. The range of actions a player can take in an RPG is often much greater than in any other form of game. There is a corresponding increase in the complexity of the interface for this reason. To compensate, the manual interface is often more involved.

The interface for role-playing games such as *EverQuest II* involves character-specific components—such as character management, inventory, and communication.

Simulation

Since all *simulation* games depend on real-world rules, how can an interface be designed so that this reality isn't disrupted? The most straightforward way to establish a seamless interface is to replicate the controls that might actually be used in a simulation. This is done most effectively in vehicle sims—especially flight simulators. Visual interfaces range from those that might include an instrument panel consisting of just a few buttons (providing altitude, speed, power, fuel, coordinates) to a more complex panel that could perform over 40 different functions! These panels often have the look and feel of the controls you might actually see in a cockpit.

Simulation games require realistic interface components, such as the cockpit controls for *Wings of Prey.*

Sports

In most genres, the interface design changes only in response to explicit actions taken by the player. However, *sports* games are unusual in that the user interface often changes by the second—depending on the conditions in the game. The most difficult aspect of sports game interface design is that it's necessary to map athletic activities (such as jumping) onto a game's input device—which might be anything

Electronic Arts

from a handheld controller with buttons to motion-sensing technology (Wii, Move, Kinect). In team sports games, the player will often control one athlete at a time—indicated by a circle or star displayed right under the athlete. Symbols might also appear on the field to help the player see exactly where a flying ball should land. Players should be able to see which athlete will be in control at any time. In this way, team sports game interfaces are similar to those of many strategy games—where players might control a set of military troops, each of whom might have different skills.

Interfaces for team sports games such as *FIFA Soccer 10* allow players to control one athlete at a time (indicated by the inverted red triangle above the player).

Strategy

Most *strategy* games involve themes of conquest, exploration, and trade. The primary player strategy in these games is resource management, where the player must make decisions involving acquiring, building, expending, and exchanging resources such as food, weapons, buildings, and units (often military troops). Interfaces for these games are extremely specific. In fact, sometimes it's difficult to differentiate

Sega

between strategy games by looking at isolated screenshots. The game view is often large-scale—displaying a landscape with terrain, structures, vehicles, and units.

Data in strategy game interfaces are presented in windows—often containing a map and a series of icons that link to more in-depth information. Since this genre focuses so heavily on managing a great deal of information, it's important to divide the information up so that players don't have to look at everything at once onscreen. One way to do this is to provide context-sensitive information that appears only when needed. Another helpful consideration is to provide both a beginner and advance mode to facilitate different levels of experience.

Interface design for strategy games such as *Medieval II: Total War Kingdoms* focus on ensuring players can effectively manage resources.

Components of strategy game interfaces include general information (such as a map and statistics related to the condition of the environment [temperature, elevation, population]), and more specific information (such as inventory, skills, and status indicators related to a particular resource or unit).

Genre Interface Restrictions?

Do you think it's necessary to have specific interface elements for each genre? Choose a genre, analyze its interface components, and consider how you might change these elements to better suit players' needs and goals. What interface components would you include in a hybrid genre—or a new genre of your own?

Usability

The primary purpose of the user interface is functionality—not aesthetics. If an interface is functional, it is considered *usable*. The concept of *usability* is a vast area of study in many areas of interactive design, including web development, DVD authoring, and wireless display design. Since games represent the highest form of interactivity, player-centered design must incorporate a high level of usability. The main idea behind designing for usability is to think more like an engineer than an artist. An aesthetically appealing interface is definitely desirable. However, an interface that looks great but is not functional will be useless both to the player and to the developer. The most important function of the interface is to allow the player to *play the game!* An interface is considered dysfunctional when it is:

- **Cryptic:** containing unintuitive controls or obscure graphics due to aesthetic over-enthusiasm
- **Complex:** providing too many options so that a starting point is unclear
- **Simplistic:** limiting player choice by including few components
- **Inconsistent:** confusing players with style and logic clashes between the interface and the game itself, or within different areas of the interface
- **Inefficient:** forcing players to interact too many times with the interface before they get to their destination
- **Cluttered:** taking up too much screen space and obstructing the game content area, or incorporating crowded controls that are physically difficult for some players to use

TS

Tom Sloper
(Producer &
Designer, Sloperama
Productions;
Educator, University of
Southern California)

Tom Sloper got his start in the game industry at Western Technologies designing GCE's 1982 LCD watch games *Game Time* and *Arcade Time*. He went on to design games for the Vectrex, Atari 2600, and other early game systems before moving on to Sega (1984) and Atari (1986) and then Activision (1988). In his career, Tom designed and produced games for most major console platforms from the Atari 7800 on up to the NES, SNES, Genesis, PlayStation, Xbox 360, Dreamcast, and DS, as well as games for PC, Mac, Internet, and IPTV. Most well-known for his work on the *Shanghai* series of mah jong tile-matching games, he produced many action games as well. His credits include *Mechwarrior, Alien vs. Predator, Blast Chamber, Sargon V,* and *Star Trek.* An author and speaker, Tom has contributed to several books on games and the industry (*Secrets of the Game Business, Game Design Perspectives, Introduction to Game Development, Mah Jong Anyone?,* and *The Red Dragon & The West Wind*), and has spoken at GDC, Serious Games Summit, Montreal Game Summit, Korean Games Conference, SIGGRAPH, and the Smithsonian.

Good user interface design is crucial. The game has to be user-friendly, intuitive, and accessible. Interface design extends to most if not all aspects of game design, starting with the title screen and running all the way through to the final game ending. As I read a GDD [*game design document,* discussed in Chapter 11] or playtest the latest build, I look for the following key things:

- ◼ Is it quick and easy to get in and start to play?

- ◼ Is it clear and obvious to the player *what* he or she is supposed to do?

- ◼ Is it clear and intuitive *how* it is supposed to be done?

- ◼ Is all crucial information visible in an intuitive way, or readily and conveniently available?

- ◼ Are there reasonable adjustment options for a wide range of players?

- ◼ Is it easy and intuitive to make option adjustments?

Some game modes may require the user to set up options prior to beginning play. I always look for those options to be minimal and to utilize the latest advances in user interface design. Once I'm in the game itself, I look at the onscreen interface and ask myself, 'Can I tell intuitively what each interface element is after a few minutes of play?' If I keep forgetting which controller button controls which action, I make a note to improve that.

Just this week, I played a new game—one that's currently in the stores. To start playing, I had to input a name. The on-screen keyboard interface took me several frustrating minutes to figure out; I finally found that I had to hit the onscreen right-arrow key to move the cursor to the right before I could enter a new letter. Then I had to sit through an interminable non-bypassable scrolling text intro story. I played the game a little while—then pulled up the in-game menu. I selected "Save and Quit." The next time I loaded the game, I discovered to my dismay that there was no saved game. I had to input my name again and sit through the scrolling intro story text again. These "user-unfriendly" elements would not be tolerated in a game that I design or produce. I would make sure that the on-screen keyboard was no more unfriendly than the average mobile phone's text inputting system. I'd make sure that the story text was bypassable. And I'd make sure that the "Save and Quit" feature actually did let you save— even if you hadn't yet reached a "save point." It's the little unfriendly things like these that can turn a player against a game—even if it's otherwise fun to play.

The key is to allow the player to interact with the game effectively. During the game development process, placeholders are often used in place of visual interfaces so that usability is tested without the distraction of aesthetics. Only later in the development process is the visual look and feel introduced. Consider the example of an aesthetically pleasing user interface that players can't figure out how to use, and contrast it with a boring interface that is simple and easy to use. Which game do you think will be played more often? Which game will ultimately be more successful?

There's a term used among designers, engineers, and programmers known as *elegance*. If a design is efficient, consistent, clear, and functional, it's elegant. Designers are really problem solvers—not beautifiers. (The difference between an artist and a designer is discussed in more detail in Chapter 10.) By connecting the player to the game itself, active interfaces provide problem-solving functions (such as saving the game, accessing a tutorial, and communicating with other players). Of course, interfaces that are both aesthetically pleasing *and* usable give the player the best of both worlds!

Task & Needs Analysis

When designing interface components, it's important to conduct a *task and needs analysis* to determine whether the interface will help fulfill player goals. One aspect of this analysis includes usability testing for frequency. Which tasks will the player need to complete most frequently? What if you designed an interface so that it took three actions to access a character's status screen—but you discovered that players needed to access that screen every time their characters added objects to their inventories? A simple redesign might allow a player to access that same screen with only one action—but you might have assumed that this screen wasn't going to be accessed that frequently. Testing your interface on prospective players or with an in-house testing team (discussed further in Chapter 10) could help you avoid doing major interface redesigns.

The Importance of Usability Testing

Usability testing *means* putting the game in front of target users early to see if they can get through the game. One of the reasons games appeal to such a narrow demographic is because they're inaccessible to most people. Usability testing lets designers see how their audience will deal with the interfaces and gameplay before they've spent much money developing it. Designers learn a lot by putting each game through usability testing and often end up drastically changing their interfaces, control systems, and play mechanics accordingly.

—*Chris Swain (Associate Research Professor, USC School of Cinematic Arts; Director, USC Games Institute)*

Jennifer Estaris on Usability in Games for Children :::::

Sam Tepperman-Gelfant

Jennifer F. Estaris (Senior Game Designer, Nickelodeon Virtual Worlds)

Jennifer Estaris worked in the software and newspaper industries before swerving over to grad school for creative writing, publishing video game-inspired fiction, and then re-swerving over to the game industry—working on casual, children, and massively multiplayer online games (MMOs) for all platforms at studios within Nickelodeon, Majesco, Atari, and Large Animal Games. An avid gamer, Jennifer is a member of the International Game Developers Association (IGDA) and the Academy of Interactive Arts & Sciences (AIAS) story panel—and she still writes game-inspired fiction for Gamasutra, The Escapists, and other fine publications.

Since I primarily develop games for children, and I am no longer a child (though I try to be), usability is of utmost importance. A child is still learning what we take for granted; however, a child is thus open to new experiences and doesn't have the same expectations that older gamers have. For example, as I found out in a usability session when I worked at Nick Jr., children may not associate the mouse and the mouse pointer, nor will they have strong hand-eye coordination. As a result, they'll lose interest in the game, even if it's the ultimate Dora vs Mickey vs Teletubbies vs Big Bird experience -- and some kids will even cry. However, immediate, perceivable consequence works best; they are happy to play with the idea that pushing a button causes something to react. A couple of games where an unknown puppy and turtle reacted to a mouse click, regardless of where the pointer was on the screen, were some of the most popular on the Nick Jr. site.

Matt MacLean on Usability vs. Aesthetics:::::

Matt MacLean wanted to be a game designer since he was five years old and spent his warm summer days hidden indoors playing *Ultima IV* on the Apple IIe. Matt has worked as a designer, writer, and quality assurance lead on *Neverwinter Nights 2, Starchamber, The Lord of The Rings Online Trading Card Game*, as well as the most popular title in the industry: *Unannounced Project*. Matt is presently a designer at Obsidian Entertainment doing systems and level design for a next-gen RPG.

MM

Matt MacLean
(Lead Systems
Designer, Obsidian
Entertainment)

Designers have two (sometimes competing) goals in interface design: immerse the player in the action, and give the player the tools to solve the game. Though these goals compete, the latter goal of usability is always the primary consideration; without the tools, nobody will bother to play the game.

A first-person shooter can have a usable interface that is entirely invisible; every action is accomplished by a controller input and all the game information is handled within the game universe. *Call of Cthulhu: Dark Corners of the Earth* has relatively simple, though by no means boring, first-person shooter gameplay and all information you need to solve the game is done invisibly. Your health is gauged by sound and visual cues (not health meters), there is no mini-map, and all your actions are guided by the Xbox controller. This is a game that immerses you into the action while giving usability in both control and interface. *Call of Cthulhu: Dark Corners of the Earth* has a functional, usable manual interface and all of the game's visual feedback needs are handled with audio and visual cues that blend into the game world.

On the opposite end of the spectrum is *EVE Online*. The gameplay in *EVE* is anything but straightforward and the player must juggle space travel, combat, production, manufacturing, chat, stock market browsing—so many actions that a console controller won't cut it—the game's interface exists onscreen as a dizzying array of icons, spreadsheets, graphs, and drop-down menus. The interface for *EVE* is shockingly intimidating to new players but it has usability in spades—when you figure out what all those buttons do, you can do all manner of tasks very quickly and even customize the settings of your interface to best manage your task at hand. While this interface risks killing the immersion of the game's sci-fi universe (hard to feel like a space ace when you're looking at the daily moving average of ore prices), the game lets you turn off the entire visual interface with a click of a button. Unfortunately, the controls of the game require this interface to be turned on to accomplish most tasks.

Heavy Rain: Effective "Anti-Usability"

Sony Computer Entertainment America

Contrary to general wisdom, some games require thoughtful and careful design of "anti-usability." When done right, a game can leverage its designed lack of usability as an integral part of an immersive and rewarding gameplay experience. Consider *Heavy Rain* for the PlayStation 3. In this interactive drama, the player is often required to hold down four of five buttons simultaneously. The awkward hand positioning is both uncomfortable and physically straining to the player. From a usability perspective, it seems terrible; however, it is highly effective in creating a more immersive gameplay experience in which the player's subtle discomfort mirrors the emotional state of the game character. The game also uses a variety of on-screen icons that float in the environment and indicate which controller actions need to be carried out. When a character is stressed or emotionally affected in some way (e.g., angry, scared), the floating icons shake, shift, and move around. The effect is unsettling because it makes the icons hard to decipher. The challenge faced by the character ('I can't think clearly, what should I do?') is passed on to the player—who can't easily figure out what the available options are, making it more likely that he or she will make a mistake. This is perfectly suited to the dramatic nature of the game, as well as the ethical dilemmas faced by the characters. Due to the careful design that went into the interface's anti-usability, the game is ultimately effective in creating meaningful experiences.

—*Jose P. Zagal (Professor, DePaul University)*

Accessibility

Accessibility is a branch of usability that focuses specifically on users with disabilities. According to the World Health Organization, an estimated 180 million people worldwide have visual impairments alone. Of these, between 40 and 45 million persons are blind. More than 40 years have passed since the first computer game was developed, yet the same player prerequisites are still assumed—full sight, hearing, and cognitive functions. The game industry excludes many (or most) potential gamers who have disabilities. Compare this to the web development industry—which has been in existence only since the mid-1990s and has focused on accessibility for years. The International Game Developers Association (IGDA) has addressed this problem by forming a Game Accessibility Special Interest Group, chaired by Michelle Hinn. There are five main disability categories addressed by accessibility: visual, audio, motor, speech, and cognitive.

Visual

Players with *visual* disabilities are those who are visually impaired, colorblind, or either partially or completely blind. To ensure that an interface addresses players with visual impairments, it must contain code that allows screen readers such as Jaws to read the information displayed on the screen to the player. As an option, games should also provide audio such as voiceover dialogue and sound effects that cue the player to what is happening in the game. Players should also have the option of making the text larger for ease of reading.

Bayonetta's saturated color scheme doesn't include any colors that would confuse a color-blind player—and players are not ever required to differentiate between colors during the game.

It's also necessary for text to be written for *scannability* so that players can read it quickly. Scannable text is concise, direct, free of unnecessary words (such as the articles "a," "an," and "the"), and it contains only those words that are essential to get the point across. Plowing through linear text dialogue and backstory is tedious for anyone! This is one of the inherent issues associated with handheld devices; to address it, keep text options within the player's control. Many Game Boy Advance titles allow players to opt out of the linear dialogue and story by clicking the start button. (This solution would not work for new players, who might need to scroll through the text information to fully understand the game.) Hard copy instruction manuals should also be available in Braille.

Audio

Players with *audio* disabilities include those who are partially or completely deaf, along with those who have hearing conditions such as *tinnitus*—which results in constant ringing in the ears and is common among concert-goers, performers, and others who regularly listen to loud noises for extended periods of time. (William Shatner and Pete Townshend are two well-known performers who have this ailment.) Audio disabilities can be addressed by *not* relying on audio as a primary gameplay cue. Subtitles and text should be provided for cut-scenes and dialogue. Visual elements for game notices and alerts help all players.

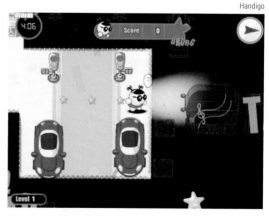

Handigo does not require audio in order to play.

Majesco

Psychonauts allows players who have physical disabilities to play the game using specialized equipment.

Sony Computer Entertainment America

SOCOM: U.S. Navy Seals—a game that focuses on speech as a communication method—allows players the option of communicating by text.

Electronic Arts

The Sims 3 utilizes an icon-based interface, although players may communicate optionally via text.

Motor

Players with some *motor* or *physical* disabilities might have difficulty using a mouse, keyboard, controller, foot pedal, or other input device. Menu systems containing small buttons might be difficult to navigate if a player has difficulty controlling a mouse in a point-and-click interface. A computer interface can allow for tab navigation as an option, avoiding the necessity of mouse clicking.

Speech

Players with *speech* disabilities have difficulty communicating through voice. Since most electronic games are visual, speech disabilities haven't yet become a primary area of accessibility research. However, games such as *SOCOM: U.S. Navy Seals* that require voice communication between players (through headset/microphone input devices) are impossible for those with speech disabilities to play without non-speech options.

Cognitive

Players with *cognitive* disabilities have difficulty with reading, writing, and envisioning spatial relationships. Complicated menu systems with several layers should be avoided to address this type of disability. Simple sentence structure and vocabulary should also be used to avoid the possibility of players misunderstanding the rules of the game. Many online multiplayer games require players to communicate with each other via chat or IM-style windows. This can pose a problem for some players, who don't feel comfortable with text communication due to cognitive disabilities such as *dyslexia*—a common condition that could cause a player to spend extra time creating correctly formulated words and sentences. Games that require time-dependent text responses would be inappropriate and unfair for these players.

Internationalization

Games that are *internationalized* attempt to be usable for players worldwide, without having to develop language-based versions. (In localization—which was discussed in Chapter 2 and will be covered again in Chapter 11—versions of a game are developed to address specific languages and cultures.) Internationalization involves techniques such as making menu buttons icon-based rather than text-based. The visual icon can be interpreted and understood much faster than the equivalent text. Buttons should specifically display universal symbols (including those that have become interface standards, such as the question mark to represent "help") to avoid misunderstandings that might result from the use of culture-specific icons, symbols, puns, and phrases. When time zones, measurements, and currency must be specified, they should not be biased toward a particular region (e.g., Pacific Time) or country (e.g., U.S. non-metric system).

Virginia Hetrick on Accessibility in Serious Games :::::

Dr. Virginia Hetrick holds three academic degrees in geography. After serving for 37 years as a faculty member in higher education and computer professional, Virginia is currently a consultant focusing on service-oriented architecture and programming for a geography game that will accept customized instructor-generated questions.

VH

Virginia R. Hetrick, PhD
(Game Architecture
& Programming
Consultant)

I find that most games are not created with accessibility in mind. I work with a lot of pediatric patients who have limited use of various parts of their bodies—and nearly always, they're hooked on a game just watching other kids play it—but when they are encouraged to try it themselves, we run into the accessibility issue. Thus far, contacting major game development companies has not led to any successes in getting accessible capabilities added to these games. The game I'm currently working on allows voice controls on a computer equipped with Dragon Naturally Speaking as well as keyboard and mouse input. Since most of these are installed in hospital pediatric areas, the DNS is on all systems just as a matter of course—so I'm not as concerned with computer capability issues in this case.

MB

Mark C. Barlet
(President &
Co-Founder,
AbleGamers
Foundation)

With over 18 years of software development experience and becoming disabled while serving active duty in the United States Air Force, Mark Barlet used the challenges his childhood friend was having with games after being diagnosised with multiple sclerosis as a catalyst for a quest to change the world. Eight years into the AbleGamers Foundations mission, Mark is pleased to have helped create a new way of thinking for content producers—who are now seeing game accessibility as something significant to think about. With nearly one in five people in the United States disabled, game developers are hard-pressed to ignore the need for game accessibility in their titles.

While there is no magic bullet that says do XY and Z and your game will be fully accessible, there are a few things that you should include in every title to give a person with disabilities the best chance to have fun, and to enjoy the fruits of your labor. Here are three things developers should do today:

- **Button remapped ability:** While this used to be commonplace, button remapped ability is often a feature that is now being left out as the schedule gets compressed, and the company executives are pushing you to get the title out the door. The absence of this feature, more often than not, will make your title out of reach to many people with physical disabilities. Why? The reason is simple: Have you seen a modern console controller? It's an 8" x 5" hunk of plastic that is almost completely surrounded on all sides in buttons. For most fully able-bodied people, the modern console controller can be a bit intimidating. For a person with disabilities, its form factor makes it almost impossible to use. To solve this problem, many people with disabilities employ specially modified controllers that allow them to remove the buttons from the confines of the controller and place them in a more accessible position. For this strategy to be truly effective, the ability to remap controls within the game is imperative.

- **Closed captioning vs. true captioning:** Closed captioning is pretty standard in most games today. This is great for gamers with hearing impairments, or for other reasons (e.g., sleeping baby in the other room) in which a player wouldn't be able to enjoy the game with the sound on. The basic closed captioning does not make a game fully accessible to those who are deaf. In order to do this, you really need to employ true captioning. What is true captioning? It is very similar to the standard closed captioning with the addition of Horton sound effects that affect the gameplay. For example;

[You hear a creek in the floor to your left]

Cindy: Did you hear that?

Simply adding this important sound effect to the caption stream will provide gamers with a hearing impairment a clue about what might about to happen, an increase in the ability to immerse themselves in the story, and the capacity to enjoy your hard work the way you truly intended for it to be enjoyed.

- **Colorblindness:** One of the most common visual disabilities out there, affecting as many as one in seven men, is colorblindness – and almost all of them (97%) are red-green colorblind. This is one of the most overlooked features in any game, which is shocking given that our work at the AbleGamers Foundation has allowed us to interact with countless developers (themselves colorblind) working on games that do not take this common disability into account. The strategy for adding colorblind accessibility couldn't be easier: Simply make sure that if you're going to use color as an indicator/ status/state, be sure to include a symbol to go along with it. An example of this is the addition of plus (+) or minus (-) signs over a monster that you are "conning," along with a red or green color indicator.

Gogan the Disturbed +++

A Field Rat ---

While these are no means the only things you should do to ensure game accessibility, these will allow far more people with disabilities to enjoy your title than they otherwise would. It is my hope that they also start getting you to think about other ways you could make your title accessible – considering that there are 60 million people with disabilities in the U.S. alone. If you'd like to go a little deeper, please check out our developer resource kit at *www.gameaccessibility.org*.

Robert Florio on Accessible Interfaces :::::

Robert Florio
(artist)

In 1996, when Robert Florio was only 14 years old, he injured his spinal cord while diving. After the accident, Robert decided to focus on pursuing his dream of becoming a game designer. Robert is a quadriplegic and creates all of his artwork with his mouth using a tool known as a mouth stick. Game accessibility to him means "finally gaining control over a world I no longer can interact with and reconnecting my senses to those actions." Robert is now 25 years old and lives in Maryland. He is working on obtaining his Bachelor of Arts degree in Game Art & Design from the Art Institute Online. He also is learning to create his own games from home. Robert feels that many players who cannot physically function to play these games are at a disadvantage—and he hopes to bridge the gap between players of different abilities by creating his own company and influencing the structure of games. Robert now works together with the International Game Developers Association Game Accessibility Special Interest Group. Together, they research and coordinate sessions at the Game Developers Conference (GDC).

The most accessible games I've played allow the rearranging of all moves, special button selections, and combos of buttons in one—all in the game options menu. Making everything much more simple not only makes it easier for me to play, but it also simplifies games for others to enjoy. So many games on the market are becoming more complicated in design—especially with regard to the design of player interaction with the controller and the environment.

Robert Florio playing *Tomb Raider: Legends* with the QuadControl mouthstick.

Game interfaces will eventually be even more interactive—with the senses implemented into the game control and environment. For example, I could use my mouth (by breathing in and out), chin, or bottom lip for certain functions. There could possibly be "mind control" through computer chips for those with complete quadriplegia. I would love to see the day where I could get a physical workout while playing a video game specifically tuned to my needs and function as a quadriplegic.

Save-Game Options

The various *save-game options* available to a game developer bring up a balance issue between *immersion* and *player control* (discussed in Chapters 5 and 6). An active in-game interface often includes a "save" menu item, which can effectively take the player out of the game and compromise the game's immersiveness. In contrast, a game could be automatically saved at different *checkpoints* (or milestones) during the game. Although this save-game option is seamless and does not take the player out of the game, it compromises player control. Game developers have debated which of these concepts might be more important to the player or to the game itself—and the answer usually depends on the game's genre and platform. Let's take a closer look at some save-game options and apply them to different types of games.

Quick-Save

In action games where the player's avatar is in constant danger (such as an FPS), the player can often *quick-save* by pressing one button on a manual interface to save instantly at any time during the game—without ever leaving the game world. In this case, no visual interface exists except for the possibility of a confirmation (the word "saved") being displayed onscreen for a moment—but this does not break the player's concentration and immersion. The disadvantage of this method is that it contains only one save slot. Sometimes, there are several additional slots available—but the player must remember to designate these after pressing the quick-save button. This also takes up extra time, which might be detrimental to gameplay during a fast-moving game. This save option allows for more immersiveness and speed at the expense of flexibility and player control.

Take=Two Interactive

When playing *Prey*, players can quick-save with a single keystroke or button press.

Auto-Save

The *auto-save* (also known as *check-point save*) option offers the most immersion and the least amount of player control. The game auto-saves as it progresses, allowing the player to leave and return at any time without explicitly having to save the game. Auto-saves can be continuous, but they more often take place at certain *checkpoints* in the game. These checkpoints are not necessarily revealed to the player—which can prevent the player from undoing earlier mistakes. However, the player is able to interrupt and resume the game at any point. Action games featuring rewind—such as *Prince of Persia: The Sands of Time* and *Braid*—allow the player to undo one action. It's very common to have a limited number of profiles stored on consoles and have the game auto-save to those profiles after a particular mission has been completed. This trend is increasing, since online gaming through console systems depends heavily on profiles.

Hothead Games

Braid uses the auto-save model—allowing for more immersion but less player control.

Save to Slot or File

Some games allow the player to interrupt play and save the game to a series of named *slots* (console or handheld) or a *file* (computer) maintained by the game. In this case, a "save" item is usually included on an in-game active interface so that the player can conveniently access this option at any time during the game. The player can save either a limited or infinite (only limited by the player's hard drive space) number of games at various points during play, and provide them with distinct names. This method of saving the game is considered the most harmful to a game's immersiveness. The interface for managing files or save slots often looks like a file management system. This can be made more visually interesting, but it will still take the player out of the game unless it is somehow integrated into the experience itself.

Electronic Arts

In *Mass Effect 2*, players interrupt game play to save the game in one of a series of slots.

To create a great game interface, keep the following guidelines in mind:

- Be consistent.

- Enable shortcuts (as options for hardcore players).

- Provide feedback.

- Offer defined tasks.

- Permit easy reversal of actions.

- Allow for player control.

- Keep it simple (and don't strain the player's short-term memory).

- Make it customizable (and allow the player to configure the interface somewhat).

- Include a context-sensitive pointer (that changes form when pointing to an object of interest).

- Implement different modes (including beginner and expert).

- Use established conventions (avoid trying to invent your own).

The "Save-Game" Debate

There is a debate among developers concerning whether or not to allow players the freedom to save the game at chosen intervals. The debate centers around how gameplay might be affected by saving the game. Developers of some puzzle games are often against the idea because they feel that the player should solve the game by skill rather than trial-and-error. Saving and reloading can also defeat the purpose of an uninterrupted action sequence. When players can save and reload at any point, some argue that nothing is really at stake in the game. What if a player's avatar dies or loses resources? Any disaster can be reversed simply by reloading the game. This definitely takes away much of the challenge!

On the other hand, some argue that making a game harder simply by preventing the player from saving the game is not an ideal way to create a challenge. It most certainly does not show respect for the player. For a more challenging game, create more difficult gameplay challenges! Forcing a player to replay a level or entire game due to a mistake made near the end wastes a player's time and condemns the player to frustration and boredom. This must be avoided—not created.

One compromise solution is to allow the player to save at any time but to somehow reward the player for not saving. *Alpha Centauri* includes an Iron Man mode. A game played in Iron Man would close automatically when saved, thereby making the save-load process an ineffective way to undo a serious mistake. As compensation, the player's final score is doubled when playing in this mode. Some games—such as *Halo*—reward players for completing the game without saving at all.

The Player Experience: Interface & Gameplay

Interface design is a specific game development discipline just like level design—and it's also closely tied to gameplay. Consider how physical and visual interfaces provide both feedback and control—allowing the player to make choices throughout the game by interacting with onscreen menus and controllers. The basic elements discussed in Chapters 2 and 3 (platforms and genres) are also closely related to interface design with regard to physical interface design and visual interface standards associated with most genres.

::

In the next chapter, you will learn about how audio can enhance the atmosphere of the game—and how it can work with the game interface to help the player connect to the game. Audio can be considered a type of interface element that can blend visual and tactile elements through a variety of sounds—effects, ambience, musical score, song soundtrack, and even voiceover dialogue.

:::CHAPTER REVIEW EXERCISES:::

1. Using one of your favorite games as an example, discuss ways in which the game's interfaces allow you to feel you have some control during gameplay.

2. There are several unique physical interfaces—such as foot pads, maracas, a microphone, and a fishing pole—that are designed to enhance the game-playing experience. Disregarding the obvious (such as guns for first-person shooters), recommend a unique physical interface that could be used as an alternative physical device for one of your favorite games. If you were asked to create an original physical interface for your own game, what would it be—and how would it make the player's experience of the game more enjoyable?

3. The area of accessibility is gradually being addressed by the game industry. Choose one of the five disabilities discussed in this chapter and come up with a unique way to address the disability in a game interface.

4. Knowing that the save-game debate hasn't been resolved, what type of save-game option would you incorporate into your game—and why? Can you think of a new way of saving the game?

5. How do the components of a game interface work together to make a game usable and functional for the player? Choose a game and analyze its usability features. Suggest at least three improvements to the interface, and create a rough sketch redesigning the interface based on your analysis.

6. Begin a task-and-needs analysis of a game by asking the following questions: What tasks does the visual interface allow the player to accomplish? Do these tasks correspond to gameplay goals? Detail a task-and-needs analysis for your original game idea. Provide a list of five necessary tasks that players must complete to advance in the game. Provide a list of the top five items or actions that players will need to accomplish these tasks during the game. How will your interface address these needs and tasks?

7. Construct a draft interface template for your original game. Define the layout, content, and navigation components of your template.

8. Choose a genre and discuss specific interface design features that correspond to that genre. Add another interface component that has not been discussed in this chapter to address a genre-specific need that might not be immediately obvious.

CHAPTER

9

Audio
creating the atmosphere

Key Chapter Questions

- Why is *audio* an important aspect of game development?

- How are *voiceovers*, *sound effects*, and *music* used effectively in a game?

- What is the difference between *looping* and *adaptive* music?

- What is the distinction between composing for games and movies?

- What are the different *formats* and *tools* used in game audio?

Audio is probably the least appreciated area of game development—and it is often overlooked. This neglect is not unusual; it happens in other industries as well. In a film, final audio is not incorporated until the post-production stage—and it is considered an enhancement rather than a core feature of the project. Game developers often focus heavily on graphics, artificial intelligence, and gameplay, without considering the many functions of audio. Once the importance of game audio is finally realized, it is often too late to make the best use of it. This chapter provides an introduction to game audio (including music, sound, and dialogue)—and how it can be utilized effectively to create a rich game atmosphere.

The Importance of Game Audio

Game audio can range from *sampled* (recorded) sound, such as voices and music; interface sounds such as beeps and button clicks; and in-game effects, such as explosions and footsteps. Audio can be extremely important for a game's atmosphere, setting the mood as well as changing it. Audio can also provide gameplay cues, heighten player satisfaction, and enhance the quality of a game. While graphics will draw a player into a scene, game audio has an immersive effect on the player that can seldom be achieved with graphics alone. This might be partially because real-life sounds can be reproduced on a computer much better than real-life visuals. (Although a digital image of a gorilla pounding on its chest can be striking, contrast this with a well-sampled gorilla's threatening roar.) Since the game's screen is limited in size, players can conceivably be taken out of the game's visual world. In contrast, players can be enveloped by the sounds of a game world—which can exist all around them.

In Chapter 8, you learned about the importance of a game's interface. Audio can also effectively reinforce a player's physical sensations, so it is an essential part of that interface. Even in menu buttons, sound can convey a solid tactile feeling of switches being flipped or buttons being pushed. Accessibility must also be considered as a usability principle with audio interfaces. Since some players have hearing impairments, make sure a visual cue is always given as a complement to an audio cue—or at least have visual cues be a potential option that the player can set. Anytime there is spoken dialogue, subtitles should also be included. Allow players the option of adjusting the game audio volume without affecting the sounds on their machines. Finally, be sure to separate volume controls for dialogue, sound effects, and music.

Great Audio Enhances Gameplay

Great audio makes a game play better. This is true for sound design, music, voiceovers, ambient effects—you name it. Players will know it and feel it instinctively, even if they're not concentrating on the audio. In fact, that's really the point: the audio is there to enhance the gameplay, not draw attention to itself.

— *Jamie Lendino (Composer & Sound Designer, Sound For Games Interactive)*

Russell Burt & John Davies on the Importance of Game Audio :::::

Russell Burt has been living in Los Angeles for 15 years and has worked extensively as a keyboardist, recording engineer, and producer. His recording credits include Warrant, Boney James, the Temptations, Bruce Hornsby, and the Doobie Brothers. Russell has also worked as a sound designer and composer for many audio dramas, including the *Star Wars* audio book series. He has programmed and produced several interactive CD entertainment titles, as well as corporate training projects. Russell now teaches full-time at the Art Institute of California–Los Angeles in the Interactive Design department.

RB

Russell Burt
(sound designer & engineer; Interactive Design Faculty, Art Institute of California– Los Angeles)

The role of audio cannot be overstated in games! As an audio engineer, keyboardist, and sound designer, I am continually amazed at how poorly audio in general is appreciated. A common adage states that people don't pay attention to sound in entertainment unless the sound is bad. Specifically with games, audio needs to be handled subtly, for it creates a mood whether or not the gamer is actively listening. Audio can be used effectively for dialogue, sound effects, and music—but if it's used ineffectively, it can ruin an otherwise great project.

With several years of experience and a string of top 10 titles under his belt, John has spent a career in audio promoting the virtues of creating dynamic and lively soundscapes. Ever the audio evangelist, he has always held that you can't force good audio on people; you have to give them the opportunity to realize that their games simply cannot be without it.

JD

John Davies
(Audio Manager, Codemasters)

If gameplay and graphics are the body of a game, then audio is the soul. A game world, no matter how beautifully rendered and realized, is an inert experience until the audio is included. The right balance of sound effects, music and dialogue are what breathe life into these worlds we play in. Audio has to be done right, though. There's nothing more jarring than when the audio clashes with the game. Audio should blend into the experience. Ambiance should create a sense of life and reality in a game level, music should capture the emotion, and dialogue should give the characters personality.

Game Audio Formats

In the 1980s, game audio was limited by game hardware to simple beeps. Early computer-based audio revolved around *frequency modulation (FM) synthesis,* which uses algorithms to re-create and combine sound waves of different shapes, frequencies, and volumes. Often, these sounds were used to approximate real-world sounds and musical instruments—and the results were less than spectacular.

Diagram by Per Olin

Yamaha Corporation of America

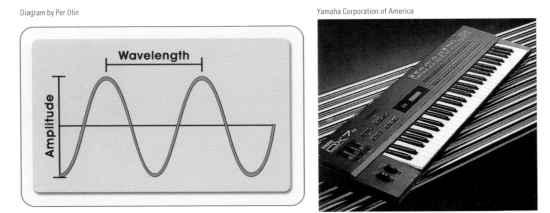

FM synthesis (used by synthesizers such as the DX7) involves generating sounds from mathematical data associated with sound waves.

The MOD (module) music format, popularized by the Amiga, used real samples instead of mathematical approximations. MOD supported four tracks, each of which could be playing one sample at any pitch. Since computers had enough memory to store instrument samples—and enough processing power to manipulate the pitch of those instruments in real-time—MOD was a vast improvement over FM synthesis. This technique was an earlier version of what is now known as *wave table synthesis,* in which the creation of audio relies on a table of sampled sound waves.

Tracked audio followed, with software such as Startrekker, ProTracker, and ScreamTracker (STM). Parallel to the development of FM synth and tracked audio, the *MIDI (musical instrument digital interface)* revolution was also taking shape. Unlike tracked audio (which is a closed, CPU-based system that stores instruments, applies effects, and plays the finished process through one device), MIDI incorporates several different devices that work together to create sound. A MIDI setup might include a drum machine, keyboard, instrument banks, computer, and effects processors—and MIDI allows them all to communicate with one another. MIDI is a sort of networking protocol that specifies how musical notes are stored and transmitted across wires to different devices. Following the advent of MIDI, many performers began using synthesizers (electronic keyboards) to control multiple instruments during live shows. MIDI has been responsible for the development of hardware and computer-based sequencers, which can be used to record, edit, and play back performances.

Instead of generating sounds from mathematical wave data, *samplers* digitized sound from an external audio source (such as an analog musical instrument) at particular pitches and played these sounds back digitally.

In the 1990s, MIDI and tracked audio were the most popular technology approaches to game audio. MIDI files are typically very small because the instruments playing the music were not stored within the files. However, this means that good playback of a MIDI song depends on the quality of the hardware/instruments; game audio would often sound great on a composer's professional setup, but would leave much to be desired on a player's system. Tracked audio was great because the instruments were contained in the audio, which sounded the same regardless of the hardware used to play it—but the audio took up way too much space and CPU power on the player's system.

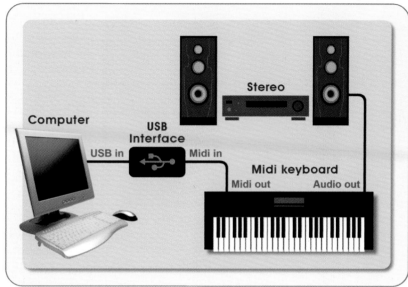

A musical instrument digital interface (MIDI) setup incorporates several different devices that work together to create sound.

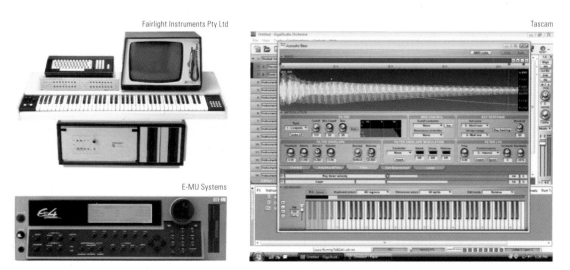

Fairlight Instruments Pty Ltd

Tascam

E-MU Systems

The Fairlight CMI (expensive hardware-based pioneer), Emu E4 (modular unit), and Gigastudio (software) represent three different eras in sampling tools.

Digidesign

Pro Tools 8 is considered to be the industry standard for audio recording, editing, and mixing.

Tracked audio and MIDI eventually merged in 1997 in the form of *DLS1 (Downloadable Sounds Level 1),* which also allowed each instrument to have multiple samples based on frequency. In 1999, *DLS2*, an even better improvement, was introduced, and is supported by Microsoft's DirectMusic.

The audio capabilities of current console systems mark a vast improvement over game audio of the past. The PlayStation 3 uses Dolby TrueHD—an advanced lossless (compression that provides an exact duplicate of the original audio stream) multi-channel audio codec intended primarily for high-definition equipment such as Blu-ray (also included with the PS3). DTS-HD Master Audio bitstreaming, which competes with DolbyTrueHD, is also utilized in the PS3—making the console the clear game audio leader. The Xbox 360 uses Dolby Digital 5.1, and the Wii is Dolby Pro Logic II-capable.

Lennie Moore & Aaron Marks on Game Audio Tools :::::

LM

Lennie Moore
(composer)

For over 20 years, Lennie Moore has been a proven force as an accomplished composer, orchestrator, and arranger of music for games, film, and television. His credits include *Star Wars: The Old Republic*, *The Walking Dead Motion Comic*, *Watchmen Motion Comic* (2009 G.A.N.G. award winner), *Magic: The Gathering – Duels of the Planeswalkers*, *Dirty Harry*, *Dragonshard*, *War of the Ring*, and *Outcast* (2000 nominee for Best Music by the AIAS - Academy of Interactive Arts and Sciences). Lennie has also developed and taught Composing for Video Games courses at USC's Thornton School of Music and UCLA Extension—and he also developed the first accredited degree program for Game Audio and Interactive Media at Pinnacle College.

Currently, I'm using Cubase 5 on a PC, four Gigastudio PCs, dynaudio acoustics surround monitors, East West Quantum Leap Symphony Orchestra Platinum, Project Sam Symphobia, Spectrasonics Stylus RMX/ Trilian/Omnisphere, Ministry of Rock, Pro Tools, Sonic Foundry Sound Forge, and tons of sample libraries such as the Project SAM Brass and Sonic Implants Strings. In addition to straight composing and orchestrating, I'm also very passionate about creating the best adaptive music possible—so I use tools such as Ableton Live and middleware engines such as Audiokinetic Wwise or FMOD to test and deliver incredibly flexible music content.

AM

Aaron Marks is not only an outspoken advocate of great audio in games, but an accomplished composer, sound designer, field recordist, voiceover artist, and owner of On Your Mark Music Productions. Aaron is also the author of *The Complete Guide to Game Audio* and lead author of *Game Audio Development* (part of the *Game Development Essentials* series), on the audio production faculty at the Art Institute of California – San Diego teaching the art of field recording and sound for interactive media. Aaron has music, sound design, field recording, and voiceover credits on over 120 game titles for the Xbox and Xbox 360, PlayStation 2 and 3, Wii, Dreamcast, CD/ DVD-ROM, touch screen arcade games, iPhone/iPad, Class II video slot machines, Class III mechanical and video slot machines, coin op/arcade, online and terminal based video casino games. Through the years, Aaron has written for Game Developer Magazine, Gamasutra.com, Music4Games.net and the Society of Composers and Lyrists. He wrote an accredited college course on game audio for the Art Institute Online, is a member of the AES Technical Committee for Games, was an AES Game Audio Workshop chairman, was on the launch committee for the Game Audio Network Guild (G.A.N.G.), and is a popular guest speaker and lecturer at game related conferences and academic functions.

Aaron Marks (composer & sound designer; President, On Your Mark Music Productions)

It is essential that you have a good audio editing program; you can't do the job without it! My main editor is Sound Forge, but I also use Audition, Wavelab and Goldwave for their unique capabilities. Whether you are doing sound design or composing, taking a final look at the sound will ensure that the file is "healthy" and doesn't have unwanted silence or clipping. Also, a good multi-track audio program such as Vegas Video, SONAR or Nuendo is a nice addition. Having the flexibility to layer various sounds and adjust their parameters separately really adds to the overall sound, and it makes it easy to go back and edit later. The one tool I can't live without is Sound Forge's Batch Converter. All of the sound effects and music are created as at least 8-kHz, 24-bit, stereo .wav files. Since I initially create up to several hundred sound effects and music cues per game, I could easily end up spending an entire day just doing sound conversions if I didn't have this awesome tool!

schedivypictures.com

Jamie Lendino
(Composer & Sound
Designer, Sound For
Games Interactive)

Jamie Lendino is an independent sound designer and music composer with 10 years of experience in the game industry. He has created audio for over 30 games, including *Monopoly: Here & Now*, *SpongeBob's Atlantis SquarePantis: Atlantis Treasures*, *Elder Scrolls IV: Oblivion*, *Zoo Tycoon 2: Endangered Species*, *Mage Knight: Apocalypse*, and the mobile version of *True Crime: New York City*. When he's not creating alien sound effects or working out drum parts for his next composition, he is busy indulging his other passions: writing, reading (both fiction and non-fiction), fast cars, and astronomy.

The introduction of the Adlib and SoundBlaster sound cards in 1989 was highly significant. Between this and the later adoption of the Roland MT-32 sound module (which actually came out a bit earlier in 1987, in pro audio circles), PCs finally sounded like viable gaming machines—not just hulking business desktops that beeped through the PC speaker every so often. Around the same time, we saw the introduction of faster 386 processors and VGA graphics cards—but you can't have real gaming without real audio! Between the CPU, audio, and video innovations that opened up the platform for seriously talented developers at studios such as LucasArts, Origin, and Sierra to jump in and get to work. Soon, the PC catapulted to the front of the pack for computer gaming with titles such as *Wing Commander*, *The Secret of Monkey Island I* and *II*, *Space Quest IV*, and *Kings Quest V*—all of which took special advantage of VGA graphics cards, 386 processors, and a slew of aftermarket sound boards. These innovations in turn led to Windows 95 and DirectX, which helped standardize game development and sealed the PC's place at the top of the heap for over decade. It's only now that the latest round of consoles, with their high-definition 1080p and 5.1-channel surround sound capabilities, can really threaten or (in some cases) surpass PC gaming. But it's really all because of the original PC sound card that this happened.

Sound Effects

Game *sound effects* are used to provide feedback and cues to a player. In a vehicle simulation game, audio representing the RPMs (rotations per minute) of an engine can be used to indicate when a player needs to shift gears. (The engine sound is recorded in different stages with multiple mics: idle, acceleration, deceleration, full throttle. The recordings are used as samples that will be generated in real-time when the game runs.) Audio can also be used to warn a player that an enemy is approaching through the sound of footsteps, heavy breathing, or a muffled roar behind a locked door.

As you read this book, what sounds do you hear around you? In real life, sound is everywhere. Pure silence exists only in artificial environments, such as soundproof chambers. In games, background sounds can be used to help immerse players in the game by providing a realistic atmosphere. Players do not focus on the background ambience in a game, but they would notice if this ambience were to suddenly cease. If you have ever experienced a sudden power outage, you have a small idea of what this feels like.

Event-based sounds serve as feedback to the actions the player takes. These sounds can be realistic, such as a vehicle accelerating—or artificial, such as a special sound that occurs only when a magical spell is cast. Sounds can also provide clues to the player. If a player's avatar is walking down a dark street and is being followed, the player might hear the sound of footsteps coming from behind the avatar—getting progressively louder.

> Without audio, the only feedback players will get during gameplay will be visual. Total immersion relies on the involvement of different senses. Therefore, having both auditory and visual feedback from a game during gameplay adds to immersion.
>
> —*Shahnaz Kamberi (Associate Professor of Game & Simulation Development, DeVry University)*

A sound designer creates the bigger sound effects (such as vehicle acceleration, explosions, and the hum of machinery) and the smaller *foley* sounds (such as a key turning in a lock, footsteps, and doors swinging shut). Foley is used in movies and is named after Jack Foley, who helped make the transition from the silent era to talkies. He recreated noises in a sound studio that were not easily captured on the movie set and then synched them to the action on the screen.

'Naughty Dog

Uncharted 2: Among Thieves has received awards for excellent sound effects.

"It's All Music"

I don't separate sound effects from music. To me it is all music. Go outside and listen to the traffic, the birds, the planes flying overhead, the people talking: It's an ever-changing sonic composition. Whenever I can, I like to I just sit and listen; I'm always amazed by what I hear.

Chad Mossholder (Composer & Senior Sound Designer, Sony Online Entertainment)

Sound designers often purchase entire sound libraries to help with both large sound effects and foley. Although these libraries can provide some highly effective sounds, they should be used only as a starting point or to provide ideas. Many game audio professionals—as well as the players themselves—have come to recognize (and sometimes grow tired of) some commonly used library sounds. The best sound designers go out in the world with a recorder, capture natural sounds, and tweak them into original sounds in a studio.

Creating an Audio Identity

Once the initial "feel" for a game is defined, it's up to the sound designer to match that vision and create an audio identity for the game. Even something as simple as a gunshot, for example, has to be unique for each game. I know a sound designer has done a good job when I can hear a sound playing in another room and I can tell what game it's from. Sometimes creating this "uniqueness" can be a difficult task. We've all heard games where the sound detracts from the experience—and we've turned the volume off altogether. Now, it's not to say that sound alone will make or break a game, but experiencing one where audio is a priority can literally be mind-blowing, and an experience a player will want to relive again and again. *Halo* and the *Medal of Honor* series immediately come to mind. These types of games are successful in totally immersing the players into the game world and giving them the ride of their lives! With sound providing one-third of the overall experience, it better be good! When I'm creating, I often find myself very focused on the task at hand. I was once creating sound effects for a sword fight in my studio, getting all the standard metal hits and scrapes recorded. The next sound on the list was a series of "sword-breaking-rock" effects, which was to be used when the swordsman missed his opponent and hit one of the many rock features in the arena. Not even thinking, I brought a bunch of rocks, bricks, and concrete blocks into the control room, pressed record, and proceeded to start smashing and throwing debris everywhere—really getting into the scene and trying to make it sound realistic. Once I felt I had enough to work with, I stopped and stood back to contemplate the session. That's when I realized dust and rock debris was covering everything! I'd made a complete mess out of the place! I'm still finding bits and pieces of that session in the oddest places.

—Aaron Marks (composer & sound designer; President, On Your Mark Music Productions)

Using a digital or analog recorder, you can capture effects for a variety of sounds—such as gunshots and footsteps—by either recording them in the environment or by using foley techniques. Here are just a few sounds that are fairly easy to capture using foley:

- *Car crash:* Fill a metal box with scrap metal and chunks of wood. Shake vigorously.
- *Fire:* Open an umbrella quickly for a burst of flames. Crumple up thick cellophane for the crackle.
- *Body collision:* Strike a pumpkin or watermelon with a piece of wood.
- *Body stabs:* Drive a knife into a soft fruit, such as a grapefruit or small cantaloupe.
- *Cocked gun:* Click ratchet wrench.
- *Gunshots:* Hit a leather seat with a thin wooden stick, such as a ruler (or fold a belt in half and snap it).
- *Bushes:* Rustle some broom straw.
- *Boiling water:* Blow through a straw inserted in water to make bubbles.
- *Bubbling volcanic lava:* Boil oatmeal.
- *Airplanes:* Run electric fans.
- *Clothes ripping:* Quickly pull apart Velcro strips.

Once you have connected your device to the computer, you can use a program such as CoolEdit to record and save the sample into the computer.

::::: *Operation Flashpoint: Dragon Rising*:
Field Recording in 100-Degree Heat

Codemasters

My most memorable experience was field recording various military battle vehicles at a U.S. Marines base in Twentynine Palms, California. The challenge was to gain access, use the correct recording equipment, brave the 110-degree desert heat, and have enough resources to complete our field recording tasks for an entire week. We hired a military adviser who was able to get us all of the vehicles on the wish list—including an M1A1 Abrams battle tank, armor-plated humvee, and armor-plated personnel trucks.

— *Watson Wu (Composer & Sound Designer, Watson Wu Studios)*

Scott Snyder
(Senior Sound
Designer,
Edge of Reality)

Scott Snyder started playing guitar when he was four, then played around with a reel-to-reel tape recorder when he was 16—discovering the wonders of speed shifting and tape reverb as if no one had ever heard it before. After many bar bands, coffee houses, and hundreds of songs (lovingly crafted, and unheard by anyone, he says), Scott formalized his audio experience in the U.S. Army as a broadcast journalist. He produced radio and television for the U.S. Army for nearly 10 years, then went back to school and ended up with an MFA in Theatre, Sound Design from the University of Illinois, Urbana-Champaign. He then landed his first game job with a great company called Accolade in San Jose. Since then, he has made the rounds as sound designer, audio director, and general sound dude for: Accolade, Infogrames, Atari, Microsoft, a stint as Marketing VP for a audio technology startup, some time working for himself (read: unemployed)—and now happily lives and works as a sound designer (he refers to himself as a sonic architect, since he feels it is more appropriate to what he actually does) for Edge of Reality in Austin, Texas. And he is back to playing guitar again. What a long, strange trip it has been.

The challenges facing any brave soul who takes on the responsibility for a game's sound are many. From a technology standpoint, consoles have been steadily increasing their power and capabilities, and likely will continue doing so for some time. While we are given more RAM, higher sample rates, more channels, and more CPU, the games we are designing have already scaled up their content to meet or surpass these increases. Where once we had five enemies on the screen, now we have 50—so we end up with the same issues: lack of resources, process starvation, and repetition that we have always faced. I believe the solution is smarter implementation.

The second part of the technology challenge is, indeed, implementation. There are third-party tools that can sometimes simplify asset and behavior creation, and put more power back into the hands of the designer. While this seems to be the easiest solution, it's important to understand that third-party audio content tools are not the ultimate solution for all your audio problems. They can bring along issues of their own, and you will need good engineering support to get them into your game engine, and keep them working throughout development. These tools provide a common set of behavior definitions for sound which can speed your initial workflow; however, if you want to do something innovative, something different than what everyone else is doing, you will need to be able to create engineering solutions outside of the middleware tool to accomplish this.

From a design standpoint, implementation designs are becoming much more complex. Getting a rich and varied world to "sound right" and meet all design expectations is a difficult but rewarding task. In order to keep a project under its budget of RAM, CPU use, and disk access, creative solutions are required from the designers and the engineers. Sound designers have to weigh the technical cost of the creative design, and decide how best to accomplish those goals within the resources they have. For a sound designer, understanding how the audio engine and audio system works is much more important now than it was even five years ago.

Audio quality is another one of those points that will come up in any discussion about game or interactive audio. Of course, it depends on the specific conversation and topic at hand what "quality" is actually referring to. As far as pure content quality, audio is miles ahead of every other system in a game engine. While graphics continues to work toward more realistic models, smoother more natural animations and lighting, audio jumped past the uncanny valley when we started using samples instead of FM synthesis. Now, when we record or create an asset, we are using absolutely "real" sounds and sound primitives. When you hear birds chirping in the world, you're probably not hearing some programmed FM Synth version of birds, but a field recording of actual birds. This verisimilitude of the audio experience that most people experience every day, can lead non-audio folks to believe that's all there is to it. Get a good sample, stick it in, and you're done. But of course, this is not true; if these realistic samples are not played back in a natural way during the course of the interactive experience, then they will sound as low quality as 8-bit sprites in a 64-bit world.

This means more than playing the right sound on the right event – but it includes concepts such as mixing that must be done dynamically and respond correctly to game states and events. Unlike linear mixing of multi-track recordings where the engineer knows precisely where every note is in time, interactive media are by nature unpredictable. We don't know when or where that event is going to happen, when that footstep will sound, when that explosion will play. So we create a set of rules, or audio system behaviors that will react accordingly to in game events and player input. I refer to this as Audio AI; you are essentially programming the mix and telling the audio engine how it should react to any given situation that arises. To me, this Audio AI concept is where the exciting future of game sound design lies -- and it will require sound designers to have a good grasp of both the creative and the technical side of their craft.

Voiceovers

Voiceovers are used in games for spoken dialogue and narration. Voiceovers are often supplied by outsourced talent. The artists are recorded as they read dialogue and narration scripts in a recording studio. Make sure the artists understand any specifics about the voices, including accents and how character development must be revealed during the reading. Voiceover talent should have previous experience in commercial voiceover work—such as film, television, games, or advertising.

As discussed in Chapter 5, game stories (unlike film) are non-linear. This means that dialogue scripts for the game (other than cut-scene scripts) will often be out of context. Voiceover artists will often speak only one or two lines at a time or make victorious or defeated sounds (such as screams or grunts) that will be used again in many parts of the game. An audio director will most likely want to record many versions of one type of sound from the voiceover artists so that the game is more realistic and varied. For example, an orc grunting in the same way each time it is clicked will sound more artificial than it would if it emitted several different types of grunts each time. Similarly, a non-player character (NPC) who states that same line of dialogue every time a player character runs into him ("You really shouldn't head in this direction!") also decreases the immersive experience of the game. Several alternate lines of dialogue should be prepared for this purpose and should be recorded by the same voiceover artist for consistency. The best games typically have 20 or more variants of common sounds.

Bob Bergen & Hope Levy on the Joys and Perils of Voice Acting :::::

BB

Bob Bergen
(voice actor)

Bob Bergen started working full time as an actor at the age of 23. His resume consists of hundreds of cartoons, commercials, promos, and games—as well as work on-camera hosting *Jep!*, the kids' version of the classic game show *Jeopardy!* on GSN.. In 1990, Bob's dream came true when he joined a handful of actors who share the job of voicing the Looney Tunes characters. Over the years, Bob has voiced Porky, Tweety, Marvin the Martian, Henry Hawk, Sylvester Jr., and Speedy Gonzales in a variety of projects. For 10 years, Bob worked as the grandstand host at the annual Hollywood Christmas Parade. His one-man show, *Bob Bergen: So, Here's the Deal!* (the story of a nice Jewish boy who wanted to be Porky Pig) has enjoyed several successful runs in Los Angeles, New York City, Chicago, and Atlanta—touring the US and Canada throughout the year. Bob has been teaching his animation voiceover workshop for over 15 years, and he is currently working on a slew of animation projects, commercials, and games.

In games, voice actors usually work solo. On an animated series, the producers try to have as many of the cast members at the session as possible. When voicing games, you need to record all the potential options a player might have in the game. This often takes a while and can get a bit tedious…. One of the most challenging things about voice acting for games in particular is the yelling—which is *very* hard on the voice at times! But the good directors will wait until the end of the session to record those. My most memorable experience during a game voiceover session was when I voiced Luke Skywalker for LucasArts. Luke had the line, "Look at the size of that thing!" I kept laughing and it took a long time to get through the line!

Hope Levy can be heard in *The Matrix: Path of Neo, Bratz, Polar Express, EverQuest II, Jumpstart, Vampires Masquerade: Bloodlines*, and as Rebecca Chambers in *Resident Evil: Biohazard.* She can also be heard in the animated features and series *Howl's Moving Castle, Madagascar, The Fairly Odd Parents, Rugrats, Ozzy & Drix, Invader Zim* and the Japanese anime series *Shin Chan.* On screen, Hope has played the Greek Wedding Girl in *My Big Fat Independent Movie*, which was co-written and produced by Chris Gore of Film Threat and G4 TV. Hope also co-stars as Pam, the wannabe rapper, in *Uncle P—* starring Master P and Lil' Romeo.

HL

Hope Levy
(voice actor and
singer)

In game voice acting, each emotion—such as laughing, crying, screaming—has to be recorded. Each action also has to be recorded; we call these "efforts"—and they include punching, getting punched, sighing, getting attacked, performing full combat, dragging bodies, and being dragged. We also perform *numerous* endings for the game so that the player has more to experience and play with. That's cool, because our characters may actually play good guys or bad guys—depending on which ending the player chooses. The energy it takes to voice act in a game is *endless.* It's a surprisingly physical job. We voice actors throw ourselves into the moment … so when we're being chased, we're running in place—huffing and puffing. After a four-hour session of screaming and really getting into the actions and emotions of what the game requires, we feel pretty spent!

"Convincing Death Noises"

I was doing voice talent for the female player character for id Software's *Quake 2.* At the time, I was working for Crack dot Com, and we occupied offices right next to a title company. For a week, I made all manner of horrible screams, gurgling drownings, leaping grunts, and other assorted tasty morsels into FX files. At one point on the first day, a rep from the title company had to come over to our offices and make sure nothing was going wrong. I make convincing death noises, apparently. Bwahahaha!

—*Carly Staehlin (artist; Owner, Burrow Owl Trading, LLC)*

Music

Game *music* is a way to tell the players how they should react to the visual images on the screen. Music can heighten the thrill of action, tell the player when danger lurks around the corner, or set a lighter tone for comedic moments. A game's *soundtrack* might consist of a *score* and *songs*. The *score* refers to instrumental music often written for the game itself that creates a mood and atmosphere. Composers often put together scores using home recording systems—including a MIDI synthesizer or keyboard that is hooked up to a computer containing recording, sequencing, and mixing software. For games with larger budgets, a composer might prepare *parts* for live instruments and record this music at a recording studio with a live orchestra or ensemble.

AM
RJ

Soundtracks are recorded in a home recording studio (Aaron Marks in studio, left) or a professional recording studio (Ron Jones conducting, right).

A *song* soundtrack usually consists of pre-existing songs with vocals (not written especially for the game) that are licensed from the respective copyright holders or publishers to be used in the game. Sometimes songs from well-known artists are used to increase the popularity of a game. This can be extremely expensive and create several royalty problems down the road. Although song soundtracks have proven to be quite effective in many films, such as *Pulp Fiction* and *Moulin Rouge,* they have not been as effective in games. There are also several alternatives to licensing well-known recordings. You can get a synchronization license, which allows you to hire your own performers to make a new version of a particular song. Or you can purchase the rights to use songs (and instrumental music) from music libraries such as Associated Production Music (APM), which provide an entire catalog of music organized by mood and scene.

Electronic Arts

Brütal Legend won awards for its epic and inventive game soundtracks.

Rob Cairns on the Function of Music Libraries :::::

Since 2002, Rob Cairns has licensed thousands of compositions and recordings into hundreds of game titles. Working closely with music professionals at many of the world's greatest video game companies, he has helped to form meaningful and multi-dimensional partnerships between APM and the game industry. Beyond game music, Rob also specializes in other new media markets such as ringtones, user-generated content, digital music retail sales, re-records (cover songs), commercials, film, television, custom music negotiations, and various mechanical models such as products featuring sound chip recordings.

Rob Cairns
(Key Account Director,
New Media & Games,
Associated Production
Music)

Developers and publishers often consider music libraries to be an extremely important part of creating a quality soundtrack. Production music is composed and recorded specifically for use with the moving image and therefore it is frequently a perfect fit for in-game forefront music and cut-scenes. A large percentage of library music heard in games is period/archival music that was recorded across the decades or even authentic national/ethnic tracks that were recorded in other parts of the world. These types of songs are often licensed as in-game source music and continue to add authenticity and depth to games of all kinds. In most cases, production music's role is to supplement the work of the featured composer and/or licensed commercial songs, helping to create a full, diverse and interesting soundtrack.

Bill Brown on Positive Challenges in the Composition Process :::::

Bill Brown began his career composing powerful scores for AAA game titles, including *Tom Clancy's Rainbow Six, Tom Clancy's Ghost Recon, Clive Barker's Undying, Return to Castle Wolfenstein, Lineage II: The Chaotic Chronicle*, and *Command & Conquer: Generals*. Bill also contributed additional music to the films *Any Given Sunday, Ali*, and *Finding Forrester*—and he scored the films *Scorcher* (CineTel/HBO), *Trapped* (USA Network), and *The Devil's Tomb* (Sony Pictures Entertainment). Bill is currently the composer for the hit CBS series, *CSI:NY*.

Bill Brown
(composer)

I always look at challenge as a good thing in the context of creativity. If it is obvious, it's not going to interest me as much. If it is complex and layered, there might be a challenge somewhere in the process—and that's good! Where there is challenge, there is growth—and I keep finding that where there is growth, there is huge reward. For me, the process of writing music for games is like mastery of anything, really. I'm just practicing, and every once in a while, I will notice that I have just stepped up to a whole new plateau. And that is a great feeling … and then I continue to practice.

Ron Jones on the Composer- Game Developer Relationship :::::

RJ

Ron Jones
(Composer, Ron Jones
Productions, Inc.)

Ron Jones has scored hundreds of animated series—including *The Flintstones, The Smurfs, The New Adventures of Scooby Doo, Superman, Duck Tales,* and *Family Guy* (which garnered an Emmy nomination for Best Original Song). After a successful four seasons scoring *Star Trek: The Next Generation,* Ron contributed to two best-selling *Star Trek* computer games—providing orchestral scores for Interplay's *Star Trek: Star Fleet Command* and *Star Trek: Star Fleet Academy.* The National Association of Independent Record Distributors & Manufacturers (NAIRD) awarded him with Best Soundtrack Album of the Year for *Star Trek: The Next Generation—Best of Both Worlds, Parts I & II,* on Crescendo Records. Ron Jones Productions maintains a state-of-the-art studio with full, updated computer systems and software located in Burbank, CA.

The most challenging aspect of game composing is filtering through the language differences of game producers and designers in order to discover not only the essence of the game, but to find the right musical approach. Composers are really on a different planet than the game team. You have to hold true to what you know will be right and what will work best—yet still manage to nail what the game developers want. This is a tricky, slippery task. It involves a great amount of patience, and the ability to really listen.

The Role of Music in Games

Music plays a very important role in games. It can help establish the entire tone and mood of the game. It can change the players' perceptions and emotions during gameplay. Music can make a huge impact on how much the player becomes immersed in the game experience.

— *Tom Salta (Composer, Persist Music)*

The Music Pre-Production Process

Each style of music presents its own unique challenges, but that's easy compared to the very first step of writing that first note. I usually spend some time researching the game and really getting into what it's all about before I even think about the music. Coming up with a concept that will fit the game, not be obtrusive, and be unique is probably the toughest thing for me. But once I have a good direction laid out, the music pours out. The next challenge is turning the faucet off!

—*Aaron Marks (composer & sound designer; President, On Your Mark Music Productions)*

As the game industry continues to reach a wider audience—and as music sales from traditional distribution channels continue to decline—record labels and independent musicians alike have begun to focus on the game industry as a new medium for music exposure. Unlike the traditional film-going and TV-watching audience, gamers are an "active" audience—manipulating characters, choosing paths, and sometimes changing the scenery in a game environment. Games are truly an immersive experience, and the music that gamers hear while playing—whether looping theme music or adaptive sounds that conform to characters' actions—can make a long-lasting impression. When you consider MMOs that might involve players for weeks or even months on end, no wonder the fan base for game music is growing tremendously!

Alex Brandon on Challenges & Successes in Game Audio:::::

AB

Alex Brandon
(President,
Funky Rustic)

Alex Brandon has been involved in game audio for 17 years as a composer, sound designer, voice actor, voice director, and audio director at companies such as Epic Games, Midway, and Obsidian Entertainment. He is also the author of *Audio For Games: Planning, Process and Production*. At the start of his career, Alex successfully used a version of Ad Lib technology that was able to take its 4-bit capabilities and convert them into pseudo 6/8 bit versions to create the soundtrack to his first game, *Tyrian*. Put it this way: The PC now sounded like a Sega Genesis! Next up was music for the Epic game *Unreal*, which went on to sell well over a million copies. The *Unreal* level pack, *Unreal Tournament*, and *Deus Ex* followed in a string of interactive MOD-based titles generating music that hadn't been heard before and hasn't been heard since. At that point, Alex began working with live orchestras, Chow Yun Fat (voice acting), and artists such as BT. The music is far more a challenge now than it ever was, but Alex continues to create unique tracks—contributing to the Big Giant Circles *Deus Ex* remix "Siren Synapse" in 2010 and interviewing Japanese rock stars Hip Tanaka and Tetsuya Mizuguchi. Alex owns his own audio production house in Georgetown, Texas and distributes music through Bandcamp—releasing an album every now and then.

Making music and sound effects is easy. Making good music and good sound effects is hard. Integrating good music and sound effects effectively is the most difficult part. *Deus Ex: Invisible War* and *Thief: Deadly Shadows* both have excellent models. In fact, *Thief*'s gameplay is driven more directly through audio. On the flip side, I really like *Ballers*. It has a very appropriate licensed soundtrack and a variety of hip-hop styles that help ease repetition.

Audio: creating the atmosphere   chapter 9

Mobile Game Audio in the Cloud?

As mobile games continue to rise tremendously in popularity, more opportunities have become available to game audio professionals. Of course, there are many challenges associated with creating audio for mobile games due to restricted memory storage, slow CPU speeds, or limited data networks. Although players have the option of using headphones during gameplay, it's more likely that audio will instead be heard through the device's speakers—which are limited in quality. In his article, "Game Audio in the Cloud," musician and composer Peter Drescher addresses the issue of mobile game audio quality and puts forth a possible solution. He asserts that mobile game soundtracks tend to be "archaic" due to bandwidth limitations and comprised of low-quality MIDI files and highly-compressed WAV file sound effects that sound lacking when compared to the streaming audio produced by the media player on the same device. Drescher's solution involves cloud-based audio -- where music is not downloaded and stored on a user's device but streamed off a cloud server.

::::: *Iron Bridge*:
Mobile Game Audio Challenges

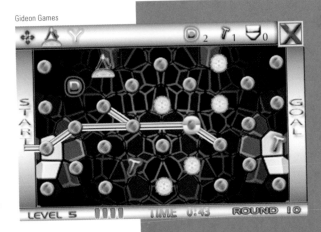

Gideon Games

The audio issue was tricky for us on *Iron Bridge*. When developing for mobile devices, keeping memory usage and file storage to a minimum is important; we wanted to avoid dreaded "forever long" load screen. We noticed that consumers/players are more hesitant to download a game that will weigh heavily on their mobile device's memory. If not done wisely, sound can take up vital system resources and/or create an unintentional ambiance that may push players in a direction contradictory to what was intended. Music plays such a vital part in creating an imaginable interactive environment. Aside from tasting or smelling, the player can only utilize three senses to enjoy any game experience: seeing, touching, and hearing. What you hear can either enhance or kill game experience. Another issue I came across was the over use of sound effects. There were times where over five different sound effects would be playing at once, depending on the circumstances within the game. This became overwhelming during more difficult levels, making concentration a bit tougher—so we had to rework sound priorities.

— *Jacques A. Montemoino (Founder & Creative Director, Gideon Games Inc.)*

Audio in Mobile Game Development

Lately I've been highly active in the iPhone realm. It's a great market with a large amount of activity and creativity—but there are limitations often relating to data size constraints but also music playback. It's not very common to have deep music features such as varying tempos, changing instruments on the fly, or adding or removing various layers.

— *Nathan Madsen (Composer & Sound Designer, Madsen Studios LLC)*

Looping Music

Some games use *looping music* to provide a continuous soundtrack. If the loops are long enough, the player might not notice that the music is repeating. A composer might also create different themes with identical beginnings and endings that are put together to provide variation. Keep in mind that a player might spend more than 100 hours with your game, and you do not want to drive the player insane with looping music. Another issue with looping music in many current games is context. Let us say you are playing a game that involves exploring a beautiful forest, and the music accompanying your exploration is a beautiful simple theme that matches the setting. What if an evil pagan god jumps out from behind a tree and starts trying to hypnotize your character with his pan pipe? What if your character falls into a hypnotic trance and starts destroying the beautiful scenery by chopping down trees? If the music has not changed by that point to complement the change of mood in the game, it will ruin the immersive experience. This problem can be addressed by providing distinct themes that relate to different events that occur in the game. To do this, the composer needs to know what paths can be taken by the player character in the game in order to provide enough musical variety to the developer.

Contractual Issues

Film composers are paid by the score, and they retain rights that provide an income stream from their music for years after they have supplied it. Game developers are leaning toward paying by the finished minute, acquiring all the rights, and avoiding any future royalty entanglements. Developers are also concerned with restrictions that prevent them from repackaging the game and managing it through its normal lifecycle. A common compromise is for developers to make a one-time payment to acquire all the rights needed for the life of the game, while the composer retains rights for non-interactive use so that he or she can sell the music again in other media.

Game vs. Film Scoring

Many film composers are interested in migrating to the game industry. Just like screenwriters who might consider writing game "scripts," film composers face an adjustment to a new, nonlinear medium. In film scoring, composers are able to watch a finished film and often meet with the director of the film for a *spotting* session. Spotting involves watching the film all the way through and deciding where music should be used by calculating each music cue's start and end points, along with any *hit* points—places where the music should be particularly dramatic and "hit" on a particular action, such as a bullet being fired from a gun or the sudden appearance of a magical creature. In contrast, there is not a way to view a finished game. For a composer to see all paths a character might take in the game, the composer would have to play the game several times—which could take hundreds of hours. Instead, the composer needs to see various characters and settings used in the game, read the story synopsis and character profiles, and be provided a list of levels and associated objectives and gameplay elements. Since cut-scenes are more like mini-movies, they can be spotted and scored like films.

Richard Jacques & Rich Ragsdale on Film & Game Scoring :::::

RJ

Richard Jacques
(composer)

Classically trained with an extensive music repertoire in orchestral, jazz, and other contemporary music genres, Richard Jacques is a multiple award-winning composer of music for video games, film, and television. A leader in the field of modern game music, Richard was the first video game composer to: secure a major budget for a live symphony orchestra; record a live orchestra for a PSP handheld video game; be featured in art galleries and live concerts in Europe, Japan, and North America; and release game soundtracks commercially in Japan, Europe, and North America. Richard has received numerous awards and accolades for his music, including Best Music awards from both GameSpot and GameSpy and the Game Audio Network Guild Recognition Award. He also has received multiple nominations, including Music of the Year, Best Original Instrumental Song, Best Live Performance Recording, and Best Original Soundtrack Album. An accomplished pianist, trombonist, percussionist, and guitarist, Jacques was classically trained at the Royal Academy of Music in London, and began his career as an in-house Composer and later Audio Director at Sega Europe in London. Widely credited with pushing the boundaries of live orchestral scores—and having worked on titles such as *James Bond 007: Blood Stone*, *Headhunter*, *Starship Troopers*, and *Mass Effect*— Richard is one of the most experienced composers working in the game industry today.

Film and television music is linear, and games are non-linear. Therefore, in film or television music, you know exactly what is going to happen at a particular time so you can score the music accordingly. In a game, you don't know what the player is going to do, so you have to make the music react to whatever situation the player is in.

Rich Ragsdale grew up in Nashville, Tennessee. He started playing guitar at age 16, and soon joined local punk and heavy metal bands with "silly" names like Soft Skull Sam and Bombshell. Deciding to get serious about his music, he studied classical guitar and then went to Berklee College of Music, where he majored both in film scoring and composition. He then completed the one-year film-scoring program at USC. After scoring a few independent films, Rich began to write music for television and games. He has also scored several commercials and has contributed music and songs to several features (both studio and independent). Now he is also a film director—with *Into Something Rich and Strange* winning Best Experimental Short Film, and a horror feature (*El Charro*) in development with Pretty Dangerous Films. Rich has composed music for several commercial game projects for Vivendi Universal Games, Fox Interactive, and Music Consultants Group. His game credits include *Aliens vs. Predator, No One Lives Forever,* and *Eight-Legged Freaks* (based on the movie of the same name). His music has been featured on the television shows *Will and Grace* and *King of Queens.*

Kevin Ragsdale

Rich Ragsdale
(composer)

In film and television, the composer usually comes in during post-production. The picture is more or less locked—so the parameters are often fixed, and your job becomes mainly about finding the correct style and sound for the picture. For game projects, I have generally been brought in closer to the beginning of production—months before I can really see what the game is going to be like. Cut-scenes and specific events can have hard and fast parameters as far as timing is concerned, but gameplay is more fluid and does not.

Temp Track Infatuation

A *temp track* is temporary music that is traditionally used in a film to provide an idea of what a director might want to hear. Usually, the film's editor adds the temp track to an early version of the film and continues to use it while editing. In fact, film editors sometimes edit the film to the music—making it more difficult to part with the temp track. The director often falls in love with the temp track—which often consists of a score to another film, or music from well-known artists that would be prohibitively expensive to license. A composer is often brought in at post-production and not only must write original music quickly so that the dialogue, music, and effects tracks can be mixed—but must also convince the director that this new music will work much better with the film than the temp track. Usually, the composer is right—but the director has already heard the temp track too many times and has difficulty parting with it. Game developers are becoming similar in this way. Advice? Get a music supervisor or composer on the project during preproduction. Do not wait until you are almost ready to release the game. One more thing: If you must use a temp track, try to not to fall in love with it!

HN

Henning Nugel
(Composer & Sound
Designer,
Nugel Bros. Music)

Henning Nugel founded Nugel Bros. Music with his brother, Ingo. The Nugel brothers have provided services in the area of composition and sound design for all media. Situated in Dortmund, Germany, Nugel Bros. Music has worked for over 12 years for major game publishers and developers such as Electronic Arts, Ubisoft, Blue Byte and Funatics on titles such as *The Settlers II 10th Anniversary Edition* (PC), *Endwar* (PSP and DS), and *Darkstar One* (PC and Xbox)—in addition to audio design for the multiple award winning Audi R8 online campaign.

It's essential or at least advantageous to integrate the composer and/or sound designer as early as possible into game development. There are many details to focus on at the planning stage of an audio production for a game where his advice can be of great help in answering questions such as, "Will we need an orchestra?" or "Should we have musical motifs for characters or situations?" Also, the more time there is to create, the more pleasing the outcome usually is.

It's also important to keep your audio team or contractors informed of all major changes to the game. Don't let them be the last to one to know that the 1st-person-high-adrenalin-gory zombie-hack-and-slash shooter is now going to be a family-oriented bubble-bobbly jump-and-run game. Treat them like you would a member of your internal team. They will reward you with a fitting atmospheric and emotionally pleasing soundtrack that will greatly enhance your game.

GO-R

Greg O'Connor-Read
(Founder,
Top Dollar PR)

Greg O'Connor-Read has been instrumental in the promotion of numerous award-winning composers and soundtracks—including *007: Blood Stone*, *Alan Wake*, *Assassin's Creed*, *BioShock*, *Dead Space*, *Deus Ex: Human Revolution*, *Dragon Age*, *Fable*, *God of War*, *Halo*, *Headhunter*, *Hitman*, *Prince of Persia*, *Resident Evil*, *Splinter Cell: Double Agent*, *Uncharted 2*, and many more. He has consulted for The Barbican's Game On exhibition (the first international touring exhibition to celebrate the art and culture of video games including soundtracks), lobbied for and secured the British Academy Award (BAFTA) for best original music in a video game, and consulted for GameTrailers TV on the induction of the "Best Original Video Game Score" category in the MTV Video Music Awards (VMAs). Greg is a consultant and moderator for The Hollywood Reporter / Billboard Film & TV Music Conference, the Computer Music Magazine monthly column "Game Overture" and MIDEM Music for Images Conference. Greg was honored as the first recipient of the Game Audio Network Guild Recognition Award. He has also contributed to or secured coverage for composers and video game soundtracks in global media such as the BBC, *Billboard*, *Hollywood Reporter*, *New York Times*, *Variety*, *Business Week*, *Red Herring*, *POST*, *Electronic Musician*, *Computer Music*, *Future Music*, *MIX*, *Sound On Sound*, *Develop*, *Edge*, *Electronic Gaming Monthly*, *Film Music Magazine*, *Game Informer*, *Play Magazine*, *Official PlayStation Magazine*, *Official Xbox Magazine*, G4TV, and Spike TV.

Similar to film, music in games establishes the emotional context—providing the player with an emotional connection to the visuals on the screen. Music feeds into the gameplay and, if implemented well, the music and visuals will fully immerse the player in the game environment.... Music is an essential component in elevating the game experience.... Unfortunately, game composers do not often get the credit they deserve for their contribution to the overall product. Most game composer deals are "buyouts," with no royalties involved. Finally, game composers working on big-budget games have smaller budgets to work with than film composers working on big-budget movies.

Adaptive Music

A more immersive way to incorporate music in a game is for a composer to write *adaptive music*—which changes to conform to a player's actions within the game. This requires writing music in very small segments and embedding flags in the code to signal the rapidly changing states in the game. In the example already discussed in the "Looping Music" subsection, the music would begin with the original beautiful simple theme that matches the pastoral setting. When the evil creature jumps out from behind the tree and begins to hypnotize the player, the music might change to reflect a mixture of playful, evil, and hypnotic themes. When your character starts to destroy the scenery, the music could rise dramatically—emphasizing the evil theme. Creating this kind of music requires very close coordination between the game designer, programmer, and composer. The composer not only will know what the game is about, but also will know the many shifting moods that must be interpreted for the player.

Game Music Popularity

Game music continues to rise in popularity—often becoming distinct from the games associated with it. Two examples of this growing trend include the continued success of concert series Video Games Live and sites such as Overclocked Remix. Video Games Live features game music performed by top orchestras and choirs throughout the world. Overclocked Remix (*www.ocremix.org*) allows game music fans to remix their favorite tracks for others to sample—highlighting the popularity of game soundtracks while also showcasing the collaborative features of the Internet.

Chance Thomas on the Essential Audio Tool Kit :::::

CT

Chance Thomas
(Principal Composer,
HUGEsound)

Chance Thomas composes original music and produces audio for smash hit titles such as *Lord of the Rings Online*, *James Cameron's Avatar*, *Peter Jackson's King Kong*, and others. His projects have won major awards, including: Oscar, Emmy, Addy, Telly, GANG, and IGN. Chance was the first game composer to score an Academy-Award-winning film and log more than one million downloads of his game music. He produced one of the first live orchestral scores and commercially successful soundtracks in gaming. Chance's efforts brought game music into the Grammy Awards and helped found the Game Audio Network Guild. His company, HUGEsound, offers comprehensive audio post and music production services to innovative developers and publishers worldwide.

- **Vivid imagination:** The most brilliant scores always take shape first in the musical workshop of the mind. There's no technology with enough horsepower to outperform the spontaneous magic of the human spirit.

- **Quality education:** Learning opens the mind, paves the path to creative flow, and forges habits of intellectual striving. Formal education can provide needed discipline, craftsmanship and volumes of relevant information. The best inspiration always comes with the best information. Reference books on orchestration, classical literature, music theory, history, great works of art—all of these enrich the mind and cultivate a fertile seedbed for compelling ideas to rise from.

- **Reliable equipment:** When your time comes—when you finally get that long anticipated opportunity to make your mark on the world—the last thing you want is trouble with your gear. When deadlines loom, busy composers may run their studios around the clock for weeks or even months on end. I've found the following categories of equipment to be very reliable over the years: Mac Pro workstations, Neumann microphones, Genelec speakers, Yamaha mixers, Dell monitors, Pro Tools hardware, Apogee hardware, and MOTU hardware. They've never let me down.

- **Riveting sounds:** Today's sample libraries offer composers so many fabulous choices. From the traditional to the supernatural, chances are you can find them in a library. I love to blend sounds from various libraries and alter them further with editing and plug-ins. It's important to have a vast arsenal of ready-made sounds on hand for quick mock-ups and demos—but it's also important to develop ways to make the sounds completely your own. In this day of sample library proliferation, creativity has to extend all the way to your source sounds.

■ **Meticulous musicians:** Live musicians can make a significant difference in the sound of a music project—for better or worse, unfortunately. A slightly out-of-tune performance on a Stradivarius will make your stomach tighten uncomfortably, whereas a passionate and accurate performance on your grandpa's old fiddle can send the spirit soaring. Nothing is more disappointing to composers than to hear their work performed poorly by a large ensemble. But when the musicians truly dial in the performance—playing in tune and in time, then pouring in a little passion—it can be absolutely exhilarating!

David Javelosa on Adaptive Music :::::

David Javelosa is a composer/technologist and game industry special- ist based in Santa Monica, California. Previously, he worked with Yamaha Corporation of America as an evangelist for its game audio technology. David is an instructor at Santa Monica College's Entertainment Technology program, teaching game development and digital audio. He also composes music for the Internet and live performances. He has created soundtracks for most of the major game consoles and has been involved with digital media since its inception. His interests include vintage synthesizers, remixing pop bands and sci-fi soundtracks, skydiving, biking, and raising his three children. As "David Microwave," he began releasing recordings in 1979 with his bands Los Microwaves and Baby Buddha representing a fusion of synth-pop ballads, vintage analog sound, "lo-fi" game music, and experimental techno grooves. His recordings have included veteran musicians Robert Williams of Capt. Beefheart, Knox Chandler of the Psychedelic Furs, and Steve Berlin of Los Lobos, among others. His game music background includes audio director positions at Sega and Inscape, as well as credits on titles from Disney Interactive, Microsoft Network, Sony Online, Crave, Psygnosis, Marvel Interactive, and Voyager.

DJ

David Javelosa (composer & music technologist)

With adaptive music, we look at both the vertical and horizontal structures of the score. The vertical structure generally describes instrumentation, arrange- ment, and mix of the music, sometimes referred to as the density or the inten- sity of the game scene. As the player gets in and out of situations, the ability of this quality to change with the state of the game is immensely effective.

On the horizontal axis, we look over the arrangement of musical segments, or sequencing of the musical development. Having different themes associated with certain scenes or the appearance of characters actually allows the player to have an unconscious hand in the playback of the arrangement. If done too sim- plistically, the player can become aware of these changes and actually "play" the soundtrack by repeating scene transitions in a non–gameplay fashion. As with most adaptive soundtracks, the more subtle and transparent the transition, the more effective the overall experience. The best soundtracks are the ones that are so well integrated that we tend not to notice them consciously.

TT

Tommy Tallarico
(President, Tommy
Tallarico Studios, Inc;
President/Founder,
Game Audio Network
Guild [GANG])

Tommy Tallarico's music has been heard all over the world on video games, television, motion pictures, radio, soundtracks—and even on floats in the New Year's Day Rose Bowl parade in Pasadena. Some of Tallarico's top titles include *Earthworm Jim 1 & 2, Disney's Aladdin, Cool Spot, The Terminator, Madden Football, Prince of Persia,* the *Test Drive* series, *MDK, Tomorrow Never Dies, Tony Hawk Skateboarding, Spider-Man, Pac-Man World, Knockout Kings and the Blitz, Unreal, Unreal 2, Metroid Prime, Scooby Doo, Maximo, Twisted Metal,* and the *Time Crisis* series. Tommy was the first musician to release a game soundtrack worldwide (*Tommy Tallarico's Greatest Hits Vol. 1* – Capitol Records). He has released five soundtrack albums since—including the highly acclaimed *James Bond Tomorrow Never Dies* soundtrack. Tommy was also the first to use 3D audio in a game (Q-Sound), and was instrumental in bringing true digital interactive surround 5.1 (6-channel) to the industry. Tommy is the founder and president of GANG (Game Audio Network Guild)—a nonprofit organization educating and heightening the awareness of audio for the interactive world (*www.audiogang.org*). He is also an advisory board member for the *Game Developers Conference* and a nominating committee member for the Academy of Interactive Arts & Sciences. In 1999, Tommy co-designed the award-winning boxing game *Knockout Kings* for the N64 with Electronic Arts, which went on to win the "Best Console Sports Product of 1999" by the Academy of Interactive Arts & Sciences (AIAS). Also in 1999, Tommy was instrumental in getting video game music categorized in the Grammys. Tommy was part of a committee that petitioned NARAS to include game soundtracks in the awards show. In his spare time, Tommy is the host, writer, and co-producer of the worldwide weekly, award-winning video-game television show, *The Electric Playground* (*www.elecplay.com*)—which airs daily on the Discovery network and MTV Canada and was the proud recipient of the 2001 Telly Award for "Best Entertainment Cable Program." Tommy is the co-host of a half-hour weekly show titled *Judgment Day,* which appears on the 24-hour video-game network G4. In 2005, he launched the "Video Games Live" tour—held at the Hollywood Bowl in Los Angeles, California.

I founded the Game Audio Network Guild (GANG) mostly because of the need for *respect*. I was so sick and tired of audio being the last thing everyone focused on in game development. It was ridiculous! I realize that the game industry is currently like the film industry was in the 1950s. We are all still trying to figure this out as we go. However, that is all changing very

chapter 9 Audio: creating the atmosphere

quickly. I felt that if something wasn't done soon, that other people that were *not* in audio were going to be the ones to decide how things should be with regard to audio—and I didn't want that to happen. I wanted the audio community to dictate to everyone how things should be—from a technical standpoint, a creative standpoint, and even a business standpoint. We can look to the film industry and see the amount of importance they put into all aspects of audio—from voice acting, to music, to sound design. Great attention to detail and care is taken to make it sound incredible because they realize the *importance* of sound. Now the game industry is starting to think the same way—thanks to all of us coming together as one voice to form GANG.

George Alistair Sanger (a.k.a. "The Fat Man") on Game Audio & the Imagination : : : : :

The Fat Man has been creating music and other audio for games since 1983. He is internationally recognized for having contributed to the atmosphere of over 130 games—including such sound barrier breaking greats as *Loom*, *Wing Commander I* and *II*, *The 7th Guest I* and *II*, *NASCAR Racing*, *Putt-Putt Saves the Zoo*, and *ATF*. He wrote the first general MIDI soundtrack for a game, the first direct-to-MIDI live recording of musicians, the first Redbook soundtrack included with a game as a separate disc, the first music for a game that was considered a "work of art," and the first soundtrack that was considered a selling point for the game. On a 380-acre ranch on the Guadalupe River, the Fat Man hosts the annual Texas Interactive Music Conference & BBQ (Project BBQ)—the game audio industry's most prestigious and influential conference. His GamePlayMusic project is aimed at redefining the business and creative models of music for games, to benefit users, developers, and musicians alike.

GS

George Sanger
"The Fat Man"
(Composer & Author)

The player's perception of the place he's in—the mood of it, the history of it—need not be limited by accurate visualization. Story takes us beyond what we see; audio takes us further—allowing our minds to fill in countless gaps in what can be rendered or told with accuracy. Resolution and realism work against imagination. Perhaps plot harnesses it. Audio sets it free.

Gamers are not only fans of games, but of game soundtracks. In fact, many have been known to listen to game soundtracks from their favorite games while playing other games. In May 2003, game composer and producer Tommy Tallarico put on a live concert at the Hollywood Bowl on the last day of the Electronic Entertainment Expo (E3) in Los Angeles. The concert featured a 90-piece orchestra, 40-person choir, fireworks—and it was shown on cable television. Tallarico is also the founder of the Game Audio Network Guild (GANG) (*www.audiogang.org*). Another influential and prolific game composer is George Sanger (a.k.a. "The Fat Man"), who is also a published author (*The Fat Man on Game Audio: Tasty Morsels of Sonic Goodness*) and coordinator of an annual game audio think tank conference known as Project Bar-B-Q (*www.projectbarbq.com*).

Audio: A New Dimension

You should now have a clear understanding of the importance of audio in game development. Consider how audio can be an interface, gameplay, and story element all at once—providing the player with the necessary interface feedback, mood, and sense of reality. Audio might even guide the player toward a certain path in the game. Music, sound effects, and voiceover work together to provide both functional and dramatic elements—heightening the playing experience.

::

This chapter concludes Part II of this book, which focuses on content creation. In Part III, you will learn about the game development process and beyond—including game production team roles and responsibilities, management, tools, documentation, the production cycle, marketing, and player communities..

Expanded assignments and projects based on the material in this chapter are available on the Instructor Resources DVD.

307

:::CHAPTER REVIEW EXERCISES:::

1. What are the many purposes audio serves in games? Why is audio an important (but often overlooked) element in game development? Can you think of a purpose of game audio that was not discussed in this chapter?

2. What is the difference between looping and adaptive music in games? Discuss how two current games use these forms of music. Why can adaptive music sometimes be more effective than looping music?

3. What are some essential tools utilized by audio professionals in the game industry? What do these tools help audio professionals accomplish?

4. How are voiceovers, sound effects, and music used effectively in a game? How would you integrate all three audio forms into your original game? Consider the genre, subject matter, style of play, platform, and mood of your game in your answer.

5. Game and film scoring are very different from each other. Analyze the differences between these processes, and discuss the major distinctions between these two media. Tie these differences into what you have learned about gameplay, story, and character development.

6. How is voice acting in games different from other media? What are the benefits and disadvantages of working as a voice actor in this medium? If you were producing a game dialogue session, how would you change the way the session was structured to get the best performances out of your actors?

7. If you were designing sound for a game, in what instances would you create your own sounds using foley (or by recording sounds from the environment) versus utilizing pre-existing material from a library? Similarly, when would you create (or hire someone to create) original music versus licensing pre-existing material from a library or label?

8. Experiment with foley and come up with new ways to create sound effects that were not listed in this chapter. Capture your foley creations with a recorder. Take the recorder with you wherever you go and capture unique sounds from the environment. Catalog your recordings in a spreadsheet and consider what types of game sounds could be reflected by your recordings. Apply some of what you have recorded to your own original game.

Part III: Strategy

team, process, and community

CHAPTER

10

Roles & Responsibilities

developing the team

Key Chapter Questions

- What are the *company roles* associated with game development studios, publishers, licensors, and manufacturers?

- What are the *team roles* and *responsibilities* associated with management, art, design, programming, audio, and testing?

- What specific *techniques* and *tools* are utilized by different team members during game development?

In Part II, you learned how to develop compelling content for games. Now, let's take a look at game development from a business perspective. This chapter introduces the many roles, responsibilities, and tools associated with a development team. Understanding all the factors associated with a strong team is the first step in moving into the real world of game production. Whether you plan to join an existing development studio or go it alone, this chapter will give you the background you need to make an informed decision.

Company Roles

For further reading on this topic, please see *Game Project Management* (Hight/Novak)—part of the *Game Development Essentials* series.

There are several roles that companies can play in the game development process. A *developer* (or *development studio*) is the company that creates the game—coming up with a game concept, creating a prototype, and producing the final product.

Frequently, a separate company—known as a *publisher*—will fund, market, and distribute a game title. Sometimes a publisher will have an *in-house* development team that creates game titles. Activision, THQ, and Atari are examples of publishers. Electronic Arts publishes and develops its own titles in-house. Bethesda Softworks developed and published the *Elder Scrolls* series—including *Morrowind*, the popular third installment—and has also published games developed by other companies (such as *Call of Cthulu*, developed by Headfirst).

Raw Creativity, Grunt Work... and Begging

I think the most challenging aspect of game development is just the raw creativity that needs to go into giving life to characters, the world, quests, and events. After that, everything is just grunt work that you can muscle through. Oh, and begging for resources. And selling someone on the idea. Then threatening them. Then begging again.

—Chris Avellone (Creative Director & Co-Owner, Obsidian Entertainment)

When a publisher funds or hires an outside developer to create a title, the developer is known as a *third-party developer*. In some instances, the developer might present a game prototype to the publisher prior to getting funding—long before beginning the production process. Examples of third-party developers include High Voltage Software, Kung Fu Factory, Liquid Entertainment, Obsidian Entertainment, PopCap Games, and Respawn Entertainment. An increasing number of developers such as Halfbrick, Spacetime Studios, Appy Entertainment, and Zynga self-fund their games; this is particularly common within the mobile and social game markets.

In Chapter 2, you learned about how console game development differs from computer game development because a *manufacturer* is involved in the process. A manufacturer develops the hardware associated with a game's platform. For a game to be developed for a particular console brand, that hardware manufacturer (e.g., Sony, Microsoft, Nintendo) would need to approve the prototype before the title goes into production. Manufacturers develop titles themselves.

Louis Castle on Running a Large Game Development Studio :::::

Louis Castle is co-founder of Westwood Studios and served as a senior studio leader at Electronic Arts–Los Angeles (EALA), GM of EA's Blueprint Studio, and CEO of InstantAction (an IAC company). As part of the management team at Electronic Arts, Louis directed programming, artwork, audio, research and development, and business strategy. Louis was the general manager of Westwood Studios from 2000 to 2003, and he served in creative, business, and finance roles while expanding Westwood from two employees in 1985 to over 250 in 2002 (including the Irvine office). In his creative roles, Louis has contributed to over 100 games created by Westwood as executive producer, creative director, technical director, programmer, and artist. His business positions include serving as the COO and finance officer for Westwood Studios between 1992 and 2000, a period in which the company negotiated four multi-national acquisitions. Louis is passionate about the products and the people who create them. His role as Vice President at EALA allowed him to leverage his considerable interactive entertainment experience to add value across the spectrum of EALA's creative and business development.

Louis Castle
(Vice President of
Studios, Zynga)

Running a reasonably large studio (75+ employees) takes you away from most of the day-to-day creative decisions. Your role is more about strategy, timing—and choosing which titles should receive the most resources and funding based on the current progress and competitive environment. You deal with legal issues, employment concerns, communicating to executives or investors—drilling down only occasionally to the details of the operations. Contrary to common belief—if you are the final point of accountability—the larger the company is, the less control you have. You are required to constantly make compromises to maximize your business. I thoroughly enjoyed running Westwood Studios at its peak size of 250 employees, but I missed the day-to-day involvement and focus I got when working with a smaller team.

A *licensor* is involved if the game's content is adapted from an original source. Licensing fees are notoriously expensive, especially if they are from well-known properties. If you are considering creating a game based on a concept that is pre-existing (and not your original idea), avoid pursuing this until you have the industry clout and funding to make this kind of deal. Even if you had the money, the deal isn't guaranteed to happen. A competitor might have already secured the rights, you might not have the credibility to convince the copyright holder that you will create something worthwhile from their property, or the copyright holder simply might not be willing to sell the rights to anyone. New Line Cinema is an example of a licensor—which licensed the rights to the film *The Lord of the Rings* to Electronic Arts.

Christopher Bretz on Game Art for Licensed Properties : : : : :

CB

Christopher Bretz
(Art Director,
Bretz Consulting)

Christopher Bretz has been creating artwork for the video game and interactive entertainment industries since 1994. He was Art Director at Sega and San Francisco-based Secret Level—developers of tools, technology, and game titles for the console and computer game markets. Chris has worked in all aspects of graphics in the game industry—from concepts, to interface design, to 3D modeling and animation. His work has been seen in game titles published by Nintendo, THQ, LucasArts, and Atari.

When you work with licenses, you are given the opportunity to bring an established creative world—full of rich detail and history—into a new medium. You are tasked with re-imagining it in a way which remains faithful to the original material. This can be an exciting challenge for a game artist, especially when you are already a huge fan of the property. But changes inevitably have to be made to accommodate an interactive game—and that's the real challenge. Licensors are hoping that the special spark that made the property such a hit in its native medium (e.g., movie, book) will simply translate well into the game space with very little change. Things as simple as scale and color become issues for an interactive character in a way which might not have mattered for the movie or book version. You must also contend with all the preconceptions and biases of the property's creators—who are very protective of their creation, even though they might never have envisioned it as a video game. However, these people are huge assets, since they understand the license like no one else, and can offer insight or solutions to problems from a unique perspective. All parties want as faithful an interpretation as possible, because it is that world we all are sold on, and the one that the audience is following. It is your responsibility as the game artist to respect whatever that special aesthetic was in the original, and ensure that it remains present throughout the metamorphosis into a game.

Both *Toy Story 3: The Video Game* (left) and *TRON: Evolution* (right) are games that have been adapted from films.

If a developer decides to publish its own title for a non-proprietary computer platform, the developer does not have to partner with or get approval from a separate company to begin the production process. This type of developer is known as an independent (or indie) developer. 21-6 Productions (*Orbz* and *GravRally*), Three Rings Design (*Puzzle Pirates*), and eGenesis (*A Tale in the Desert*) are all award-winning indie game developers.

If you are interested in starting your own game development company so that you can produce your own titles, you need to approach a funding source to have enough capital to create the game (unless you happen to be independently wealthy!). However, to get interest from a prospective funding source, you will have to show them something tangible. If you decide to go in this direction, make use of the Web as an inexpensive and efficient marketing source. (Marketing strategies will be discussed further in Chapter 12.)

More likely, you might be interested in approaching a publisher—who can be both a funding and a distribution source for your title. Publishers are usually not interested in reading unsolicited proposals. Unless you know someone in the industry who can get you in a meeting with a publisher, you will need to focus on getting a prototype of your title completed so that you can show something tangible to your prospective publishers. You can reach these people through conferences and organizations—such as GDC (Game Developers Conference), E3 (Electronic Entertainment Expo), and IGDA (International Game Developers Association). (A list of conferences and organizations is available in the Resources section at the end of this book.) Even successful developers often need to develop prototypes to secure a publisher.

JM

Justin Mette
(President,
21-6 Productions)

Over his 18-year professional engineering career, Justin has held the titles of Senior Software Engineer, Lead Architect, and Development Manager. Justin's hard-core gaming history really started with the Atari 2600. Although he had used other game platforms previously, the 2600 really unlocked his addiction to gaming. Finding a profession that combined his passions for software development and games has been a life-long dream for Justin—a dream that has finally been realized in his latest role as President of 21-6 Productions.

I believe that the online distribution market for games is where most independent developers can get started and make a good living. Developing a game in four to six months with a small remote team means that your costs stay low and your return on investment does not have to be as large as the box or console industry.

You don't have to just build puzzle games anymore to succeed in online game distribution. Many companies have proven that true—with games like *Orbz*, *Marble Blast*, and *Tennis Critters* (all available from GarageGames).

We've also seen an incredibly strong rush of Mac gamers this past year in the online market. For our title *Orbz*, we saw almost a 50/50 split in revenue between Windows and Mac sales during 2003.

It's a great time to be an indie. The Internet allows you to find amazing talent, and work together without an office; technology like Torque makes game development a reality for small inexperienced teams; and a booming online game distribution market all lay out the best opportunity in years for game developers to live their dreams.

Jason Kay on Maximizing Revenue in the Game Industry:::::

Jason Kay is the co-founder of Monkey Gods, a social/mobile game developer based in Los Angeles. Previously, he co-founded Flektor (acquired by MySpace) with Jason Rubin and Andy Gavin—the creators of Crash Bandicoot and Jak & Daxter. Prior to Flektor, Jason served as a consultant to Home Box Office, Inc., the largest pay television service in the world, where he consulted on a variety of projects in games and new media. Prior to his work at HBO, he was involved in the sale of direct marketer Columbia House, Inc., which is now owned by BMG Direct, Inc. Jason began his career in entertainment as a Producer and Business Development Executive for Activision. Jason holds a Juris Doctor degree from the University of Southern California Law Center, and a BA *magna cum laude* with honors in English from Tulane University.

JK

Jason Kay
(Chief Business
Monkey,
Monkey Gods LLC)

People frequently say that the game business is rapidly becoming like the movie business. While this is true to some extent—the hits are bigger than ever, and the flops more painful—this analogy is imperfect. The feature film business (and to a lesser extent, television) derives revenue through a carefully crafted and maintained "windowing" strategy. Movies are first released at the box office in foreign and domestic markets, then on home video, then on pay-per-view—and eventually on cable and broadcast television. This strategy maximizes revenues across a variety of markets and at multiple price points. There is no analogy to this in the game business. Titles are sold at retail at full price, then at discount prices until they eventually are sent to the bargain bin and/or removed from distribution. While Disney can re-release "classic" animated movies to a new generation of young viewers every few years on various home video platforms (including VHS and DVD) at a fairly low cost, the only way to exploit older game properties is to either produce sequels or remakes at increasingly higher costs. In the last year, digital distribution of games through services like Valve's Steam and Onlive have made a windowed strategy more viable and have started to prove that windowing can generate incremental revenue once packaged goods are removed from the equation. Onlive even allows users to select from a combination of rental, ownership, or subscription bundles that allow access to multiple games.

Stephanie Spong on Game Industry Business Models :::::

SS

Stephanie Spong
(Founder,
Moksa Ventures)

Stephanie Spong is a venture capitalist with a passion for the game sector. She is currently raising a micro-venture fund, Moksa Ventures, focusing on the digital game industry and the application of game technologies and mechanics to non-game sectors. Formerly with EPIC Ventures (and with over 20 years professional experience in financial, operating and consulting roles from her tenure at Goldman Sachs, Citibank, McKinsey and Monitor), Stephanie brings seasoned business judgment and financial skills. Before joining EPIC, Stephanie gained operating experience and immersion in the digital media space as Managing Director of Razorfish's Los Angeles office. She earned a B.S. degree in Economics and Asian Studies from Brigham Young University and an M.B.A. from Harvard Business School.

Not so long ago, game business models were rather simple. "The Box" [tangible product sold through stores] retailed for $50 and contained premium game content from a major publisher. With the rise of interconnected gaming, either through PC-based MMOs or connected consoles allowing team play through a proprietary network, subscription-based business models emerged—generally $5 a month or less for small games, and $10 to $15 monthly for premium games. Today, dozens of business models compete for attention in mobile, multi-platform, casual, and social game segments— enabled by advances in micropayment systems, the emergence of alternate online game platforms, the falling cost to launch smaller games, the rise of the open social graph [term generally described as "global mapping of everybody and how they're related," which is used to explain the way social media platforms such as Facebook benefit], and the increasingly frictionless infrastructure for distributing digital downloadable content.

Primary among the newer models is the "freemium" business model, which offers a free play experience and the option to buy additional virtual goods, expansions, and the ability to unlock access to a premium or enhanced version of the game through micropayments and/or subscriptions. A small percentage of paying players and a large active population of free players can often cover development and distribution costs quite well for a smaller, low cost game. So far so good; payment of currency for goods or recurring access is an obvious continuation of the old Box or Subscription business models. New platforms enable variants of subscription business models, allowing access to multiple games within a given platform for a flat subscription fee. While straightforward from a player perspective, complexity lurks in the background for developers and publishers sorting through royalties and licenses for distribution through the platform.

Things really get interesting from a business model perspective when freemium models collide with powerful game platforms and the open social graph. From this collision emerges new ways for players to "pay" for access to game content in addition to forking over cash—by trading off either their attention (time spent in game or time spent with targeted advertisers) or reputation (referring friends and acquaintances to the game and essentially becoming marketers). For publishers and developers, the challenge is to avoid having their products priced at free or at iTunes rates of a few dollars (which is becoming common for many mobile apps). To avoid this industry-destroying fate, developers are experimenting wildly to find the right combination of free and paid access to their content and to discover the right combination of markets in attention and reputation to capture player interest and drive conversions to paying players.

Team Roles

In theory, a game could be created by just an artist and a programmer—but it takes a lot more than programming and art skills to create a working prototype that will form the basis of a successful game. Let's look at the various roles and responsibilities associated with those who work together to develop a game. Keep in mind that not all of these roles are always assumed by different people!

Production

A *producer* is someone who makes things happen. Producers are responsible for making sure the game is released on time and on budget—and that everyone involved is doing what they're supposed to be doing. One of the important, yet overlooked, responsibilities of a producer is the ability to manage people through conflict resolution, to communicate clearly, and to teach consensus-building skills. The lack of these skills can pose a big problem for a project, resulting in a decrease of team morale and an increase in employee attrition. A producer is responsible for balancing time, money, and quality on a project. An *external* producer is the liaison between the game development team and the publisher, while an *internal* producer works for the developer and leads the entire game development team in-house.

Executive Producer

An *executive producer* is usually the highest-level producer on a project. Responsibilities include production management, proposal and prototype management, and project support. The executive producer often oversees multiple projects. At some companies, the executive producer might also be the studio head.

For further reading on this topic, please see *Game Industry Career Guide* (Moore/Novak)— part of the *Game Development Essentials* series.

John Hight on the Role of Executive Producer:::::

JH

John Hight
(Director of
Product Development,
Sony Computer
Entertainment America)

In 1991, John Hight built his first game, *Battleship*, for the Philips CDi player. Since that time, he has worked on over 25 games and 9 edutainment products on various consoles and PCs. He's been fortunate to experience game development from many different roles: programmer, artist, writer, designer, and producer. Prior to joining Sony, John held management and creative positions with Atari, Electronic Arts, Westwood Studios, and 3DO. In his role as Executive Producer and Director of Design for Electronic Arts, John contributed to the design and production of *Nox, Command & Conquer: Red Alert 2*, and *Yuri's Revenge*. He is currently working on games for the PlayStation 3 for both retail sale and direct-to-consumer digital distribution. John holds a BSE in Computer Science from the University of New Mexico and an MBA from the Marshall School of Business at the University of Southern California.

A executive producer decides which games to produce, which developers to work with, and how much money to put into a given property. The job can involve scouting for new talent, negotiating deals, creative problem-solving, building teams, and, yes, playing games. I have a team of top-notch producers; each one manages a single game like it's their own business. Every game starts with an idea—whether my own, one of my producer's, or one pitched by a developer. I work with my producers and their developers to draft a *high concept*. From concept we go into *pre-production* and a working *prototype*. Our goal at the end of pre-production is to have a solid grasp of the game design and the look and feel of the game. If the game has the potential to be a success, then we green-light it into production. I stay with each game until it ships, and then the process of looking for the next "big thing" starts all over again.

I've done both internal and external production—and I like to switch back and forth. In internal production, you really get into the details of your game. You have a personal relationship with every member of the development team. You get involved in the daily decision making, and you have a strong awareness of the technology and talent going into your game. In external production, you have a broader view, and it's easier to maintain objectivity. You see the works of many studios and see more of the business side. In external production, you have a much better sense of industry trends and consumer tastes.

Producer

The *producer* is responsible for meeting project goals and establishing policies. This position focuses on priorities, due dates, contractual requirements, payments, budgeting, scheduling, staff support, and reporting to upper management (usually the executive producer). The producer sometimes interfaces with the press and resolves communication problems with partners (e.g., publisher, developer, hardware manufacturer, licensor).

Frank Gilson on the Role of Producer:::::

Frank Gilson is Senior Producer at Kabam—a developer focusing on massively multiplayer social games (MMSGs), including *Kingdoms of Camelot*. Prior to Kabam, Frank was Senior Producer for online and mobile games at Wizards of the Coast and a producer at Atari's Santa Monica, California office—managing aspects of third-party development, contracting with talent (such as composers and writers), and overseeing external development. Frank was also Associate Producer at Blizzard for *Warcraft III: Reign of Chaos* and the *Frozen Throne* expansion. He also worked in quality assurance as QA Technical Engineer (*Diablo 2*), QA Lead Analyst (*StarCraft: Brood War*), and QA Analyst (*StarCraft* and *Mac Diablo*). Before joining the game industry, Frank was a graduate student at the University of California, Irvine in Mathematical Behavioral Sciences—studying formal models for economics, voter choice, and psychology.

FG

Frank T. Gilson
(Senior Producer,
Kabam)

Part of my role as producer involves business development. We need to look to the future to determine what projects the company should finance, and who should develop them. This involves looking at existing licenses, potential new licenses (e.g., TV, film, fiction), or original intellectual property developed internally. Once a project exists, I manage the relationship between my company, a publisher, and the game developer. I will contract for music composition and performance, voice work and audio engineering, and writing with various groups and individuals. I make sure that the project has a sound schedule for the development of all of its parts, and I correct problems as they occur. I also work to promote the project internally, assuring that our public relations and marketing personnel worldwide have proper visibility of the project.

Grant Collier on Running a Third-Party Development Studio :::::

GC

Grant Collier
(former President,
Infinity Ward)

Grant Collier has been in the game industry for a decade. After spending a year in marketing and advertising, he made the transition to production, at various publishers. After several years and many titles, he moved over to the development side of the business. Shortly thereafter, Grant and company created Infinity Ward.

My duties often involve empowering team members so that they can do their jobs efficiently—from ordering equipment and hiring staff to basic human resources. I eliminate obstacles in project development to provide a positive work environment. A lot of my time is spent collaborating with my partners and publisher on the direction of our products…. Currently, the initial planning for the scope of the game is pretty challenging—although this might change depending on the stage of development. Our design team, our management, and our publisher all have to do a lot of compromising.

Associate Producer

The *associate producer* assists a producer on a particular project—providing research, interfacing with the development team, and making sure all areas of the project are running smoothly. Some specific tasks might include managing assets, generating screenshots for the public relations team, and reviewing milestones. The associate producer also works with outsourced producers for motion capture or cinematic video.

Assistant Producer

The *assistant producer* often works under the associate producer, handling any paperwork or other administrative requirements associated with budgeting and scheduling a project. Depending on the company, the assistant producer and associate producer roles might be interchangeable.

"A Hive Mind!"

The biggest challenge is probably maintaining a coherent vision. For a game to work, it has to feel like the work of one mind (or at least a hive mind!)—but, in fact, games are (often) created by 30, 40, 100 people or more. Communication is critical and, as in all human endeavors, communication is hard, hard, hard.

—*Warren Spector*
(*Vice President & Creative Director, Junction Point - Disney Interactive Studios*)

Design

Game *design* is often confused with game *art*. Design and art teams are often separated from each other, and some designers do not have any art-related experience whatsoever. Game designers are often more like engineers—taking a problem-solving approach to design functional systems (worlds and interfaces). Some designers also have scripting or even programming experience, which helps them turn the gameplay events they design into reality. *Game designers* focus on gameplay, levels, and interfaces (Chapters 6, 7, and 8). Some game designers are the visionaries behind some very successful games. Sid Meier (*Civilization*), Will Wright (*The Sims*), Warren Spector (*Deus Ex*), Richard Garriott (*Ultima*), and Peter Molyneux (*Black & White*) have formulated game concepts, created compelling storylines, and incorporated gameplay mechanics into successful game worlds.

Creative Director

The *creative director* ensures that the overall style and game content is consistent with the original vision for the project. The creative director might also help maintain the art style of the game through working closely with the art director (discussed later in this chapter).

Vision & Quality: The Role of Creative Director

As game teams have expanded over the past few years, many teams have added the role of Creative Director—which tends to focus on the overall vision and quality of the product. I develop the initial vision of the product, along with the supporting product pillars—and communicate that vision to the internal team and external partners. Throughout production, I am responsible for overseeing the overall quality and playability of the game—as well as assisting the Executive Producer in prioritizing features to ensure they meet the goals and needs of the market, the consumer, and the company.

—Christian Allen (Design Director, WB Games)

Design Director

A *game design director* is another management position that focuses less on hands-on design tasks and more on staff support, documentation, and guiding the design team in creating a game prototype. Depending on the company and project, this role might be taken on by the lead designer, creative director, or a producer.

Lead Designer

A *lead designer* usually supervises the game design team and is also often involved hands-on in the daily game design process. Some lead designer responsibilities include gameplay development, documentation assembly, and level design.

Chris Avellone on the Role of Lead Designer :::::

CA

Chris Avellone
(Creative Director, Lead
Designer & Co-Owner,
Obsidian
Entertainment)

Chris Avellone wanted to develop computer RPGs ever since he saw one of his friends playing *Bard's Tale 2* on a Commodore 64. After receiving a BA in English at the College of William and Mary, Chris started writing several short stories and RPG material—some of which got published. His writing got him noticed at Interplay, where he worked for seven to eight years before co-founding Obsidian Entertainment, Inc., with other ex-Interplayers. Chris has worked on *Starfleet Academy, Die by the Sword, Conquest of the New World, Red Asphalt, Planescape: Torment, Fallout 2, Icewind Dale 1, Icewind Dale: Heart of Winter, Icewind Dale: Trials of the Luremaster, Icewind Dale 2, Baldur's Gate: Dark Alliance, Lionheart, and Champions of Norrath, Knights of the Old Republic II: The Sith Lords*, and *Neverwinter Nights 2, Neverwinter Nights 2: Mask of the Betrayer, Alpha Protocol*, and *Fallout: New Vegas.* He says that his mom still isn't exactly clear on what he does on a day-to-day basis—and neither is he.

As lead designer, the actual duties vary on a day-to-day basis. Overall, I'm responsible for keeping the vision for the game, the game mechanics, and the "fun" of the game; the overall story (and any specific elements about the game designed to propel the overall story, such as companions, key locations, etc.); and then breaking down the remaining elements into digestible chunks for the other designers in terms of area briefs and area overviews ("This planet is X, the following things need to happen on it," etc.), breaking up the mechanics and play-balancing ("I need you to oversee the feat and class advancement systems as long as they accomplish the following goals," etc.)—and then managing all the parts so programmers, artists, and the producer are getting everything they need to keep moving.

Narrative Designer

One or more narrative designers might be part of the design team. These designers are writers who might have background writing in other media such as television or film—but they also understand how games differ from traditional, linear media. In other instances, writers might be outsourced when needed to help develop the story and characters for a particular project. The narrative designer has become an essential asset to most design teams as game developers have become better able to integrate storytelling with gameplay—and as screenwriters and other professional writers have learned to apply their skills to this very different medium. Depending on the genre and the extent of story and character development needs, though, members of the game design team might still be tasked with writing story and dialogue without any narrative designers on hand. The demarcation between the gameplay designer and narrative designer should eventually disappear as the design team truly integrates story and gameplay into one cohesive whole.

Anne Toole on the Roles of Writer & Narrative Designer:::::

AT

Anne Toole focuses on bringing fun, meaningful, and relevant content to games. Her credits include the MMO *Wizard 101* and *The Witcher*, an RPG that earned her a Writers Guild nomination. As a contract writer and designer, she has written games for the DS, 360, Wii, and PC in a variety of game genres including adventure, simulation, serious—and narrative genres such as fantasy, science fiction, and horror. Anne also served as the first head writer for the MMO *Stargate Worlds* and also has a television background—writing for the NBC serial, *Days of Our Lives*. Due to her transmedia experience, Anne has spoken about games and entertainment for the inaugural Nokia OpenLab 2008, South by Southwest (SXSW), ION Game Conference, and Comic-Con International. She has contributed chapters to the IGDA's *Writing for Video Game Genres* and *Professional Techniques for Video Game Writing* books, and she has served as Mentorship Chair for the Women in Games SIG. A citizen of both the EU and US, Anne holds a degree in Archaeology from Harvard.

Anne Toole
(Writer & Designer,
The Write Toole)

As a writer and narrative designer, my responsibilities could include anything from crafting the entire narrative, providing gameplay and art suggestions to bolster the narrative, to writing in-game text or dialogue. When creating the broad strokes of a game, a writer/narrative designer is ideally brought in early, during pre-production. However, I'm often brought in mere months before the ship date – and I'm usually crunching to get dialogue and story revisions in place before the game is finalized. While being brought in early seems like it would be the most fun creatively, I do enjoy the challenge of writing under pressure on a game that is near completion.

Atlus

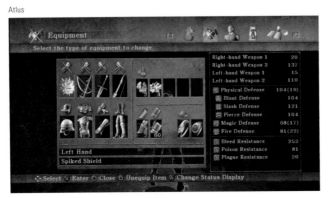

Inventory management user interface for *Demon's Souls*

Interface Designer

An *interface designer* determines the layout, content, navigation, and usability features of the game interface (see Chapter 8). The art team might be involved in creating the style of the interface, but this happens after the design stage.

James Owen Lowe on the Role of Content Designer in MMOs : : : : :

JOL

James Owen Lowe
(Content Designer,
ZeniMax Online
Studios)

James Owen Lowe is a writer and MMO content designer. He has a BA in Communication & Culture from Indiana University and a BS in Game Art & Design from the Art Institute of Pittsburgh–Online Division (formerly the Art Institute Online). His credits include *Fallen Earth* and the *Fallen Earth: Blood Sports* update while working at Icarus Studios. He now is designing content on an unannounced title for ZeniMax Online Studios. He lives with his wife Mandy and daughter Nora.

A content designer for a massively multiplayer online game (MMO) can specialize in certain aspects of the job, but it mostly boils down to creating interesting quests and spaces for the player. In general, the content designer writes a document that describes an area, the story, and the nature of the quests in that area. This document gets passed to the art and world-building teams, and they all collaborate on constructing the play space. Once the space has been blocked out, the content designer places creatures, quest-givers, and targets to meet a more refined design. The next steps are iteration. As the art gets more refined, the content must change and be polished. As an MMO content designer, I must work to create an interesting quest players must feel heroic doing. All players are heroes of their own MMOs, and other players are just the supporting cast. I have to ensure that the players are doing something cool that has an impact on the world without impacting the world of other players too much.

Level Designer

A *level designer* focuses on building the game environment or world (see Chapter 7). Some level designers only build the physical environment; others incorporate gameplay into the game world (see Chapter 6). Level designers might also be involved in writing the stories (and even dialogue!) associated with missions or campaigns that they design.

Level for *Warhammer 40,000: Dawn of War II.*

Mary-Margaret Walker on the Level Designer Shortage :::::

As CEO, Mary-Margaret leads the new business endeavors for Mary-Margaret Network. She brings to the role 14 years of experience in career and hiring services and 6 years of experience in video game development. Prior to creating Mary-Margaret Network in 1996, Mary-Margaret was Manager of Studio Services for The 3DO Company—managing the milestones and development process of all projects in production and the hiring of over 200 employees. Previously, she was at Origin Systems where she created the company's Human Resources department and contributed to titles in development as a Design Manager. Mary-Margaret is a regular speaker at international trade shows and has authored numerous articles. A founding member of the IGDA, Mary-Margaret holds a Bachelor of Arts degree from Texas Christian University and an M.B.A. from Sacred Heart University.

MMW

Mary-Margaret Walker (Chief Executive Officer, Mary-Margaret Network)

I have been in the industry for 20 years and have watched all of the cycles of hiring in their ups and downs throughout the years. There has always been a shortage of engineers of all types. As the industry has matured, companies have actively reached out to make diversity hires especially in engineering. With the latest growth in the industry we have seen a new shortage: Level Designers have become crucial to game development in ways that we have not seen before. When I started in the industry in 1991, I was a level designer on *Ultima VII* at Origin Systems. Now, 20 years later, there is an amazing shortage in this highly specialized position that requires imagination and creativity as well as an understanding of the tools, platform, and players.

Patricia Pizer on the Greatest Design Challenge :::::

PP

Patricia A. Pizer
(Creative Director,
ZeeGee Games)

Patricia Pizer debuted in the game industry at Infocom in 1988, making games back when you didn't even need graphics. Over the next decade, she worked at Boffo Games, THQ/GameFX, CogniToy, and Harmonix Music. Patricia moved into massively multiplayer online games at Turbine Entertainment, Ubisoft, and Disney's VR Studio. Currently, She then applied her design skills to Alternate Reality Games for 42 Entertainment. Patricia returned to Disney to design *Dgamer* (a social network cross-platform application for children) and *Club Penguin: Elite Penguin Force* (the top-selling third-party title on the Nintendo DS). Currently, she consults with various firms to improve the social aspects of their games. Mostly though, she just likes to play games.

The most challenging part of game design is not letting go of a pet idea because it's not technically feasible—or even trying out a game idea that simply does not work and having to start over. No, I think the most challenging part is the time and effort involved. You frequently don't see a game on a shelf for years after you've begun. The process has an extremely extended gestation period, unless you're creating Facebook-style games where the challenge shifts to producing great games within a very short timeline. But seeing it all come to life is incredibly rewarding.

Game Design: A Common Thread

Every programmer and artist should spend some time on game design early in their career, even as a hobby. They may never pick it up again or make that game, but that experience will improve them so much in their jobs. The programmer who understands design better understands the game designer's vision—what makes the designer's contribution different and fun. Anyone can make an orc run across a field, but the artist and programmer can convey a story through the little extra creative efforts that they give that orc, from a scar, to a limp, to a cautious glance over an armor-plated soldier. They convey history and backstory to a gamer without ever writing it down in a manual or cut scene. Every game developer, in any role, should always put a part of themselves and their creativity into the game. It makes it real, and draws the gamer into the world they've created as a team.

—*Mark Chuberka (Director of Business Development, GameSalad)*

Art

Game *art* involves creating concept art or assets that will be used in the game. There are four basic art tasks that differentiate game artists: drawing (analog or digital), modeling, texturing, and animation. There are also different applications that artists focus on—including characters, props, vehicles, interiors, exteriors, environment, effects, cinematics, and interface. Artist roles are often distinguished by their task and application focus. A *2D artist* creates and refines two-dimensional art assets used in the game itself—including textures for characters, environments, objects, interfaces, and game packaging (also handled by the marketing department). A *3D artist* creates and refines three-dimensional art assets—including modeling, texture-mapping, and lighting.

Art Director

The *art director* usually operates the art department, overseeing scheduling, development, budgeting, and hiring. Responsibilities of an art director include directing the style of the game's art—including determining the mood, look, and feel of the game. The art director improves the process, quality, and productivity of art development throughout the company.

Lead Artist

A *lead artist* usually supervises the game art team and is also often involved hands-on in the daily game art production process. Most lead artist positions are based on specialty—such as Lead Concept (or Storyboard) Artist, Lead Modeling Artist, Lead Texture Artist, and Lead Animator.

Marc Taro Holmes on the Role of Art Director:::::

Illustrator and concept artist Marc Taro Holmes was Art Director at Ensemble Studios, Lead Artist at Obsidian Entertainment, and Art Director/Production Designer at Turbine Entertainment and BioWare—contributing to RPGs such as *Neverwinter Nights* and *Neverwinter Nights 2*. He holds a BFA in Graphic Design from the Alberta College of Art & Design. Marc's neglected hobbies include traveling and filling sketchbooks.

MTH

Marc Taro Holmes
(art director, concept
artist, and illustrator)

The art director role, as I have experienced it, is very bipolar. Art directors have to be equally interested in the creative aspect of production design and in planning and monitoring the project schedule. I actually spend a lot of my time drawing during the brainstorming stage. My goal is to create a tangible example to direct the team's efforts—a set of images that define a visual language. It's about setting limits and boundaries, by actual example. Over on the other side of the brain, I do a lot of project scheduling. Excel sheets, meetings, email, design docs—all that fun, fun administration that goes on behind the scenes. In my experience, the actual game takes so much time and energy that the [creative] work has to be handled on nights and weekends. There seems to be some unwritten rule that if artists want to make the pretty pictures, they have to suffer for that privilege!

Concept Artist

A *concept artist* usually creates drawings and sketches of the game environment, props, and characters. Storyboards are used during the concept development process and are often included in concept documentation. (See the Documentation section in Chapter 11 for more details.) The concept artist can be key to securing a publishing deal by providing a low-cost way to visualize the game before it is made.

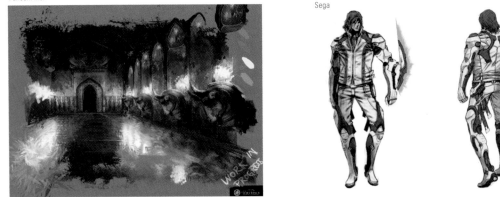

Funcom Inc.

Sega

It all starts with concept art—such as the Temple of Erlik from *Age of Conan: Hyborian Adventures* (left) or Leo images from *Anarchy Reigns* (right).

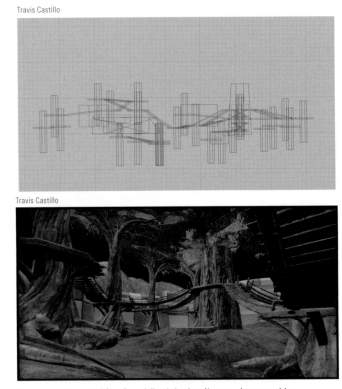

Travis Castillo

Travis Castillo

A wiremesh model (top) and final design (bottom) created by environmental artist Travis Castillo.

Modeler

Modeling involves creating 3D assets from 2D drawings—often for game characters, props, environments, and structures. Modelers create all of the final art assets for the game, unless the system being used to create the game is a 2D (or *sprite-based*) system. Modelers create 3D wire meshes from the concept art, and apply textures to the meshes in a process known as *skinning*.

Sometimes models are created from scratch within a software package, or they are created from scanning a real-world 3D clay model into a software program such as 3D Studio Max or Maya. Environmental modelers build 3D spaces and worlds through which characters move, starting with geometric shapes which are combined and re-formed to create the game environment. After completing a

3D mesh for the environment, the modeler provides shading, texturing, and lighting. Types of modelers based on application include Character Modeler, Environmental Modeler, and Structures Modeler.

Texture Artist

Texturing involves generating 2D image maps that are applied to 3D models. These texture maps include surfaces for characters (skin, clothing), structures (building interiors/exteriors), and objects (vehicles, props). Sometimes texture artists photograph an existing surface, scan it into a software program such as Photoshop, and then touch it up. Another method of texturing involves creating a texture from scratch and building it up by layer.

Animator

Animation involves applying movement to objects and characters in the game world. In addition to in-game motions and performances, some animators also get involved with *cinematics*. In Chapter 5, you learned that a character's movement can reveal personality. Animators need to understand character development. Techniques used in animation include *keyframing* (where an animator makes each pose of a movement and sets sequential keyframes to generate animation files) and *motion capture* (where an animator captures the motions of real people, placing markers on joints of the person to track movement and create motion data). Types of animators based on differing applications include Character Animator, Cinematics Artist, and Effects Artist.

Sony Computer Entertainment America

An alternative to keyframing, motion capture (*Heavy Rain* mocap studio, shown) allows animators to capture actors' motions and live performances.

Technical Artist

Some artists bridge the divide between art and programming. They understand the 3D technical requirements and game engine. They help set standards with the tools, work on the art "pipeline," and make sure assets are created and stored in the appropriate formats. They are often experts with particular art packages and scripting.

Programming

Game *programming* can involve anything from creating the *game engine* (the core code for the game) to in-house database, graphics, audio, and world-building *tools* that other team members can use during the game production process to manage assets and create art, sound, and game worlds.

Technical Director

The *technical director* creates the technical design for the project, oversees its implementation throughout all phases of production, and selects the tools, hardware, and code standards.

Jason Spangler on the Role of Technical Director :::::

JS

Jason Spangler
(Technical Director,
BioWare /
Electronic Arts)

Jason Spangler is a Technical Director at the BioWare studio of Electronic Arts, where he has worked on the *Star Wars: The Old Republic* MMO project. Jason has performed a variety of technology leadership roles at different studios, including Director of Technology at Origin Systems and Technical Director at Mythic Entertainment. Jason also worked on the original version and many expansions of *Ultima Online*. In his spare time, Jason enjoys hiking, native plant landscaping, and conservation—and he is the board president of a non-profit conservation group.

As Technical Director, I work with people throughout the development team—most frequently software engineers, product managers, producers, and QA—to help ensure that the technical design and implementation of systems and code in the game and supporting infrastructure (such as tools, build systems, patching systems, and installers) are of high quality and ready for the customer. I also help to identify technical risks and potential solutions, and I highlight areas that need more work and improvement.

Lead Programmer

The *lead programmer* usually supervises the programming team (and often reports to the Technical Director) and is also often involved hands-on in the daily programming process.

KyungMin Bang on the Role of Lead Programmer :::::

After graduating from Seoul National University with a degree in electrical engineering and computer science—and a focus on networking and graphics—KyungMin Bang started as a game programmer at Nexon in 2000, where he led *Project NG*. KyungMin founded J2M in December 2004—where he developed *Raycity*, *TAAN*, and *Debut*. J2M was acquired by Electronic Arts in December 2008. KyungMin is currently GM of EA's Seoul Studio.

KyungMin Bang
(General Manager,
Electronic Arts -
Seoul)

As Lead Programmer, I focused primarily on system design and time management. There are many technical ways to implement one gameplay feature. It was my responsibility to design the whole system to implement the feature and lead the programming process. At Nexon, I had four programmers on my team, and I needed to make a very detailed task list and schedule for them. For instance, if I needed to implement a task (from the design team) such as "two characters are playing golf through the online environment," then the tasks to be done would include:

- 3D max plug-in to export character model
- Enhance rendering engine
- Play scripting
- Network sync design
- Network protocol design

I would make these separate tasks, assign them to the programmers, and check to see how much of each task has been completed on a daily basis.

Network Programmer

The *network programmer* specifically enables the multiplayer component for online games and should understand database management, client/server architecture, security, and writing code using network protocols such as TCP/IP, Winsock, and UDP. DirectPlay (the DirectX interface to networking) is a popular tool for network programming. Sometimes a network programmer will also need wireless protocol knowledge (BlueTooth, Infra-Red).

Graphics Programmer

The *graphics programmer* (a mix between a programmer and an artist) is also known as the 3D Programmer—and is responsible for programming solutions to specific graphical game issues. This programmer must understand code animation and effects using 3D graphics APIs such as DirectX or OpenGL.

Engine Programmer

The *engine programmer* creates the core game engine, which usually handles graphics rendering as well as collision detection between game objects. Collision detection involves checking the intersection between game objects and calculating trajectories, impact times, and impact points. The term "game engine" arose in the mid-1990s when id Software began to license its core software for *Doom* and *Quake* games, which allowed the company to have an additional revenue stream. Other developers were able to design their own game content and assets using id's game engine instead of working from scratch.

Tools Programmer

The *tools programmer* designs tools to assist art and design team members incorporate their work into code so that it can be included in the game. This programmer might create level editors to help designers create worlds—or write plug-ins for graphics software like 3D Studio Max and Maya to make it easier for artists to create game assets. The tools programmer also designs performance tracking tools, as well as script engines.

John Ahlquist & Denis Papp on Engine & Tools Programming :::::

JA

John Ahlquist
(Founder, Ahlquist
Software)

John Ahlquist developed the tools and engine for Electronic Arts' *Command & Conquer: Generals - Zero Hour* and *The Lord of the Rings: Battle for Middle-Earth*. John currently runs Ahlquist Software—developing game software for a variety of clients. John previously worked for Altsys/Macromedia on Aldus FreeHand and was one of the creators of Macromedia Fireworks. Prior to Macromedia, John spent seven years working at Texas Instruments, programming Integrated Circuit CAD tools in the Design Automation Department. He is a second-degree black belt in Tae Kwon Do and has been playing video games since *Pong*.

My first responsibility is to analyze what the designers and artists need the game engine and tools to do—and I design and implement efficient solutions. There are two keys to *efficiency:* The first is to develop the code quickly, since we are always longer on features and shorter on time. The second is runtime performance for the engine. The tools are less critical, but engine performance is very important. Tasks include anything from designing and implementing a map layout tool (we call ours Worldbuilder), to creating a motion blur transition from a movie trailer clip. As we get closer to shipping the game, debugging and, optimization become my main responsibilities.

Denis Papp has been with TimeGate Studios since 1999, during which time it has earned awards for RTS of the Year, Strategy Game of the Year, and Expansion of the Year. At TimeGate, Denis has worked on multiple titles—including *Kohan* and *Section 8*—and he has been responsible for engine architecture, game design, and development of an Agile methodology for video game project management. Denis started in the game industry professionally at BioWare in 1996, working as Lead Programmer for *Shattered Steel*. Following that, he developed one of the first strong poker AIs, *Loki*, for his M.Sc. thesis with the University of Alberta Game Research Group. Denis's favorite game is *NetHack*. Here are Denis's tips for managing game projects using engines and tools.

Denis Papp
(Director of
Programming &
Executive Producer,
TimeGate Studios)

With the engine:

■ Design a framework that minimizes the chance of writing expensive bugs, and maximizes the chances of tracking them down when they occur.

■ With C++, focus on memory and pointer bugs.

■ Clean object-oriented design (OOD): code with dependencies that stretch between multiple modules is brittle and difficult to understand.

With tools:

■ Keep things intuitive.

■ Automate as much as possible—don't expect users to memorize procedures.

■ Understand the distinction between user data errors and programming logic errors.

■ Check for and provide descriptive error messages for data errors.

■ Make warnings visible and try to enforce a zero warnings policy.

Artificial Intelligence Programmer

The *artificial intelligence (AI) programmer* focuses on the creation of behaviors that give the impression of intelligent behavior. This "intelligence" is most commonly exhibited by the game's non-player characters (NPCs) and "virtual players" (those that aren't perceived by players—such as a chess opponent in a traditional computer chess game). Game AI involves logical responses to stimulus, pathfinding, strategic planning, and even dialogue. Gameplay design elements such as balance and flow are also incorporated into a game by the AI programmer so that it's challenging and fun to play.

Audio Programmer

The *audio programmer* implements sound and music into the game. Responsibilities include effectively accessing the sound card, loading different sound formats, and programming music.

Physics Programmer

The *physics programmer* researches, develops, and optimizes efficient physics, collision systems, particle systems, and body dynamics. A game's physics needs might include gravity, water viscosity, and even motions attributed to NPCs.

Interface Programmer

The *interface programmer* designs and creates expandable, customizable, graphical user interface systems. Advanced game user interface (UI) systems might allow scripting and special effects—such as transparency, animation, or particle effects for the controls—such as inverse kinematics (IK), which is the process of determining that the game characters connect physically to the game world (such as their feet landing firmly atop terrain).

MMO Programming Challenges

The complexity of developing, running, and maintaining MMO games is a great challenge. A wide range of customer computer capabilities (CPU, memory, video cards), network bandwidth (from slow DSL, to cable models, to fast fiber), and the dynamic nature of the games (difficult to control how many player characters and what equipment and thus models and textures are on-screen) makes developing a high-quality game client that runs on such a variety of hardware difficult. The servers need to handle thousands of player clients at once while still performing well enough to give a great gameplay experience. And many people forget the back-end systems needed to support a large online product—including a reliable tools pipeline, patching systems and servers, a variety of boxed and digital download installation options, build and deploy systems that can efficiently publish a new build and data to thousands of servers, among many others.

Jason Spangler (Technical Director, BioWare / Electronic Arts)

Associate Programmer

The *associate* (or junior) *programmer* adds small elements to a game project, using a game company's own scripting tools and languages to program events or actions in a game. Sometimes, this scripting responsibility is assigned to members of the game design team who have the required skills. A game designer with some programming experience can then make gameplay events happen in a particular mission or campaign.

Jay Gawronek on the Evolution of Programmer Roles :::::

JG

Jay Gawronek has been a part of the game industry since 1988 when he was first hired as an assembly programmer for Icon Design, Ltd, a UK company responsible for creating 8-bit games for the Commodore 64, Sinclair Spectrum, and the Amstrad CPC. Less than a year later, his first game was published. Since then, Jay has had published games on all the major consoles and most of the popular home computers. In 1995, he moved from the UK to Austin, TX when he started working for Acclaim Studios–Austin. He is now an independent contractor at Rainbow Studios, a THQ subsidiary in Arizona.

Jay Gawronek
(Independent
Contractor,
Bluepoint Games)

Over the 19 years or so that I have been in the industry, my roles have changed quite a lot. Originally as an 8-bit assembly programmer, I was the only programmer on the game with maybe a supporting artist if I was lucky. All the design was done by either me or an artist; I don't ever remember working with a full-time designer until the SNES/Genesis era.

Then as teams got bigger, we had the lead roles. Throughout my career I have had many lead programmer roles. This was the person who did the most work and the "go-to" guy management needed to speak to in order to add features (and extended working hours!) to the game.

Now we have much bigger teams with multiple leads specializing in different areas such as network, AI, tools, and rendering. The lead programmer role has changed over the years. Now it's heavily based around working with the schedules and delegating tasks.

As Technical Director, I manage multiple groups of programmers. I work at a higher level now and do not get time to program at work anymore, which I miss.

Audio

As discussed in more detail in Chapter 9, *audio* for a game project might include music, sound effects, and dialog. Some companies do not have audio departments or teams of their own, and will instead outsource audio services.

Audio Director

The *audio director* is responsible for managing the audio department; interfacing with the audio programmer (or team) to ensure that the audio assets get properly incorporated into the game; hiring personnel such as composers, sound designers, and voice-over artists; and licensing pre-existing songs for use in game soundtracks.

Composer

A *composer* writes the musical score for a game and is often outsourced. Unlike a film composer—who writes music to fit various scenes in a linear medium—a game composer is unable to preview the entire game before writing the music. As discussed in Chapter 6, there are often many paths players can choose to take within a game. Music must be written to fit each of the possible paths and events that could occur.

Sound Designer

A *sound designer* is responsible for creating sound effects and ambient sound for a game. This position often involves collecting sounds from the environment with an audio recorder, editing them, and incorporating them into the game engine (or providing audio assets to the audio programmer for this purpose). Unfortunately, many sound designers make all-too-frequent use of pre-existing sounds collected in libraries that can be purchased or sometimes downloaded at no charge. Although these sounds can be helpful, they can be overused because they are so easy to obtain.

Voiceover Artist

A *voiceover artist* (also known as a *voice actor*) is often outsourced to provide spoken-word narration and dialogue for the game. There may be several voiceover artists involved in one game project, providing the voice for each character.

For further reading on this topic, please see *Game Audio Development* (Marks/ Novak)—part of the *Game Development Essentials* series.

Role Variance in Game Audio

I'm a freelance composer and sound designer. When I started in 1999, there was a 50-50 split between staff audio positions and freelancers. I still see a good bit of variance in this, mainly because of the ebb and flow of audio work during game development. It's important to have the composer and sound designers on board early for any game using interactive and adaptive audio. On the other hand, you can find yourself with downtime over the course of a year or two—which leads to some companies relegating that aspect to the freelance side. Other studios may hire just an audio director, while the larger companies may keep an entire department on board to work on multiple titles concurrently.

—Jamie Lendino (Composer & Sound Designer, Sound For Games Interactive)

Testing & Quality Assurance

Game *testing* involves playing a game before its release to determine whether or not it is *playable*—bug-free, consistent, and entertaining. Similar to starting out in the mailroom in the film industry, beginning your game development career as an in-house tester is an opportunity to network with company decision-makers. Furthermore, these people care what *you* think! If a tester doesn't feel a product is playable, a producer will often take this information very seriously—and have the development team make any changes necessary to pass the playability test. Company management sees testers as a sample of the players that will be buying the game. If the players don't like the product, it will flop. Testers focus on the game's "fun factor," usability, logic, and functionality. Techniques for testing include *black box* or *white box*. In black-box testing, the tester does not know what is wrong with the game and must figure it out during the testing process. In white-box testing, the tester can see the problems with the game almost immediately by running it with a debugger turned on, which reveals code errors.

Quality assurance (QA) is often confused with testing. Unlike testing for playability and compatibility, QA involves establishing standards and procedures for the development of a game. Functions of QA include process monitoring, product evaluation, and auditing—ensuring that games meet the documentation, design, programming, and code standards set by the game developer and publisher. The roles of QA and testing are often combined into the same team, though sometimes one or both roles will be outsourced. Compliance is all-important in console publishing and legal/contractual agreements.

For further reading on this topic, please see *Game Testing & QA* (Levy/Novak)—part of the *Game Development Essentials* series.

Testing Manager

The *testing manager* is responsible for managing the testing and QA teams on multiple game projects. Several lead testers report to the testing manager—who might also manage the testing budget and interface with upper management to ensure that products being tested are completed in a timely manner.

Lead Tester

The *lead tester* usually supervises the testing team and is also often involved hands-on in the daily testing process for a particular game project. Responsibilities of the lead tester include searching for errors and inconsistencies related to 3D geometry, modeling, texturing, aesthetics, and game logic. The lead tester also manages the data entry process of playability testers, ensures that testers are looking for bugs in the correct areas of the product, and summarizes the status of the project when requested in written and verbal form. The lead tester might interface with the project's producer, who often determines whether bugs are important enough to be fixed.

Compatibility & Format Testers

Compatibility (computer games) and *format* (console games) *testers* work for a publisher and focus on whether a game has cross-platform compatibility—functioning equally well on all target platforms and manual interfaces. If a game has been developed for all console platforms, does it run equally well on all? Do all the controllers allow the game to be played smoothly? Compatibility testers might test joysticks, mice, controllers, operating system standards, and video/sound cards—and they also need to be familiar with the underlying programming and scripting languages associated with any systems being tested. For computer games, compatibility testers might also ensure that the game runs adequately on machines that comply with the minimum hardware specifications of a game.

The "Fun Factor"

Making games fun is the most challenging aspect of the game development process. Everything else pales in comparison. Games have to be familiar enough so that they are accessible to the audience, but different enough to be novel and challenging. It's such a balancing act when making a game—to find and iterate through game systems, be strongly self-critical of features that aren't adding to the fun of the game, and still be able to defend those that just need a little bit more work to gel into something great.

—*Mark Terrano (Design Director, Hidden Path Entertainment)*

Production, Quality Assurance & Regression Testers

Production (developer), *quality assurance* (publisher), and *regression testers* are usually in-house, paid positions that last perhaps four to six months at a time. These testers also make suggestions for improving, adding, or deleting features—and they might also compare the game to prospective competing titles. Since these positions are in-house, they do provide many opportunities for networking. Company executives and management visit the testing department, observe the reactions of testers, and listen to testers' opinions. Tools used in the position include spreadsheets such as Excel and bug-tracking software such as TestTrack Pro. Regression testers specifically focus on verifying that certain bugs (such as severe and high-priority) have been fixed.

Playability, Usability & Beta Testers

When a game is at the Beta stage (discussed in Chapter 11), volunteer *Beta testers* are recruited (usually via the Internet) to test the game in the privacy of their own homes. Beta testing is the easiest way to gain industry experience. Since Beta testing does not occur in-house, Beta testing doesn't involve face-to-face networking opportunities—but it still allows for feedback and communication with some company decision makers online. A drawback of Beta testing for the developer is that a tester's reactions can't be observed during the process. Beta, playability, and usability testers usually consist of members of a game's target market who are not unfamiliar with the game. Stress or progression testing is a form of Beta testing that involves playing a game thoroughly from start to finish to determine whether the game is usable and playable.

Focus Testers

Focus testers are target customers (and sometimes other groups) who are recruited on-site at little or no compensation to play the game to determine which aspects are most appealing. The marketing department usually conducts focus testing—which is similar to assembling a focus group to discuss a target market's opinions on a new product or service.

Marketing

Separate from roles associated with the development team are those associated with marketing the game to the public. Chapter 12 discusses all of these roles (including promotion, sales, advertising, public relations, and community management) in detail.

Tools

The game development team uses a variety of tools during each phase of development to plan, budget, schedule, create, and test games.

Design

Tools used in design are either proprietary— such as *level editors* built in-house by tools programmers—or publicly available development suites such as GameSalad Creator that allow for game creation and prototyping. Versions of level editors are often released with the game so that players can use them to build their own worlds. Level- and world-building tools are packaged with several games—including *Neverwinter Nights* (Aurora Toolset), *Half-Life* (Valve Hammer Editor), and *Unreal* (Unreal Editor), and *Far Cry* (CryENGINE's Sandbox Editor).

Crytek GmbH

GameSalad

Game design tools include level editors such as CryENGINE's Sandbox Editor (left) and development suites that can be used for game creation or prototyping such as the 2D drag-and-drop authoring tool, GameSalad Creator (right).

Game Engine Programming

Programmers use a variety of tools to build game engines. Here are just a few examples:

- *Compiler:* This tool takes the source code written by the programmer in the "source" language and translates it into a different "target" programming language that the computer can understand so that it can be executed. Part of the GNU Project, the GNU Compiler Collection (GCC) is part of the GNU Project, supported by the Free Software Foundation. Some compilers used in game programming include freeware DOS compiler DJGPP (a port of the GCC compiler), as well as Microsoft Visual Basic (VB) and Visual C++.

- *Debugger:* This tool is used after a program is compiled to find any *bugs* (defects) in the code and help fix them. The GNU Visual Debugger (known as GVD) is free. Microsoft VB contains a debugger, and the GNU Debugger (GDB) is the most common UNIX system debugger.

- *IDE (Integrated Development Environment):* An IDE is a tool that integrates applications into one environment for the programmer, allowing increased productivity by not forcing time-wasting swaps of applications. IDEs such as NetBeans and RHIDE will work with GCC and DJGPP, respectively. Microsoft Visual Studio contains a built-in compiler and debugger.

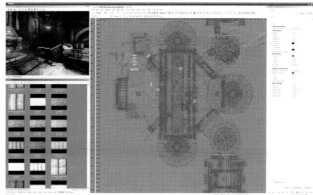
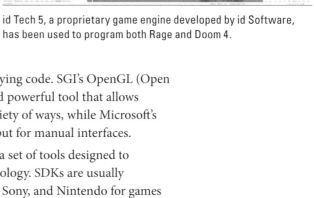

id Tech 5, a proprietary game engine developed by id Software, has been used to program both Rage and Doom 4.

- *API (Application Programming Interface):* An API is an interface that makes life easier for the programmer by allowing for a pre-built solution, so that the programmer does not have to use the underlying code. SGI's OpenGL (Open Graphics Library) API provides a flexible and powerful tool that allows high-quality graphics to be rendered in a variety of ways, while Microsoft's DirectX handles 3D graphics, sound, and input for manual interfaces.

- *SDK (Software Development Kit):* An SDK is a set of tools designed to help with development for a particular technology. SDKs are usually platform-specific—available from Microsoft, Sony, and Nintendo for games created specifically for their systems. Mobile SDKs include those available specifically for iOS (Apple) and Android-based smartphones.

::::: *Shattered Galaxy*: The "Minus" Bug

Nexon Corporation

As a programmer on *Shattered Galaxy,* I once had to apply a big game patch. (This is common in MMOGs—where new content, regions, graphics, interface improvements, and other features need to be added on a regular basis to keep the game evolving.) Right after patching, I encountered a strange game bug, and I had no clue why it happened. I tried almost everything I could to fix it. Since the game was commercialized (people were paying subscription fees to play), I had to find the bug no matter how long it might take. After about almost 12 hours of searching, I finally found that I had made a simple mistake by putting a "minus" sign ("–") before a "1" in the code. Due to a single "minus" sign mistake, over 5,000 concurrent players had big trouble playing the game!

—KyungMin Bang (General Manager, Electronic Arts - Seoul)

In our Gaming and Mobile Apps Concentration (GMAC), we use the Unity 3 development environment to leverage the deployment of games to multiple platforms. I believe the adoption of platforms such as OpenGL and Mono (to mention just two) will promote the development of a family of games that can be seamlessly deployed to multiple platforms.

—*Dr. Arturo Sanchez-Ruiz (Associate Professor of Computing, University of North Florida)*

Game Engines for Indie Development

With the erratic work schedules of indie developers (which is usually in the evenings after a day job or on weekends), there isn't enough time to develop a game engine yourself and still make money with your business. Instead, spend the time designing and developing a fun game. Even with a full-featured game engine like Torque (from GarageGames), our first 3D game *Orbz* took three months to develop version 1.0, and another three months to develop version 2.0 with a five-person team. Our latest title, *GravRally*, which also uses Torque, has a team of eight and has been in development for nine months already, with a few more to go before it's complete. As you can see, even with experience and a great game engine under our belt, it still takes a long time to design and build fun games. The other reason to use an existing game engine is testing liability. Developing computer games comes with the large burden of testing on many different hardware combinations (e.g., CPU, memory, operating system, video card, sound card). Using a proven game engine will greatly reduce your testing liabilities and make it worthwhile to take on computer game development.

—*Justin Mette (President, 21-6 Productions, Inc.)*

XNA: Leveling the Playing Field for Programmers

In 2006, Microsoft opened the door for indie developers to create their own games for the PC and the Xbox 360 platform using their XNA Game Studio Express. While it was not the first console development suite ever to be made available, it was certainly the cheapest—requiring only an annual subscription of $99 (or free for students with DreamSpark) to gain access to thousands of game assets from Microsoft and other key partners. XNA allows amateur game developers to bring their creative ideas to life and share their creations with friends via the Xbox Live network. In 2009, Microsoft created a peer review submission system for XNA based games and formed the Xbox Live Marketplace—a platform allowing indie developers to sell their XNA based games online and keep 70% of their total sales revenue. With the release of XNA Game Studio 4 in 2010, Microsoft further expanded the reach of the XNA framework into the mobile world—allowing developers to create games targeting the Windows Mobile operating system. This expansion has led Microsoft to rebrand its XNA Creators Club as App Hub, which continues with the original spirit of supporting independent game development—now on a wider variety of devices.

—*Jason Bramble (Founder & President, Deadman Games, Inc.)*

Popular programming languages used by game programmers include C, C++, Visual Basic, and Java. Operating systems include Windows 7, Vista, 95/98/2000, XP and NT, Macintosh OSX, UNIX, and Linux. In Chapter 2, you learned about the various platforms used in game development, along with associated brands. Most game programmers are familiar with requirements associated with programming games for home console, personal computer, and handheld systems. Major brands include Sony (PS3, PS2, PSP), Nintendo (Wii, GameCube, DS, Game Boy Advance SP), Microsoft (Xbox 360, Xbox), Apple (iPhone, iPad, iPod Touch)—and Android-based brands such as HTC, Motorola, Samsung, and Dell.

Unity Technologies   GarageGames

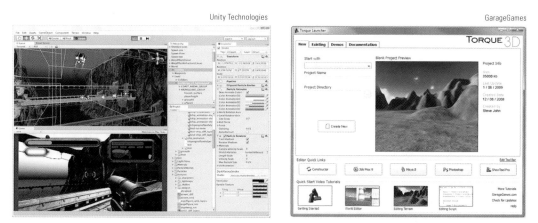

Basic Unity 3 (freeware) and Torque 3D ($99 license for indie developers) are excellent low-cost game engines.

The Multi-User Capabilities of Flash Media Server

Flash has always been a great tool for game development because of its versatility in methodology. One can design almost any type of game with graphics, animation, text, and interactivity, created all in the same program. I use Flash to teach interactive programming concepts, and students are able to generate both simple and complex games during the course. They learn fundamental and advanced programming concepts in ActionScript, while enjoying the challenge of implementing a game idea—and they get to see and share the fruits of their labor at the end of the course. Flash Media Server provides more flexibility in gaming with its multi-user functionality. It allows users to communicate and play the same game over a network—even on the Internet. It is fairly easy to implement, as long as the server itself is configured and managed correctly. Having such capabilities expands the possibilities for game design, and challenges game creators to go beyond their previous horizons. Multi-user programming is available for everyone now.

—*Russell Burt (Interactive Design Instructor, Art Institute of California–Los Angeles)*

Art

Popular 3D software tools used by game artists include 3D Studio Max and Maya; these tools have become standards in the industry—with a large installed customer base, world-building and character modeling utilities, and animation enhancements. Lightwave is another popular game-art software program; its modeler and layout modules provide powerful solutions for animating and modeling. Other programs include Bones Pro (skeletal deformation plug-in), Zbrush, SoftImage, and Mirai. Adobe Photoshop is standard bitmap and vector-based graphics software used by 2D game artists. Other Adobe products used in the industry include Painter, After Effects, Illustrator, and Premiere.

Autodesk, Inc.   Autodesk, Inc.

Autodesk 3ds Max (left) and Maya (right) are industry standard game art modeling and animation tools.

Game Engines as Art Tools

When it finally comes to putting artwork into a game engine, being able to iterate rapidly on the target platform is key—preferably by doing the authoring within the engine itself. For Secret Level, the Unreal engine has been an important tool, which allows our artists to quickly transfer their work and see it "in the game"—giving them a maximum amount of control over their artwork. It is also versatile enough to provide a framework for more than just first-person shooters.

—*Christopher Bretz (Art Director, Bretz Consulting)*

Game Worlds Depend on Tools

If your tools make great trees, but suck at architecture, then your game is going to be set in a forest—regardless of what the design doc says. Conversely, if your particle effects editor crashes constantly and doesn't save values, then you will find yourself in a game world that only has ten spells. Make particle effects fun to work with, and you might find yourself in a glowing fantasy world full of mist, fireflies, and paper lanterns.

—*Marc Taro Holmes (illustrator, concept artist, and art director)*

Audio

Popular game audio creation tools include Audacity (free, open source, and cross-platform—available for Windows, Mac, and Linux), Microsoft's DirectX Audio (and its authoring tool, DirectMusic Producer), Digidesign's ProTools (a standard in almost all music-related industries, including film and studio recording), and Emagic's Logic (a sequencer, which is a device that records and plays back control information for an electronic instrument such as a synthesizer). Analog Devices' SoundMAX Smart Tools allows sound designers to create interactive and nonrepetitive audio content, so that game sound effects neither sound the same every time nor occur at regular intervals—like a bird chirping the same exact way every five seconds. For more detail on audio tools, refer to Chapter 9.

Propellerhead

Reason is one of the most widely used software programs for game audio.

::::: *Orbz*:
       Better with a Bug!

21-6 Productions

One of the most memorable moments in developing *Orbz* happened in the early design stages for the game. We were originally developing a quirky golf game. One day, a couple of us were playing a new prototype course together. We were testing out some new scoring code when hitting the targets with the golf ball. I inadvertently introduced a bug in the prototype where the target disappeared after you hit it. During this test session, we realized this bug and started playing the game a different way than we had before—to see who could get the most stars before time ran out. We had so much fun with this new way of playing the game that we changed gears on the game design. Instead of building a golf game, we decided to build a game completely based around this simple concept of getting the most stars/points. A couple months later, out came *Orbz*—a unique game that has met with critical acclaim for originality and fun factor (including Best Game of 2003 from *PC Magazine*). We learned a great lesson on *Orbz*: to prototype our ideas early and often. [*Author's Note*: Prototyping and playtesting will be discussed in more detail in Chapter 11.] What's written on paper doesn't always translate well into gameplay, and it's better to find that out sooner rather than later.

—*Justin Mette (President, 21-6 Productions)*

Roles & Responsibilities: developing the team   chapter 10

The Business Side of Game Development

This chapter focused on the components needed before developing a game. You learned about the industry from a business standpoint—including company and team roles, responsibilities, and tools necessary for a solid development studio. Whether you plan to work for an established developer or publisher—or you want to explore your entrepreneurial side and start your own company—consider this chapter your first step!

:::

Now that you have a background on the roles and responsibilities associated with the game development team, let's focus on the process of developing a game from start to finish—and beyond. The next chapter discusses the phases of game development—from concept to release.

Expanded assignments and projects based on the material in this chapter are available on the Instructor Resources DVD.

:::CHAPTER REVIEW EXERCISES:::

1. How do game development studios, publishers, licensors, and manufacturers work together to bring a game to market? Compare and contrast business models as part of your answer.

2. The roles of artist and designer are sometimes confused with one another. How do these roles differ? Using one electronic game as a reference, discuss three examples of how art is used in the game, and three examples of how design is used in the game. Does the game utilize art and design successfully?

3. Put together a team for your original game. Analyze each sub-team (art, design, tech, audio, testing) to determine the number of people you will have on each, along with their specialized roles. Consider the unique features of your game idea.

4. Experiment with some of the game engines, level editors, and development suites discussed in this chapter (e.g., Game Maker, Torque, CryENGINE, Unity 3D, GameSalad Creator, Unreal), and list their features—comparing and contrasting them with each other. Which tool are you most comfortable with, and why?

5. What are the benefits and disadvantages of running an independent game studio? How does this structure differ from third-party developers and publishers? If you were running an independent studio and you could initially hire only two team members, what roles would you assign to them?

CHAPTER

Production & Management
developing the process

Key Chapter Questions

- What are the phases and associated components in the game development *cycle*?

- What are some effective ways to *lead* and *manage* game development teams?

- What are the different types of *documentation* used in game development?

Now that you have a basic understanding of the roles and responsibilities of game development team members, let's take a look at the game development process itself. This chapter concentrates on all phases of game development—including concept, pre-production, prototype, production, alpha, beta, gold, and post-production. Management techniques used by game producers is also covered; the development of leadership skills in this industry cannot be overlooked. The final section of this chapter focuses on the functions and features of game documentation.

For further reading on this topic, please see *Game Project Management* (Hight/Novak)—part of the *Game Development Essentials* series.

Development Phases

There are several phases in the development process: concept, pre-production, prototype, production, alpha, beta, gold, and post-production. Each phase involves certain members of the game development team and focuses on specific objectives.

Concept

The *concept* development phase begins when an idea for a game is envisioned—and it ends when a decision is made to begin planning the project (also known as the *pre-production* phase). During the concept phase, the development team can be quite small—perhaps only consisting of a designer, programmer, artist, and a producer. The goal of concept development is to decide what the game is about and convey the idea to others in written form. The concept document, discussed later in this chapter, is the result of the concept development phase. The goals are to identify a target market, assess company resources, and identify a concept that resonates with developers as well as having a potential market. Often, many short game design treatments are considered.

Daniel James on the "Conceptual Click" :::::

DJ

Daniel James
(Chief Executive
Officer & Designer,
Three Rings)

Daniel James is founder and CEO of Three Rings, a San Francisco developer and operator of massively multiplayer online games for the mass market casual audience. Three Rings' *Yohoho! Puzzle Pirates* combines accessible and fun puzzle games with the depth of a social persistent world, while *Bang! Howdy* is an online strategy game set in a steam-powered wild west world. Prior to Three Rings, Daniel consulted on game design, toiled for many years on *Middle-Earth Online,* and co-founded two profitable UK Internet startups: Avalon and Sense Internet.

For me, the most memorable moment in developing a game is that moment of conceptual "click"—the beginning of the process of development, mirrored by the moments with actual players in the real game, when you feel that "click" reach its fruition. The most challenging part? The last five percent, the polish…getting things just right.

Pre-Production

Once you have received interest in the concept, it's time to develop the proposal and enter the planning (or *pre-production*) phase of development. Additional documentation developed during this phase includes the art style guide and production plan. This phase ends with the creation of the game design document (GDD) and technical design document—discussed later in this chapter.

Rade Stojsavljevic on the Challenge of Pre-Production :::::

Rade Stojsavljevic has worked on a variety of games in different genres—including massively multiplayer online role-playing, real-time strategy, adventure, strategy, and military simulation games. At Electronic Arts, he worked on *The Lord of the Rings: The Battle for Middle-Earth* and *Command & Conquer: Generals - Zero Hour*. At Activision, he worked on *X-Men* and *True Crime: New York City*. At Westwood Studios, he worked on *Earth & Beyond Online, Command & Conquer: Tiberian Sun, Firestorm,* and *Blade Runner*. Before joining Westwood and Electronic Arts, Rade worked as a sound designer and video editor for a couple of smaller game developers.

Rade Stojsavljevic
(President, Jet Set
Games, Inc.)

I used to think that wrapping up a project was the hardest process, but that's not the case any more. After you've shipped a couple of titles, you know what you need to do to get a game out the door. Now I think the hardest part of the development project is pre-production. Generating new ideas for a game is difficult, but the real challenge is figuring out which of those ideas is really good, and which will work together to make a hit. If you don't nail your pre-production goals, you wind up working so much harder in the long run to try and make the game fun and successful.

Making *Great* Games

We need to make our games more *fun* and of much higher quality. Next, we need to work in themes beyond medieval fantasy and sci-fi.... Finally, developers need sufficient *time and resources* to make a great—versus only good—game.

—Gordon Walton (Vice President & Executive Producer, Playdom)

Prototype

The next goal for most game development teams is to create a tangible *prototype*. The usual definition of a prototype in the game industry is something like this: "A working piece of software that captures onscreen the essence of what makes your game special, what sets it apart from the rest, and what will make it successful." However, before moving into the digital realm, it's arguably beneficial to initially create a *low-fidelity* prototype (often paper-based—using cards, boards, tiles, and/or miniatures) of the game and test it in-house to ensure that the gameplay mechanics are tight—and that the game is fun and compelling. Concern about visual style and programming features in a digital prototype can often cause game designers to be distracted from focusing on the game's foundation—the gameplay itself.

Whether or not you decide to begin with an analog prototype, the creation of a digital prototype is essential in the development process—and it could be the single greatest item that influences whether or not the project gets to the next level. Publishers and other funding sources like to be able to look at a screen and understand the game idea right away. If they can't see the vision within a minute or two, they're less likely to fund the rest of the project. Sometimes a development team will be creating new technology during the development process that will be used in the final game. Since the prototype stage is too early for this technology to be available, just try to simulate the feel of the game without it. For example, you could pre-render any material that will be rendered in real-time during the final game.

You might also want to prepare standalone demonstrations proving that the various pieces of planned technology are feasible. The finished prototype shows your vision and establishes that your production path is working—and that you're able to go from idea to reality. Game engines are often used for prototyping, even if entirely new technology will be used for the shipped game.

Is the Industry a Victim of Its Own Success?

Developing a game is like trying to assemble an airplane while learning how to fly it. I think that the hardest task is integrating all the disparate pieces—gameplay, sound, 3D engine—in a cohesive format in what seems to be an impossible time frame. I think that the industry has been a bit of a victim of its own success. The great game designers and programmers out there have consistently blown the socks off of people so many times that when a really solid game comes out that *isn't* a breakthrough in some way, fans are disappointed.

—*Jason Kay (Chief Business Monkey, Monkey Gods LLC)*

Brenda Laurel on "Make-Believe" Playtesting : : : : :

A designer, writer, researcher, and performer, Brenda Laurel is active as a consultant in interaction design and research. Since 1976, her work has focused on experience design, interactive story, and the intersection of culture and technology. In 1996, Brenda co-founded Purple Moon (acquired by Mattel in 1999) to create interactive media for girls. The company was based on four years of research in gender and technology at Interval Research Corp. In 1990, Brenda co-founded Telepresence Research—which developed technology and applications for virtual reality and remote presence. Other employers include Atari, Activision, and Apple. Brenda edited *The Art of Human-Computer Interface Design* (Addison-Wesley, 1990), and authored *Computers as Theatre* (Addison-Wesley, 1991 and 1993) and *Utopian Entrepreneur* (MIT Press, 2001). Her latest book is *Design Research: Methods and Perspectives* (MIT Press, 2004). In addition to public speaking and consulting, Brenda is a Board of Advisors member at several companies and organizations—including Cheskin, the Communication Research Institute of Australia, and the Comparative Media Studies program at MIT. She serves on the Executive Committee of the Digital Storytelling Association and is active in the Association of Computing Machinery (ACM), the International Game Developers Association (IGDA), and the American Institute for Graphic Arts (AIGA). Prior to her position at California College of the Arts, Brenda was the Chair of the Graduate Media Program at Art Center College of Design.

BL

Brenda Laurel, PhD
(Chair, Graduate Design Program, California College of the Arts)

During the prototype testing for the *Secret Paths* series at Purple Moon, we gave kids paper dolls that represented animals, plants, and other outdoor objects and asked them to make us a play about them. We were expecting *Secret Garden*-type stuff where kids would have magical adventures together. But the girls surprised us; they consistently felt that a place "in nature" would be a place where they would go alone. They wouldn't be taking care of the animals (there goes that nurturing thing); they expected animals and magical creatures to take care of them. What they *wanted*—and what we gave them—was a refuge and a space for personal reflection.

Tracy Fullerton on the Prototyping & Playtesting Process :::::

TF

Tracy Fullerton
(Associate Professor,
USC School of
Cinematic Arts;
Director,
Game Innovation Lab)

Tracy Fullerton is an experimental game designer, writer and associate professor in the Interactive Media Division of the USC School of Cinematic Arts, where she directs the Game Innovation Lab. This design research center has produced several of the most influential products to be released in the emerging field of independent games—including *Cloud*, *flOw*, *Darfur is Dying*, *The Misadventures of P.B. Winterbottom*, and *The Night Journey*—a collaboration with media artist Bill Viola. Tracy is also the author of *Game Design Workshop: A Play-Centric Approach to Innovative Games* (a design textbook in use at game programs worldwide) and holder of the Electronic Arts Endowed Chair in Interactive Entertainment. Recent projects include: *Participation Nation*, a game that teaches U.S. history and civics developed in collaboration with Activision-Blizzard and KCET; *Pathfinder*, a strategic college preparation game; and *Walden*, a simulation of Henry David Thoreau's experiment at Walden Pond. Prior to joining USC, Tracy was the president and founder of the interactive television game developer Spiderdance—which produced NBC's *Weakest Link*, MTV's *webRIOT*, the WB's *No Boundaries*, History Channel's History *IQ*, Sony Game Show Network's *Inquizition*, and TBS' *Cyber Bond*. Before starting Spiderdance, Tracy was a founding member of the New York design firm R/GA Interactive, Creative Director at the interactive film studio Interfilm, and a designer at Robert Abel's early interactive company, Synapse. Notable projects include Sony's Multiplayer *Jeopardy!* and Multiplayer *Wheel of Fortune*, and MSN's *NetWits*. Tracy's work has received numerous industry honors, including an Emmy nomination for interactive television and Time Magazine's "Best of the Web."

The most significant elements in prototyping and playtesting are: *when and how often* you do it, *who* you do it with, and *what* you do with the feedback you get. Prototypes are often created these days as demos to sell ideas. While there's value in getting an idea funded, this is one of the worst reasons to do a prototype.

Prototypes are a chance to ask wild, unusual questions, to try ideas that may seem fundamentally unsound, but appeal to you anyway. They provide an opportunity to learn—for game designers to experiment with entirely new mechanics. I encourage prototyping at the earliest possible stage of an idea. And I encourage testing that prototype—no matter how rough or unseemly it feels.

Who should you playtest it with? Playtesting with your core design team is an option, of course—but what type of feedback will you get? Informed, but not really objective. As soon as a prototype is functional and stands, albeit precariously, on its feet as a game, I encourage you to recruit objective playtesters from your target group. These are people you don't know. What you will learn from them will be invaluable—and probably hard to hear.

Incorporating feedback is one of the most critical elements to making prototyping and playtesting worthwhile. There is no point to the process if you are not open to change. There is also no point to the process if you don't have player experience goals you are trying to reach—and so are swayed by playtester comments that try to force the game to be a copy of the last game they enjoyed. The bottom line is: prototype early, playtest often, and have clear goals that you are trying to reach, so that you'll know how best to incorporate the feedback you get.

Early Prototyping

Early prototyping means focusing a team's attention on crude, playable prototypes at the beginning of the design process, before a full production crew is on board. A small group of designers can create a playable version of an idea quickly, using very low production values. The idea is to test and revise the crude prototype over and over using the small team, until you've developed a really interesting play system. Then and only then should the idea be put into production and a full team be brought on board.

—Chris Swain (Associate Research Professor, USC School of Cinematic Arts; Director, USC Games Institute)

Knowing When to Start Over

I was working on a game project within an established IP. With a major milestone looming, the IP-holders made a drastic change to their world, such that it effectively cobbled the plans the entire development team had made. What did we do? We started over. We turned around a new story and completed it in time to make the first milestone.

—Anne Toole (Writer & Designer, The Write Toole)

Production & Management: developing the process   chapter 11

Production

Once the prototype has been approved, the development team should be ready to enter the longest phase—*production*—in which the game is actually developed. This phase often lasts six months to two years, and the result is a completed game. You've probably heard about "crunch-time"—involving 100-hour weeks required of most team members during the tail end of this phase, where many employees might as well sleep on cots at the office for weeks straight. This disaster does not have to happen. In reality, many development teams make the mistake of miscalculating how long it will really take to complete a project. Some projects are given an impossible cycle of under six months due to an attempt to make the holiday rush or some other time-sensitive deadline. An even bigger disaster can occur when projects that have a two-year (or more) cycle have the same last-minute scrambling—often resulting in employees quitting, leaving other overworked employees to take up the slack. Initially, two years might sound like a long time—and the initial 1½ years might be spent with team members working a little more "leisurely" than normal. As discussed in Chapter 10, it is management's job to ensure that a project is completed under budget and by the scheduled release date—without causing a mass exodus of dissatisfied employees. (*Note:* The following phases in the game development cycle may differ by project and publisher.)

Localization

If a game will be sold into a market containing a language other than that for which it was originally developed (e.g., an American game being sold in the German market), the development team needs to ensure that the game's content has been *localized* for each respective market. Localization involves language translation (text and voice) and content modification necessary for that market's particular regulations (e.g., on violence, profanity, and adult content). Keep in mind that some languages, such as German, require more characters per word than others. Gameplay is also often adjusted to suit the tastes of a market.

Balancing Act: Creativity & Business

The most challenging aspect of the game-production process is balancing creativity with the real business and professional requirements of making a game. Creating an environment where we can be artists and have fun while still getting our work done on time and on budget is quite challenging. However, I believe that achieving this balance is how great games are made.

—*Starr Long (Executive Producer, The Walt Disney Company)*

Alpha

The *alpha* phase is the point at which a game is playable from start to finish. There might be a few gaps and the art assets might not be final, but the engine and user interface are both complete. Instead of focusing on building and creating, the alpha stage is about finishing and polishing the game. If any features need to be dropped to make the release date, this is the time to do it. During alpha, the testing department: ensures that each game module is tested at least once; creates a bug database and test plan; and records bugs and performance results. Temporary playability testers are brought on during this phase to check for bugs. This is the first time the game is seen by people outside the development team. To pass the alpha phase, the following elements should be complete:

- One gameplay path (playable from beginning to end)
- Primary language text
- Basic interface with preliminary documentation
- Compatibility with most specified hardware and software configurations
- Minimum system requirements tested
- Most manual interfaces tested for compatibility
- Placeholder art and audio
- Multiplayer functionality tested (if applicable)
- Draft of game manual

Mark Mencher, in his book *Get in the Game,* does an excellent job of outlining what items are needed (such as the preceding list) to pass one development phase and go to the next. (*Note:* Some studios consider *demo creation* to be a phase right after *alpha* and it is required by some publishers.)

"Are We There Yet?!"

Every facet of the game production process must be handled well or the entire process suffers. If you don't adequately plan during your pre-production phase, you suffer later. If you don't do a good enough job of frontloading your tasks, you'll get bitten later. If you don't manage the team so that they don't peak too early or late, you suffer later. The part I like the least is the middle portion. When you're thinking up cool ideas and planning, you're having fun. When you're at the end and the hours are hideous, at least you have a mostly finished game and light at the end of the tunnel. The middle part, though, is rough. The game isn't quite there yet, and you have a long way to go—but expectations are high and you constantly have executives breathing down your neck...much like kids on a road trip repeating, "Are we there yet?!"

—*Graeme Bayless (General Manager, Big Ego Games)*

Beta

After the game has passed the alpha phase, it enters the *beta* phase. During this phase, the focus is on fixing bugs. All assets are integrated into the game, and the entire production process ceases. The goal during beta is to stabilize the project and eliminate as many bugs as possible before shipping the product. Beta testers are recruited online to test the game for playability. Objectives of this phase include isolating all significant bugs and performance problems; complete testing, bug fixing, and performance tuning; and tests on all supported platforms. If the game has been developed for a proprietary hardware platform—such as a console system—the corresponding hardware manufacturer will test the game to ensure that it meets its own quality standards; this is done right before the game goes gold (see the next section) and is known as *certification* or *submission* (first, second, final). Games developed for the personal computer platform are tested for compatibility to uncover whether there are any hardware configurations under which the game will not operate.

The last few days or weeks of this phase are sometimes referred to as the *code freeze* period, in which all the work is done and the preparation of master game media begins. The media (usually in disc form) is sent to testing, and the only changes allowed to the game are those that address urgent bugs that show up during this final testing process. The following are elements that must be complete to pass the beta phase:

- Code
- Content
- Language version text
- Game path navigation
- User interface
- Hardware and software compatibility
- Manual interface compatibility
- Art and audio
- Game manual

The primary improvements during the beta phase include the development of the game's final code and content, along with the manual and visual interfaces.

Game Art Trade-Offs

As a game artist, you are frequently making designs and hoping that the technology will work as advertised—or, conversely, you have made a lot of assets, and late in the game some new thing becomes available that suddenly makes them pale by comparison. Now you have to decide: Do you keep to the plan and risk looking dated—or throw out the old work and try and master the new approach in the time remaining? This is always a tough call.

—Marc Taro Holmes (art director, concept artist, and illustrator)

A Memorable Test of Will

A strangely banal yet memorable experience involved me, alone in the Atari testing lab, playing open-world, single-player driving games for a straight month, as part of my research analyst job (checking out and comparing the competition). Since I despise driving games and playing alone, the challenge was to filter through my hatred and become objective in my deconstruction of each of these games. Besides being a mental test of will, it was also a good exercise finding the strong game design, finding the fun, despite my immediate negative reaction. Oh, and now I enjoy open-world single-player driving games.

—Jennifer F. Estaris (Senior Game Designer, Nickelodeon Virtual Worlds)

The "Golden Spike" Method

I use the "Golden Spike" method of schedule planning. First, working from the back end, I determine the timeframes that cannot be reduced between Beta and the target ship date. Then, I create a plan that permits the project to reach Beta before that Golden Spike date.

—Tom Sloper (Producer & Designer, Sloperama Productions; Educator, University of Southern California)

Knowing When to Stop

The most challenging part of development, to me, is deciding when to stop. In the end, every game could have a bit more of this or another feature or two. You have to draw the line, finish the title up, and get it into the market. This always results in crunch time for passionate teams, and a good management team ensures that the long hours are being put in to make a good product great, not just to get any product out the door.

—Louis Castle (Vice President of Studios, Zynga)

Gold

Once the game has passed the beta phase, it is considered *gold*. The game is sent to be manufactured after one of the master game discs has been thoroughly tested and is found to be acceptable. At gold, senior management has reviewed the product and bug database ("bugbase")—and agrees that the product is ready. Manufacturing takes several weeks, as the media is created and packaged. After the game "goes gold," it is released into the marketplace. It is becoming more common to skip the manufacturing phase altogether, since the popularity of digital downloads has shifted the marketplace to online rather than offline (brick and mortar).

::::: *Civilization II:*
Exceeding Expectations

Firaxis Games

Back in 1995 when I was working on *Civilization II*, I lived for a year in Yorkshire (England) during my wife's teaching fellowship—so I was basically just tapping away on a little portable computer in our living room. Management was telling us this game wasn't going to sell very well at all, so it was a very low priority for resources, marketing, etc. But then I came back to the U.S., and one day I happened to be walking around the studio. I saw all sorts of people playing the *Civilization II* beta—including lots of people who had nothing to do with the *Civilization II* team and worked in other departments like marketing and documentation. When I saw how thoroughly we had "infected" the company, it was great—because at that moment I knew we were going to do well in spite of the low sales projection (which we exceeded by a factor of 40)!

—*Brian Reynolds (Chief Game Designer, Zynga)*

Watching the Sunrise

The most memorable experience I had developing a game was watching the sunrise from a conference room. It wasn't a good experience; it was the middle of doing 90 hours in five days. I'm happy to report that those days are long behind me now. The industry is learning and crunch is going the way of sprites.

—*John Comes (Creative Director, Uber Entertainment)*

:::::Aladdin: The $100 Million Piece of Code

On *Disney's Aladdin*, I was with a group of great guys trying to meet a really tough deadline. There on my computer was a small file that was worthless to the world. But when I hit the return key, our work was done, we could all relax, the data was heading for a cartridge—and that little piece of code that we had lovingly built was going to be worth over $100 million. It still amazes me to this day.

—David Perry (Chief Executive Officer, Gaikai, Inc.)

Sega

Rapid Development

The need for rapid development is the most challenging aspect of game programming. Time is always short, and getting shorter. Console game development took a few weeks to develop a game feature. Now online social games such as Zynga's *CityVille* develop and release game features in a matter of days. Game designs are always changing because each iteration brings up new gameplay and visual issues. Designers can always think of more cool improvements and fixes than we can possibly code up. The game team has to identify the subset of possible features that will give us the most bang for the programming buck. The engineers then get these coded up so the designers can start to build the game and identify what is missing—and they repeat this until it is time to polish. There are always more things to polish than time, but polish is what makes a game feel great.

—John Ahlquist (Founder, Ahlquist Software)

Cookies at Crunch Time

I was working on an interactive project for a food-service provider, and the lead programmer quit at the worst possible moment: just a few weeks before the deadline. Guess who stepped in? The fact that we were short one programmer meant that I had to work a lot of overtime to get the job done. Fortunately, the project ended well, but those few weeks are a blur in my memory. Thank goodness the producer understood our needs and supplied us with anything we needed. I remember I ate a lot of cookies.

—Russell Burt (Interactive Design Faculty, Art Institute of California–Los Angeles)

:::::*Utopia:*
A Perfect Future

Mattel, Inc.

Creating the first computer baseball game and the first computer role-playing game was a lot of fun, but at the time I never realized that anyone would notice or care. We were college students creating games for classmates on mainframe computers, and we had no idea this would ever become an industry. I remember being surprised when my games were shared with other universities across the country and I started getting letters from players. When my first Intellivision game, *Utopia*, was a surprise hit in 1982, I felt like pinching myself—thinking, "How can someone possibly get paid to write games?"

—*Don Daglow*
(Chief Executive Officer & Creative Director,
Daglow Entertainment LLC)

:::::Shipping *Age of Empires:*
"An Enormous Breakfast at Denny's"

Reprinted with permission from
Microsoft Corporation

Ensemble Studios was a new company, and it was our first title....Everyone was very passionate and driven to make the game the best it could be. The dozen of us worked crunch hours for nearly a year and were completely exhausted in those last few days. The testers at Microsoft were matching us step-for-step, and we'd play multiplayer games until 4:00 a.m. pretty much every night. We set a goal for ourselves of 100 back-to-back multiplayer games without crashing, hangs, or multiplayer problems—and we'd call it good to ship. We were sleep-deprived, going without stopping the last 48 hours—but fueled by being so close to finishing, that we felt like mountain climbers nearing the peak. When the test team called it gold, we all cheered—then got an enormous breakfast at Denny's. We toasted with orange juice, laughed, and slept for a solid week. It was terrible and wonderful at the same time. I'll never forget it.

—*Mark Terrano*
(Design Director, Hidden Path Entertainment)

Post-Production

During the *post-production* (or *post-release*) phase, several subsequent *versions* of the game might also be released that replace and improve upon the original game—increasing its longevity. These new versions are free of charge and are created by applying patches to the original game to upgrade it with additional content that enhances the original game. A *patch* can also be applied to fix software bugs—which are not necessarily major software glitches, but issues as innocuous as making the game run properly on an unusual hardware combination. *Updates*—additional content created to enhance the original game—are also released during this phase. These are usually created to extend the life of the original game. *Expansions* are self-contained games requiring their own software (and sometimes the original game software as well) to run. These adaptations usually cost less than the original game, but are free in rare cases.

Downloadable Content

Once developed during the post-production phase, *downloadable content (DLC)* is now being created during production. Although the Dreamcast was actually the first console to support DLC as a standard, Microsoft was the first to charge for this content with the 2002 game, *Mech Assault*, and was the first to develop a "points" system (Microsoft Points) so that players didn't have to pay for DLC directly with credit cards. (This strategy was later utilized by both Sony's PlayStation Network Card and Nintendo's Wii Points.) DLC has been criticized as being overpriced, providing an incentive for developers to leave items out of the initial release, and consisting of only content keys used to unlock content already sitting on the game disc (which gives the impression that customers are paying to unlock content they already purchased). Music games such as Rock Band have utilized DLC extensively by providing new songs on a regular basis.

After Crossing the Finish Line...

Like most developers, my fondest memories are usually when the team is gathered around, bleary-eyed from lack of sleep, cheering when our game finally gets released to manufacturing. After a few beers are consumed, we inevitably recount the events, both humorous and dramatic, that led up to that day. My best friends are my colleagues.

—*John Hight (Director of Product Development, Sony Computer Entertainment America)*

Management

As mentioned in Chapter 10, the producer needs to balance time, money, and value during the course of a project. If the game has a short production cycle, the producer must make sure that the quality of the product does not decrease due to the lack of time available. This can be done by adjusting the budget, extending the release date, or by restricting or restructuring the game's feature set or scope. The producer also needs to come up with a structured development plan for the project.

> I'm often asked about my management methods. My response: "I treat them like humans."
>
> *Jennifer F. Estaris (Senior Game Designer, Nickelodeon Virtual Worlds)*

John Comes on Managing for Success :::::

John Comes
(Creative Director,
Uber Entertainment)

John Comes was born in Reading, Pennsylvania and grew up near Cleveland, Ohio. He received a BS in Mechanical Engineering from the University of Akron. After college, John and his older brother wrote *Wolfshade MUD* from scratch—which led to a position as Senior Content Designer on *Earth & Beyond* at Westwood Studios. At Electronic Arts—Los Angeles, he shipped *Command & Conquer: Generals – Zero Hour* and *The Lord of the Rings: The Battle for Middle-Earth*. At Gas Powered Games, he helped produce *Supreme Commander* and *Demigod*. Most recently, as Creative Director at Uber Entertainment, John developed the Xbox Live Arcade hit *Monday Night Combat*.

Drop waterfall development processes and embrace agile ones. Games are about iteration—*not* writing a huge design tome and handing it off to the production team. Getting your team agile and keeping the game playable early is a great way to have success.

Get your designers in the engine. All artists know how to use the tools of their trades—and this should be no different in games. A painter knows how to use brushes and paint. Musicians know how to play their instruments. Movie directors are on the set directing, sitting in the editing room, looking into the camera. Game designers should be editing data, building levels, and changing gameplay. Get your designers out of Word and Excel and into the game engine.

Iterative Development

Game development is more like software development than other forms of entertainment. Just like games are not films in content, the process by which they are developed is also not anything like film production. The *iterative* development process—used in software and web development (and discussed in detail in Van Duyne, et al., *The Design of Sites*)—also seems to work well for game development. This model incorporates a circular three-stage process: design, prototype, evaluate.

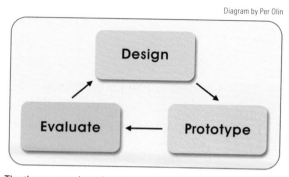

Diagram by Per Olin

The three-stage iterative development process.

After the *design* phase (which involves planning and pre-production), a *prototype* is developed. After the prototype has been played and tested during the *evaluation* phase, the team decides what works and what doesn't—then goes back to the design phase and modifies the prototype (making it available again for testing). This process is repeated over and over again as needed until the game is no longer a prototype—but a completed game. The key to this model is to continuously refine the design of the game, based on what has been created so far. Don't build assets that you might not need later. Each prototype should have its own cycle of full development—including associated requirements, deliverables, and schedule. This iterative approach is the opposite of *gold-plating*—in which members of the team add "bells and whistles" to a product, costing time and money. When possible, involve prospective players in the evaluation phase so that you can get a player's perspective on usability, gameplay, and the game's "fun factor." This allows the player to take part in the development process (supporting the player-developer connection discussed in earlier chapters)—and it is commonly utilized in games that can be easily beta-tested online.

Code Competitions at Four in the Morning

I was the programmer on a SNES title that really took a whole lot of blood, sweat, and tears to ship. At the time, the Genesis programmer and I worked side by side. We would both work in different areas of the game for our specific consoles and then port each other's work across. (In other words, he would write the collision on the Genesis in 68000 assembly—and I would convert it to run on the SNES in 65816.) What made this fun was that the competition between me and the other programmer really heated up. About halfway through the project, he began to write the code in a unique way that was really to the advantage of the Genesis; for me to convert it to SNES was awkward and time-consuming. Not to be outdone, I began to do the same thing. Since the project was already late and behind schedule, we both put in an extraordinary amount of work to get the title shipped. One night at around 4:00 a.m. while converting assembly code, I remember hitting the assemble key and seeing hundreds of errors. When I looked at the code I had written, I realized I was so tired that I had converted the 68000 to both 65186 and Z80 (the Sinclair spectrum processor)!

—*Jay Gawronek (Independent Contractor, Bluepoint Games)*

Ed Del Castillo on Being a Valuable Team Member :::::

EDC

Edward A. Del Castillo
(President & Creative
Director, Liquid
Entertainment)

Ed Del Castillo founded Liquid Entertainment in 1999 and has worked as President and Creative Director on *Battle Realms*, *The Lord of the Rings: War of the Ring*, and *Dungeons & Dragons: Dragonshard*. At Origin Systems, Ed worked on *Sid Meier's Gettysburg*, *Alpha Centauri*, and *Ultima: Ascension*. He was also the producer of the original *Command & Conquer*, *Command & Conquer: Red Alert*, and all the ports and expansions of those titles. Ed's first job in the industry was at Mindcraft Software – where he started in Customer Support and worked his way into Design, which resulted in credits on several RTSs and RPGs. Ed received a BA in Economics, with a double minor in Psychology and Visual Arts, from the University of California, San Diego (UCSD). Ed's recent games include *Rise of the Argonauts* and *Thor* (released alongside the 2011 movie).

When I was starting out, I was given a job answering phones and shipping orders from a folding table. The job had down times, when I read magazines and waited for a call or order. Instead of wasting the time, I offered to write the game manual for *Siege*, promising that if they didn't like it they could just throw it away. It was a no-risk proposition for them. They liked my work, so I asked to help with the game, under the same rules as the manual. I ended up building all the levels in the game, and I did a large chunk of the design. After that, my boss came to me and said, "I don't know why we're paying you to answer phones!" I was promoted, and that's how I became a designer.

The story is important for two reasons:

1. The best way to get a promotion, raise, etc. is to do the job you want in addition to the job you have.

2. Never gauge your success on how well you are fulfilling your job description. If you're doing what you are paid to do, that's what is expected. You're only passing your "job" class—getting a C-, not an A. If you want to push your career forward, you need to consistently do something extra to earn the A. Trust me, your boss will see it that way, too!

Meeting Deadlines

The most challenging aspect of game development is getting the game done on time. It's easy to spend five years experimenting with what you do and don't like—but it's a whole different game when you have a date to meet. Time is something we still find challenging, and I think always will. That said, if it was easy, *everyone* would be making games!

—*David Perry (Chief Executive Officer, Gaikai, Inc.)*

Common Mistakes

In his book, *Rapid Development,* author Steve McConnell identifies several classic mistakes that managers make on software projects, and discusses the problems that these mistakes cause. Game producers should keep some of these mistakes in mind:

- **Lack of motivation:** Know the team members on your project, and give them reasons to do a good job.

- **Lack of skill:** Make sure team members are highly skilled, instead of hiring people who can get onto the project the fastest.

- **Difficult employees:** If an employee doesn't work well with the rest of the team, it can destroy morale and project efficiency. Removing a problem member from a team will allow for more productivity, even if other team members have to do a little more work to compensate. (They'll be happier!)

- **Restricted environment:** Most game development offices suffer from noisy and crowded bullpens, or even employees crammed together into small rooms without any privacy. It has been debated whether it's more productive for team members to work in their own offices (or uncrowded spaces) or to establish a culture that encourages frequent communication among team members.

- **Insufficient tracking:** Make sure you track the progress of all team members to determine whether you are on schedule.

- **Incomplete task list:** Some time-consuming tasks are overlooked and omitted from the project plan. Examples include interviews, meetings, reviews, and missed days due to conferences or other special events.

- **Misunderstandings:** Make sure that each task is clearly explained. What does it mean to create a demo for a trade show? What does this entail?

- **Unplanned tasks:** Management may ask for unexpected (and sometimes last-minute) tasks that have not been accounted for in the project plan. Assume that this will happen and budget time for this in the project plan.

- **Waiting to fix bugs:** Some developers feel that there's no point in fixing bugs until close to the end of the development process. However, fixing bugs often uncovers other hidden bugs—and it can also create more bugs!

Ed Magnin on the Virtual Studio:::::

EM

Ed Magnin
(Director of
Development,
Magnin & Associates)

Ed Magnin has been in the game industry for over 30 years. After working at companies such as MicroProse, Cinemaware, Virgin Games, and Park Place Productions, he started Magnin & Associates in 1993 to focus on handheld game development. Magnin & Associates started out as an authorized Nintendo developer and is now developing games for the iPhone and iPad. For the past 12 years, Ed has also made time to teach game studies classes to the next generation of game programmers. Ed is proud to serve as a Trustee of the International Game Developers Association (IGDA) Foundation.

We work more like a virtual company, but we need to meet once a week (either in person or online) to make sure we are focusing on the things we need to—ensuring we release our games on schedule. It's difficult to find people who can work well independently; perhaps they need to work in a more traditional environment first, and then they'll appreciate the freedom a company like ours offers.

Recovery from Mistakes

Game producers also need to avoid falling into the trap of attempting to recover from common management mistakes by doing the following:

- **Planning to catch up later:** This often happens at the beginning, after there's been an unexpected delay that does not conform to the schedule. Don't plan to catch up later, but address problems immediately.

- **Requiring mandatory overtime:** While asking for small amounts of overtime can sometimes be effective for a short time just prior to a major milestone, extended periods of mandatory overtime can result in a significant drop in productivity. As team members tire out, they make more mistakes—which results in more testing and reworking. The most important issue is motivation—thought of as the most significant predictor of productivity—which begins to plummet as a result of forced overtime. Instead of requiring overtime, ask employees to concentrate on making the best use of their standard workweek.

- **Adding people to the project:** This can work at the beginning of an understaffed project. However, if the project has fallen behind after you are well into it, adding people will almost never help you catch up. New people have to come up to speed on the project, and other people might have to take time out to train them. Meetings can take longer, and more misunderstandings might occur.

- **Holding more meetings:** Disrupting a team's workflow by holding status update meetings can greatly reduce productivity. Every time you interrupt people who are immersed in intellectual work, all of the problems they are trying to solve are dropped—and the problem-solving process has to begin all over again later. A workday full of meetings, reports, and other interruptions almost guarantees a drop in productivity.

Managing game projects takes a great deal of inspiration, energy, passion, patience—and the ability to delegate. If you're interested in managing a game development team, consider gaining education in the areas of leadership, project management, business management—and even general "people" skills!

Management vs. Leadership

Management and leadership are two very, very different things. A good manager understands that he or she is a servant to the rest of the team. Management consists of helping a team of people be better at what they do. That does involve directing them at times, but most often it involves maintaining communications, removing unnecessary distractions, and solving problems before they become crises. Good management is a skill set, and can be taught and learned. A leader, on the other hand, sets the goals for a team. Sometimes the leader is high up in the organization, and is also a manager. But most often true leadership comes from within the team, from people who are doing the work and setting the bar for others. This is leading by example, and it's a rare but magical thing. Leadership is a talent, and must be cultivated.

— *Kevin Perry (Executive Director of Production, Alelo)*

Know Your Limitations

Most game developers are also gamers—and we're always saying things like, "I can make that better," when we play our favorite games. In our early years, we thought we could build these full-blown AAA [high-quality] box/console titles, but we were wrong. We needed much more experience with technology, running remote teams, and harmonizing all the creative talent required to make a great game. Understanding the limits of your team is imperative to the success of the project. Don't design features into your game that nobody on your team has developed before or that your technology (e.g., game engine) does not support. You are just asking for trouble, and the project can easily spin out of control as you get deeper into it.

—*Justin Mette (President, 21-6 Productions)*

Effective Management

Here are just a few guidelines for effective management:

- Ask for input instead of issuing orders.
- Involve the team in the planning stage, and be flexible with the scheduled deadlines when necessary.
- Encourage employees to discuss problems with you so that they do not grow into unmanageable ones.
- Don't panic when problems arise, and don't personalize problems.
- Before making decisions, get the facts and see if the team can reach consensus.
- Make sure employees have several uninterrupted hours of work each day.
- Be forthcoming with your team, and do not hide information from them (even if you feel that they might not be able to handle it).
- Don't just work regular hours when you've asked your team to work overtime.
- Don't make promises to employees to get them to make personal sacrifices for the project.
- Provide significant rewards to employees after the project is completed.

Sheri Graner Ray on Building Team Trust:::::

SGR

Sheri Graner Ray
(Studio Design Director,
Schell Games)

Sheri Graner Ray has been designing computer games since 1989. She has worked for such companies as Electronic Arts, Origin Systems, Sony Online Entertainment, and Cartoon Network—and she has worked on titles such as *Star Wars Galaxies*, *Ultima*, and *Nancy Drew*. She is author of the book, *Gender Inclusive Game Design: Expanding the Market*, and is the game industry's leading expert on gender and computer games. In 2005, she was awarded the International Game Developers Association's (IGDA) Game Developer's Choice award for her work in gender and games and she is the founder of the IGDA Women's SIG and Women in Games International (WIGI).

For the past several years, I have had the following Lao Tzu quote on my wall: "A leader is best when people barely know he exists, not so good when people obey and acclaim him, worse when they despise him. But of a good leader who talks little when his work is done, his aim fulfilled, they will say: We did it ourselves." I wholly believe this and work to live by it as a manager. I believe building trust from your team is the key part of being a good leader. Your team should trust you to stand up for them and you should trust them to do their very best work. If you do this, and have hired the best people you can, then you will not be disappointed.

Using SCRUM Methodology

I think what works best with most game development teams is some form of adapted SCRUM methodology, where tasks are broken down into weekly or bi-weekly sprints. In our team, we also added sticky notes task-tracking on a common whiteboard in the lab, which avoids the overhead of daily reporting and allows everyone in the team to see the progress of each member or whether they are currently blocked. Each task on a sticky note has a certain time frame (3 hours) and is marked with a red sticker if it is blocked. Each member of the team is assigned a portion of the whiteboard and encouraged to update their tasks at least twice a day. This method has provided us with tracking and visibility that allow better management of complex projects.

—Dr. Lennart E. Nacke (Assistant Professor, Faculty of Business and Information Technology, University of Ontario Institute of Technology)

Get Out of Their Way

Experience has shown me that the best way to manage a project is to pick the right people and then get out of their way. I'm fond of telling my teams that an executive producer of a project is just the highest-ranking slave—that my job is to make sure they have the time, equipment, and breathing space to do theirs. This method of management has never failed me. Given the opportunity to take ownership, most teams will not just blossom; they will kick butt and take names. This means that the leaders have to hold themselves back and let their people do the fun stuff; the temptation is always there to stick your finger in the pie and swirl it around a bit. That's why we got into game development in the first place; to make cool games. However, the top managers have to resist that temptation and give their teams room to stretch and be creative.

—Jessica Mulligan (Executive Consultant, Frogster America)

Inspire Them!

As Creative Director, my most important job is communication and inspiration. If I can't communicate the vision of the game both internally to my team and externally to the people responsible for financing and marketing it, then the game won't be successful. Inspiring folks is hugely important. While I am ultimately responsible to ensure that the game is fun, development teams these days number in the hundreds—and you can't implement everything yourself. The people on your team are the ones that will come up with the coolest ideas—and it is your job to absorb, sort, prioritize, and turn them into game features. In addition, if your team members are inspired and excited about your project, they will put in 110%—taking the features they are tasked with implementing from "just good enough" to outstanding. Great games are polished games, and if your team does not understand the vision or is not inspired by it, you won't get a polished product.

—Christian Allen (Design Director, WB Games)

GB

Graeme Bayless
(General Manager,
Big Ego Games)

Graeme has been directing computer game development for 18 years, and has been in game development for over 25 years. He has shipped over 60 games in his extensive career and has worked on nearly every type of game, ranging from military simulations to action games, from RPGs to sports, and from interactive films to strategy games. Graeme has been a programmer, producer, director, lead designer, and even a quality assurance manager. Prior to Kush/2K, Graeme worked for Crystal Dynamics, Eidos, Sierra, Sega, and Electronic Arts. Graeme is a self-admitted gamer geek, and when he's not at work poring over management documents, he can be found playing nearly every type of game on the market. Beyond computer games, Graeme is a board-miniatures gamer, movie nut, avid reader, and astronomy enthusiast.

Rule #1: Be honest…especially with yourself. This may seem ridiculously obvious, but it really isn't. Your integrity is critical to your success in life—both business and personal. If you don't have that, you don't have anything. Beyond this, however, is a more subtle aspect: the amazing ability for all humans to delude themselves. Let's say you are the Producer on a big project that is into the mid-production cycle. Upper management comes to you and requests a significant change that you don't have adequate time budgeted for. Assuming that no additional resources are given and no additional time is allocated, this means that you'd probably have to cut something to fit in this change—right? Well, all too often, producers will simply accept the change and expect to "find the time somewhere"—basically convincing themselves it isn't as difficult or large a change as they know it is. Result? A death march and a burned-out team. Simply put, never try to delude yourself or others into believing things aren't as they are. If you're honest at all times, you will save yourself a lot of heartache.

Rule #2: Learn to step back. Producers nearly always come from "the ranks"—former programmers, artists, designers, writers, or testers. However, the job of Producer is not one of these anymore. Unless you're pulling double duty (and if you are, please stop—and re-read Rule #1), you should not be trying to be a producer and still keep your old job. If you're an ex-designer, please leave the design job to the designer. Comment and carry the vision—but let them do their job. You are a facilitator now—not a "doer."

Rule #3: If you do nothing else … communicate. You've taken a huge step towards success if you keep everyone informed and talking—even if you do nothing else on the team. Every day that is wasted because someone didn't understand that the orders had changed is a day you threw away because you failed to keep the team communicating. Do that too many times and you'll hurt your game…badly. There are a million methods for keeping the communication pathways open. Find the best one for you, and use it constantly!

MC

Mark has been in the game industry for 20 years, in both business development and sales roles. During his career, he has worked for a variety of companies—including Electronic Arts, Activision, Sony Online, and Metrowerks. He is currently the Director of Business Development for GameSalad, a coding-free development tool for mobile and connected systems.

When it comes to people, I believe in the "give them enough rope to hang themselves with, but hold on to the end so they don't" philosophy. People don't thrive under micromanagement, but they like guidance and support. Plus, you can identify trouble spots by keeping connected before they become issues. Hire great people, learn from them on new ways to do things (even if you don't end up doing it that way), mentor them where they need it, trust that they can do their job, advise them early on where they need to improve, keep an open door (and mind) to address their questions and concerns—and you'll bring them (and your team) success.

Mark Chuberka
(Director of Business Development, GameSalad)

A Few Small Rules for Team Leads …

1) No surprises.

2) Provide your team with the authority to succeed with the responsibilities you have given them.

3) You are the coach—not the "boss"!

4) Your team members are the rock stars, and you're the road manager. Your job is to keep the team supplied with the constant experience of being "on stage"—so you'd better be sure they have enough strings, guitar picks, and gigs!

Create a healthy space for creativity to flourish. Let brainstorm meetings be brainstorm meetings. Encourage everyone to question authority, as long as they know that it's not really a democracy. Healthy disagreement is a good thing. It's constructive feedback, not constructive criticism. Share your enthusiasm. Let people see what you are working on as often as possible. Celebrate milestones. And finally, remember that you are not the customer—and neither is your team. You're creating commercial art for people that want a fun experience; entertain them.

—*Billy Joe Cain (Chief Creative Officer, Sneaky Games)*

BG

Brandii Grace
(Game Designer,
Engaging Designs)

Brandii Grace is a game designer, programmer, and executive producer overseeing multiple teams. She was a design instructor at DigiPen Institute of Technology with expertise in the field of design analysis. Currently, Brandii works as a consultant while she forges connections between the game industry and Hollywood. A member of the International Game Developers Association – Los Angeles (IGDA-LA) Board of Directors and Writers Guild's Video Game Caucus, Brandii is also Founder and President of the Los Angeles branch of the Electronic Consumers Association (ECA).

1) Believe in your employees' excellence: People rise to the expectations that are set for them. I expect excellence where I know people can deliver it, and I reward excellence when they do deliver it. If someone is failing to meet expectations, I start conversations from a mutual assumption that these expectations can be met. "We both know you are able to deliver assets as fast as the rest of your team. Let's see how we can both help you get there."

2) Reward excellence: Rewarding someone doesn't always mean promotions or bonuses (although those can be nice). I've worked with volunteers for years; it's amazing to see how hard people will work for no money. Praise, a chance to work on desired projects, public displays of trust and support: All of these low-cost rewards can create amazing environments full of enthusiastically motivated people.

3) Say yes to saying "yes" to excellence: People generally start from a position of "no" and need to be convinced to say "yes." It's a natural defense to risk-taking. It's also easy to come up with reasons *not* to do something; after all, everything takes time, effort, or money to some degree or another. Starting from a cooperative place can open you up to a whole range of wonderful ideas and make your employees feel supported. Next time an employee suggests something, start from a mental position of "let's see how we can make that happen." From there, you can discover if there are any pressing reasons not to move forward. Bottom line: You don't have to (or want to) agree to support every little suggestion (your game would never ship!), but you should give every serious suggestion some reasonable consideration.

4) Create an infrastructure of excellence: Train your managers, directors, producers, supervisors, and leads to follow the above advice. It is not useful if the CEO is positive and supportive but the immediate boss is a brutally insulting naysayer.

Starr Long on Game Management Mantras :::::

Starr Long has been in the business of making games for nearly 20 years. He was the original project director for the longest-running MMO in history, *Ultima Online*, working alongside Richard Garriott, the creator of the *Ultima* series. Starr worked his way up through the ranks of Origin Systems, starting in quality assurance on *Wing Commander*, *Ultima*, and many other titles. After Origin, he worked for NCsoft on various titles—including *City of Heroes*, *Lineage 2*, and *Tabula Rasa*. Starr currently works for The Walt Disney Company on a series of unannounced learning projects.

SL

Starr Long
(Executive Producer,
The Walt Disney
Company)

Mantra 1: "No amount of ego is worth any amount of talent." Developers with professional attitudes are a must. Nothing slows down teams more than intra-team friction—most often created by ego clashes. Ego prevents valuable feedback loops and causes people to get locked into ideas—making them unwilling to be flexible.

Mantra 2: "If you are not having fun making the game, the players won't have fun playing it." Provide a relaxed, professional atmosphere for your team. Engage in team-building and bonding events. Always keep your team at a reasonable size; more than 25 on a team is very risky. Large teams have trouble communicating and staying in synch. With larger teams, managers (including Leads and Producers) spend too much time managing people instead of managing the project.

Mantra 3: "Be a leader, not just a manager." Admit and learn from your mistakes. Use inspiration, not degradation. Positive reinforcement is much more powerful and motivating than negative reinforcement. Ensure that the entire team is always aware of the current status of the project by maintaining a consistently high level of communication; always "show and tell" at team gatherings, and provide regular reports to your team (e.g., daily, weekly, monthly).

Mantra 4: "Fiction explains gameplay—so gameplay should not have to explain fiction." Game design should be about how the game plays, first and foremost. Even genre doesn't need to be defined until the mechanics are sketched out.

Mantra 5: "No plan survives contact with the enemy." Only do enough pre-production on the game design to build an overall schedule. Only do detailed designs in conjunction with the programming team as they are implementing a given system.

Mantra 6: "It's a game and a service." Online games have some unique needs. Know that an online game is both a service and a game—not just one of these. Remember that an online game is a game—not a world, and not a simulation.

Mantra 7: "Stable, fast, fun—in that order." If the game is not stable and does not have a reliably fast frame rate, it won't matter how fun it is.

Richard Garriott on Memorable Moments in Game Development : : : : :

RG

Richard "Lord British" Garriott (Creative Director, Portalarium)

A true veteran of the computer game industry, Richard Garriott is best known for creating and publishing the best-selling *Ultima* series— including the first commercially successful online game, *Ultima Online*. In a career that spans more than two decades, Richard has received numerous awards, including *Computer Gaming World*'s "15 Most Influential Industry Players," *Next Generation*'s "America's Elite," PC Gamer's "Game Gods," and *PC Games*' "Designer of the Year." He and his brother, Robert, were also awarded the "Entrepreneur of the Year" award by *Inc. Magazine*. In an industry that now rivals the movie industry in popularity, Richard Garriott is one of the few well-known "stars." Richard's first game was published when he was still a teenager. Under the pseudonym "Lord British," Richard created *Ultima I* (and subsequently the entire *Ultima* series). By the time *Ultima II* was released in 1982, he was sought after by publishers for his expertise and creative vision. In 1983, Richard and his brother, Robert, established Origin Systems, Inc. The company, based in Austin, Texas, is recognized as one of the innovation leaders in the ever-changing world of entertainment software. In 1992, Origin was acquired by Electronic Arts, a global leader in the entertainment software industry. At Origin, Richard continued to add to the *Ultima* series, making it one of the most successful and longest running series in entertainment software history. In 1997, Richard and his team created a new genre with the technologically groundbreaking title, *Ultima Online*. The game's continued success is measured by the hundreds of thousands of people who enjoy playing the game from all over the world, and by the explosion of online games that have followed since its release. Richard retired from Origin in April of 2000 and, with his brother Robert, formed Destination Games, which became part of NCsoft in 2001. In 2009, he co-founded Portalarium for the purpose of developing and publishing online social games, virtual worlds, and related services and products.

After 25 years, there are many memorable moments! Some of my favorite experiences include the following:

- Being killed (unexpectedly and in game, of course) at the end of the *Ultima Online* beta

- The large-scale protest "drunken, naked sit-in" in *Ultima Online*

- Late-night jam sessions back at Origin

- The "Killing Children" scene that's been in every *Ultima* since *Ultima IV*. When I made *Ultima IV*, I created the game to test players' virtues. One of the things I did was to put in a room full of evil children who would attack you if you walked your character into the room. I knew players would debate on how to get out of the room alive without having to harm the children and possibly lose points for their morality. In the end, the players could not be harmed. However, my own family thought this was terrible. They felt like I would be portrayed as some sort of evil advocate for child abuse. But it turned out to be a non-issue. No one complained. And so in every *Ultima* following *Ultima IV*, we always created a room full of "Killing Children" as a memory to this special situation.

- Catching one of our developers putting in their own back door (secret room) in an early *Ultima* and then our team quickly modifying the room just before release to keep this cheat out of the hands of players. One of our developers created a back door where he could keep all the equipment he needed to win the game. If this had leaked out, it would have provided a cheat for players to finish the game without really completing it. So what we did was to modify the room so that—when players went through the back door—instead of finding a load of free equipment, Lord British made an appearance and exclaimed, "How dare you cheat in this game!" and summarily killed the player. An *Ultima* saved at the 11th hour.

- Playing lots of practical jokes on employees and "modifying" their offices a bit while they were out of town. Ah, those were the days!

Trusting Your Team

To be a good producer, you cannot be emotionally invested in the game – but you must be emotionally invested in seeing it ship. This is what most junior producers lack, the ability to divorce themselves enough from their game in order to redline their favorite features and cut the parts of the game that are going to drive it off schedule and over budget. The key to this is trusting your team: They'll make sure that the game is great; you just have to make sure that you're streamlining the process and reining in anything that will jeopardize the project as a whole. Everyone one your team is better at their field than you are; that's why you hired them as artists, game designers, programmers, etc. Trust them and don't second guess them ...

—*James Portnow (Chief Executive Officer, Rainmaker Games; Professor, DigiPen Institute of Technology)*

Game Documentation

Game documentation is created during the concept, pre-production, and production phases to convey components of the project to team members and prospective partners (such as a publisher, manufacturer, or licensor). The documentation serves two purposes: to ensure that team members understand their roles in the development process; and to convince companies to develop, fund production, or otherwise help make the game a reality. Keep in mind that the following documentation descriptions and elements are guidelines only. No strict documentation standards exist yet in this industry—although the following represents all the essential components needed for a strong foundation.

Don Daglow on the Relationship Between Technology & Creativity :::::

E. Dalage

Don Daglow
(Chief Executive
Officer & Creative
Director, Daglow
Entertainment LLC)

Don Daglow serves as CEO and Creative Director at Daglow Entertainment LLC, a new studio that creates innovative online and downloadable games. Don's work was selected for an Emmy Award for Technology & Engineering in 2008 for his creation of *Neverwinter Nights*—and he received the CGE Award in 2003 for "groundbreaking achievements that shaped the Video Game Industry." Don served as CEO of Stormfront Studios for 20 years after founding the company in 1988, selling over 14 million units and generating over $500 million retail and online game sales. Prior to founding Stormfront, Don served as Director of Intellivision Game Development for Mattel, a producer at Electronic Arts, and head of the Entertainment division at Broderbund. Don designed and programmed the first-ever computer baseball game in 1971 (now recorded in the Baseball Hall of Fame in Cooperstown), the first mainframe computer role-playing game (*Dungeon* for PDP-10 mainframes, 1975), the first sim game (Intellivision *Utopia*, 1981), and the first game to use multiple camera angles (Intellivision *World Series Major League Baseball*, 1983). He co-designed Computer Game Hall of Fame title *Earl Weaver Baseball (1987*, with Eddie Dombrower) and the original *Neverwinter Nights* for AOL (1991-97).

The new generation of online games is re-living old conflicts between creativity and technology. In the early days of gaming, we had big dreams for wonderful eye-popping games—but the limits of screen resolution, memory, cartridge or disk size, and processor speed doused those dreams in the cold shower of reality. Today, console teams still have big dreams—but it is the big budgets (not the small machines) that inhibit our ability to bring those games to life. Few publishers will risk $10 million on a project in an industry where most games lose money. Even as this new check and balance system evolves, the explosion of online games has introduced a new era of limitations. Once again, we have big dreams—but many of them require bandwidth and response times far beyond the reach of most players.

There is much debate in the industry on the effectiveness of creating extensive game documentation during the planning process. In reality, many elements of a game change drastically during the pre-production and production phases—whether due to problems related to implementation, scheduling, budgeting, market trends ... or even a senior executive's change of mind. Lengthy game design document "tomes" should be avoided if at all possible. During the pre-production phase of *Ultima Online II,* Producer Starr Long and his team spent almost three months building "a massive 150-page design document. We ended up completely changing at least 75% of the design, making a lot of that work useless." It's still good practice to put a game project into a structured framework early on so that the development team understands the project's initial vision—even if that eventually changes. Just avoid the unnecessary "documentation dissertation syndrome"!

Brian Reynolds on Starting From Scratch :::::

A 15-year industry veteran, Brian Reynolds is recognized as one of the industry's most talented and productive game designers. Honored by PC Gamer magazine as one of 25 "Game Gods," Reynolds has masterminded the design of an unbroken stream of hit strategy games—including the multi-million-selling *Civilization II*, *Alpha Centauri*, and *Rise of Nations*, as well as such new games as *Rise of Legends* and *Catan Live*. Highly regarded for his mastery of the art of programming, Reynolds' dual specialty gives him the substantial advantage of being able to bring his own visions to life—and he has built a reputation for finely tuned strategy games. As CEO of Big Huge Games, Brian concentrates on the creative side of the company—devoting most of his time to hands-on development of new game concepts and prototypes.

BR

Brian Reynolds
(Chief Game Designer, Zynga)

I think starting a brand new game from scratch is the most daunting part of the process. On the one hand, you have infinite possible choices; on the other hand, most of them are dead ends. Trying to come up with something that's going to be new and innovative—but still functional, and recognizable as a game people will want to buy and play—can be very challenging. You have to break the problem down into smaller steps and then solve it one bit at a time.

Concept

The *concept* document (also known as a *pitch* document) is the result of the concept development stage. The main goal of this document is to convey the goal and purpose of the proposed game. The document helps management (or a prospective investor or publisher) assess whether or not the game idea is viable, timely, and feasible. The purpose of this document is to sell the idea to funding sources, publishers, or other decision makers in the company. This document should be no more than five pages in length, and it should take no more than a week to create. The producer or creative director is usually responsible for putting together this document. Following is a description of several components that should be included.

Premise

The *premise* or *high concept* (discussed in more detail in Chapter 5) encompasses the basic idea of a game. The ideal premise consists of 1-2 sentences addressing the player directly—describing the mood and unique "hook" of the game. Think of the premise as something that will be used on posters and on the front of the game's packaging, near the title.

Player Motivation

You learned in Chapter 6 that there are victory and loss conditions in most games. A *player motivation* statement should briefly discuss the game's victory condition. How does the player win? What will drive the player to actually play the game to the end? For example, the player could be driven by a desire to compete, solve puzzles, or explore.

Unique Selling Proposition (USP)

What makes your game unique? Why will your audience choose to play your game over your competitors' titles? Your *unique selling proposition (USP)* is that one thing that makes your title stand out from the others. Why should your game be developed? Why is it special? Briefly state your USP and support it in no more than one paragraph. You might also want to list the features that will make your game particularly exceptional—anything from an unusual graphic style to advanced engine technology. Think of the USP as content that would be included on the back of the packaging for the game.

Target Market

The *target audience* is the portion of the game-playing audience that will be most likely to play your game. In Chapter 4, you learned about player demographics, psychographics, and geographics. Apply this information to the type of player who will enjoy your game the most. Make sure you include a specific age range. The target audience will also tie into the game's genre. This section should be no more than one paragraph in length.

Getty Imagees

What age group will you target?

You Want Them to Sneeze!

Don't assume that everyone will play your game—because they won't! The key here is to hone in on smaller groups of people that will not only want to play your game, but who will get their friends to play it as well. Marketing guru Seth Godin calls these people "sneezers," who spread an "ideavirus" to others. (Marketing strategies are discussed further in Chapter 12.)

Genre

In Chapter 3, you learned about all the primary *genres* that have been used to classify games. These genres are not based on setting or mood—as in those associated with traditional media, such as film—but on gameplay or style of game. What genre will you choose for your game? If you're considering combining genres (creating a *hybrid*) or inventing a new one, keep in mind that the industry might consider this a risky undertaking. If you are approaching outside funding or partnerships, remember that publishers and financial backers might need to be convinced that your innovative hybrid or brand new genre will be a success. Without the ability to analyze the sales performance of games in the same genre, your prospective partners might be hesitant to put money and credibility behind something that isn't a "sure thing." If the genre you've chosen is already established, take a few words to name and define the genre with respect to your game. If you are using an original genre or hybrid, discuss it in a paragraph.

Secret Exit Ltd.

Mobile games like *Zen Bound* tend to have much shorter development schedules and smaller budgets, which significantly lowers the risk of creating a new genre.

Target Rating

In Chapter 4, you learned about the various ratings provided by the Entertainment Software Rating Board (ESRB). Indicate what the expected ESRB rating for your game will be, and why.

Reprinted with permission from Microsoft Corporation

Will your game be rated "E" for "Everyone" (*Viva Piñata*, shown)?

Target Platform and Hardware Requirements

In Chapter 2, you learned about several platforms used in game development—including arcade, console, handheld, mobile, and computer. Most platforms require a relationship with the hardware manufacturer associated with that platform. As discussed in Chapter 2, the computer platform does not require this because it is not a proprietary platform. The mobile platform requires a relationship with a service provider who acts like a publisher. Major manufacturers of console platforms currently include Sony, Microsoft, and Nintendo. Handheld manufacturers include Nintendo, Sony, and Nokia.

WindySoft Co., Ltd.

Will your target platform be a handheld device such as the iPhone? (*Strikers 1945 Plus*, shown)

Choose a target platform for your game, and indicate whether you plan to port the game to another platform as well. If you're developing an iPhone game, consider whether you plan to develop an Android-based version. Will your game be optimized to run on smartphones and tablets? Your choice of primary platform will have a lot to do with your target audience and genre. Discuss your primary target platform and support your choice in one paragraph. If you also plan to develop for other platforms, discuss your reasons for these choices as well. Make sure you also include the minimum and recommended technical requirements for the primary platform you choose.

::::: *Iron Bridge:*
Testing the Mobile Waters

Gideon Games

On my first released game, *Iron Bridge*, I wanted to test the waters of mobile game design and development. A relatively small team operated under my direction, but organizing and directing that team proved to be a challenge in many ways. The game's initial concept and general design had to be functional yet have a simple goal. It was my responsibility to write a technical document that accurately conveyed the intended purpose of the application and all technical functionality to the team. I was also responsible for overseeing staff productivity, since a few members of the team worked remotely. Many reports, updates, requests for approval on completed tasks, and/or submissions from the sound department were emailed daily—and timing of the response could make or break a week's worth of development, or prevent a misunderstanding that could cost time and money. One of my more important responsibilities was to select and maintain a friction-free development team. Months of production can wear on a team that's under the gun, so I discovered that maintaining team morale and camaraderie was imperative; problem-solving disputes between team members came up occasionally but were easily remedied. Occasionally, there are updates needed for the app; months after release, I still monitor review posts and player feedback to determine which changes to the mechanics might better the gameplay experience, and I assign such tasks to in-house staff to facilitate playability.

Jacques A. Montemoino (Founder & Creative Director, Gideon Games Inc.)

Listen to Your Team!

Good project leads are masters of their discipline; great project leads are easy-going, approachable managers. Game developers tend to be united by their passionate view of what's best for a game, as well as their almost suicidal work ethic. Every good artist, programmer, designer, producer, and tester likely has strong views about how a project "should be." It's impossible to please everyone, but it's critical that every team member is listened to and considered—even if their ideas aren't viable. Project leads that can listen patiently and accept and deny ideas with diplomacy are crucial for getting the best work (and the best game) out of their teams.

—*Matt MacLean (Lead Systems Designer, Obsidian Entertainment)*

License

If your game will be adapted from a licensed property, indicate this. Have you made an exclusive deal with the licensor? Include any additional information about the property's popularity and appeal to particular markets. Almost all sports games are also licensed properties for team logos, names, and likenesses.

Sega

Will you license a film property like Sega did with Marvel's *Iron Man*?

Reprinted with permission from Microsoft Corporation

Is one of your competitors a top-selling game such as Epic Games' *Gears of War 3*?

Competitive Analysis

Select three to five successful titles currently available on the market and discuss how your title will be able to compete with each of them. Make sure you relate this competitive edge to your game's USP. Provide one paragraph per game—and include the title (as a subheader), genre, and a description of the game's premise. Most important, discuss why your game will effectively compete with each game. How will it distinguish itself from the others—and how will it be better?

Goals

What are your expectations for this game as an experience? What mood are you attempting to achieve? Make sure you go beyond the idea of "fun." Are you trying to provide excitement, tension, suspense, challenge, humor, nostalgia, sadness, fear, or a "warm fuzzy" feeling? Do you want players to create their own stories and characters? Discuss how the game will achieve these goals.

Game Proposal

The game *proposal* is a follow-up to the concept document—describing all the components of the earlier document in more detail. The purpose of the proposal is to present the details of the game to a company or prospective partner that is already interested in the idea (perhaps after reading the concept document). This document is much longer than the concept document—usually 10 to 20 pages in length—and it can also be used to explain the game in detail to prospective team members before they begin to plan the game's development. The producer and directors of the art, programming, and design teams are involved in putting this document together. (Sometimes a story-based *treatment* is created at this stage—focusing specifically on the premise and story elements discussed in the following sections, such as the backstory, story synopsis, and character descriptions.) All of the sections included in the concept document should be in the proposal. In addition, include the following sections:

Hook

A *hook* is an element that will attract players to the game and keep them there. Why would anyone buy this game? Choose the three to five best features that answer this question. Hooks can be based on visuals, audio, gameplay, storyline, mood—anything that you feel will grab and hold onto a player's attention.

Gameplay

In Chapter 6, you learned about some basic elements of *gameplay*. This section should list 10 to 20 elements that describe the experience of playing the game. What types of challenges are in the game? What paths can a player choose from? Discuss any activities the player can engage in—such as exploration, combat, collecting, puzzle-solving, construction, management, or cooperation with other players.

Online Features

If your game will include an *online* multiplayer component, discuss any pertinent features in this section. You might include elements related to cooperative teamwork, player matching services, and player vs. player (PvP) modes here.

Technology

The *technology* section is optional and should be included only if you plan to incorporate any special software or hardware technologies into the game. If you plan to license a game engine from a third party, discuss its features here. Will you incorporate innovative features such as a custom controller, highly-sophisticated artificial intelligence (AI), or voice recognition?

Art & Audio Features

Discuss any unique art and audio features of the game in this section—especially if they might be selling points for the game. Will you license any pre-existing music for the game? Do you plan to hire a well-known game composer to write the score? Will you use motion-capture techniques of relevant real-world people in the character animation process? You might want to discuss related popular media examples.

Production Details

Include a section discussing production details—including your development team, budget, and schedule. What is your current production status? Have you already developed a prototype, or are you at the concept development stage? Spend a few sentences introducing your development team as a whole, and then use subheads for each team member and his or her expected title on the project. Write brief paragraphs (one to three sentences in length) describing each team member's background, credits, and skills related to the role. Provide a rough estimate of how much you expect to spend overall. As a guide, $500,000 means you see this as a small project—and $5 million means you expect the game to be a huge hit. (If you are developing the game independently, your budget would be considerably smaller.) Also, your budget will depend heavily on platform. An AAA web-based or mobile game might only cost $100,000—but an AAA PS3 title might cost $25 million. (Consider that an AAA MMOG could easily cost twice this amount!) You can also offer a proposed ship date for the product and some key milestones. Keep in mind that the budget and schedule elements you include in the proposal are not final. Instead, they serve as guides to the publisher regarding the project's level of ambition. A rough budget breakdown for each phase is also typical.

Backstory

In Chapter 5, you learned about the backstory—which is a brief overview of everything that has taken place prior to the beginning of the game. Summarize your game's backstory briefly in a short paragraph. (The backstory would also be included in the treatment, if applicable.)

Story Synopsis

Chapter 5 discussed the components of a compelling storyline. Describe your story synopsis in one paragraph. Do not include details on various plot points; just stick to the main story idea. Focus on aspects of the story that might be unique or emotionally compelling. Also incorporate a discussion of how gameplay (discussed in Chapter 6) will reflect the story. What will the player do in the game? What type of environment or scenarios will the player encounter. (The story synopsis would also be included in the treatment, if applicable.)

Character Descriptions

In Chapter 5, you learned about putting together a brief description of each character. Incorporate these short, one-paragraph character summaries into your proposal (and in your treatment, if applicable). Include each primary character's name (as a header), physical description, personality characteristics, background/history, and relevance to the game's story.

Risk Analysis

This section discusses all the things that could possibly go wrong with the project, and how you should plan to deal with these problems should they arise. Some common risks that threaten projects include the following:

- Difficulties recruiting personnel
- Late delivery of materials (such as software development kits from console manufacturers)
- Reliance on external sources for key technology components
- Competitive technology developments
- Experimental technology or design decisions that could impact the schedule
- Asset-protection provisions

This section should also include your comments on which parts of the project are relatively safe. If you have any of the traditional risks covered, indicate this. For example, you might have a full team already in place.

Development Budget

A publisher is likely to require a *development budget* (or profit and loss [P&L] analysis) at the proposal stage. This is an estimate of all the costs of bringing the game to market, along with estimates of all anticipated income. Your company will most likely have a P&L statement available. If you're an independent developer presenting a proposal to a publisher, you will not have access to that publisher's cost structures. Instead of a P&L, you will need to include your development budget. Here are some items you'll need to list. (A detailed discussion of the following is beyond the scope of this book, but this list should give you a general idea of what's expected.)

- *Direct costs:* These are derived by multiplying person-per-month estimates by the group's salaries, then adding in equipment costs, overhead costs, and any external costs (licensing fees and outsourcing—such as sound, music, writing, and any special graphic effects).

- *Cost of goods sold (COGS):* These are the costs of physical materials that go into the tangible game product—including the box, disc, jewel case, and manual.

- *Marketing:* The marketing team will need to put together an estimate of how much it will spend to promote the game in print, television, online, point-of-purchase displays, and/or sell sheets.

- *Market development fund (MDF):* These are costs that the publisher pays stores in the retail channel for prime shelf space, end caps, shelf talkers, and circular ads.

- *Income estimates:* Consider the game's unit price and the size of your target market. Assuming only a portion of your target market will purchase your game, what do you expect your income to be from sales of the game? If you are proposing an online multiplayer game that uses a monthly subscription-based financial model, include your expected monthly income from this revenue stream as well.

  - *Allowances:* Provide allowances for returns, corporate overhead, and calculations for royalty payments if the game is based on an external license.

  - *Return on investment (ROI):* This must show that the company can make more money investing in your game than in some less risky venture, such as putting the money in the bank and drawing interest for two years.

Concept Art

If possible, include concept drawings and sketches of characters and scenes related to the game. The characters should be shown from front, side, and back views. Also, provide a few 2D mock-ups of screen shots depicting the game environment and primary characters. Discuss the style of the character and background art you plan to use in the game. Will it be cartoon-like, gothic, realistic, surrealistic, hyperreal?

Trion Worlds

Werewolf concept art from *Rift*

Game Design Document

The *game design document (GDD)* is much longer than the concept or proposal documents. Often running 50 to 200 pages in length, the GDD is not meant to sell your idea. Instead, its sole purpose is to be the reference guide to the game development process. The GDD focuses on the gameplay, storyline, characters, interface, and rules of the game. The GDD should specify the rules of playing the game in enough detail that you could, in theory, play the game without the use of a computer. (Playing a paper version of the game is actually an inexpensive way to get feedback on the design of your game—and paper prototyping should always be considered during the development process.) Due to the length of the GDD, a table of contents should follow the title page. This document will change on almost a daily basis as the project develops. Make sure the document is sitting on a network, and members of the development team are able to make changes to it at any time. In addition to the items in your project proposal, the GDD should include the elements discussed in the following sections.

Game Interface

In Chapter 8, you learned about the elements of a functional game interface. In this section, discuss each passive and active interface you plan to include in the game. Include the following elements:

- Elements you plan to include in each interface
- Production time required
- Cost to produce
- Need for each interface and associated elements
- Viability of interface for target audience and genre
- Usability features

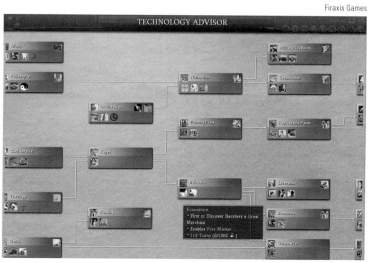

Firaxis Games

Will you utilize a tech tree as part of your interface, similar to the one used in *Civilization IV?*

Game World

In Chapter 7, you learned about levels associated with the game world. Describe the elements present in each level—including cinematics, art, gameplay, animation, characters, pick-up items, and background danger items.

Warner Bros.

Will characters carry items symbolizing their skills or powers (such as Harry's wand in *LEGO Harry Potter: Years 1-4,* which evokes his magical skills)?

Character Abilities and Items

In Chapter 5, you learned about character abilities and items that might exist in a game. Discuss the acquired, non-acquired, combat, and defense abilities of each player character and non-player character (NPC). What weapons and pick-up items might each character control or find during the game? Incorporate concept art and the synopsis that you included in the proposal for each discussion.

Game Engine

Many misunderstandings arise between programming, design, and art teams over limitations associated with the game engine. It's important for all teams to be on the same page—and for designers and artists to create game worlds and art assets knowing these limitations. In this section, include information from the programming team on what the game engine can and cannot do. Elements in this section might include:

- Number of characters that can be present onscreen at once
- Number of animations per character
- Camera and game view restrictions
- Polygons available per level and character
- Number of colors per texture map
- Support for special controllers (manual interfaces)

Keep in mind that a GDD can vary based on the details of a particular project—and there are many different templates available. (See this book's companion DVD for a GDD template and real-world example.)

GameSalad

Unity Technologies

Will you use a 2D authoring tool such as GameSalad (left) or a 3D game engine such as Unity (right) to develop your game?

Command & Conquer: Generals—Zero Hour: Developing a Proprietary Game Engine

Electronic Arts

The key challenge associated with developing a proprietary game engine [as opposed to licensing a pre-existing engine] is that you have to implement every single feature from scratch. As a result, there is usually not enough time left for polish. Sometimes you can squeeze some of that into the expansion pack. I thought we did a pretty good job with *Command & Conquer Generals: Zero Hour* in that respect. Given a decent engine to license, I would go for the license. We created the *Command & Conquer: Generals* RTS Sage engine from scratch—in part because there weren't any RTS engines available for license. However, we did reuse the 3D library and art pipeline from another Electronic Arts title. I'm in favor of using as much existing code as possible. Generally, adapting existing code is much faster than writing it from scratch.

—John Ahlquist (Founder, Ahlquist Software)

Art Style Guide

The purpose of the *art style guide or art plan* (which consists primarily of a set of visuals) is to establish the look and feel of the game and provide a reference for other artists to work from. This document is usually assembled by the concept artist and art director—and it ensures that a consistent style is followed throughout the game. Depending on the genre, some of the art in this document can take the form of pencil sketches, but it's also useful to have some digitized images that capture the final look of the game. A visual reference library should also be included that reflects the direction the art should take. Images in this library can come from any print publication or web site—but they should be used only for reference, and not for the final product!

Technical Design Document

The *technical design* document is based on the game design document and is usually written by the game's technical lead or director. This document describes the specifics of the game *engine*—the software in which the game is built—and compares it to other engines on the market. It establishes: how the game will transition from concept to software (known as the *technology production path*); who will be involved in the development of the engine; what tasks each person will perform; how long it will take to complete each task; what core tools will be used to build the game; and what hardware and software must be purchased.

Project Plan

The *project plan*—usually assembled by the producer—outlines the path taken to develop the game. It begins with the raw task lists provided by the technical design document, establishes dependencies, adds overhead hours, and turns all of this into a real-world schedule. The final project plan is broken down into a resource plan, budget, schedule, and milestones that will help track the project.

The *resource plan* is a spreadsheet that lists all the personnel on the project, when they will start, and how much of their salaries will be applied to the project. It takes from the technology design document the timing of the hardware purchases to support those personnel, and it estimates when the external costs (such as outsourced personnel) will be incurred. After applying the overhead costs, you can use these numbers to derive your monthly cash requirements and the overall budget for the game. The project plan is revised and updated throughout the project. Some producers use project management software for this (such as Microsoft Project). Keep in mind that sticking to this schedule and meeting your release date is imperative. If the project is delayed due to poor planning, you might sell fewer units than expected because all the advertising, cover stories, reviews, and previews are timed by the marketing and public relations teams to appear at certain times based on when the product is expected to be released.

Test Plan

A *test plan* is usually created by the QA department. It involves constructing test cases and creating a testing checklist—itemizing each aspect or area that needs to be focused on during the testing process. The test plan documents the procedures describing how the game will be tested. It is consistently revised throughout the process to cover new and modified areas.

Making It Happen

In Chapter 10, you learned about the components needed to build a strong development team. In this chapter, you discovered how that team should function once it's in place. You should now be able to identify elements related to the game production process—including phases, leadership/management strategies, and documentation. Whether you're a producer, lead, designer, or a team of one, understanding the "big picture" is essential.

::

This chapter took you through the intricacies of the game development process—including the phases, management strategies, and documentation. In the next chapter, we'll move from the inner workings of the game development studio to a more public topic: supporting and marketing to the player community before and after a game is released.

Expanded assignments and projects based on the material in this chapter are available on the Instructor Resources DVD.

:::CHAPTER REVIEW EXERCISES:::

1. Distinguish between the different phases of the game development process, and discuss the purpose and importance of each phase.

2. Leadership is a significant but often under-utilized skill in game development management. Why is this the case, and what strategies do producers and other managers utilize when leading game development teams?

3. Choose three forms of game documentation and discuss the importance of each in the development process. Discuss three components of each form of documentation. Why do you think these components are necessary to include in the documentation? Now choose one form of documentation and gear it toward your original game idea. Make sure that your finished document serves its intended purpose.

4. What is the importance of iterative design? Discuss the three phases of iterative design and what occurs during each phase. How are these phases connected with each other? How is the player market involved in the iterative design process?

5. Develop an analog (tabletop version) or digital prototype for your original game. What elements will you include in the prototype? Give reasons you won't include certain elements at this time. Have a group of people playtest your game and provide comments on elements related to gameplay mechanics, story/character, mood, functionality, and the "fun factor"!

CHAPTER

12

Marketing & Maintenance
developing the community

Key Chapter Questions

- What are the respective functions of the roles associated with *marketing*—such as advertising, promotion, public relations, and sales?

- What are the functions of *customer support* and *community management* in the game industry?

- What are the characteristics of *player communities*—and how are they created and maintained?

After the production team has successfully shipped a game, additional teams take over to market it and maintain its player base. (A game's marketing campaign can often start earlier in the process—causing some overlap between production and marketing.) Cultivating a game's player community as part of the marketing process will extend its longevity, increase its popularity—and allow for the release of expansions, upgrades, and even new games to a loyal customer base. Online player communities are essential for all types of games—and all channels of online communication (e.g., social networks, blogs, discussion forums, email, instant messaging, chat, newsletters) should be available to players at all times. This chapter provides an overview of what happens as a game is being launched—and beyond.

Marketing

Marketing involves targeting the game for a particular player market (discussed in Chapter 4) and persuading that audience to purchase the game. The game's publisher usually handles marketing responsibilities (whether the publisher is separate or a part of the game development studio). In Chapter 4, you learned about geographics, demographics, and psychographics—methods used to segment a market into a smaller niche that is most likely to purchase the game. There are several functions that exist under the marketing umbrella—including advertising, public relations, sales, and promotion—all of which utilize these methods while supporting and cultivating player communities. Sometimes these functions are split up into separate departments, but each of them use marketing principles to accomplish their goals.

Ivo Gerscovich on Effective Game Marketing Strategies :::::

IG

Ivo Gerscovich
(Vice President of
Global Marketing,
Paramount Pictures
Interactive & Mobile
Entertainment)

Before entering the game industry over 12 years ago, Ivo Gerscovich worked for Professional Sportscar Racing—a car racing series featuring Porsche, Ferrari, Lamborghini, and other high-end sports cars. He then helped start Fox Sports Interactive and then went on to work at Vivendi Universal Games, where he helped launch games based on *Ghostbusters*, *The Simpsons*, and other movie and TV properties. Currently, Ivo is Vice President of Global Marketing at Paramount Digital Entertainment working on mobile/tablet, social media, downloadable, and retail console products such as *Star Trek* (based on the J.J. Abrams reboot of the franchise).

Here are my recommended strategies for effective game marketing:

Know Your Audience: This is one of the most basic, yet important elements of marketing. The more you know about your target audience, the better—especially it can vary greatly based on game and platform. The potential audience for a shooter is different from the potential audience for a puzzle game—and the Wii audience is very different from the PS3/Xbox 360 audience.

Create Excitement About Your Product Using Game Content: There are many ways to generate buzz about a title, but game content itself is ultimately what gets audiences most interested in purchasing a product. Spend time choosing great screenshots, gameplay videos or concept art—and offer exclusive content to those who pre-order your game.

Get The Audience Involved: Social media offers many ways to engage audiences that were once much more fragmented and difficult to reach. It can greatly help get word out about your title—but at the same time, it's like handing a bullhorn to someone on a street corner. Make sure your engagement strategy will be appreciated by the fan base, and allow them to evangelize your products.

Be Bold, Be Different: "Me too" products and campaigns don't get much notice or attention. Being different is key. Make sure there are standout game features that are meaningful and marketable to your audience. Once you've got a list of cool new features, "show and tell" everyone about them -- or better yet, reveal them over time leading up to launch.

Create Killer Advertising: Creating great ads and running them (e.g., TV, print, online, in-theater) is very expensive and generally takes up the largest portion of an overall marketing campaign -- so make sure the creative elements are very strong. There are ways to test TV ads to make sure they are really helping to sell your game effectively; this may cost a bit -- but when you're spending a lot of money to run TV spots, you need to make sure your ads will really sell the game.

Work with Partners: Gone are the days of "casting a wide marketing net," only to find that a small amount of the people you reached even play video games. Today, working with Apple, Microsoft, Sony or Nintendo can help you reach your target player audience relatively simply and inexpensively.

Allow Respected Sources Speak for Your Product: Gamers are a savvy and connected bunch. From reading blogs, reviews, and spreading the word via Twitter and Facebook, these gamers only trust credible sources. When a game gets a "Best of E3" award or any other type of accolade from a reputable source, check with that source to see if it can be quoted in marketing materials.

Let Consumers Play the Game: Ultimately, the game will live or die by the gameplay experience it delivers. Put out a great demo that represents the game accurately; let gamers enjoy the experience and then tell all their friends about it. Word of mouth is one of the best marketing weapons you have in your arsenal—and now that social media is a huge part of the discovery process, a game with great gameplay will spread like wildfire.

As discussed in Chapter 4, traditional mass marketing focuses on getting the largest number of people to purchase your product. In contrast, niche marketing focuses on targeting that smaller segment of your market who will become die-hard fans of your product. Marketing analyst Seth Godin, author of *Purple Cow,* calls these early adopters "sneezers," because they will spread your marketing message (or "ideavirus") to friends, family, and colleagues through word of mouth. Instead of trying to get all people who play games to buy your game (this will not happen!), think about the specific type of person who would not pass up the opportunity to play your game. You can start by looking at your game's genre. If your game is an RPG, do you really think action gamers will be interested in playing it? Maybe some of them will, but why waste time focusing on action gamers when you have developed a game that has more appeal for RPG gamers? You can hone in further on your market niche by looking at the setting, story, and characters of your game—as well as the environment, levels, and gameplay you have incorporated.

Godin also suggests that marketing should start with the product itself. Examples of what Godin calls "remarkable" products are those with a unique industrial design—such as the Mini Cooper, a car that markets itself just by being driven around by its owner. The marketing process actually starts at the concept stage, when a game's *premise* (or *high concept*) and *unique selling proposition (USP)* are incorporated into the *concept* document (discussed in Chapter 11). What is it that truly makes your game unique? Why would your target market be compelled to play it—and tell others about it? Why might they prefer your game to competing titles? Marketing teams often use the game's premise to help the public form a mental image of the game.

Belinda Van Sickle on the Expanding Player Market :::::

BVS

Belinda Van Sickle
President & Chief
Executive Officer,
GameDocs;
Chief Executive Officer,
Women in Games
International)

Belinda Van Sickle is President & CEO of GameDocs – which specializes in distribution, consulting, packaging, localization, web promotion, and b-to-b documents. She began her game career in 1996 at Activision and was one of the founding members of Ignited Minds in 1999. Belinda started volunteering for Women in Games International in 2006 and has since become CEO of the organization. Belinda has an undergraduate degree in Feminist Studies and Psychology from the University of California at Santa Cruz and a Master's in English with a focus in Creative Writing from Sonoma State University. She has spoken at industry conferences such as the Game Developers Conference (GDC), Casual Connect, National Association of Broadcasters (NAB) and has appeared in several articles on the game industry for publications such as *Wired*, *GameSpot*, *GameCareerGuide*, *Chicago Tribune*, and *Los Angeles Times*. She has lectured or taught at the University of Southern California (USC), California State University-Fullerton, the Art Institute of California-Los Angeles, and Westwood College.

My experience began when the game industry was still focused on the hardcore PC market. I worked on packaging and watched the process change as the console revolution took place and advanced. The biggest improvements in video game marketing and advertising came when the industry hired from the outside—professionals experienced in consumer product marketing. For too long, publishers were making packages for a small segment of the market: PC gamers. As the installed base of consoles grew, publishers learned to advertise to their expanding market. The industry is in the process of expanding the video game market even further, and it is experimenting with newer kinds of messaging for this new audience.

Billions, Save Them All: Marketing a Facebook Game

We launched 3DVIA Studio with a game engine demo—Billions, Save Them All, which was published on Facebook as a fully 3D, multi-level, action/puzzle game. It was intended solely to demo the engine's capabilities, but it ended up being a success on Facebook—attracting 130,000 users in the first month. We attribute this success to the marketing push behind it. Through our experience on Facebook, we learned that a successful game needs to have an interesting story and/or gameplay – which must be communicated well through targeted promotion. Billions was the first game published on 3DVIA Studio, was one of the only fully 3D games on Facebook, and had unique gameplay and graphics. We ran advertising that drove traffic—but what really helped was the editorial content published in the top trade publications, namely IGN. From there, it was word of mouth: friends sharing the game with friends.

—Emmy Jonassen (Marketing Manager, 3DVIA/Dassault Systemes)

Dassault Systemes

One of the most significant elements of any marketing campaign is the effective use of a Web site for the company or game itself. As discussed later in this chapter, online fan communities form the basis of much of a game's word-of-mouth marketing. Godin's notion of spreading an "ideavirus" through sneezing is so easily accomplished in the online world. This is due to what Malcolm Gladwell (author of *The Tipping Point*) calls *network effects.*

You learned in Chapter 2 that online games are "networked" games. This means that players can interact with each other through a network (the Internet) to which their computers are connected. The Internet is not a broadcasting system, but a communication system—more like the telephone than the television. Rather than a two-person phone call, the Internet provides the ability to connect freely with people all over the world simultaneously. This capacity for *viral* communication is shown particularly well in email—in which one message can easily be sent simultaneously to thousands of people, who can then forward it to more people, and so on (hence the existence of spam)! Online strategies that take advantage of network effects include newsgroups, forums, chat rooms, blogs, newsletters, reciprocal linking, affiliate programs, fan sites—and, most importantly, social networks such as Facebook and Twitter. These strategies are discussed in the Community Management section, later in this chapter.

SB

Sara Borthwick
(Marketing & Insights
Director,
CBS Interactive)

Sara Borthwick worked as Online Marketing Manager at Atari and Encore Software. She was also a marketing consultant for Fandango and Accenture Strategy Consulting. Sara has promoted nearly 100 games, including *Dragon Ball Z: Budokai, Neverwinter Nights, Enter the Matrix, Civilization III, Test Drive, Unreal Tournament 2003, Backyard Sports, Horizons,* and *Sacred.*

At larger game companies, the online marketer would be responsible for crafting the strategy and the marketing communications, while an online producer would create the sites, ads, and other online assets. At smaller publishers, my day-to-day responsibilities would involve almost everything that relates to the Internet—which can be broken down into six basic areas:

1. Online advertising

2. Websites

3. Online retail

4. Newsletters and loyalty programs

5. Community support/grassroots outreach

6. Research

During a typical week as Online Marketing Manager, I have done the following:

■ Communicate a *marcom* (marketing/communications) strategy to the VP to secure a budget for online advertising, negotiate a campaign with ad sales reps from targeted gaming sites, and kick off creative product with a designer, while optimizing a campaign currently in progress. Tweak copy for search engine optimization purposes, and surf targeted sites to see how the competitors are advertising their products.

■ Create product pages, or gather information from producers and brand managers, to update the website. Work to incorporate beneficial new technology and ensure that the sites are easy to use, relevant, and portray the publisher in the desired light. Hire designers to create title-specific sites that provide users with enough information to make a purchase decision.

- Design promotional campaigns to increase revenue at the corporate online store. Ensure that the site navigation is intuitive and persuasive. Work with the sales team to increase buy-in and sell-through at the publisher's online retail partners (such as *Amazon.com, EBgames.com, BestBuy.com*).

- Grow the customer database with qualified opt-in consumers. Encourage repeat purchases at the online store through promotions, and encourage multiple product purchases through targeted and informative newsletters.

- Provide a framework for fans of the publisher's products to interact with each other, the publisher, and the developer. Listen. Address valid concerns as forthrightly as possible. Find and leverage the existing fan base for similar products by establishing relationships with key influencers within the gamer community through grassroots advocacy outreach.

- Estimate the level of consumer excitement for a game prior to release by gathering and analyzing internal and syndicated log file (information on Web site pages accessed) data. Gather qualitative opinions from gamers on similar competitive products and on preliminary experiences of our games. Investigate new technologies, consumer attitudes and behaviors, and marketing opportunities.

The game industry is extremely fluid. Games are a mix of art and technology. At any moment, an unexpected problem can pop up that forces production delays and/or the elimination of key elements from the game. This, in turn, can force the ship date to be pushed out by months or years, and the marketing team to re-evaluate and sometimes re-do the entire marketing campaign. The ability to react quickly to changes, while still planning ahead—in addition to extremely strong communication skills—is essential to success in game marketing. Finally, knowledge of games and the player mentality is also necessary to creative effective marketing communications, and also to gain the respect of the developers—some of whom have rock star mentalities!

::::: Game Packaging Art

Some game artists specialize in creating art for marketing materials, such as game packaging. These artists are not necessarily on the development team, but they are often in the publisher's marketing department. For this reason, game box art might consist of illustrations that do not necessarily reflect art seen within the game itself.

Electronic Arts / BioWare   Sony Computer Entertainment America

Box art from *Dragon Age II* (Xbox 360) and *Killzone 3* (PlayStation 3).

Casual vs. Hardcore Market

As discussed in Chapter 4, there is a tradition in the game industry to divide the player community into two segments: *casual* and *hardcore* gamers. The casual gamer is someone who seldom plays games and might be attracted more by the commercial appeal of the game (e.g., an adaptation of a popular film or book like *The Lord of the Rings*). The hardcore gamer is someone who plays games on a regular basis and who often enjoys competitive features and deep gameplay. Mass marketing would be the approach used for casual gamers, while niche marketing would be more appropriate for hardcore gamers. However—as mentioned in Chapter 4—this casual vs. hardcore market segmentation is not ideal. A better approach would be to divide the market up by genre, platform, geographics, demographics, and pyschographics.

Advertising

The *advertising* team focuses on reaching the market through paid ads in media outlets such as television, radio, magazines, newspapers, and web sites. In a niche marketing approach, ads would be purchased in game-related or even genre-related outlets—such as *GamePro* (magazine), IGN (web site), and *Attack of the Show* (television series).

Deep Silver, Inc.

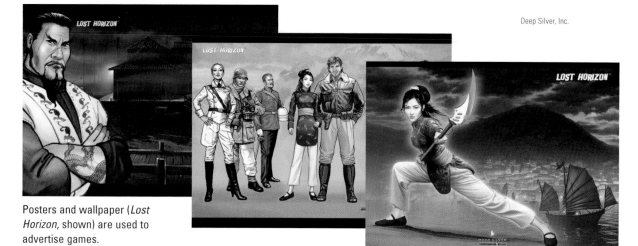

Posters and wallpaper (*Lost Horizon*, shown) are used to advertise games.

Effective Game Advertising

Word-of-mouth supported by clever ads that show some degree of gameplay—but not too much—work best. Think Mr. T playing *World of Warcraft* (*WoW*), the *Fallout* commercials, and the odd *Katamari Damacy* commercials where real life office mates are pleasantly rolled up. Think of game advertisements as a classy and elegant strip-tease: teasers, less hype, nothing too in-your-face.

—*Jennifer F. Estaris (Senior Game Designer, Nickelodeon Virtual Worlds)*

Reprinted with permission from Microsoft Corporation

Although developers may purchase ad space on external web sites that focus on the player market, some use their own web sites as a form of advertising (Lionhead Studios' *Fable III* site, shown).

Promotion

Promotion involves putting together events, contests, trials, giveaways, and merchandise to get the public excited about a product. Promotional merchandise might include stickers, posters, hats, and T-shirts portraying the cover art of the game; these might be provided to prospective customers at game retail stores or offered along with the product itself. Giveaways might include iTunes promo codes; almost every iPhone/Android launch provides these, if not similar items. Contests might involve providing cash or merchandise prizes to players who win tournaments involving the game. One of the most common forms of promotion for subscription-based online games is to provide a downloadable 10- to 30-day free trial version of the game to prospective customers. Special events might include in-store game signings, preview demonstrations at conferences, online chats with game developers, and educational panels for players interested in learning how games are created.

ceres47 (Photobucket)

Consumer events can be effective promotional tools—especially when fans are encouraged to attend in costume (Mario and friends at Gen Con, shown).

From "Merchandising" to "Transmedia"

Marketing for big-budget games and franchises—especially those with well-known game characters (such as Lara Croft and Mario)—are often supplemented by companion products such as movies and novels set in the game world, action figures, or licensed properties such as cartoons and *manga* (Japanese comic books). More recently, *transmedia* techniques have been used by game marketing to heighten awareness of a title and increase market base. Transmedia has traditionally been used as a cross-media storytelling device—where a product (or spin-offs containing its characters or world) is released in different media formats such as a game, film, television series, and book. While at MIT, media studies professor Henry Jenkins espoused the view that the coordinated use of storytelling across multiple platforms may result in making the players more compelling to the audience. While marketing has long been releasing promotional merchandise to supplement the launch of a game title, they are now often involved in the release of multiple products in various media that are not consciously considered promotional items by the audience.

Public Relations

The *public relations (PR)* professional (or team) focuses on letting the public know about the game—often long before it is released. PR involves targeting the news media and game-related press at magazines, newspapers, radio, television, and websites. Goals include securing previews, reviews, interviews, features, and cover stories. The PR team often uses assets produced by the art, design, and programming teams—such as demos, videos, concept art, and screen shots—to help assemble analog and digital press kits for media outlets.

During the pre-launch period, a PR professional or firm requests assets in order to generate buzz and may offer "first looks" or previews to the press. A month or so before launch, the review program kicks in—and the media is invited to take advantage of custom accounts and game discs. Additional services usually provided by a PR professional or outside firm include *corporate PR*

Game press releases (*Vindictus,* shown) are posted on news sites and directories such as MPOGD.com so that players can find out about new releases.

(focusing the messaging and positioning for the studio and team behind the product), *commentary* (where team members are given the opportunity to comment on hot news topic or respond to a statement—such as "games aren't art!"), and *media tours* (setting up in-person meetings with journalists and interfacing with the media at trade shows).

Sue Bohle on Pre-Launch Public Relations Campaigns :::::

Sue Bohle has been providing counsel to game companies since 1983. Her company has served hardware, software, tools, conference producers and online game sites—launching titles in all genres and for all platforms. Among the companies Sue has counseled include Warner Bros., Atari, Activision, IGN/Fox Entertainment, Game Developers Conference (GDC), Penny Arcade, and numerous indie studios.

Building anticipation and enthusiasm for a game before launch is extremely important with titles for the hardcore market. An asset calendar can keep the studio and the agency on track and increase efficiency. Media tours ensure that studios get the attention of the right reporters and always significantly increase both coverage and scores/ratings. Social media has come on strong as a tool for big games—with in-house blogs, sneak previews, and YouTube videos and trailers high on the list of important activities.

SB

Sue Bohle
(Chief Executive Officer,
The Bohle Company)

Luis Levy on Game PR Strategies That Work :::::

JN

Luis Levy
(Co-Founder,
Novy Unlimited;
Director, Novy PR)

Luis Levy is the co-founder of Novy Unlimited and the director of Novy PR—a public relations firm specializing in mobile and indie game developers and high technology clients including Appy Entertainment and Liquid Entertainment. At Novy, Luis manages strategy, planning, media placement, speaking opportunities, and trade show bookings. Prior to Novy, Luis was an account executive at The Bohle Company – where he represented game and high-technology clients such as Spacetime Studios, The Voxel Agents, SRRN Games, Muzzy Lane, TimeGate Studios, and Dr. Fun Fun. Luis has also worked in advertising, sales, film and television editing, and as a game tester. Luis co-authored *Play the Game: The Parent's Guide to Video Games* and *Game Development Essentials: Game QA & Testing* with Jeannie Novak. Luis was born in São Paulo, Brazil and attended Fundação Armando Álvares Penteado (FAAP), where he received a B.A. in Film & Television.

The best game PR strategy is to stagger the release of assets such as screenshots and trailers. The studio should make sure to hit journos every six weeks or so to stay "top of mind" (i.e., helping them remember you exist). It all starts with the announcement press release plus some concept art. Then you can move on to screenshots, the first trailer, more screenshots, multiplayer details (when applicable), and finally a launch trailer/press release combo. The idea is to make the game interesting enough for members of the press so they set aside some time to review it. This is what we call a review program. Of course, any game will benefit from extras such as previews at trade shows like E3 and GDC, media tours, and editor days (when editors are flown to the company's offices for face-to-face interviews and playthroughs). Such activities usually cost extra—so apart from meetings at trade shows, they may be too expensive for indie developers.

Developer Diaries: A Unique PR Strategy

Developer diaries, such as those found on game and game news websites (such as *gamespy.com*), can be seen as a way for developers to communicate their experiences to players—thereby strengthening the developer-player bond. The diaries are also a great PR strategy that lets the public know about a game before it is released. Having the developers become directly involved in the PR process allows the news to be seen as legitimate information—rather than "hype."

::::: Pocket Legends: The Little Android in All of Us

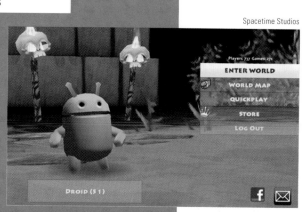

Spacetime Studios

Launching the 3D mobile MMO *Pocket Legends* on Android was a dream come true! Not only did I get to push my PR skills to the limit, I was also able to come up with an idea that worked really well: a cute in-game Android costume—the kind of exclusive item players would kill to get their hands on. Spacetime Studios, a savvy studio if there ever was one, knew this would fly with the "Android Army" and executed the plan with the utmost care in no time at all. At launch, Bohle (the firm I worked for at the time) made sure to let everyone in the press know about the very exclusive Android costumes available for both Android and iPhone users. For almost two weeks straight, sites and blogs conducted giveaways of the costume non-stop with their readers via comments, Twitter and Facebook—resulting in almost 500,000 downloads and much in-game spending. To this day, we credit the huge success of *Pocket Legends* on Android, in part, to this creative—and uncommon—idea, straight from the mind of a PR pro that happened to be a huge Android fanboy.

—Luis Levy (Co-Founder, Novy Unlimited; Director, Novy PR)

Marketing Multi-tasking

The most challenging part of the video game marketing process is launching many titles in a short window. Naturally, Quarters 3 and 4 are the biggest launch months because that is when the game industry does the vast majority of its business—and marketing teams must be able to effectively juggle multiple titles, tasks, and work under tight time constraints at any given moment in order to make those crucial dates. There are a tremendous number of things that need to be done on the marketing side to prepare for a game launch. When you have multiple titles releasing around the same time—and you need to familiarize yourself with new properties, conduct market analyses, develop marketing plans, create great packaging, create great advertising, manage budgets, on and on—it can mean many early mornings and late nights. But this is also what makes marketing games very exciting and rewarding!

—Ivo Gerscovich
(Vice President of Global Marketing, Paramount Pictures Interactive & Mobile Entertainment)

Sales

The *sales* team maintains relationships with buyers from online and offline retail stores, wholesalers, discount stores, video rental chains, and hardware manufacturers. This team focuses not only on getting the game into these outlets, but also on positioning the game in stores so that it gets priority shelf space. The team also tries to secure deals with game hardware manufacturers to bundle the game with the hardware platform.

Sony Computer Entertainment America

The most visible shelf space and freestanding displays are at a premium in retail outlets.

Why Is It Important to Reach the Millennial Market?

Millennials are the largest generation by population. As they mature and define a unique generational style, they will overturn many standard cultural formats popular during the Xer era of the 1980s and 1990s. Those who do not understand the unique aspects of this generation will be caught fighting the "last war," and creating media for a youth culture that no longer exists. In addition, Millennials are more comfortable with games than any earlier generation, and are likely to make them their dominant media as they mature.

—*Pete Markiewicz, PhD*
(Instructor, Interactive Media Design, Art Institute of California-Los Angeles)

The Art & Marketing Relationship

The worst thing that could happen to you is that you've got a great game, but nobody's heard of it. We don't want that, but we don't want to be distracting the team from the tight deadlines—so it's usually up to the Art Director to fuel the voracious marketing machine with screenshots, illustrations, the occasional bit of concept art that turned out well … whatever you can dig up to put the best face forward for your project.

—*Marc Taro Holmes (illustrator, concept artist, and art director)*

Community Management & Customer Support

The customer support team is responsible for fielding questions and concerns related to the game. Issues can range from technical difficulties in loading the game software to complaints about disruptive behavior of other players (specifically in an online multiplayer game). It used to be common practice in massively multiplayer online games (MMOs) to hand over some of the customer support duties to experienced gamers who might offer to participate voluntarily as *game masters (GMs)*—also known as guides, counselors, or companions. As discussed in Chapter 3, GMs originated in *Dungeons & Dragons*® as those able to change the course of the game. Online GMs are at the forefront of customer service, acting as mediators between game developers and customers. Responsibilities include disciplining players who take part in harassment and cheating; helping new players get situated; answering in-game questions; and accepting feedback from players.

Maintaining a Balance in Community Management

For an online game, it is extremely important to manage the community after launch. This means many different things. You must constantly fix game bugs and balance the game to keep people happy, but you must also constantly try to keep both the hardcore and casual players happy in the same game. You must also continue to expand the game content for most games, which leads to ongoing balance problems. In most online games, players join and continue to play because it is where their friends are—which means that sometimes if you lose a single person, they can take all their friends with them. Online games are now much more about selling a service than a product. However, it will always be impossible to keep everyone happy—so this is a difficult balance to strike when managing the needs and requests of the community.

—Troy Dunniway (Vice President & General Manager; Globex Studios)

The Player Community Feedback Loop

I don't recommend muddling up a game concept and design with too many "must-haves" based on what's currently popular with the player community. This feedback loop works best for a persistent world that thrives on ever-changing elements that provide a challenge for the veterans and ease-of-entry for the new.

—Jennifer F. Estaris (Senior Game Designer, Nickelodeon Virtual Worlds)

CS

Carly Staehlin
(artist; Owner, Burrow
Owl Trading, LLC)

Former game developer Carly Staehlin participated in the computer game industry for more than eight years from 1998 to 2005. At Origin Systems, she pioneered the first online community services department in the massively multiplayer online game industry—which served as the model that many other companies, in games and other industries, have since emulated. Having worked on many titles in the *Ultima* series, she was also the producer of *Ultima Online* during the height of its commercial success.

The online community that exists because of an MMO, *but outside of it*, tends to represent no more than 30% of the player base. That means that 70% of the player base will likely never look at the website, communicate with game support personnel, submit bugs, or otherwise interact with the developer other than to play the game.

Given these figures, one might imagine that the out-of-game community isn't that important. After all, it's standard practice is to only spend your energy on those things that are seen and enjoyed by 70% of the players and to place lower priority on those that impact the remaining 30%. However, I believe that the out-of-game community that grows around a game actually enriches the in-game environment for all players. Out-of-game community "leaders" tend to be highly active in the in-game environment. Their relative level of happiness and satisfaction with the game can be somewhat measured by the number of in-game activities and groups that they also participate in or create. These leaders provide more content and entertainment within the game environment for all players—even those who do not realize that they are interacting with a "community leader" of some type. On the other hand, I believe that an MMO could do fine without any kind of additional out-of-game Web support—especially if that game includes the traditional out-of-game features within itself. Once the concepts of community begin to be well understood, they may need to be less distanced from the game itself, and in fact might benefit from a tighter integration.

Any way for a player to get more content, features, attention, or opportunities for fun related to a game will absolutely help that game to be more successful than it would have been otherwise. I don't believe that this is limited to MMOs either, as evidenced by the FPS and Modder communities.

Drew Davidson is a professor, producer, and player of interactive media. His background spans academic, industry and professional worlds—and he is interested in stories across texts, comics, games and other media. Drew is the Director of the Entertainment Technology Center at Carnegie Mellon University and the Editor of the ETC Press. He serves many advisory boards, program committees and jury panels—and he has written and edited books, journals, articles, and essays on narratives across media, serious games, gameplay analysis, and cross-media communication.

Drew Davidson, PhD
(Director,
Entertainment
Technology Center,
Carnegie Mellon
University)

With everything connecting to the Internet, players can speak up more than ever about what they want in the games they are playing. This provides developers with interesting opportunities to decide whether they want to tweak their games in response to player input. Granted, with games shipped, this isn't often a real-time process—but with more and more games being created with an online connectivity, the community management aspect takes on added dimensions. An ARG [alternate reality game— discussed later in this chapter] is a good example of a genre in which developers are able to almost instantly adjust their game based on player input. Now, this can be both good and bad. On the one hand, it could be useful to get this extra bit of player testing and feedback—and developers may be able to iterate a better game after the fact. On the other hand, we don't want the tail wagging the dog; being overly responsive to lots of player feedback could devolve into game design by community. That said, I think we're not only going to see player input have more explicit impact, we're also going to see more games such as *Spore* and *Little Big Planet* that incorporate player-generated content as a foundational part of the playing experience.

Andy Nealen is an architect, civil engineer, professor, and an independent game designer. He is a computer graphics, animation and modeling researcher and has previously worked on the critically acclaimed iPhone/iPad/PC/Mac/Linux game *Osmos*.

For small, independently developed video games, community is essential. Without it, there is no word-of-mouth—which is crucial to the commercial success of an indie game, since it's the main channel for advertisement. Indies have become quite skilled at using social media and other means to spread the word and thereby circumvent the need for a publisher.

AN

Andy Nealen
(Assistant Professor,
Rutgers University)

AT

Allison P. Thresher
(Community Moderator,
Harmonix Music
Systems, Inc)

Alli "HMXThrasher" Thresher has been a member of the Harmonix Community and Public Relations team since 2009. Prior to working with Harmonix, Alli was an administrator at a small music school as well as a researcher and ghost writer at a large tech and consulting firm. She's worked as a freelance writer and social media consultant for a variety of small start-ups and non-profits. Alli also has a Masters' Degree in Irish Studies which serves her well in the land of video games.

My role is a varied mix of community management – both online and in person, public relations, customer support, content building, and social media. Community moderators (also known as community managers) are both the conduit of information about our games and company to the outside world as well as the voice of the fans in-house. We staff public demos, speak at and attend large scale gaming conventions and fan events, moderate our online community forums, provide customer support, produce videos and podcasts for our web sites, manage the company Twitter and Facebook accounts, and interact with members of the gaming and traditional press. We also provide feedback throughout the development process to ensure that the needs of our fans (whether casual or hardcore) are met.

We pride ourselves on the level of interactivity we have with our community. We're always looking for ways to improve upon the overall Rock Band experience, and community feedback is an important part of that. We host threads on our forums letting fans "request a feature" and pass this feedback along to our design team for consideration. Many of these wishes were addressed, for example, when we moved from *Rock Band 2* to *Rock Band 3*. During development, we also reach out to individual "power users" of certain features, such as our character creator and art maker, to find out about how they'd like to see that feature improved or changed and bring that feedback back to the production team. We make our games for our fans, so we see their input as instrumental to the ongoing iteration on all our franchises.

Following the launch of one of our games, feedback from our community is particularly important. In the days following a release, we spend a great deal of time reviewing feedback not only on our own site but on major gaming forums and other community sites as well. In addition to this tracking, our team manages one-on-one support via social media (Twitter and Facebook)—

ensuring that our most vocal brand ambassadors and power users feel that their reactions to changes or improvements we've made to the games they love are heard and communicated back to the studio.

Christian Allen started in games in the late '90s creating mods for the *Tom Clancy's Rainbow Six* franchise. He parlayed his mod work into a job at Red Storm Entertainment/Ubisoft—quickly working his way up to Lead Designer and then Creative Director on the *Tom Clancy's Ghost Recon* franchise. Christian then went on to work at Bungie as Design Lead on *Halo: Reach* before joining WB Games, where he currently works as Design Director on an unannounced title. Christian's games have shipped over 10 million units on various platforms and have won several awards—including the British Academy of Film and Television's (BAFTA) Best Game gong in 2006 for *Tom Clancy's Ghost Recon Advanced Warfighter*. Christian is married to Angeline Fowler – his wife of over 15 years who also works in the industry – and he has a young daughter, Isabel.

CA

Christian Allen
(Design Director,
WB Games)

Game communities consist of the folks that will evangelize your title, since they tend to be opinion leaders among their less tech-savvy social networks. Having worked in games with extremely strong and vocal communities, notably Ghost Recon and Halo, I can say that the community can be an invaluable resource if you manage the relationship properly. The key is to directly hook developers up with community members and allow them to communicate directly, while effectively managing the messaging to ensure that the community gets a strong and unified message from the developers. You must also have a way of cohesively gathering community feelings and comments—and present that information back to the development team so they can act on it. You must always remember that just because someone in a game community is the loudest or most persistent poster, it doesn't mean that their views represent the community as a whole. You must spend time becoming intimately involved in the community to effectively filter the feedback you receive.

MMO Communities: Walking a Fine Line

Player markets for a massively multiplayer online game (MMO) are vital—even more so after the game is launched. Since an MMO lives and breathes on retaining players, doing everything you can to please the community without alienating too large a section of that community is a fine line to walk. Some have done it well, and others have done it spectacularly poorly—creating situations where new player experiences trumped veterans' enjoyment of existing gameplay, which led to a mass exodus from the game.

—*James Owen Lowe (Content Designer, ZeniMax Studios)*

BC

Billy Joe Cain
(Chief Creative Officer,
Sneaky Games)

Billy Cain started in the game industry in 1992 at Origin Systems. He has worked on hundreds of games over his career for such companies as Origin Systems, Electronic Arts, Sony, and THQ. He was a co-founder of BigSky Interactive, Critical Mass Interactive, and now Sneaky Games—a world-class game developer of Facebook games. He frequently speaks at game conferences and serves on multiple university-level advisory boards in the field of game education to assist students with practical guidance on breaking into the video game industry.

Community management is an amazing tool that improves the play experience for the players – allowing them to provide input, interact with the team, and get immediate information about the game; it enhances the game itself, since the developers can listen to what the players want, what is causing them frustration, and other issues they might be experiencing. It is vital in community management to listen to the players' pain or frustration rather than their exact comments and suggestions. For instance, if a player wants to jump farther, it may be that there's a particularly difficult jump in their path—so this might be all you really need to adjust. Remember that your players are *why you exist*; listening to them with compassion, being completely honest with them about what you can and will do, and maintaining a healthy communication style all pay off in a real relationship between fan and development team—and that's a beautiful thing. Community management is a mindset that must be bought into all the way up the chain of your organization. Sharing our limitations with our players is sometimes uncomfortable for many managers, owners, and shareholders—so be sure you know where the line is drawn for your organization and for the health of your relationship with the fans. Telling people you cannot share something is all right, too. Just be honest—because fans *will* find out if you are not, and this could irreparably damage the relationship. Getting player feedback prior to launch helps playtesting because really, who has that many people in their building? After launch, players want to be connected to the game and assist with further adjustments—or they might provide new ideas to be added later, or in the sequel. Remember: Your players are *why* you exist!

"It's Not Your World Any Longer": Community Control in MMOs & Social Games

In social and massively multiplayer online games (MMOs), the key is to realize that as a designer, the moment you ship, it's not your world any longer: it's the player's. Embrace the players' decisions and support them in how they want to play. Don't force your story in the direction you think it should go; build it around what your players do. With the level of metrics that we can build into games today we can tell everything about what our player base is doing, from the number of times they click per play session to how many of them buy blue hats rather than red. Use this information as you are crafting the expansions to your world, it will tell you what players find compelling and what they find tangential to their experience. This sort of clear numerical data will, if analyzed well, give you a much better insight into what your community truly finds compelling about your game than any trawling of your message boards or listening to the crowing in your forums.

—James Portnow (Chief Executive Officer, Rainmaker Games; Professor, DigiPen Institute of Technology)

The most challenging aspect of game online marketing is managing the player community. Game publishers and developers know that most game purchase decisions are heavily influenced by recommendations from friends and general word-of-mouth buzz. Online communities of players provide a window into these interactions, and of course publishers and developers want to influence these communities and the corresponding word-of-mouth buzz to promote their products. However, players are highly resistant to corporate marketing communication. It is one thing for a publisher to say that they will leverage an online community to generate interest in a game, but it is very hard, if not impossible, to make people care about a product. If and when a community of players does latch onto a particular game, the publisher and developer have to be extremely responsive to the players' needs. Players are highly informed, intelligent and fanatical. If the product communications are not consistent, this can cause problems for the success of the product. Finally, when players create a community around a particular game, they are actually shaping the brand. Marketing must be okay with not having complete control over the product image and product communication....I firmly believe that player communities can never be built by design. Instead, the developer and the publisher can stimulate a community through their own enthusiasm for the product and by actively listening and respecting the fan base. A publisher/developer can aid a community by providing tools for players to interact with each other and the game. This can range from simple forums, to mod tools, to easy map exchanges. Most of all, the publisher/developer can aid the player communities online by becoming part of those communities.

—Sara Borthwick (Marking & Insights Director, CBS Interactive)

Sequels & Community Direction

For sequels, community direction and ideas are critical. Being able to look at user data and correlate it with comments on the Internet and those submitted directly to the community manager is gigantic; in several cases, this has directly affected features we have developed for future games, and it's always awesome to prove to your customers that you listened to them.

— *James Stevenson (Senior Community Manager, Insomniac Games)*

Post-Launch Budget for Community Management

Some games need little community management, and some games need a lot! If your game is subscription or micro-transaction based, then community management is essential to keep people playing (and paying!). Modern games need one budget to get them to launch, and another ongoing budget after launch, to add new features and to manage the community.

—*Jesse Schell (Professor, Carnegie Mellon University; Chief Executive Officer, Schell Games)*

The Attack of the Santa Clauses

One of my favorite memories is from *Ultima Online* during one of the first in-game Christmas celebrations we performed. We created Santa Clauses giving gifts to player characters. Unfortunately the spawn rate of the Santa Clauses was set a little too high and they started to fill up the towns. We had to quickly turn them off!

—*Jason Spangler (Technical Director, BioWare / Electronic Arts)*

Games as a Service

Community is a becoming a vital part of game development. Many game companies will need to become familiar with the concept of "Games as a Service" in order to survive the next game generation. *[Author Note: The epitome of this concept involves community—in particular, user-generated content and game amplifiers involving team management away from the game itself.]*

—*Anthony Borquez (Chief Executive Officer, Grab Games; Faculty Member, University of Southern California)*

Official Web Site

One of the single most important marketing tools is the game's official site—which can also be a great source of customer support. Whether or not your game is played online, customers will most likely check the website first for any news, updates, or technical assistance. Customers will also want to provide feedback on their game-playing experience, so make sure that a discussion forum is available on the site for that purpose.

Reprinted with permission from Microsoft Corporation

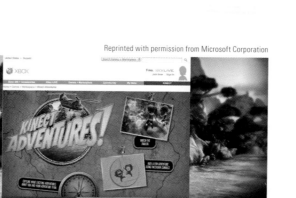

Microsoft's official *Kinect Adventures!* web site provides trailers and previews, tutorials, news for existing and prospective players, and connections to social networks such as Facebook.

The Community Web Site: Up Close & Personal

If you don't have a community site built for your players when your game launches, it's easy for your title to become a flash in the pan—even if it's great. When your game comes out, people will want to be talk about it and sharing information with one another – and one of the first places they'll look to do this is on your game's web site. If you don't provide the nesting ground for a community, they're less likely to start their own. Players sometimes form their own fan sites and communities, but don't count on them doing your own community building for you. You want to establish a place for them to come together while the energy from your game is hot. Even better, in the Internet age players absolutely love being in close touch with the developers. At the bare minimum, you should put up a web site with basic information about the game. Include a discussion forum only if you're planning to invest the energy to moderate it; otherwise, it will quickly fill up with spam. The best thing to do is to put up a development blog a few months before the game launches and show people the internals of your design process; players love this—especially those video game mavens that like to tell their friends about the hottest new thing.

Lars Doucet (educational game designer)

Tutorials

If you have released an online multiplayer game, provide real-time tutorials to new players. Weekly tutorial play sessions were established for the online game, *Shanghai Dynasty*. Not only did these play sessions provide needed customer support for new players, they also allowed developers to receive feedback on the game content, programming, design, and player psychographics—including the thoughts and preferences of the player community.

Astraware Limited

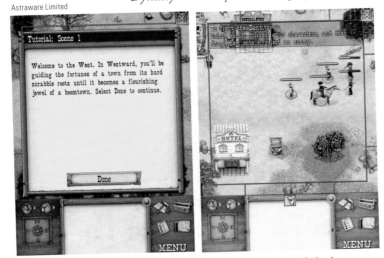

Tutorials (*Westward*, shown) provide useful customer support in both multiplayer and single-player games.

Player Forums

Player forums existed on the Internet long before the commercialization of the Web, so group members who joined during that time do not take kindly to overt marketing techniques. However, these groups contain ideal viral marketing candidates, because the group members are so highly focused on the group's topic. If a newsgroup has not been formed around your game, create one yourself and moderate it. Join other newsgroups (*groups.google.com*) that focus on your game's genre or platform, and participate in the group—providing fans with any information they need without trying to sell them the game or associated material. Do not create new threads (which might be seen as overt marketing), but participate in discussions begun by fans and explicitly identify yourself as a company representative or developer. Elicit feedback from the group on how to improve on the game. Although not official player forums, a Facebook page and/or group can sometimes provide a similar sense of community—depending on your game's market.

CCP

The *EVE Online* player forum allows players to share their experiences within the game.

Astroturfing the App Store

It has become common for not only developers and publishers—but even some outside firms—to use a tactic known as astroturfing to increase sales by having a team of (usually) interns crawl through iTunes and other community forums posing as players and posting positive reviews for the company's game. So ... do a little more research before downloading that 5-star iPhone game! (The term "astroturfing" was originally used to identify a form of advocacy or propaganda in support of a political or corporate agenda that was in the guise of a grassroots movement.)

::::: *Shattered Galaxy*: Supporting Player Communities Through Interactive Communication Channels

Nexon

One of the most effective methods of supporting player communities is through *interactive* communication channels. Opening a dialogue with the players serves two primary purposes. First, it can be an effective method of learning what the players' opinions and wishes are. Second, it provides the players with a sense of empowerment, increasing their loyalty to the game and the developer. Interactive communication channels need not be high maintenance. In *Shattered Galaxy,* we polled players as they logged out of the game to learn their views on game elements or new changes. We also allowed players to vote through the website on which features or issues they most wanted us to address. Through these methods, players had a voice, and we could hear what they were saying with minimal effort on our part. Online forums are, in my opinion, a very ineffective method of interacting with player communities. We found that fewer than 5% of the players participated actively on the in-game forum, while over 30% would take part in the polls. Online forums can be important, but remember that they are dominated by the vocal minority. Finally, always remember that players will complain. This is good— but don't take it personally. It means that they care about the game and want to make it better. If your players suddenly become silent, then you have a serious problem.

—*Kevin D. Saunders (Creative Director, Alelo)*

Newsletters

Allow players the option of signing up to receive online *newsletters* that are sent out to players on a regular basis. Do not automatically put players on the newsletter list, but allow them to *opt-in* (and *opt-out* if they are no longer interested). The newsletter could contain information on updates, expansions, gameplay tips, other products released by your company, Beta testing invitations, promotions, and anything else related to the game (or your company). Newsletters allow your player community to be reminded about the game and will show them that you care about your customers.

Player Matching

If your game is online, consider offering a *player matching* service for your customers. Xbox Live uses player matching to make it easy for players to find prospective opponents and team members with similar skill levels. During GameSpy Arcade's matching process, players can determine which other players are online and what games they are playing at the moment. Players can also send out invitations to other players requesting a game session. (It is interesting that player matching services utilize many of the features found in online dating sites!)

Lennart Nacke on Marketing Through Gamification & Reciprocity :::::

LN

Dr. Lennart E. Nacke (Assistant Professor, Faculty of Business & Information Technology, University of Ontario Institute of Technology)

Dr. Lennart Nacke received one of Europe's first Ph.D. degrees in Digital Game Development from Blekinge Institute of Technology, Sweden. He is currently working on affective computing and applying game design methods to create entertaining interfaces as a postdoctoral research fellow in the Human-Computer Interaction Lab of the University of Saskatchewan, Canada. Lennart frequently chairs and organizes workshops and panels with academics and industry experts on such topics as applying game design to user interfaces, affective computing, measurement of fun, joyful interaction design, game usability and, UX (user experience) at venues such as CHI, DiGRA, Future Play, and GDC Canada. An avid gamer, Lennart is a passionate researcher and consultant whose scientific interests include affective player testing and physiological interaction (e.g., using EEG/brainwaves and EMG/facial muscle contractions or eye tracking as well as gameplay experience in player-game interaction, technology-driven innovation, and interaction design in digital entertainment technologies).

Gamification is the application of game design principles in non-gaming contexts. While this includes all areas of life, it is especially interesting in commercial areas, such as marketing and sales. When a sales process is gamified, people are encouraged to either purchase a product or sign up for a service by engaging them in a playful process. Often this includes the use of achievements, badges, progress bars or other visual indicators of clear goals and current status. For example in December 2010, Valve's online game distribution service Steam gamified its sales by creating a treasure hunt over a period of several days. Players were encouraged to gather achievements by contributing to the community or reaching a certain status in advertised games that were on sale during the timeframes for each treasure hunt objective. As a motivation for individual treasure hunt objectives, players could win games every two days by completing four objectives. As a larger motivation for the players, at the end of the treasure hunt, 100 games were given away for the completion of a certain number of individual objectives during the hunt—which could be completed after the individual timeframes, but before the end of the hunt.

Another strategy that works especially well for social games is the reciprocity effect known from social psychology. This means if you receive a gift, you feel the need to send a gift back. This is probably most familiar to us during Christmas, when we are especially encouraged to provide gifts to others. If the gift giving is well-integrated into game mechanics, the sending and receiving of gifts must provide some in-game rewards that are good enough to trigger this process regularly. A good example of this is *FarmVille* (or any Zynga game for that matter), where gifts can be posted to the Facebook walls of non-players, urging them to sign up for the game. Another example is Steam's gift promotions—where 10 copies of a game can be bought for the price of one, allowing players to gift the other copies to friends (which will hopefully trigger the need to gift back to you at some point).

Social Networking

Using *social networking* tools such as Facebook pages and Twitter can be the quickest and most effective way to communicate and engage with the outside world—but also the riskiest (e.g., careless late-night updates). Although each post or tweet can be created quickly, a great deal of dedication is required when looking for suitable topics—with much time and effort spent replying to customers and fans. However, the benefits of using social networking tools are many. For example, a Twitter account can transform a daily, neverending flow of information into viral content if you hit the right note—a great way to keep your game or company in the spotlight (especially if you're addressing timely topics). Social networks are also extremely effective for customer support. Customers can just tweet when they have an issue—rather than filling out a complicated form, or worse, placing a phone call!

Blogs

Unlike the short-form nature of tweets and Facebook posts, *blogs* usually consist of long-form posts (sometimes article length) that require much more detail and reflective thought. Developers can use blogs effectively to share challenges, wins, discoveries, and much more. Blogs also allow for comments, which is a great way to engage with fans. Since there isn't a limit on how long a blog post can be (unlike the 140-character limit of a tweet), there's more than enough room to express your thoughts to members of the press, fans, investors—and even to other developers. On the other hand, a blog post takes a while to prepare (45 min for a short post to 2 hours or more for a longer article). It's important that a blog post be polished and free of grammatical errors so that it doesn't reflect badly on the studio. Blogs can be standalone sites or part of a larger company web site—and they should always be referenced in the company profile on social networking sites, ensuring that followers and Facebook friends can find you easily.

Online Community: Real or Virtual?

The online world is very real to many players. You learned in Chapter 6 that some will pay tens or thousands of real-life dollars for in-game items and money. (There is an exchange rate between *EverQuest* "platinum" and U.S. dollars.) Players even meet online, fall in love, and then marry in real-life—more often than you might imagine. The social goals of players vary greatly; some players make new friends, while others connect with family (such as grandmothers playing with their grandkids thousands of miles away).

Prosumerism: Player as Developer

In his book, *The Third Wave,* futurist Alvin Toffler coined the term *prosumer*—which refers to the combination of a producer and consumer. The roles of players (consumers) and developers (producers) are usually separated from each other. But sometimes the line between player and developer can become blurred. Chapters 5 and 6 discussed how players are able to take part in the development of storylines by making certain decisions while playing the game; customize their characters, right down to personality traits; and build physical environments and levels based on a particular game. In these cases, the player becomes a prosumer—a combination of player and developer. Examples of prosumerism that help cultivate a player community also include modding, fan sites, fan art, and "fan fic" (fan fiction).

Rocksan Lessard on Players as Prosumers in Virtual Worlds :::::

Rocksan Lessard is a 35-year-old single mother of three who started out in the field of audio and video production. After moving to interactive media design, she discovered the virtual world of *Second Life* and began creating content for it, which she has been doing for almost five years. As CEO of Secrets of Gaia, Rocksan creates jewelry, clothing, furnishings, and roleplay-specific accessories. She also communicates with players in certain roleplay markets to determine their needs and concerns — creating items based on the results of her research. This process allows her to work closely with the end users of her products in order to improve standards and provide items fitting market needs.

RL

Rocksan Lessard
(Chief Executive Officer,
Secrets of Gaia)

The ability given to the "residents" in virtual worlds such as *Second Life* to be involved as creators is highly significant because it is the end user who needs to be impressed and involved in the experience. *Second Life* is responsive to the needs of the community by allowing residents to create needed items; in many cases, these items might be wholly original but nonetheless important in the eyes of the end users. Additionally, the ability for users to have some effect on the world as well as the potential to make even small amounts of money from item creation brings long-term interest that might otherwise not exist. The investment of time and energy to make and sell items can create a type of loyalty and devotion that cannot be found in a game or world that only involves play experiences created by the developer.

Beta-Testing: Community & Career Path?

In Chapter 10, you learned about the importance of Beta testers in the game development process. Many of these testers are recruited from online player communities. In addition to providing a link between the player and developer, Beta-testing can be the first step in a new career. (At least one of the prominent industry professionals profiled in this book started out as a Beta-tester!)

Alternate Reality Games

Alternate reality games (*ARGs*) are interactive narratives that use the real world as a platform, often involving multiple media and game elements, to tell a story that might be affected by participants' ideas or actions. These games evolve according to players' responses and characters that are actively controlled by the game designers—rather than non-player characters (NPCs).

Modding

Allowing the user community to modify, expand, and otherwise customize the content of your game (*modding*) can heighten the value of your game. New missions, models, and settings for a game can also extend its lifespan. Supporting the modding community includes providing players with the ability to customize game variables, scripts, animation, textures, models, audio, and levels.

Electronic Arts

Electronic Arts

Command & Conquer: Red Alert 3 Synergy mod (left) and *Battlefield 2142* BattlePaint2 mod (right)

The Modding Origins of Machinima

The *machinima* movement (discussed in detail in Chapter 5) was actually an outgrowth of modding. Player communities making mods from *Quake* and other game engines (such as *Unreal* and *Half-Life*) began to create mini-movies within their mods—inspiring people such as Strange Company founder Hugh Hancock to blend game engines with cinema.

Fan-Produced Content

It is not uncommon in Japan for dedicated fan communities to build on the game world—extending or tweaking the mechanics of popular games. Sometimes these fans even produce *doujinshi*—books and fanzines that contain stories and art based on the characters in their favorite games. These publications are often produced in small quantities and sold to fans at conventions, by mail, or through specialty shops. Fans in Japan have also produced games based on other popular games that have achieved a cult status. The *Queen of Heart* series is one example of fan-produced fighting games that star characters in the popular game *To Heart*.

Reviews: Players as Experts

Online game communities such as Evil Avatar, NeoGAF, and Just RPG recruit players from their discussion forums to write reviews for their site: Here is an excerpt from a review of *Dungeon Siege: Legends of Aranna,* submitted by player-reviewer Kevin O'Connor to Just RPG: "To help with the vast inventory management, some new convenient features were added, such as the redistribute potions function, which, at the press of a button, shifts health potions to fighters and mana to casters—a time saver, indeed, and something other RPG designers should consider implementing." Opportunities to review games can give budding writers and designers some early exposure and credibility.

Western game development companies have not thrown enough support in the direction of this sort of fan-produced material, which would provide a great deal of word-of-mouth marketing for a game. There are plenty of spin-off fan art or "fan fic" (fan fiction) works from U.S. game fans based on *Final Fantasy*. The size of this market segment is growing, and this type of fan activity will most likely increase dramatically. The player community gets information and opinions on games from other fans more than from traditional channels such as magazines or television ads. Cultivating these fans would help build a terrific marketing strategy. Game studios receive free publicity from fan activity, and these fans act as a marketing force for the game—endorsing it and encouraging all other members of your target market to play it.

laughinggamesjack (Photobucket)

Fan-created art of Fox McCloud, the protagonist of the *Star Fox* series.

Fan Sites

Encouraging players to construct their own sites centering around your game can greatly increase a game's visibility. This method has been used successfully by independent filmmakers and musicians to create a buzz surrounding the release of a product. Sometimes, pseudo-fan sites have been created by the producers (ironically

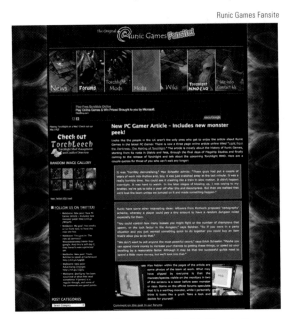

Runic Games Fansite

posing as consumers) to generate hype. A notorious example of this was when *The Blair Witch Project* filmmakers and colleagues created a series of fan sites that perpetuated the legend surrounding the film—and managed to convince people that the legend really existed. This marketing strategy snowballed into a major campaign (involving plenty of real fan sites) that brought a huge audience into theaters across the nation. Most fan sites contain graphics, audio, video, storylines, character descriptions, and even up-to-the-minute news (usually more current than the official site, which does not get updated nearly as much!) on a game—including rankings, sales figures, reviews, versions, and expansions. Fans might also include a *blog* on the site, containing daily entries and thoughts on the experience of playing your game. Other players visiting the site can contribute to the blog, adding their own experiences with the game.

Runic Games Fansite focuses on' *Torchlight* and other games created by the development studio.

With a lot of effort and some luck, the player community will continue to flourish years after the original game has been released—and supporting it effectively might be the most significant factor in a game's continuous success. How will you support your player community?

Community is King

In this chapter, you learned that producing a game is only the beginning; it's what comes afterward that gives a game staying power. It takes a combination of reaching the target player community by marketing to the public—along with maintaining that player community once it has been reached—for a game to be successful well beyond launch. Third-party developers often rely on publishers to provide many of these services, but independent developers who self-publish must learn these skills.

After reading Part III, you should now have a wide range of knowledge about the roles and responsibilities of the game development team; production elements and management of the development process; and the marketing and maintenance associated with player communities. Earlier in this book, you learned about all areas of game content creation—as well as the history, player market, and game development options available to you. Where do you think all of this is going? Read the Conclusion for some thoughts on the future of games.

Expanded assignments and projects based on the material in this chapter are available on the Instructor Resources DVD.

:::CHAPTER REVIEW EXERCISES:::

1. What are some effective strategies game companies use to market to player communities? What are some distinctions between the roles associated with marketing—such as promotion, advertising, public relations, and sales?

2. How do community management and customer support enhance a game's credibility and extend the life of a game? What are some techniques used by community managers to encourage prosumerism in players?

3. Applying what you learned about geographics, demographics, and psychographics earlier in this book, create a player community profile for an original game idea. How would you market to this community? Consider concepts such as viral marketing, generational marketing, prosumerism, and player-developer interactivity.

4. What is the significance of the modding and Beta-testing communities with regard to the player-developer relationship?

5. Search for player communities centered around one of your favorite games—and participate in some forums. What sorts of topics are discussed? How do players create a bond with one another? Do players keep up with news related to the game that is provided through marketing?

6. Look through one of the news sites listed in the Appendix and find three examples of how developers connect with players. How are the players able to provide direct feedback to the developers? How do developers reveal "behind the scenes" information to the players?

7. Create a fan site for your favorite game and have it hosted on a low-cost (or free) hosting service. Produce content related to the game—such as a short story, animated sequence, or character art. Market your site online through player forums, and invite other players to contribute content to your site.

8. Search for a modding community site associated with one of your favorite games. Develop a mod using the editor shipped with the game, and post it on this and other community sites.

Conclusion

The Future
where are we going?

Throughout this book, you've learned about the history of the electronic game industry, significant features of compelling game content, and the reality of game development cycles. Now let's speculate on the future of game development. This conclusion focuses on my personal opinions as well as those of other game industry professionals as we attempt to predict trends in this growing industry.

What Types of Games Will Be Played in the Future?

How will game content continue to evolve? Will content continue to expand beyond the restrictions of genre? Will developers take more risks with story, character, and gameplay? Content convergence between games and film can be seen in the proliferation of the Machinima movement, increased use of cinematics and cut-scenes, creation of Hollywood-style studios to entice the professional film community, use of well-known celebrities to provide character voiceovers, and a focus on licensing pre-existing film content (such as *The Matrix, Star Wars, King Kong, The Lord of the Rings,* and *James Bond*).

What about the continued focus on violent content? Will censorship of games rise? As the market continues to widen, games could become as common as going to the movies. There will be plenty of violent games—just like there are plenty of violent movies—but there will be a large number of commercially successful, ground-breaking games, such as *The Sims,* that don't focus on violence.

How will game audio evolve? Will it continue to become more interactive—diverging away from looping "cinematic" underscoring? At the same time, will composers garner higher budgets in order to hire live orchestras to record game scores?

iStock Photo

Will games draw us even closer to players around the world?

What about serious games—and the idea that *all* games can be learning applications? The financial model for MMOs could easily be transformed into a *business-to-business* model rather than a *business-to-consumer* model by being developed for the online-distance-learning (ODL) industry. This would not only allow MMOs to have additional ways of incurring revenue and expand upon existing content, but would help the ODL industry grow—allowing students to join a game rather than joining a class. What about the use of smartphones and tablets in the classroom to supplement the learning experience—or even as *augmented reality* applications? The possibilities for revolutionizing education are endless.

David Brin (science fiction author and futurist; Owner, Epocene.com):

Technology-driven realism will push the top game boxes forward as we flow toward full virtual reality. That's a long path, though—full immersion won't come overnight. Each year will feature sports games, shoot-'em games, and zoom games that are slightly more vivid than the previous year's—unfortunately, without a trace of story or originality. The one interesting new development in this area is involvement by the U.S. military. Certain games will appear that spin off from genuine virtual reality software used by soldiers, sailors, airmen, and marines, who are training to use actual equipment in realistic scenarios. Not just combat simulation, but also problem situations that may require judgment calls—for example, decisions: whether to use force, not just how fast you can shoot. Some of these will not only be cool, but vastly more interesting than your typical tactical gameplay.

Bill Brown (composer):

Games are reaching new levels of emotional expression. More cinematic story-telling is becoming a natural part of the process now. That part of the experience is going to open up a whole new level of creative expression for developers. Audio storytelling will be creative mixing in real-time that goes deeper ... more to the subtextual experience ... more to the soul of the narrative, and the player.

Louis Castle (Vice President of Studios, Zynga):

The game industry will clearly continue to grow and expand as it becomes an entertainment alternative to film, music, and literature. I predict that the current move toward more simulation-like products that rely on convincing worlds where the player's reasonable expectations are rewarded is a trend that will continue. Future products will rely more strongly on artistic style and theme than technology to sell their worlds as convincing places to tell a story.

Edward Castronova, PhD (Associate Professor of Telecommunications, Indiana University):

Interactive computer-mediated entertainment will continue to merge with film and toys into multimedia entertainment products. *Yu-Gi-Oh* is a likely future model—with cartoons, cards, merchandise (e.g., backpacks), and games all sharing the same theme, maybe as part of a single purchase package.

Grant Collier (former President, Infinity Ward):

The future of games will be shaped by what is selling today. Currently, games that have identifiable human characters (sports titles, for example, as well as *The Sims,* and *Counter-Strike*) are very popular. All of these games have characters that could be you and me. Their constant popularity gives publishers a good grasp of what is marketable. Similarities can be seen with other forms of entertainment, like books and movies. As technology moves along, realistic depictions of people will grow in the games industry. While this has exciting prospects, there will be poor side-effects. As games reach heightened levels of realism, people will probably try to increase censorship of games.

Ed Del Castillo (President & Co-Founder, Liquid Entertainment):

Of all the entertainment industries, the game business is the hardest to predict—due mainly to the constant change in technology. As new technology is invented, our business has to reinvent itself. As a result, we tend to see an oscillation of what the consumer wants. I think the one thing that is certain is that, eventually, technological advances—or more importantly, *perceived* advances—will slow; as that happens, content will become a more dominant part of the purchasing decision. In other words, eventually we'll get to the point where players won't perceive the differences in technology any longer and will start buying games because they have good stories or gameplay rather than because they look cool.

Troy Dunniway (Vice President & General Manager, Globex Studios):

More cross media titles need to be developed; this will leverage a wider variety of platforms. We need to shift away from just porting games to other platforms and find ways to make all online games part of a single cohesive experience—so that both casual and hardcore players can experience the same game world from different perspectives but still be able to play with each other.

James Paul Gee (Mary Lou Fulton Presidential Professor of Literacy Studies, Arizona State University):

The big dilemma for the future is this: Will we dumb games down and standardize them more to reach a mass audience via well-known brands and sequels, thanks in part to game companies becoming monopolies—or we will encourage smarter and smarter games with increasing levels of innovation? I believe that if we build strong niche markets for different types of games and gaming experiences, we can have our cake and eat it too: profits and innovation.

Ivo Gerscovich (Vice President of Global Marketing, Paramount Pictures Interactive & Mobile Entertainment):

The game industry is in such flux right now with many emerging platforms, technologies, and business models. The changes are happening very quickly and make for an intense and exciting time to be working in this field. Obviously, connectivity and community are two of the main pillars that most games will incorporate in the future. There is also a big push toward lower-priced and free games with monetization through selling virtual items. These directions seem to be rapidly migrating across all platforms.

John Hight (Director of Product Development, Sony Computer Entertainment America):

We're making fewer games and spending more on each game that we make. Advances in hardware have made it possible to create worlds so realistic and compelling that they rival film. We also have an ever-growing pool of very talented artists, engineers, and designers to push the creative envelope. Games are no longer a niche form of entertainment. They are here to stay, and millions of people buy and play games on a regular basis. I expect to see a convergence of games, Internet, and cinema in the near future.

Stephen Jacobs (Associate Professor of Interactive Games & Media, Rochester Institute of Technology):

When we get to the point where our AI and our writing is good enough, and powerful enough—to have the characters in our games seem truly truly real, responsive and interactive—this will be significant. In many ways, all of what's come so far has been incremental, evolutionary and derivative. That doesn't mean it hasn't been hugely entertaining; it has. It doesn't mean that games aren't a true medium; they are. But we're only just a little way down the road of where we (or at least I) want them to be.

Chang Liu (Associate Professor & Founding Director of the Virtual Immersive Technologies & Arts for Games & Learning Lab, Ohio University):

I believe game-like simulations and learning materials will become a significant part of the computing industry. Every child will grow up with these materials in the future. Game development will improve rapidly and significantly due to the amount of investment the society will put in this area.

Aaron Marks (Composer; Founder, On Your Mark Music Productions):

Interactive audio is a concept that has caught on quickly. What better game-playing experience can we have where the music changes as we explore new levels, a door opens where a bad guy is waiting in ambush, or a throng of evil creatures attacks us? Having music change to fit the mood of what we are experiencing is a fantastic element, which adds an incredible amount to the experience. Surround sound is also becoming more of a standard than previously, and this trend will definitely continue. Being totally enveloped by sound really adds to the believability of what we are seeing on screen. And important clues and foreboding can be conveyed through this type of playback. Knowing that a bad guy is sneaking up from behind makes for a great gaming experience, and that's what the audio side of the industry is all about.

Lennie Moore (composer):

I'm seeing larger commitments from game developers and publishers for live musicians and higher production quality. In the same manner that big feature films require world-class composers and performers, game developers are [becoming] more innovative with audio and are seeking out the best talent to make their products outstanding. Games are growing up, in my opinion— pushing the envelope with innovative audio design and helping to position [game composers] as a truly unique group of artists.

Scott Snyder (Senior Sound Designer, Edge of Reality):

Contextual events and contextual action have only been very roughly realized at this point in game development. Events that mean something, to each other and to the action—and actions that carry through and have ramifications to the story and to the experience that you as the player take away from your playing. I see a future: where you don't kill the same bosses over and over again; where monsters don't stand around in the open waiting for you to come and kill them; where enemies hide from you, and use strategy against you; where if your actions are those of a hero, you become a hero—but if your actions are those of a villain, you become a villain … and both paths are valid and lead to success in the game. I think the future lies in less use of random and more contextual event creation—determined by the results of the player's actions.

Warren Spector (Vice President & Creative Director, Junction Point—Disney Interactive Studios):

This is where I'm supposed to say, "Bring on the holodeck," right? Actually, I don't think that's coming any time soon. (Not sure it's such a great idea, actually!) It seems inevitable that we'll see better virtual actors—more humanlike in appearance and behavior. I think we'll see more and more convergence of games and other media, with the lines between games and movies and television blurring in ways we can only begin to imagine.

Chance Thomas (Principal Composer, HUGEsound):

We live in an amazing society, and the future is never what you expect. Today, in fact, someone may be inventing a new technology that will change all our lives. When I was in music school in the 1980s, who would have predicted that video games would provide major artistic and career opportunities for orchestral composers? Who could have predicted that sold out video game music concerts would one day fill the great classical concert halls of the world? What's next? No one knows for sure. But I think user-generated content will swell in casual games, certain kinds of MMOs, etc. AAA titles will continue to demand top musical talent and stellar production values. You'll see more and more ingenuity and attention funneling into smart music design, which will result in revolutionary new ways to think about dramatic scoring. And I think music education programs in colleges and universities will begin to teach music design and courses in adaptive composition. Whatever happens, it will be exciting to behold.

Jennifer Wadsworth (author; Instructor, Art Institute of California – Los Angeles):

As an educator, I am excited to see the coming explosion of more advanced educational games. At this point we have mostly simple educational games that test recall and application of concepts. There are also all kinds of high-level problem-solving and strategic thinking in MMOs. The next wave of educational games will delve into the challenge of using community dynamics and group interaction to reach new levels of critical and creative thinking.

Who Will Develop the Games of the Future?

How will the game industry be structured in the future? Will there still be a relationship between publishers, third-party developers, and hardware manufacturers? Will industry consolidation occur—or will the independent game movement continue to rise? Or could both happen and co-exist in parallel?

Will indie developers prevail?

As the founder of a company that markets, licenses, and distributes the works of independent arts and entertainment professionals of all types (game developers, musicians, filmmakers, performers, visual artists, and authors)—as well as being an independent musician and composer—I have a stake in the future of the independent games movement. Companies such as GarageGames that provide indie developers with the freedom to create, market, and distribute their games without losing ownership or creative control are making a substantial difference in the game community. Events and awards competitions such as the Independent Games Festival provide recognition for indie developers—and the trend of building startup game companies (often with the intention of remaining privately held) is on the rise.

Graeme Bayless (General Manager, Big Ego Games):

In my opinion, there are a number of challenges facing our industry. Probably the greatest challenge we currently face is the requirement of a company to remain agile and flexible. With ever increasing development costs, and a rapidly changing marketplace (particularly due to the continued evolution of the online space), a company must be able to constantly change its own development practices and evaluate its own methodologies. A company that remains static and fixed in how they approach development is at serious risk with the industry evolving at the rapid pace that it is.

Mark Chuberka (Director of Business Development, GameSalad):

As games continue to become part of our everyday lives, game development will become a part of our communication. Organizations, news, media, and individuals will incorporate game mechanics into their communication with the world and implement them on the ever-expanding list of connected devices, from HTML5 browsers to phones to portable game players to high-end consoles. Independent developers will continue to bring innovation to the community, which will then be copied by a thousand other devs and leveraged into huge games as 'new features.'

Greg Costikyan (freelance game designer):

If games are to become what I think they can be—the most important popular art form of the 21st century, as film was of the 20th and the novel of the 19th—we need to find a way to innovate, on smaller budgets, in order to find new, successful game styles. Other media do this by supporting a separate, "independent" industry with parallel distribution channels: independent music through small record stores, independent film through art houses and the like. To my mind, finding a way to create a vibrant independent game industry, where innovation and the offbeat are prized, with lower production values than the conventional industry, is the key business issue the field faces today. There are, however, some hopeful signs: The downloadable and mobile game markets are growing rapidly. And both in the industry—through venues like the Independent Games Festival—and in academia, there is an increasing interest in games developed outside the conventional industry.

Drew Davidson, PhD (Director, Entertainment Technology Center at Carnegie Mellon University)

In the future, there will be a small group of large companies knocking out "blockbuster" next-gen titles—and smaller development teams pushing the envelope in other categories, as well as independent game developers using digital distribution methods to get games uniquely delivered.

Jason Kay (Business Monkey, Monkey Gods LLC):

The game business is much more highly fragmented than ever. On the one hand, AAA console games are trending toward the $40+ million range—making it nearly impossible for most developers to earn additional royalties beyond their advances. For the games that can achieve "escape velocity," the rewards are enormous—over $1 billion in retail sales in a week, and upwards of $3 billion across the product lifespan. But only one or two games per year can achieve those numbers, leaving hundreds of games as loss-makers. The opportunity for entrepreneurs for the next few years is on the other side of the spectrum—building more complete "mid-core" games for platforms such as Facebook and Xbox Live, with varying business models (paid, subscription, microtransaction) and 700 million eager customers who may or may not have ever even owned a game console.

Nathan Madsen (Composer & Sound Designer, Madsen Studios LLC):

It looks as though the game industry is just going to keep growing; there will be more money involved, along with larger and larger teams. In some ways this is a very good thing—but in other ways, I see this as a major distraction and negative. I don't like product placement in games—and it bothers me that some studios seem more concerned with quantity rather than quality. My hope for the future is that we can filter out some of these distractions and get back to making solid, fun, and memorable games.

Justin Mette (President, 21-6 Productions):

I believe that the online distribution market for games is where most independent developers can get started and make a good living. Developing a game in 4 to 6 months with a small remote team means that your costs stay low and your return on investment does not have to be as large as the box or console industry. You don't have to just build puzzle games anymore to succeed in online game distribution. We've also seen an incredibly strong rush of Mac gamers this past year in the online market. For our title *Orbz*, we saw almost a 50/50 split in revenue between Windows and Mac sales during 2003. It's a great time to be an indie; the Internet allows you to find amazing talent and work together without an office; technology like Torque makes game development a reality for small inexperienced teams; and a booming online game-distribution market all lay out the best opportunity in years for game developers to live their dreams.

Chris Swain (Associate Research Professor, USC School of Cinematic Arts; Director, USC Games Institute):

The game industry is in a position similar to the film industry from the early 1980s. At that time movie studios were producing a lot of formulaic pictures and were not taking much creative risk. Independent film started to blossom, and companies such as Miramax took off by producing unconventional films that went on to become hits. The game industry today feels like the film industry from the early 1980s. Players are hungry for something different. Fortunately, a budding independent scene is developing that is starting to make waves. It isn't developing as quickly as the independent film scene did in the 1980s because, among other reasons, producing games is harder than producing movies. However, it is starting to move, with the Independent Games Festival, Xbox Live Arcade, and the online casual game movement leading the way. The industry will really start to move when we have some big hits come out of the independent scene.

How Will Games Be Developed in the Future?

Innovations in the game-development process itself may change the way games are created—through new processes, tools, and team structures. What are some likely advances in game art, design, and programming? As graphics technology continues to get more sophisticated, some game artists have felt the pressure to imitate the latest successful 3D game in color, style, and texture. But, as a close game industry colleague of mine once said: "Where are the Picassos of game art?" Techniques such as cel-shading represent a refreshing, eye-catching departure from the grayish, sometimes even cold world of many popular games. Will we see even more focus on replicating the human environment and less on imagining fantastic worlds? Will "synthespians" replace actors as filmmaking and game art share technology? Will non-player characters become more "real" as artificial intelligence becomes more sophisticated? Will story and gameplay both become more complex and compelling?

iStock Photo

Will future game development rely less on standard conventions and more on imagination?

John Ahlquist (Founder, Ahlquist Software):

I see the game programming process using more software engineering practices. The game engines and tools have grown to be large-scale software projects, and seat-of-the-pants methods aren't going to work any more. At the same time, I see it continuing to be a very fluid and dynamic development process. The processes from software engineering that allow quick turnaround, such as rapid prototyping and automated test, are very useful. Complex design processes are not as useful as our design changes on the fly, as the game evolves. One technique that has been very useful on a variety of games from console to social media is the use of code reviews. Peer review of code requires some time and commitment up front, but it actually reduces development time and improves game quality.

Michael Blackledge (Worldwide Studios Quality Assurance Director, Electronic Arts):

I believe the future generation of "Gamemakers" will be able to look beyond conventional games as entertainment and recognize the social and humanitarian potential of the interactive medium. I'm also convinced that the medium of games is taking a giant evolutionary leap from a left-minded technology dominant industry to a creativity-driven juggernaut.

Christopher Bretz (Art Director, Bretz Consulting):

The past few years have seen an explosion in graphics processing power. It is allowing games to have ever more complex visuals, approaching that of rendered images previously seen only in movies. The challenge before this was to use what you had available to approximate a real or imagined world with limited polygons and texture space. To use the tools effectively to create a believable simulacrum. Your skills as an artist were all about this filtering. Now these walls are coming down. With talk of the new systems in the millions of polys per second and mountains of memory, the old constraints are less of a concern and the real question for the artist becomes: "How the heck can I build all that—on the same schedule!?" A million-polygon reference character is a wonderful freedom for an artist, but what if you need 50 of them for a game? If environments can have tens of millions of triangles, and hundreds of unique shaders and properties, not to mention realistic lighting setups, how long does that take to make? Many of the new issues for artists beg solutions for these authoring challenges. And what to do with all this power?

As a visual artist, the challenges continue to be compelling characters and inspiring environments, tied to an engrossing narrative. But what is changing is the degree of reality that games can employ to bring you this vision (reality not being "realistic"). "Immersion" is the buzzword from the past few years, and I think it will continue. For the player, jumping into a believable world is the rewarding escapist experience—be it *Unreal* or *Mario* or *Silent Hill*. Coming games, for example, will have characters which can have more than simple scripted/animated responses, but emotional states and automated behaviors. This allows them to express their personalities visually, as the artist envisioned, and not the stilted responses common to past games. True digital actors which can react to, and interact with, their world. All of the things artists previously had to conceal or hint at in their work in the past can now be expressed with these new technologies.

John Byrd (Principal, Gigantic Software):

The most radical change you will see in game development in the next 10 years is the quality and stability of development environments; as they become faster, simpler, prettier, and easier to use, they will open up the field of game development to more people.

John Comes (Creative Director, Uber Entertainment):

In the future, we'll spend less time on the technology and more time on the artistry of the game. I believe we'll get to the point where engines are more like movie cameras. You don't have to reinvent the camera every time you make a movie, so why do we reinvent the engine every time we make a game?

Troy Dunniway (Vice President & General Manager; Globex Studios):

In the future, companies will need to find a balance of cost and creativity. Building hybrid teams with core creative people in the US, Europe, Japan or other region with a long history of development, with lower costs areas in Asia, Eastern Europe, South America and other lower costs areas will be the only way to develop games in the future. Teams will need to learn how to work globally and how to manage teams worldwide when there are language and cultural issues, time zone differences, and other factors. This will lead to some significant changes in the US game development community for teams hoping to develop AAA titles, and allow budgets to come back down to a reasonable level where profits are possible for more games.

Tracy Fullerton (Associate Professor, USC School of Cinematic Arts; Director, Game Innovation Lab):

The game industry has come to a point where it needs to reach new markets if it's going to continue to grow. This means designing for different types of players; those outside the traditional gaming audience. The problem with this is that while the industry is extremely skilled at maintaining steady technological innovation and cultivating consumer demand for those innovations, the same isn't true when it comes to developing original ideas in player experience. And, in order to reach new types of players, there are going to have to be breakthroughs in player experience just as surely as there had to be breakthroughs in technology in order for the industry to come this far. The best way I see to approach this problem is to adopt the type of rigorous user testing seen in other forms of software and industrial design, right from the beginning of the design process. Another important way to create innovation in player experience is to encourage diversity in game design teams.

Jay Gawronek (Independent Contractor, Bluepoint Games)

Usually, a game development cycle looks roughly like this: The designers start with the hard work, then the artists start creating the assets. Finally, the programmers who had been waiting for art and design take [the project] to the end—often working many hours to get it done in time. With the right tools and process in place, there's no reason that we can't all (artists, designers, programmers) work more consistently from beginning to end, as well as [being less dependent] on each other. There will be a time when periods of extended workdays are the exception and not the rule.

Emmy Jonassen (Marketing Manager, 3DVIA/Dassault Systemes):

Game development technology will be used in non-gaming applications such as training simulations, configurations, and large-scale immersive environments. These types of applications will span across virtually all industries, including those that you might not suspect. Part of this equation involves the democratization of 3D, where design and development tools are becoming more and more accessible to the average consumer. The problem with 3D now is that it's difficult to learn, expensive, and time-intensive. In the future, this won't be the case because tools will be designed to avoid these pitfalls; they will be accessible, easy to use, and still produce incredible results—allowing more and more businesses and consumers to create 3D applications.

David Perry (Chief Executive Officer, Gaikai, Inc.):

I expect there to be incredible investment and progress in these topics:

- **Physics**—Everything begins to function. You stick a lamp in a fan and it cuts the top off the lamp; you stick a log in the fan and the blades break.
- **Particles**—Better environmental disturbances—including the air-flow disturbances from your body. Also, better destruction—meaning you can break up a building brick by brick and it collapses correctly.
- **Lighting**—Better self-shadowing, better ambiance, and better cognition of shadows—meaning enemies know what they are and how they work.
- **Tactical AI**—They learn how you play. They actually have memory. They also see your strengths and weaknesses. If you shoot 10 times and miss, they change their opinion of you—if it felt to them like you were aiming.
- **Speech Recognition**—Beyond just a small subset of "chosen" words.
- **Speech Production**—Having them form sentences back to you.
- **Speech Cognition**—Understanding what you said. Is it, "It's fun to recognize speech?" or did I say, "It's fun to wreck a nice beach?"

- **Speech Conversation**—They hear you, get what you mean—and reply.
- **Immersion**—A high level of people achieving a mind state of flow. Time stops for the gamer—like a movie ending and the audience being amazed that two hours have passed.
- **Much Better Storytelling**—You will become more emotionally attached to the game characters. Expect to feel real loss if they die for good.

Arturo Sanchez-Ruiz, PhD (Associate Professor of Computing, University of North Florida):

Throughout the history of software development, building compilers, web applications, and mobile applications (to name just a few classes of software systems) were considered to be very difficult tasks. These application classes are now considered to be part of the mainstream of software development. This is now happening with game development. In the near future, comprehensive development environments will be used to build a wide variety of "games" associated with anything ranging from entertainment to other, more fundamental, human needs.

Mark Soderwall (Game Industry Consultant, Mark Soderwall's Authority 5 Consulting):

You will see incredible breakthroughs in dynamic lighting and shading passes that will create incredible moods and tones inside the gaming universe. I see the next level of in-game characters seamlessly interacting (in real-time) with every aspect of their environment through dynamic physics, collision routines, and real-time Inverse Kinematics—a feature that allows a character's hand to actually touch and turn a doorknob instead of just floating in front of it.

Warren Spector (Vice President & Creative Director, Junction Point— Disney Interactive Studios):

We will see great strides on the simulation front (encompassing rendering, sound propagation, physics, and object interaction)—so games can look, sound, and feel more like the real world. However, my hope is that all that game engine power can be turned to ends other than increased realism. I think we'll see game artists creating all sorts of non-representational games, too. Honestly, though, there's probably some kid out there somewhere with an idea so revolutionary I can't even imagine what it might be—that's the real future of gaming, something completely and utterly unpredictable and marvelous.

Marc Taro Holmes (illustrator, concept artist, and art director):

Real-time 3D technology is getting more and more sophisticated every month. We can pretty much count on our next game looking better than the one before—poly counts go up, new lighting models, in-game physics, material shaders offering added realism—and soon there will be fur on game animals and hair on characters. We're gradually improving toward true photographic realism. The technology has come a huge distance in only five years, and will likely begin to grow even faster. The opportunity to do better and better looking games creates an interesting tension for teams. The minimum bar for artistic skill grows higher every month, as do the requirements for technical training. People can literally be left behind if they are unable to invest in their skill sets. We are finding the need for technical people—artists who write MEL scripts for instance—is growing rapidly, but the requirement for traditional skills (color sense, anatomy, composition) is not going away either. So your team is becoming harder and harder to fill with the right people, and the budget required is growing larger and larger. This has set up a situation similar to Hollywood film, in which big budget games have to live within a mass market creative space. You have to know your potential set of fans is big enough to warrant the investment. This has led to the proliferation of licensed properties—movie games, *Harry Potter, James Bond* … IP [intellectual property]—which has a proven fan base. That is one trend that is going to rule the business for a few years.

However, I feel it is very likely that a related phenomenon mirroring independent film will come to exist. Just as fans of indie film excuse the lack of high-end effects or big-money stars, there are a category of sophisticated consumers that are looking for something different in their games. (Especially as the gaming market widens to include more of the general population, through the emergence of more mainstream platforms like the Web or mobile gaming, for instance.) Fan Mod teams, or small developers who lack a publisher's financial backing, may not be able to make a blockbuster, but they have the benefit of being agile. A ten-person studio can do a game for a niche market, while keeping their costs down. Something that the large studios have no interest in doing—feeding a monster studio means they must seek high-calorie food. Enter *Brittany's Dance Beat.* I'm looking forward to the emergence of an independent game movement that provides a creative infusion—something to keep the big budget mainstream games moving forward and trying new ideas.

Mark Terrano (Design Director, Hidden Path Entertainment):

Gaming techniques and systems are powerful tools for entertainment and education. I think we'll see some spectacular blunders in attempts to inappropriately "gamify" every possible activity, but this will open up many new opportunities for fundamentally improving education, training, and products. An understanding of game design fundamentals—how people learn and process information with appropriate feedback systems—will be useful in all human-centered designs. Technology will not only allow more immersive simulations but a better connection to the human state. Brain-computer interfaces, motion capture, and new ways of recognizing player intent will open up new genres and experiences.

Richard Wainess, PhD (Senior Research Associate, UCLA/CRESST):

My interests are from the cognitive perspective; that is, how our brains process information and how that knowledge can improve video games—games that educate and games that are played simply for fun. All gameplay is subject to our mental limitations, and virtually no game designer or developer is aware of the nature of these limitations or what has been discovered that can be used as guidelines to improve gameplay from the standpoint of game mechanics, interface, and sound. *Craft* is the application of prior experience to solve real-world problems. *Technology* is the application of science to solve real-world problems. Currently, game design is craft—but it should be a blend of technology and craft. This is the paradigm currently used in video game programming, where computer science works hand-in-hand with creative vision. It will not become the model for design until those who develop games through craft become aware, and confident, that science now exists that can support, and not hinder, their efforts. Then, much of the developer's guesswork will be replaced by the application of sound scientific principles.

How Will Games Be Played in the Future?

Will we continue to play games on a variety of platforms? Will we see further hardware convergence? Companies such as Nintendo, Microsoft, Sony, and Apple continue to manufacture new game platforms that expand our idea of "living room" entertainment—blending television, computer, console, and the online world—or allow us to play nomadically through smartphones, tablets, and other handheld devices. Will online multiplayer gaming increase? Could this cause games to transcend cultural boundaries—forming a global gaming community? As content continues to diversify and MMO developers explore new financial models and business development opportunities (e.g., partnering with the online distance learning industry), could MMOs bypass console games as the dominant form of interactive entertainment in the United States? Or will the console platform remain on top—with games becoming home entertainment centers with a cinematic impact?

Emotiv Systems

Will games receive input directly from our brains?

David Brin, PhD (science fiction author and futurist; Owner, Epocene.com):

The MMO world is vast, intricate, and immensely capital-intensive. Very few big players can step up to invest in creating these worlds that are driven by a need for huge numbers of subscriber-addicts. Fear of losing their investment makes these companies very conservative and imitative when it comes to story and game design. The problems of social interaction in these games—like dealing with deliberate maliciousness—would be better solved if there were dozens of smaller experimental worlds, trying new things under a rich variety of story-scenarios. That won't happen until somebody realizes that there is a market in offering game *templates*—a "MUD in a box"—that would let much smaller groups create their own online worlds. When this happens, authorship will simplify and the range of products will expand. Many of the problems that plague the online world will be solved by trial and error.

Don Daglow (Chief Executive Officer & Creative Director, Daglow Entertainment LLC):

The difference between game consoles, PCs, and set top boxes will continue to blur. Apple now looks like a TV network and a record company—streaming TV and music to your TV and to your phone. Microsoft and Sony make it easy to access Netflix from your console game machine. I can watch the World Series on my living room TV, my computer or my iPhone—and I can play games on the same three platforms. In the second decade of the 21st Century, game design is much more about the size of the screen you're looking at right now—not the size of the screen in your living room.

Jennifer F. Estaris (Senior Game Designer, Nickelodeon Virtual Worlds):

The word "game" becomes fuzzy or meaningless as the industry develops. What people do—whether from the safety of their desktop, with their mobile devices, or installed in their brains while they dream—becomes simply human activities, solo or with the world. It returns to play. Rules, mechanics, story may or may not exist—but there is challenge, reward, and emotional linking. Also, aliens will usher in a bunch of cool games for us to play!

Richard "Lord British" Garriott (Creative Director, Portalarium):

MMOs represent *the* growth segment in my mind—not only from a revenue standpoint, but also a place to look for cool creative innovation. MMOs are in their infancy, and we are only just beginning to see the variety of play styles and genres the online space will offer in the future.

Titus Levi, PhD (Associate Professor, United International College):

Online gaming will continue to grow from a niche to a serious market segment. First, some of these most interesting innovations will arise from collaboration through these games. Second, I think this move toward collaboration points to a new kind of interaction and communication between people, particularly groups (or tribes) of persons who bond over the games. The primary draw in connecting people will continue to be games, but other taste and lifestyle connections will come into play. And now that many persons have broadband access in North America, we will begin to see these groups coalesce and interact more frequently—both in online and offline environments. So far, these groups continue to attract new persons, but understanding the process by which newcomers integrate into well-formed social networks seems like a rich area of inquiry—both for game developers and academics.

Jessica Mulligan (Executive Consultant, Frogster America):

The popularity of single-player games in the 1980s and 1990s was an aberration that came about only because of the way PC and game console technology developed; historically, most games were designed to be played between two or more people. Let's face it: There's no opponent more challenging than the chaotically intelligent random-number generator that is the human brain. Now that technology is beginning to catch up to that reality and is ready to enable it, the future of game development is that games will become increasingly more connected. There will be more people playing on more devices and in more situations until the line between real life and "game life" is blurred beyond recognition. Old media and new will combine to provide experiences we barely dreamed of even 10 years ago. Digital communications such as online worlds, email and the Web will combine with the analog devices of radio, television, faxes, music, movies, books, newspapers—even billboards and flyers—to create not just a game, but a *lifestyle* that is a game. We can see the beginnings of this in geo-caching and advert-stunts such as *I Love Bees*. From this point on, it only gets stranger … and far more interesting than we might have prepared for.

Watson Wu (Composer & Sound Designer, Watson Wu Studios):

I envision a future in which iPhones or some other handhelds can project beyond HD quality displays larger than 100 inches. These handsets will have the ability to combine multiplayer audio and visual experience everywhere you go.

Who Will Play the Games of the Future & How Will We Reach Them?

We're entering an exciting new phase in game development, where the stereotypical gamer is no longer an adolescent boy but a whole range of players—where women over 35 top the online game market, a common form of local play involves a mother sitting at a computer with a child on her lap, and people of all cultures compete worldwide in MMOs. The market for games is growing rapidly. One of the greatest untapped markets consists of players who might have limited visual, audio, speech, cognitive, and physical/motor abilities. Steps are already being taken to address this community of players, and the majority of the games of the future should incorporate a high degree of accessibility.

iStock Photo

Will Millennials be the new dominant player market?

Robert Florio (artist):

Games of the future will need to be designed so that they incorporate everyone's needs. Game design needs to explore new technology such as the ability to use minimal movement, input devices and additional controllers specifically designed for people with limited functions (such as not being able to use one's hands, eyes, ears, or even cognitive senses completely). These people who are "different," like myself, want to play video games but are being ignored by the industry. It's time for developers to start exploring this avenue without seeing it as something completely bizarre and abnormal. Undoubtedly, technology is being developed everyday that will make it easier for people to see the relevance, importance and even the exciting factor in this new development of game accessibility. Before I was injured, I was oblivious to this kind of need. I didn't understand how people survived with severe injuries and viewed them as outcasts. I might be viewed as an extreme visionary—but when you have sat in my position and lived as many years as I have after a devastating paralyzing injury, especially at such a young age, you are forced to see things differently. There is something wonderful to be said about accessible game design.

Brenda Laurel, PhD (Chair, Graduate Design Program, California College of the Arts):

The definition of "play" has a key component: that one's actions do not have serious consequences. The innate problem with gaming as part of a curriculum is that one's play may indeed have the serious consequence of affecting one's grade for a course. Another difficulty with gaming in an educational setting is our desire for transgressive play. (Eric Zimmerman brought this issue to light for me.) We often like to feel that we are coloring outside the lines when we play. Again, this is a problem in an educational context where following the rules has high value. Solution strategies exist for each of these challenges. In the first instance, informal or extra-curricular learning with oblique relationships to coursework may serve to distance a game sufficiently from the "serious" consequences of grading. In the case of transgression, we must remember that literally everything we are taught—from science to civics—is the artifact of some seriously transgressive behavior like Copernicus' outrageous assertions about the solar system or Jefferson's bold strokes in shaping our democracy. The spirit of transgression—of productive change—is the essence of engagement, both in play and in life.

Patricia Pizer (Creative Director, ZeeGee Games):

At the simplest level, I think we'll see greater diversification in games. Casual games are becoming rapidly more widespread. Short but satisfying game experiences will be available on virtually every platform. As games surpass movies and even music sales, I think we'll see more of what equates to niche magazines: games intended to satisfy relatively small groups of players. While many have aimed for giant killer apps, thoroughly appealing to smaller numbers of players in a more meaningful way has tremendous potential.

Rade Stojsavljevic (President, Jet Set Games, Inc.):

There's a generation of gamers who grew up with video games and continues to play as they age. This will be a key element that will make gaming a more socially-acceptable activity. Right now you would probably still be labeled a geek or nerd if your friends invited you to dinner or a movie and you turned them down to play the latest *Zelda* game. That's slowly starting to change, and I believe it will impact the types of games that are created.

Mary-Margaret Walker (Chief Executive Officer, Mary-Margaret Network):

I love the cycles in our industry—watching the growth of careers, creation of companies, development of school programs, and newer generations of players. When many of us started in the industry, this was not a career that our parents understood. Today, it is a career that many parents are encouraging for their children. As Doctor Who says, "The future is this way"!

::

The Future of Entertainment?

Opinions on where the industry will go are varied—and the mood of most developers ranges from excitement to concern—but everyone agrees that the industry could dramatically change the face of entertainment as we know it. Will games become the dominant form of entertainment in the next 5–10 years? How will you participate in this exciting revolution? I hope this discussion and the topics in this book have shown you the limitless potential of game development, and have sparked an interest in you to contribute to this creative and boundless industry. Read on for some valuable resources that will help you apply what you've learned!

Resources

There's a wealth of information on game development and related topics discussed in this book. Here is just a sample list of books, news sites, organizations, and events you should definitely explore!

Communities & Directories

APM Music   www.apmmusic.com

Apple Developer Connection   developer.apple.com

ArtBarf.com   www.artbarf.com

Betawatcher.com   www.betawatcher.com

Beyond3D   www.beyond3d.com

Bitmob.com   www.bitmob.com

CG Society   www.cgtalk.com

CG Textures   www.cgtextures.com

Destructoid   www.destructoid.com

DevMaster.net   www.devmaster.net

DevShed Forum   forums.devshed.com/game-development-141

EntertainmentCareers.net   www.entertainmentcareers.net

Gamasutra   www.gamasutra.com

Game Audio Forum   www.gameaudioforum.com

Game Audio Pro Tech Group   groups.yahoo.com/group/gameaudiopro

GameDev.net   www.gamedev.net

Game Development Search Engine   www.gdse.com

GameDevMap   www.gamedevmap.com

GameFAQs   www.gamefaqs.com

Game Music.com   www.gamemusic.com

Game Music Revolution (GMR)   www.gmronline.com

Games Tester   www.gamestester.com

GarageGames   www.garagegames.com

Giant Bomb   www.giantbomb.com

iDevGames Forum   www.idevgames.com/forum

Indiegamer Forum   forums.indiegamer.com

IndustryGamers   www.industrygamers.com

International Dialects of English Archive (IDEA)   web.ku.edu/idea/

LinkedIn   www.linkedin.com

Machinima.com   www.machinima.com

Mayang's Free Texture Library   www.mayang.com/textures

MobyGames   www.mobygames.com

Monster   www.monster.com

NeoGAF   www.neogaf.com

Northern Sounds   www.northernsounds.com

Overclocked Remix   www.overclocked.org

Professional Sound Designers Forum   psd.freeforums.org

PS3   www.ps3.net

Reddit (gaming.reddit)   www.reddit.com/r/gaming

Sound Design Forum   groups.yahoo.com/group/sound_design

3D Buzz   www.3dbuzz.com

3D Total   www.3dtotal.com

VGMix   www.vgmix.com

Video Game Music Database (VGMdb)   www.vgmdb.net

Voicebank.net   www.voicebank.net

Wii-Play   www.wii-play.com

Xbox.com   www.xbox.com

Xbox 360 Homebrew   www.xbox360homebrew.com

XNA Creators Club   creators.xna.com

Career Resources

BlueSkyResumes www.blueskyresumes.com

Craigslist www.craigslist.org

Creative Heads www.creativeheads.net

Dice www.dice.com

Digital Artist Management www.digitalartistmanagement.com

Entertainment Technology Source www.etsource.com

Game Career Guide   www.gamecareerguide.com

GameJobs www.gamejobs.com

Game Recruiter www.gamerecruiter.com

Games-Match www.games-match.com

Hot Jobs www.hotjobs.com

International Search Partners www.ispards.com

LinkedIn www.linkedin.com

Mary-Margaret Network www.mary-margaret.com

Monster www.monster.com

Premier Search www.premier-search.net

Prime Candidate, Inc. www.primecandidateinc.com

Resumé Samples   www.freeresumesamples.org

Sample Resume www.bestsampleresume.com

Colleges & Universities

Academy of Art University   www.academyart.edu

American Intercontinental University   www.aiuniv.edu

Arizona State University   www.asu.edu

Art Institute of Pittsburgh Online   www.aionline.edu

The Art Institutes   www.artinstitutes.edu

Austin Community College   www.austincc.edu

Becker College   www.becker.edu

Bunker Hill Community College   www.bhcc.mass.edu

California College of the Arts   www.cca.edu

Carnegie Mellon University/Entertainment Technology Center   www.cmu.edu

Champlain College   www.champlain.edu

Cornell University   gdiac.cis.cornell.edu

Dartmouth College   www.dartmouth.edu

DePaul University   www.depaul.edu

DeVry University   www.devry.edu

DigiPen Institute of Technology   www.digipen.edu

Ex'pression College for Digital Arts   www.expression.edu

Full Sail Real World Education   www.fullsail.edu

Georgia Institute of Technology   dm.lcc.gatech.edu

Guildhall at SMU   guildhall.smu.edu

Indiana University - MIME Program   www.mime.indiana.edu

International Academy of Design & Technology   www.iadtschools.com

Iowa State University   www.iastate.edu

ITT Technical Institute   www.itt-tech.edu

Lehigh Carbon Community College (LCCC)   www.lccc.edu

Los Angeles Film School   www.lafilm.edu

Massachusetts Institute of Technology (MIT)   media.mit.edu

Mercyhurst College   www.mercyhurst.edu

New England Institute of Art   www.artinstitutes.edu/boston

Northeastern University   www.northeastern.edu

Rasmussen College   www.rasmussen.edu

Rensselaer Polytechnic Institute   www.rpi.edu

Ringling College of Art & Design   www.ringling.edu

Rochester Institute of Technology   www.rit.edu

SAE Institute   www.sae.edu

Santa Monica College Academy of Entertainment & Technology   academy.smc.edu

Savannah College of Art & Design   www.scad.edu

Tomball College   www.tomballcollege.com

University of California, Los Angeles (UCLA) Extension   www.uclaextension.edu

University of Central Florida - Florida Interactive Entertainment Academy   fiea.ucf.edu

University of North Florida   www.unf.edu

University of Ontario Institute of Technology   www.uoit.ca

University of Southern California (USC) - Information Technology Program   itp.usc.edu

University of Southern California (USC) School of Cinematic Arts   interactive.usc.edu

Vancouver Film School   www.vfs.com

Westwood College   www.westwood.edu

Worcester Polytechnic Institute   www.wpi.edu

Development Tools

Adobe: Audition/Flash/Dreamweaver/Illustrator/Photoshop www.adobe.com
Autodesk: 3ds Max/Maya/Mudbox/MotionBuilder/Softimage usa.autodesk.com
Bethesda Softworks: Elder Scrolls Construction Kit www.bethsoft.com
Crystal Space: Graphics engine www.crystalspace3d.org
Crytek: CryENGINE www.crytek.com
Dassault Systemes: 3DVIA www.3dvia.com
DigiDesign: Pro-Tools www.digidesign.com
Emergent Game Technologies: Gamebryo www.emergent.net
Epic Games/Unreal Technology: Unreal Engine www.unrealtechnology.com
Game Maker: 2D game engine www.yoyogames.com
GameSalad www.gamesalad.com
Gamestudio: 3D game engine www.3dgamestudio.com
Genesis 3D: 3D game engine www.genesis3d.com
Havok www.havok.com
id Software: id Tech www.idsoftware.com
Irrlicht Engine: 3D game engine irrlicht.sourceforge.net
Monolith Production: Lith Jupiter Engine www.lith.com
Nvidia: PhysX www.nvidia.com
Panda3D: 3D game engine panda3d.org
Pixologic: Zbrush www.pixilogic.com
RAD Game Tools www.radtools.com
RealmForge: Game engine sourceforge.net/projects/realmforge
Relic Entertainment: Essence engine www.relic.com
Sony Creative Software: Sound Forge www.sonycreativesoftware.com
Steinberg: Cubase Studio/ WaveLab www.steinberg.com
Torque 2D Game Builder/3D Game Engine Advanced www.garagegames.com
Unity www.unity3d.com
Valve Software: Source Engine www.valvesoftware.com

Organizations

Academy of Interactive Arts & Sciences (AIAS)   www.interactive.org

Academy of Machinima Arts & Sciences   www.machinima.org

Association of Computing Machinery (ACM)   www.acm.org

Audio Engineering Society (AES)   www.aes.org

Business Software Alliance (BSA)   www.bsa.org

Digital Games Research Association (DiGRA)   www.digra.org

Entertainment Software Association (ESA)   www.theesa.com

Entertainment Software Ratings Board (ESRB)   www.esrb.org

Game Audio Network Guild (GANG)   www.audiogang.org

Game Audio Technical Committee   www.aes.org/technical/ag

Interactive Audio Special Interest Group (IASIG)   www.iasig.org

International Computer Games Association (ICGA)   www.cs.unimaas.nl/icga

International Game Developers Association (IGDA)   www.igda.org

News, Reviews & Research

The APPera   www.theappera.com

Appolicious   www.appolicious.com

Ars Technica   www.arstechnica.com

Blues News   www.bluesnews.com

CNET   www.cnet.com

Computer & Video Games   www.computerandvideogames.com

Computer Games Magazine   www.cgonline.com

Curse.com   www.curse.com

Develop Magazine   www.developmag.com

Digital Playroom   www.dplay.com

DIYgamer   www.diygamer.com

Edge Online   www.edge-online.com

Electronic Gaming Monthly (EGMi)   www.egmnow.com

The Escapist   www.escapistmagazine.com

Eurogamer   www.eurogamer.net

FingerGaming   www.fingergaming.com

GameDaily   www.gamedaily.com

Game Developer Magazine   www.gdmag.com

Gamers Hell   www.gamershell.com

Game Industry News   www.gameindustry.com

GameInformer.com   www.gameinformer.com

Game-Machines.com   www.game-machines.com

GamePolitics   www.gamepolitics.com

GamePro   www.gamepro.com

GameRankings   www.gamerankings.com

Game Revolution   www.gamerevolution.com

Games.com (blog)   blog.games.com

GamesBeat (VentureBeat)   www.venturebeat.com/category/games

GameSetWatch   www.gamesetwatch.com

GamesIndustry.biz   www.gamesindustry.biz

GameSlice Weekly   www.gameslice.com

GameSpot   www.gamespot.com

GameSpy   www.gamespy.com

Games Radar (PC Gamer)   www.
   gamesradar.com/pc

GameTrailers   www.gametrailers.com

Gamezebo   www.gamezebo.com

GamingAngels   www.gamingangels.com

GayGamer   www.gaygamer.net

Girl Gamer   www.girlgamer.com

Guide to Sound Effects   www.epicsound.
   com/sfx/

IndieGames.com   www.indiegames.com

Internet Gaming Network (IGN)   www.
   ign.com

Jay is Games   www.jayisgames.com

Joystiq   www.joystiq.com

Kotaku   www.kotaku.com

The Loop   www.theloopinsight.com

Mac|Life   www.maclife.com

Macworld.com   www.macworld.com

Mayang's Free Texture Library   www.
   mayang.com/textures

MCV   www.mcvuk.com

Metacritic   www.metacritic.com

Microsoft/Monster Career Center
   office.microsoft.com/en-us/help/
   FX103504051033.aspx

MMOGChart.com   www.mmogchart.com

MMORPG.com   www.mmorpg.com

MPOGD.com   www.mpogd.com

MTV Multiplayer   multiplayerblog.mtv.
   com

Music4Games.net   www.music4games.net

Nine Over Ten   www.nineoverten.com

148Apps   www.148apps.com

1UP   www.1up.com

PC Gamer   www.pcgamer.com

Pocket Gamer   www.pocketgamer.co.uk

Penny Arcade   www.penny-arcade.com

Planet Unreal   planetunreal.gamespy.com

PolyCount   www.polycount.com

Recording History: The History of
   Recording Technology   www.
   recording-history.org

Ripten   www.ripten.com

Showfax   www.showfax.com

Slashdot   games.slashdot.org

Slide to Play   www.slidetoplay.com

Star Tech Journal   www.startechjournal.
   com

Ten Ton Hammer   www.tentonhammer.
   com

Tongue Twisters   www.geocities.com/
   Athens/8136/tonguetwisters.html

TouchArcade   www.toucharcade.com

TouchGen   www.touchgen.net

UnderGroundOnline (UGO)   www.ugo.
   com

Unreal Technology   www.
   unrealtechnology.com

Unreal Wiki   wiki.beyondunreal.com

Voiceover Demos   www.
   compostproductions.com/demos.html

Xbox Developer Programs   www.xbox.
   com/en-US/dev/contentproviders.htm

Wired Game | Life   blog.wired.com/games

WorkingGames   www.workinggames.co.uk

Events

Consumer Electronics Show (CES)
January   Las Vegas, NV
www.cesweb.org

Game Developers Conference (GDC)
March   San Francisco, CA
www.gdconf.com

D.I.C.E. Summit (AIAS)
March   Las Vegas, NV
www.dicesummit.org

Penny Arcade Expo (PAX East)
March   Boston, MA
east.paxsite.com

SIGGRAPH (ACM)
Summer   (location varies)
www.siggraph.org

E3 Expo
June   Los Angeles, CA
www.e3expo.com

Game Education Summit (GES)
June   location varies
www.gameeducationsummit.com

Origins Game Fair
June   Columbus, OH
www.originsgamefair.com

Casual Connect
July   Seattle, WA
seattle.casualconnect.org

Comic-Con
July   San Diego, CA
www.comic-con.com

BlizzCon
August   Anaheim, CA
www.blizzcon.com

Gen Con
August   Indianapolis, IN
www.gencon.com

Tokyo Game Show (TGS)
Fall   Japan
tgs.cesa.or.jp/english/

GDC Online
September   Austin, TX
www.gdcaustin.com

Penny Arcade Expo (PAX Prime)
September   Seattle, WA
www.paxsite.com

IndieCade
October   Los Angeles, CA
www.indiecade.com

SIEGE - Southern Interactive Entertainment
& Game Expo
October   Atlanta, GA
www.siegecon.net

IGDA Leadership Forum
October   Los Angeles/San Francisco, CA
http://www.igda.org/leadership/

Project Bar-B-Q
October   Lake Buchanan, TX
www.projectbarbq.com

Game Companies

2015 www.2015.com

21-6 Productions www.21-6.com

2K Boston www.2kboston.com

Activision Blizzard
   www.activisionblizzard.com

Alelo www.alelo.com

Amaze Entertainment www.amazeent.com

Apogee Software / 3D Realms
   www.apogeeosoftware.com

Appy Entertainment
   www.appyentertainment.com

ArenaNet www.arena.net

Atari www.atari.com

Atlus USA www.atlus.com

Bethesda Softworks www.bethsoft.com

Big Fish Games www.bigfishgames.com

Big Huge Games www.bighugegames.com

BioWare Austin www.bioware.com

Bluepoint Games www.bluepointgames.com

Boost Mobile www.boostmobile.com

Breakaway Games
www.breakawaygames.com

Bungie Software www.bungie.net

Cafe.com www.cafe.com

Capcom Entertainment www.capcom.com

Carbine Studios www.carbinestudios.com

CDV Software www.cdvusa.com

Chronic Logic www.chroniclogic.com

Codemasters www.codemasters.com

Crave Entertainment www.cravegames.com

Cryptic Allusion Games cagames.com

Cryptic Studios crypticstudios.com

Crystal Dynamics www.crystald.com

Cyan Worlds, Inc. cyanworlds.com

Disney Interactive Studios disney.go.com/
disneyinteractivestudios/

Double Helix Games www.
doublehelixgames.com

DreamWorks www.dreamworkanimation.
com

EA Mobile www.eamobile.com/Web/

Eidos Interactive www.eidosinteractive.com

Electronic Arts www.ea.com

Enemy Technology
www.enemytechnology.com

Enspire Learning www.enspirelearning.com

Epic Games www.epicgames.com

Firaxis Games www.firaxis.com

Foundation 9 www.foundation9.com

Frogster America
www.frogster-america.com

Funcom www.funcom.com

Gameloft www.gameloft.com

GameSalad www.gamesalad.com

GarageGames www.garagegames.com

Gas Powered Games www.gaspowered.com

Gideon Games www.gideongames.com

Glu Mobile
www.glu.com/noram/Pages/home.aspx

Gravity Interactive
www.gravity.co.kr/eng/index.asp

Hanako Games www.hanakogames.com

Hands-On Mobile www.handson.com

Harmonix www.harmonixmusic.com

Hidden Path Entertainment
www.hiddenpath.com

Icarus Studios www.icarusstudios.com

id Software www.idsoftware.com

Insomniac Games
www.insomniacgames.com

Interplay Productions www.interplay.com

I-play www.iplay.playp.biz

iWin www.iwin.com

Koei Corporation North America www.
koei.com

Konami www.konami.com/mobile

Large Animal Games www.largeanimal.
com

Last Day of Work www.ldw.com

LucasArts Entertainment www.lucasarts.
com

Mad Monkey Militia www.
madmonkeymilitia.com

Majesco Entertainment
www.majescoentertainment.com

Max Gaming Technologies
www.maxgaming.net

Microsoft Corporation www.microsoft.com

Mine Shaft Entertainment, Inc.
www.mineshaft.org

Mobile Deluxe mobiledeluxe.com

Monkey Gods www.monkeygods.com

Monolith Productions www.lith.com

MSN Games
zone.msn.com/en/root/default.htm

Namco Bandai Games
www.namcobandaigames.com

Namco Mobile www.namcomobile.com

Naughty Dog www.naughtydog.com

NCsoft www.ncsoft.net/global/

NetDevil www.netdevil.com

Neversoft Entertainment www.neversoft.com

Nexus Entertainment www.nexusent.com

Nintendo of America www.nintendo.com

Oasys Mobile www.oasysmobileinc.com

Obsidian Entertainment
www.obsidianent.com

Paramount Pictures Interactive & Mobile
Entertainment www.paramount.com

Petroglyph Games
www.petroglyphgames.com

Pixar www.pixar.com

Playdom www.playdom.com

PlayFirst www.playfirst.com

Playfish www.playfish.com

PopCap Games www.popcap.com

Rainbow Studios www.rainbowstudios.com

Raven Software www.ravensoft.com

Red Storm Entertainment
www.redstorm.com

Reflexive Entertainment
www.reflexive-inc.com

Retro Studios www.retrostudios.com

Rockstar San Diego rockstarsandiego.com/

Sega of America www.sega.com

SkyZone Entertainment
www.skyzonemobile.com

Smith & Tinker, Inc.
www.smithandtinker.com

Sneaky Games www.sneakygames.com

Snowblind Studios
www.snowblindstudios.com

Sony Computer Entertainment America
www.us.playstation.com

Sony Online Entertainment
www.soe.com/en/soe.vm

Sony Pictures Animation
www.sonypictures.com

SouthPeak Interactive www.
southpeakgames.com

Spacetime Studios
www.spacetimestudios.com

Square-Enix USA
www.square-enix.com/na/

SRRN Games www.srrngames.com

Stardock www.stardock.com

Star Mountain Studios
www.starmountainstudios.com

Sucker Punch Productions
www.suckerpunch.com

Surreal Software www.surreal.com

Take-Two Interactive www.take2games.com

Tecmo www.tecmogames.com

THQ www.thq.com

3DVIA/Dassault Systemes www.3dvia.com

Three Rings www.threerings.net

TikGames www.tikgames.com

TimeGate Studios www.timegatestudios.com

Uber Entertainment www.uberent.com

TubettiWorld Games www.tubettiworld.com

Twisted Pixel Games
www.twistedpixelgames.com

Uber Entertainment www.uberent.com

Ubisoft www.ubi.soft

Unity www.unity3d.com

Valve www.valvesoftware.com

Vicarious Visions www.vvisions.com

Walt Disney Animation Studios
www.disneyanimation.com

WildTangent www.wildtangent.com

WorldWinner www.worldwinner.com

Yahoo! Games games.yahoo.com

YoYo Games www.yoyogames.com

ZeniMax Online Studios www.
zenimaxonline.com

Zynga www.zynga.com

Books & Articles

Adams, E. (2003). *Break into the game industry.* McGraw-Hill Osborne Media.

Adams, E. & Rollings, A. (2006). *Fundamentals of game design.* Prentice Hall.

Ahearn, L. & Crooks II, C.E. (2002). *Awesome game creation: No programming required. (2ⁿᵈ ed).* Charles River Media.

Ahlquist, J.B., Jr. & Novak, J. (2007). *Game development essentials: Game artificial intelligence.* Cengage Delmar.

Aldrich, C. (2003). *Simulations and the future of learning.* Pfeiffer.

Aldrich, C. (2005). *Learning by doing.* Jossey-Bass.

Allison, S.E. et al. (March 2006). "The development of the self in the era of the Internet & role-playing fantasy games. *The American Journal of Psychiatry.*

Atkin, M. & Abercrombie, J. (2005). "Using a goal/action architecture to integrate modularity and long-term memory into AI behaviors." *Game Developers Conference.*

Axelrod, R. (1985). *The evolution of cooperation.* Basic Books.

Bartle, R.A. (1996). "Hearts, clubs, diamonds, spades: Players who suit MUDs." *MUSE Multi-User Entertainment Ltd* (www.mud.co.uk/richard/hcds.htm).

Bates, B. (2002). *Game design: The art & business of creating games.* Premier Press.

Beck, J.C. & Wade, M. (2004). *Got game: How the gamer generation is reshaping business forever.* Harvard Business School Press.

Beshera, T. (2008). *Acing the interview: How to ask and answer the questions that will get you the job.* AMACOM.

Bethke, E. (2003). *Game development and production.* Wordware.

Birn, J. (2006). *Digital lighting and rendering (2ⁿᵈ ed.).* New Riders Press.

Boer, J. (2002). *Game audio programming.* Charles River Media.

Brandon, A. (2004). *Audio for games: Planning, process, and production.* New Riders.

Brin, D. (1998). *The transparent society.* Addison-Wesley.

Broderick, D. (2001). *The spike: How our lives are being transformed by rapidly advancing technologies.* Forge.

Brooks, D. (2001). *Bobos in paradise: The new upper class and how they got there.* Simon & Schuster.

Busby, A., Parrish, Z. & Van Eenwyk, J. (2004). *Mastering Unreal technology: The art of level design.* Sams.

Byrne, E. (2004). *Game level design.* Charles River Media.

Campbell, J. (1972). *The hero with a thousand faces.* Princeton University Press.

Campbell, J. & Moyers, B. (1991). *The power of myth.* Anchor.

Castells, M. (2001). *The Internet galaxy: Reflections on the Internet, business, and society.* Oxford University Press.

Castillo, T. & Novak, J. (2008). *Game development essentials: Game level design.* Cengage Delmar.

Castronova, E. (2005). *Synthetic worlds: The business and culture of online games.* University of Chicago Press.

Chase, R.B., Aquilano, N.J. & Jacobs, R. (2001). *Operations management for competitive advantage (9ᵗʰ ed).* McGraw-Hill/Irwin

Cheeseman, H.R. (2004). *Business law (5ᵗʰ ed).* Pearson Education, Inc.

Chiarella, T. (1998). *Writing dialogue.* Story Press.

Childs, G.W. (2006). *Creating music and sound for games.* Course Technology PTR.

Christen, P. (November 2006). "Serious expectations" *Game Developer Magazine.*

Clayton, A.C. (2003). *Introduction to level design for PC games.* Charles River Media.

Co, P. (2006). *Level design for games: Creating compelling game experiences.* New Riders Games.

Cooper, A., & Reimann, R. (2003). *About face 2.0: The essentials of interaction design.* Wiley.

Cornman, L.B. et al. (December 1998). A fuzzy logic method for improved moment estimation from Doppler spectra. *Journal of Atmospheric & Oceanic Technology.*

Cox, E. & Goetz, M. (March 1991). Fuzzy logic clarified. *Computerworld.*

Crawford, C. (2003). *Chris Crawford on game design.* New Riders.

Crowley, M. (2004). "'A' is for average." *Reader's Digest.*

Csikszentmihalyi, M. (1991). *Flow: The psychology of optimal experience.* Perennial.

Dawson, M. (2006). *Beginning C++ through game programming.* Course Technology.

Decker, M. (2000). "Bug Reports That Make Sense." *StickyMinds.com* (www.stickyminds.com/sitewide.asp?Function=edetail&ObjectType=ART&ObjectId=2079).

DeMaria, R. & Wilson, J.L. (2003). *High score!: The illustrated history of electronic games.* McGraw-Hill.

Demers, O. (2001). *Digital texturing and painting.* New Riders Press.

Dickens, C. (April 1, 2004). "Automated Testing Basics." *Software Test Engineering @ Microsoft* (blogs.msdn.com/chappell/articles/106056.aspx).

Dickheiser, M. (2006). *C++ for Game Programmers.* Charles River Media.

Digital Media Wire. *Project Millennials Sourcebook (2nd Ed.).* (2008). Pass Along / Digital Media Wire.

Duffy, J. (April 2009). "8th Annual Game Developer Salary Survey." *Game Developer Magazine.*

Duffy, J. (August 2007). "The Bean Counters." *Game Developer Magazine.*

Dunniway, T. & Novak, J. (2008). *Game development essentials: Gameplay mechanics.* Cengage Delmar.

Eberly, D. H. (2004). *3D game engine architecture: Engineering real-time applications with wild magic.* Morgan Kaufmann.

Egri, L. (1946). *The art of dramatic writing: Its basis in the creative interpretation of human motives.* Simon and Schuster.

Eischen, C. W. and Eischen, L. A. (2009). *Résumés, cover letters, networking, and interviewing.* South-Western College Pub.

Eisenman, S. (2006). *Building design portfolios: Innovative concepts for presenting your work.* Rockport Publishers.

Erikson, E.H. (1994). *Identity and the life cycle.* W.W. Norton & Company.

Erikson, E.H. (1995). *Childhood and society.* Vintage.

Escober, C. & Galindo, J. (2004). Fuzzy control in agriculture: Simulation software. *Industrial Simulation Conference 2004.*

Evans, A. (2001). *This virtual life: Escapism and simulation in our media world.* Fusion Press.

Fay, T. (2003). *DirectX 9 audio exposed: Interactive audio development,* Wordware Publishing.

Feare, T. (July 2000). "Simulation: Tactical tool for system builders." *Modern Materials Handling.*

Friedl, M. (2002). *Online game interactivity theory.* Charles River Media.

Fristrom, J. (July 14, 2003). "Production Testing & Bug Tracking." *Gamasutra* (www.gamasutra.com/view/feature/2829/production_testing_and_bug_tracking.php).

Fruin, N. & Harrigan, P. (Eds.) (2004). *First person: New media as story, performance and game.* MIT Press.

Fullerton, T., Swain, C. & Hoffman, S. (2004). *Game design workshop: Designing, prototyping & playtesting games.* CMP Books.

Galitz, W.O. (2002). *The essential guide to user interface design: An introduction to GUI design principles and techniques.* (2nd ed.). Wiley.

Gamma, E., Helm, R., Johnson, R. & Vlissides, J. (1995). *Design patterns: Elements of reusable object-oriented software.* Addison-Wesley.

Gardner, J. (1991). *The art of fiction: Notes on craft for young writers.* Vintage Books.

Gee, J.P. (2003). *What video games have to teach us about learning and literacy.* Palgrave Macmillan.

Gershenfeld, A., Loparco, M. & Barajas, C. (2003). *Game plan: The insiders guide to breaking in and succeeding in the computer and video game business.* Griffin Trade Paperback.

Giarratano, J.C. & Riley, G.D. (1998). *Expert systems: Principles & programming (4th ed).* Course Technology.

Gibson, D., Aldrich, C. & Prensky, M. (Eds.) (2006). *Games and simulations in online learning.* IGI Global.

Gladwell, M. (2000). *The tipping point: How little things can make a big difference.* New York, NY: Little Brown & Company.

Gladwell, M. (2007). *Blink: The power of thinking without thinking.* Back Bay Books.

Gleick, J. (1987). *Chaos: Making a new science.* Viking.

Gleick, J. (1999). *Faster: The acceleration of just about everything.* Vintage Books.

Gleick, J. (2003). *What just happened: A chronicle from the information frontier.* Vintage.

Godin, S. (2003). *Purple cow: Transform your business by being remarkable.* Portfolio.

Godin, S. (2005). *The big moo: Stop trying to be perfect and start being remarkable.* Portfolio.

Goldratt, E.M. & Cox, J. (2004). *The goal: A process of ongoing improvement (3rd ed).* North River Press.

Gorden, R. L. (1998). *Basic interviewing skills.* Waveland Press.

Gordon, T. (2000). *P.E.T.: Parent effectiveness training.* Three Rivers Press.

Guilfoyle, E. (2007). *Half Life 2 mods for dummies.* For Dummies.

Guilfoyle, E. (2006). *Quake 4 mods for dummies.* For Dummies.

Habgood, J. & Overmars, M. (2006). *The game maker's apprentice: Game development for beginners.* Apress.

Hall, R. & Novak, J. (2008). *Game development essentials: Online game development.* Cengage Delmar.

Hamilton, E. (1940). *Mythology: Timeless tales of gods and heroes.* Mentor.

Hart, S.N. (1996-2000). "A Brief History of Home Video Games." *geekcomix* (www.geekcomix.com/vgh/main.shtml).

Heim, M. (1993). *The metaphysics of virtual reality.* Oxford University Press.

Hight, J. & Novak, J. (2007). *Game development essentials: Game project management.* Cengage Delmar.

Hofferber, K. & Isaacs, K. (2006). *The career change résumé.* McGraw-Hill.

Hornyak, T.N. (2006). *Loving the machine: The art and science of Japanese robots.* Kodansha International.

Hsu, F. (2004). *Behind Deep Blue: Building the computer that defeated the world chess champion.* Princeton University Press.

Hunt, C.W. (October 1998). "Uncertainty factor drives new approach to building simulations." *Signal.*

Jensen, E. (2006). *Enriching the brain: How to maximize every learner's potential.* John Wiley & Sons.

Isla, D. (2005). "Handling complexity in the *Halo 2* AI." Game Developers Conference.

Johnson, S. (1997). *Interface culture: How new technology transforms the way we create & communicate.* Basic Books.

Johnson, S. (2006). *Everything bad is good for you.* Riverhead.

Jung, C.G. (1969). *Man and his symbols.* Dell Publishing.

Kennedy, J. L. (2007), *Résumés for dummies.* For Dummies.

Kent, S.L. (2001). *The ultimate history of video games.* Prima.

King, S. (2000). *On writing.* Scribner.

Knoke, W. (1997). *Bold new world: The essential road map to the twenty-first century.* Kodansha International.

Koster, R. (2005). *Theory of fun for game design.* Paraglyph Press.

Krawczyk, M. & Novak, J. (2006). *Game development essentials: Game story & character development.* Cengage Delmar.

Kurzweil, R. (2000). *The age of spiritual machines: When computers exceed human intelligence.* Penguin.

Laramee, F.D. (Ed.) (2002). *Game design perspectives.* Charles River Media.

Laramee, F.D. (Ed.) (2005). *Secrets of the game business. (3rd ed).* Charles River Media.

Levy, L. & Novak, J. (2009). *Game development essentials: Game QA & testing.* Cengage Delmar.

Levy, P. (2001). *Cyberculture.* University of Minnesota Press.

Lewis, M. (2001). *Next: The future just happened.* W.W.Norton & Company.

Mackay, C. (1841). *Extraordinary popular delusions & the madness of crowds.* Three Rivers Press.

Marks, A. (2008). *The complete guide to game audio.* Elsevier/Focal Press.

Marks, A. & Novak, J. (2008). *Game development essentials: Game audio development.* Cengage Delmar.

Maurina III, E. F. (2006). *The game programmer's guide to Torque: Under the hood of the Torque game engine.* AK Peters Ltd.

McConnell, S. (1996). *Rapid development.* Microsoft Press.

McCorduck, P. (2004). *Machines who think: A personal inquiry into the history and prospects of artificial intelligence (2nd ed).* AK Peters.

McKenna, T. (December 2003). "This means war." *Journal of Electronic Defense.*

Meigs, T. (2003). *Ultimate game design: Building game worlds.* McGraw-Hill Osborne Media.

Mencher, M. (2002). *Get in the game: Careers in the game industry.* New Riders.

Meyers, S. (2005). *Effective C++: 55 specific ways to improve your programs and designs (3rd ed).* Addison-Wesley.

Michael, D. (2003). *The indie game development survival guide.* Charles River Media.

Montfort, N. (2003). *Twisty little passages: An approach to interactive fiction.* MIT Press.

Moore, M. & Novak, J. (2009). *Game development essentials: Game industry career guide.* Cengage Delmar Learning.

Moore, M. E. & Sward, J. (2006). *Introduction to the game industry.* Prentice Hall.

Moravec, H. (2000). *Robot.* Oxford University Press.

Morris, D. (September/October 2004). Virtual weather. *Weatherwise.*

Morris, D. & Hartas, L. (2003). *Game art: The graphic art of computer games.* Watson-Guptill Publications.

Muehl, W. & Novak, J. (2007). *Game development essentials: Game simulation development.* Cengage Delmar.

Mulligan, J. & Patrovsky, B. (2003). *Developing online games: An insider's guide.* New Riders.

Mummolo, J. (July 2006). "Helping children play." *Newsweek.*

Murray, J. (2001). *Hamlet on the holodeck: The future of narrative in cyberspace.* MIT Press.

Negroponte, N. (1996). *Being digital.* Vintage Books.

Nielsen, J. (1999). *Designing web usability: The practice of simplicity.* New Riders.

Nomadyun. (February 23, 2006). "Game Testing Methodology." *CN IT Blog* (www.cnitblog.com/nomadyun/archive/2006/02/23/6869.html).

Novak, J. & Levy, L. (2007). *Play the game: The parent's guide to video games.* Cengage Course Technology PTR.

Novak, J. (2003). "MMOGs as online distance learning applications." University of Southern California.

O'Donnell, M. & Marks, A. (2002). "The use and effectiveness of audio in *Halo:* Game music evolved." *Music4Games* (www.music4games.net/Features_Display.aspx?id=24).

Omernick, M. (2004). *Creating the art of the game.* New Riders Games.

Oram, A. (Ed.) (2001). *Peer-to-peer.* O'Reilly & Associates.

Patow, C.A. (December 2005). "Medical simulation makes medical education better & safer." *Health Management Technology.*

Peck, M. (January 2005). "Air Force's latest video game targets potential recruits." *National Defense.*

Pepastaek, J. "The PlayStation Gamemaker: Disassembling Net Yaroze" *Gamespot* (www.gamespot.com/features/vgs/psx/yaroze).

Pham, A. (October 20, 2008). "Mom, I Want to Major in Video Games." *Los Angeles Times* (www.latimes.com/business/la-fi-gamesschools20-2008oct20,1,1900670.story).

PHP Quality Assurance Team. "Handling Bug Reports?" *PHP-QAT* (qa.php.net/handling-bugs.php).

Piaget, J. (2000). *The psychology of the child.* Basic Books.

Piaget, J. (2007). *The child's conception of the world.* Jason Aronson.

Pohflepp, S. (January 2007). "Before and after Darwin." *We Make Money Not Art* (www.we-make-money-not -art.com/archives/009261.php).

Poole, S. (2004). *Trigger happy: Videogames and the entertainment revolution.* Arcade Publishing.

Prensky, M. (2006). *Don't bother me, Mom: I'm learning!* Paragon House.

Rabin, S. (2009). *Introduction to game development.* Concept Media.

Ramirez, J. (July 2006). "The new ad game." *Newsweek.*

Rheingold, H. (1991). *Virtual reality.* Touchstone.

Rheingold, H. (2000). *Tools for thought: The history and future of mind-expanding technology.* MIT Press.

Robbins, S.P. (2001). *Organizational behavior (9th ed).* Prentice-Hall, Inc.

Rogers, E.M. (1995). *Diffusion of innovations.* Free Press.

Rollings, A. & Morris, D. (2003). *Game architecture & design: A new edition.* New Riders.

Rollings, A. & Adams, E. (2003). *Andrew Rollings & Ernest Adams on game design.* New Riders.

Rouse, R. (2001) *Game design: Theory & practice (2nd ed).* Wordware Publishing.

Salen, K. & Zimmerman, E. (2003). *Rules of play.* MIT Press.

Sanchanta, M. (2006 January). "Japanese game aids U.S. war on obesity: Gym class in West Virginia to use an interactive dance console." *Financial Times*.

Sanger, G.A. [a.k.a. "The Fat Man"]. (2003). *The Fat Man on game audio*. New Riders.

Saltzman, M. (July 23, 1999). "Secrets of the Sages: Level Design." *Gamasutra* (www.gamasutra.com/view/feature/3360/secrets_of_the_sages_level_design.php?page=3).

Saunders, K. & Novak, J. (2007). *Game development essentials: Game interface design*. Cengage Delmar.

Schell, J. (2008). *The art of game design: A book of lenses*. Morgan Kaufmann.

Schildt, H. (2006). *Java: A beginner's guide (4th ed)*. McGraw-Hill Osborne Media.

Schomaker, W. (September 2001). "Cosmic models match reality." *Astronomy*.

Sellers, J. (2001). *Arcade fever*. Running Press.

Shaffer, D.W. (2006). *How computer games help children learn*. Palgrave Macmillan.

Standage, T. (1999). *The Victorian Internet*. New York: Berkley Publishing Group.

Strauss, W. & Howe, N. (1992). *Generations*. Perennial.

Strauss, W. & Howe, N. (1993). *13th gen: Abort, retry, ignore, fail?* Vintage Books.

Strauss, W. & Howe, N. (1998). *The fourth turning*. Broadway Books.

Strauss, W. & Howe, N. (2000). *Millennials rising: The next great generation*. Vintage Books.

Strauss, W., Howe, N. & Markiewicz, P. (2006). *Millennials & the pop culture*. LifeCourse Associates.

Stroustrup, B. (2000). *The C++ programming language (3rd ed)*. Addison-Wesley.

Szinger, J. (1993-2006). "On Composing Interactive Music." *Zing Man Productions* (www.zingman.com/spew/CompIntMusic.html).

Trotter, A. (November 2005). "Despite allure, using digital games for learning seen as no easy task." *Education Week*.

Tufte, E.R. (1983). *The visual display of quantitative information*. Graphics Press.

Tufte, E.R. (1990). *Envisioning information*. Graphics Press.

Tufte, E.R. (1997). *Visual explanations*. Graphics Press.

Tufte, E.R. (2006). *Beautiful evidence*. Graphics Press.

Turkle, S. (1997). *Life on the screen: Identity in the age of the Internet*. Touchstone.

Unger, K. & Novak, J. (2011). *Game development essentials: Mobile game development*. Cengage Delmar Learning.

Van Duyne, D.K. et al. (2003). *The design of sites*. Addison-Wesley.

Vogler, C. (1998). *The writer's journey: Mythic structure for writers. (2nd ed)*. Michael Wiese Productions.

Weems, MD. (October 5, 2008). "10 Steps to Becoming a Video Game Tester." *Bright Hub* (www.brighthub.com/video-games/pc/articles/9819.aspx).

Welch, J. & Welch, S. (2005). *Winning*. HarperCollins Publishers.

Weizenbaum, J. (1984). *Computer power and human reason*. Penguin Books.

Wilcox, J. (2007). *Voiceovers: Techniques & Tactics for Success*. Allworth Press.

Williams, J.D. (1954). *The compleat strategyst: Being a primer on the theory of the games of strategy*. McGraw-Hill.

Wolf, J.P. & Perron, B. (Eds.). (2003). *Video game theory reader*. Routledge.

Wong, G. (November 2006). "Educators explore 'Second Life' online." *CNN.com* (www.cnn.com/2006/TECH/11/13/second.life.university/index.html).

Wysocki, R.K. (2006). *Effective project management (4th ed)*. John Wiley & Sons.

Yuzwa, E. (2006). *Game programming in C++: Start to Finish*. Charles River Media.

Extended Copyright & Trademark Notices